International Organisations

- International [illegible]
- Human Rights [illegible]
- A Concise Book on International [illegible]
- Kashmir Problem [illegible]
- State Succession [illegible]
- अन्तर्राष्ट्रीय [illegible]
- मानव अधिकार [illegible]

80, [illegible]

C/27/1, Connaught Place, [illegible]

Published by [illegible]

International Organisations

Dr. H.O. Agarwal
Formerly Professor, Faculty of Law
University of Allahabad

THIRD EDITION
Reprint 2023

CENTRAL LAW PUBLICATIONS

ISBN : 978-93-90735-03-7

By the same author :

- International Law and Human Rights (Twentieth Edition) (2016)
- Human Rights (Fourteenth Edition) (2014)
- A Concise Book on International Law (Second Edition) (2009)
- Kashmir Problem : Its Legal Aspects (Reprint) (2011)
- State Succession : A Study of Indian cases
- अन्तर्राष्ट्रीय विधि एवं मानव अधिकार (भारत सरकार द्वारा पुरस्कृत) (ग्यारहवाँ संस्करण) (2010)
- मानव अधिकार (भारत सरकार द्वारा पुरस्कृत) (चतुर्थ संस्करण) (2008)

First Edition : 2011
Reprint : 2014
Second Edition: 2016
Third Edition : 2021
Reprint : 2023

Price Rs. 290.00

Sole Distributors for Delhi
M/s Universal Book Traders
80, Gokhale Market, Opp. New Courts, Delhi - 110 054
&
C/27/1, Connaught Place, Middle Circle (Between Odeon and Plaza), New Delhi - 110 001

Published by : **Central Law Publications**, 107, Darbhanga Castle, Prayagraj—21100
Laser Typesetting by : **N & T Computers**, Prayagraj
Printed at : **Caxton Press**, Prayagraj

PREFACE TO THE THIRD EDITION

It gives me pleasure in presenting the Third Edition of the book which has been thoroughly revised and updated.

The book is useful not only to law students but to the students of political science and military science as well. It is equally useful to the candidates appearing in competition examinations and to all those who are interested in the study of international organisation.

I am thankful to Mr. R.N. Arora and Mr. Rajiv Arora of M/s. Central Law Publications for having published the book quickly. I must acknowledge my gratitude to my wife Dr. Alka Agarwal, former Professor and the Head, Department of Economics, University of Allahabad for rendering her cooperation at every stage of the book.

9-A, Panna Lal Road
Prayagraj—211 002.
(India)

H.O. Agarwal

PREFACE TO THE FIRST EDITION

International organisations and International Law are closely related to each other. Former has bearing upon most of the principles of the latter. The importance of the study of international organisations in the contemporary World politics and international legal system is such that it will not be inappropriate to state that the study of International Law remains incomplete without understanding the different aspects of international organisations. This has necessitated the study of international organisations for the students of International Law. Keeping this point in mind writers of the books on International Law, included the discussion of international organisations in their work. The same practice was followed by me at the time of writing the book on International Law and Human Rights. Different aspects of international organisations were discussed. However, limited space was given to them.

With the introduction of international organisations in the recent past by the Bar Council of India as a separate subject in the LLB curriculum students are required to study the subject in detail and analytically which the books on International Law do not serve their purpose. The present book has been written mainly to fulfil their this very aspiration. Critical analysis has been done especially of the working of the League of Nations, United Nations and its principal organs, subsidiary organs and bodies, regional organisations and non-international organisations. The book covers nearly all the topics which the Bar Council of India have indicated for the LLB Course.

I must admit that many topics discussed in the present book have been borrowed from the book International Law and Human Rights. However, they have been systematically arranged, up-dated and expanded where deemed necessary.

United Nations presently having 193 members has achieved nearly universatization. Its effective role in resolving a number of conflicts and disputes between the States is undeniable. Its working has proved that it is not merely a 'talking shop'. It being an institution of more than sixty five years, no doubt, requires reforms to fulfil the aspirations of the third World countries and to make more effective force in contemporary World politics. They have been discussed at appropriate places.

United Nations has established a number of bodies, commissions, committees and working groups to perform a large variety of functions including the promotion of economic, social and cultural development of the present and the most disadvantaged of the World population. However it has not been possible to deal all of them in order to bring the book in the present size.

The book is useful not only to law students but to the students of political science and military science as well. It is equally useful to the candidates appearing in competitive examinations and to all those who are interested in the study of international organisations especially United Nations.

I am thankful to those who inspired me to write the book and gave me valuable suggestions in the preparation of the book. I am also thankful to Mr. R.N. Arora and Mr. Rajiv Arora of M/s Central Law Publications for having published the book quickly.

I must also acknowledge my gratitude to my wife Dr. Alka Agarwal, Professor, Department of Economics, University of Allahabad for rendering her cooperation at every stage of the book. In the end, I owe my thanks to Gaurav and Saumya without whose cooperation the book in the present form might not have completed.

H.O. Agarwal

August, 2011
9-A, Panna Lal Road
Allahabad—211 002.
(India)

CONTENTS

CHAPTER 4
GENERAL ASSEMBLY

CHAPTER 5
SECURITY-COUNCIL

CHAPTER 6
ECONOMIC AND SOCIAL COUNCIL

CHAPTER 7
TRUSTEESHIP COUNCIL

CHAPTER 8
THE SECRETARIAT

CHAPTER 9
INTERNATIONAL COURT OF JUSTICE

CHAPTER 10
SPECIALIZED AGENCIES

CHAPTER 11
OTHER RELATED ORGANISATIONS OF THE UNITED NATIONS

CHAPTER 12
SUBSIDIARY ORGANS AND BODIES OF THE UNITED NATIONS

CHAPTER 16
NON-GOVERNMENTAL ORGANISATIONS

APPENDICES

TABLE OF CASES

Chapter I

Concept of International Organisations

One of the promising developments of the twentieth century in inter-State relations has been in the proliferation of international organisations. They have been created and developed in order to achieve cooperation amongst independent States. Their actions have bearing upon all the aspects of the life of peoples throughout the World whether they are political, economic, social, cultural, educational or scientific. They also have a bearing upon travel and communications, health and nutrition and demography and environment. They are the centres for discussion, study and preparations on all these issues.

International organisations are created by the States on the basis of international agreements for certain specific tasks and therefore they are the association of States for the performance of specific functions. They do not supersede or dictate the States, and therefore, they do not acquire the character of international government. They have separate legal personality and, as such, are the subjects of international law. International organisations may be defined as associations of States established on the basis of a treaty in accordance with international law in order to achieve specific objectives. They possess a system of organs and rights and duties that are distinct from those of member States.[1] The above definition contains the following elements.

1. International organisations are the associations of States. Generally, membership of the international organisations is open to sovereign States only. But it is not necessary that members should always be sovereign. Not-fully sovereign States may also be admitted as members. For instance, Byelorussia and Ukrain who were the republics of USSR were the members of the United Nations. International Organisations being the associations of States are also sometimes called as Inter-Governmental Organisations (IGOs) whose members are official government delegations of States. From the view point of legal validity there is hardly any difference between inter-governmental agreements and inter-State agreements.

International Organisations may include members, in addition to States, other entities such as international organisations, territories or private entities as additional members of the organisation. For instance, European Community became a member of Food and Agriculture Organisation (FAO) whose constitution was amended in 1991 in order to allow the admission of regional economic integrated organisations. The amendment allows World Meteorological Organisation (WMO) under Article 3(d) and (e) 'territories' and 'groups of territories' to become members'. Further, World Tourism Organisation

1. *See* Tunkin, 'International Law' (Edited) p. 183.

includes States as 'full members', territories and group of territories as 'associate members' and international bodies (both inter-governmental and non-governmental) as affiliate members.

In addition to such organisations, there is another category of international organisations which are called non- governmental organisations (NGOs).[1] They are known as private international associations and consist of private groups of religious, scientific, cultural, philanthropic, technical or economic orientation. They do not involve direct government participation. Examples of NGOs are the International Chamber of Commerce, the Inter-Parliamentary Union, the World Veterans Federation, Federation of Trade Unions, the Women's International Democratic Federation and the International Red cross. Literally speaking, non-governmental organisations are not inter-State or international organisations and as such they are not international organisations in the true sense.

2. International Organisations are set up by the States through treaties which are the constituent instruments and character of the international organisations. It was clearly stated in the Advisory Opinion of the International Court of Justice in the Legality of the Threat or Use by a State of Nuclear Weapons in Armed Conflict that the constituent instruments of international organisations are also treaties of particular type.[2] The constituent instrument describes the structure, purposes and main guidelines of the organisation's activities. International organisations being the product of treaties, in principle, establish rights and duties only between the contracting States. Only in limited cases, non-parties can be committed to a treaty. Although it might be looking unnatural to call United Nations Organisation and International Labour Organisation as multilateral treaties it is a reality which cannot be denied. Sometimes, organisations are set up not on the basis of treaties, but through other instruments governed by International Law such as the resolutions of international organisations or by a conference of States.[3] For instance, the United Nations Conference on Trade and Development (UNCTAD) and the United Nations Environment Programme (UNEP) were established by the resolutions of the General Assembly within the framework of the United Nations. They do possess the structure of the International organisations in the sense that they perform their functions as stipulated in the resolutions.

3. International organisations are established for specific purposes. The purposes of an international organisations are important in establishing its legitimacy. There cannot be any organisation without any purpose.

4. International organisations possess international personality by virtue of having distinct rights and duties. Sometimes they proclaim their personality in their constitutions or atleast assert capacity in law for autonomous action. In

1. Economic and Social Council of the United Nations by adopting a resolution (288(x)) on February 27, 1950 defined the non-governmental organisations as "any international organisation which is not established by inter-governmental agreements shall be considered as a non-governmental organisation." For detail *see* Chapter 'Non-Governmental Organisations'.
2. ICJ Reports (1996) para 19.
3. Examples of such organisations are Pan-American Institute of Geography and History (1928) and the Organisation of Petroleum Exporting Countries (OPEC).

Reparation case[1] it was made clear that the United Nations Organisation possesses rights and duties distinct from the rights and duties of its members, and as such it possesses international personality and is therefore a subject of International Law.

5. International organisations are not States. They are established and empowered by States in accordance with the rules of International Law. The term international law means public international in contrast to private International Law. It implies that their activities are generally confined within the generally recognised principles and norms of International Law.

Kinds of International Organisations

International organisations may vary in their functions, type and size of membership. They may be classified in different ways. For instance, they may be divided in accordance to the intended duration, *i.e. ad hoc*, provisional or permanent organizations, or in accordance to the nature of their powers, that is, judicial, conciliatory, governmental administrative, co-ordinative or legislative organizations, or in accordance to the character of their objectives, *i.e.*, single purpose or multi-purpose organizations, or according to the geographical scope *i.e.*, universal (global) or regional organisations.

After taking into account of all the above factors, particularly the basis of membership and purposes, international organisations may be divided into following four categories :—

1. General Membership and General Purpose Organisations

Such organisations are global in scope and are open to all the States. They serve a variety of functions, such as peace and security, socio-economic co-operation, protection of human rights, growth and exchange of cultural, educational and scientific activities. Examples of such organisations are the League of Nations and the United Nations Organisation.

2. General Membership and Limited Purpose Organisations

Such organisations are also known as functional organisations because they are devoted to a specific function but they are open to all the States of the international community. Examples of such organisations are the specialized agencies of the United Nations such as International Bank for Reconstruction and Development, International Labour Organisation, World Health Organisation.

3. Limited-Membership and General Purpose Organisations

Such organisations are open to the States of a particular region and therefore, they are known as regional organisations. They are created for a wide range of security, political, and socio-economic functions and responsibilities. Examples of such organisations are the Organisation of American States (OAS), the African Union (AU) and the Arab League.

4. Limited Membership and Limited Purpose Organisations

There are organisations which are open to the States of a particular region

1. ICJ Reports, (1949) p. 179.

and which are set up to perform specific or limited functions. Examples of such organisations are the North Atlantic Treaty Organisation (NATO) and the Warsaw Treaty Organisation (the Warsaw Pact).

Powers and Functions of International Organisations

Powers and functions of the international organisations are laid down in their constituent instruments. There are organisations, such as the United Nations which may perform a number of functions in relation to economic, social, cultural and political matters. There is hardly any international matter which the General Assembly is not competent to discuss and on which it is not competent to make recommendations. However, there are international organisations which are governed by the principle of speciality, that is to say, they are invested by the States which create them with powers, with a special purpose, and therefore, they may perform functions in order to fulfil that very special function. The powers which are performed by international organisations as laid down in the constituent instruments are called express powers. In addition to them the necessities of international life may point to the need for organisations, in order to achieve their objectives, to possess subsidiary powers which are not expressly provided for in the basic instruments. The International Court of Justice in the Advisory Opinion given in the Legality of the Threat or Use by a State of Nuclear Weapons in Armed Conflicts[1] stated that such powers of international organisations are known as "implied powers.[2] As far as the United Nations is concerned, the Court expressed itself in the following terms in this respect :—

> Under international law, the organisation must be deemed to have these powers, which though not expressly provided in the Charter, are conferred upon it by necessary implication as being essential to the performance of its duties.[3]

The above principle of law was applied by the Permanent Court of International Justice to the International Labour Organisation[4] in the Advisory Opinion and must be applied to the United Nations.

International Organisations : A Subject of International Law

Any entity which possesses international personality is called an international person or a subject of International Law. Possession of international personality is therefore the determining factor in deciding as to which entities are the subjects of International Law. An entity may be deemed to possess international personality if it is capable of possessing international rights and duties and having the capacity to maintain its rights by bringing international claims.[5] Oppenheim says that an international person is one who

1. ICJ Reports (1996).
2. *Ibid.*, para 25.
3. *Ibid.*
4. Advisory opinion No. 13 of July 23, 1926 (Series B, No. 13, p. 18).
5. *See* Brownlie, 'Principles of Public International Law', (1990) Fourth Edition, p. 58. Also *see* Schwarzenberger who says that 'International personality means capacity to be a bearer of rights and duties under International Law'. 'A Manual of International Law', Vol. I, Fourth Edition, p. 47.

possesses legal personality in International Law, meaning one who is a subject of International Law so as itself to enjoy rights, duties or powers established in International Law, and, generally, the capacity to act on the international plane either directly, or indirectly through another State (as in the case of a protected State).[1] The concept of international person is thus derived from International Law.[2] The question as to what are the entities which possess the above three capacities, *i.e.*, rights, duties and capacity to maintain its rights by bringing international claims, is solely determined by the rules of International Law. Thus, International Law itself selects the different entities to which it grants international personality by endowing legal functions.

It is significant to note that it is not necessary for an entity to possess all the rights and duties recognized by International Law. If an entity is competent to perform only a few acts or even a single act as provided by the rules of International Law, that entity would be regarded as to have possessed capacity to become a subject of International Law. At the most it can be said that such entities possess restricted or limited capacity in contrast to unlimited or full capacity which is possessed by those entities which have been endowed most of the rights and duties, if not all, by the rules of International Law. It would be improper to say that the former does not possess personality in International Law at all, since it lacks the capacity to perform totality of rights and duties recognized by International Law. International Law being dynamic has, at present, granted international personality to certain entities, which at a time did not possess it. In future, a few other entities may be granted personality, as and when they acquire capacity, which at present do not possess it.

It is true that International Law addresses most of the rights and duties to States. However, in the last seventy years or so, substantial changes have taken place in it. There is a proliferation of new participants in international relations. International organisations distinct from States, have been endowed rights and duties, in addition to States. International organisations perform certain legal functions and they have distinct legal personality in International Law separate from that of the member States. In the Advisory Opinion on the Interpretation of the Agreement of 25th March, 1951 between the WHO and Egypt, the International Court of Justice clearly stated that :

> International organisations are subjects of International Law and, as such are bound by any obligations incumbent upon them under general rules of International Law, under their Constitutions or under international agreements to which they are parties.[3]

Similarly, in the Advisory Opinion requested by the World Health Organisation, on the Legality of the Threat or Use by a State of Nuclear Weapons in Armed conflict, the International Court of Justice stated that :

> The Court need hardly point out that International organisations are subjects of International Law which do not, unlike States, possess a general competence. International organisations are governed by the "principle of speciality", that is to say, they are invested by the States

1. Oppenheim, 'International Law, Vol. I, Ninth Edition (1992) pp. 119-120.
2. *Ibid.*
3. ICJ Reports (1980) p. 73 at pp. 89-90.

which create them with powers, the limits of which are a function of the common interests whose promotion those States entrust to them.[1]

However, it has to be conceded that while States have been endowed totality of rights and duties under International Law, and therefore they have 'unlimited personality', that is, they have full capacity, and they are therefore the primary subjects of International Law. International organisations possess 'restricted personality', since they perform only a few rights and duties.

It is true that International organisations have been granted rights and duties in most of the cases, by the States themselves, and they therefore are the instruments in the hands of States. They would cease to exist as the subjects of International Law on the day States decide to get rid of them. It follows that International organisations are derivative subjects or passive subjects in the sense that they draw their existence from the formal decisions of States who may be called active subjects because law is created exclusively by them. Thus active members possess the monopoly of the creation of International Law, the merely passive members of the community of States are simply creatures of International Law.[2] However, it does not matter much as to who gave them rights and duties. The material point is that if they are capable of performing rights and duties under International Law, they would be regarded as subjects of International Law. Such rights and duties may be in their possession either because of the customary rules of International Law or because of the conclusion of international conventions.

It is significant to note that International organisations as subjects of International Law differ from other subjects of International Law such as States. International organisations do not possess territory and population, and therefore, they do not exercise territorial supremacy and sovereignty. However, it is not necessary that in a given system of law, all the entities should be identical in their nature. They may differ in nature from one to another. The International Court of Justice in Reparations for Injuries Suffered in the Service of the United Nations case[3] clearly observed that :

> 'the subjects of law in any legal system are not necessarily identical in their nature or in the extent of their rights, and their nature depends upon the needs of the community. Throughout its history, the development of International Law has been influenced by the requirements of international life, and the progressive increase in the collective activities of States has already given rise to instances of action upon the international plane by certain entities which are not States'.[4]

In the opinion of the Court, the Organisation was intended to exercise and enjoy, and is in fact exercising and enjoying, functions and rights which can only be explained on the basis of the possession of a large measure of international personality and the capacity to operate upon an international plane. The Court came to the conclusion that the United Nations is an international person in spite of the fact that it is not a State. What it does mean that the United Nations

1. ICJ Reports 1996 p. 66 at p. 78.
2. Verdross, 'On the Concept of International Law', AJIL, Vol. 43 (1949) p. 439.
3. ICI Reports (1949), p. 174.
4. *Ibid* p. 179.

is a subject of International Law and it is capable of possessing international rights and duties, and that it has capacity to maintain its rights by bringing international claims.

It is apparent from the above discussion that the position of subjects of International Law has greatly changed with the passage of time. Originally, States were the only actors in the international community, but in the present century, new non-State entities such as International organisations and institutions and individuals have been given the status and rank of international legal subjects.

International Organisations and Member States and Non-Member States

International organisations are set up by the representatives of the States at a meeting or conference by adopting a treaty. Later, the treaty signed by the representatives of the States is confirmed by the States. The act of confirmation is called ratification. Thus, the treaty is the constituent instrument which describes the structures, purposes and main guidelines of the organisation's activities. Such treaties are called multilateral treaties and are binding only to the parties thereof. This is the general rule and this rule applies in principle to the constituent instruments of organisations of States.

It implies that the rights and obligations arising from a treaty do not bind third States which are not parties to the constituent instruments without their consent. This customary law principle has been expressed in a Latin maxim which is called *pacta tertis nee nocent prosunt*. International Law Commission considered that there appears to be almost universal agreement upon such a general rule, which is based not only on a general concept of the law of contract but also on the sovereignty and independence of States.[1] This rule has been incorporated under Article 34 of the Vienna Convention which says that a treaty does not create either obligations or rights for a third State without its consent. However, a treaty may create right and obligations to a third State (a) when a treaty imposes obligations on a State which is not a party to a treaty if it accepts the obligations in writing;[2] or (b) when a right is given to a third State from a provision of a treaty and third State gives its assent thereto. The assent of the third State shall be presumed so long the contrary is not indicated; and (c) when a treaty creates a customary rule of international law. Perhaps, because of this rule, the Charter of the United Nations is binding to non-members of the United Nations when it lays down under Article 2 para 6 that Organisation shall ensure that States which are not members of the United Nations act in accordance with the principles laid down under Article 2 of the Charter so far as may be necessary for the maintenance of international peace and security.

Law of International Organisations

International organisations have grown with the development of international law. The set of rules governing the activities of international organisations is called the law of international organisations. Although the term

1. *See* Year book of International Law Commission, 1966, Part II, p. 226.
2. Article 35 of the Vienna Convention on the Law of Treaties (1969).

law of international organisations is extensively used in the juridical literature, nature and mode of the law is not fully determined in view of the fact that this branch of International Law is of recent origin. The term law of international organisations combines principles and norms regulating the establishment, legal status and activities of international organisations. Law of international organisations therefore has two aspects external and internal law.

External law includes rules, regulations, relations of an international organisation with member States, non-member States and other international organisations. This branch of law has been considerably codified. International conference held in Vienna in 1975 adopted the Vienna Convention on the Representation of States in Their Relations with International Organisations of a Universal Character. Earlier, two Conventions were also adopted : Convention on Privileges and Immunities of the United Nations of 1946 and the Conventions on Privileges and Immunities of the Specialized Agencies of 1947. The Convention on the Law of Treaties to which International Organisations are parties prepered by the International Law Commission was adopted on March 20, 1986. The Convention applies to those treaties which are concluded between States and international organisations or treaties concluded between international organisations.

Internal law of international organisations includes rules regarding internal legal relations such as rules of procedure, finance rules and staff regulations. Each international organisation has internal law of its own, that is why Jenks has called it as proper law of international organisations.[1] Internal law explains aims, terms of reference, powers, functions, organisation, *i.e.*, the inner mechanisms of international organisations. As to the legal nature of internal law, it may be primary or secondary. It is primary when the constituent instrument is the direct source, or secondary when the decision of an organ of an international organisation is the basis.[2] In the latter case the rules of internal law must be regarded as international rules since they govern international relations, albeit within the organisations.[3]

The sources of the law of international organisations are (1) treaties, (2) international customs and (3) resolutions of international organisations.

International treaties are the most important source of international organisations. Treaties containing basic principles derived from general international law have been incorporated in many constituent instruments of international organisations. These general international law rules operate along with Article 5 of the Vienna Convention on the Law of Treaties of 1969 which lays down that the Convention applies to any treaty which is the constituent instrument of an international organisation without prejudice to any relevant rules of the organisation. It is to be noted that the Charter of the United Nations is the principal source of the law of the international organisations which lays down general principles and norms related not only to the United Nations but also to the other international organisations. In addition to the U.N. Charter a

1. *See* 'Proper Law of International Law', (1962).
2. *E. Shibaeva, 'Law of International Organisations in the System of Modern International Law'*, IJIL Vol. 17 (1977) p. 227 at p. 233.
3. *Ibid.*

number of multilateral treaties concerning the activities of international organisations also serve as a source of international organisations. Vienna Convention on the Representative of States in Their Relations with International Organisations of a Universal Character of 1975 serves as a norm setting source.

Custom is not the basic source of international organisations as most of the customary rules have been transformed into treaty rules. However, they were of immense value and were operative prior to this transformation

Resolutions and decisions adopted unanimously or by overwhelming votes sometimes have normative value. They contribute to the formation of customary rules. A large part of the rules of the internal law may be found in such resolutions of the organs of the international organisations.

Legal Personality of the Organisations

Personality of an entity as a legal person is decided in accordance with the provisions of the constitution. As such, the question as to whether international organisations possess any legal personality could have been answered expressly had international community been regulated through a constitution. In the absence of any constitution, at present, primary test for recognizing an entity as legal person is functional.[1] In Reparations for Injuries Suffered in the Service of the United Nations,[2] commonly known as Reparation case, the International Court of Justice was asked for an advisory opinion on the capacity of the United Nations, as an Organisation, to bring an international claim in respect of injury to its personnel, on the lines of diplomatic protection, and in respect of injury to the United Nations caused by the injury to its agents. The Court observed that :

> "the Organisation was intended to exercise and enjoy, and is in fact exercising and enjoying, functions and rights which can only be explained on the basis of the possession of a large measure of international personality and the capacity to operate on an international plane. It is at present the supreme type of international organisation, and it could not carry out the intentions of its founders if it was devoid of international personality. It must be acknowledged that its Members, by entrusting certain functions to it, with the attendant duties and responsibilities, have clothed it with the competence required to enable those functions to be effectively discharged."[3]

Accordingly, the Court came to the conclusion that the Organisation is an international person. It is a subject of International Law and capable of possessing international rights and duties, and that it has capacity to maintain its rights by bringing international claims. Further, in the Advisory Opinion requested by the World Health Organisation on the Legality of the Threat or Use by a State of Nuclear Weapons in Armed Conflict the International Court of Justice stated that international organisations are subjects of international law which do not, unlike States, possess a general competence. International

1. Brownile, 'Principles of Public International Law', Fourth Edition (1990) p. 680.
2. ICJ Reports (1949) p. 174.
3. ICJ Reports (1949) p. 179.

organisations are governed by the principle of speciality, that is to say, they are invested by the States which create them with powers, the limit of which are a function of the common interests whose promotion those States entrust to them.[1]

Similarly, many other important institutions including the specialized agencies of the United Nations proclaim their personality in their constitutions, or atleast assert capacity in law for autonomous action. For instance, Article 15(1) of the Food and Agricultural Organisation Agreement provides that 'The Organisation shall have the capacity of a legal person to perform any legal act appropriate to its purpose which is not beyond the powers granted to it by this Constitution. Further, Agreement of the International Monetary Fund under Article 9(2), and of the International Bank for Reconstruction and Development under Article 7(2) state that both the entities "shall possess full judicial personality, and in particular the capacity : (a) to contract; (b) to acquire and dispose of immovable and movable property; (c) to institute legal proceedings"; Article 47 of the International Civil Aviation Convention provides that the International Civil Aviation Organisation shall enjoy in the territory of each contracting State such legal personality as may be necessary for the performance of its functions. Full juridical personality shall be granted wherever compatible with the Constitution and laws of the State concerned. Further, the Charter of the United Nations Organisation provides under Article 104 that "The Organisation shall enjoy in the territory of each of its Members such legal capacity as may be necessary for the exercise of its functions and the fulfilment of its purposes."

Further, European Economic Community (EEC), a regional organisation provides under Article 210 that the Community shall have legal personality.[2] In *Maclaine Watson* v. *Department of Trade and Industry, Kerr*, LJ observed that "There can be no doubt that EEC has legal personality in International Law.... there is equally no doubt that the EEC exercises powers and functions which are analogous to those of sovereign States.[3]

It is to be noted that the legal capacity of international organisations derives from instituting treaties and from general International Law. The former are normally provided for in the constitutions of the organisations. As to general rules, a Convention has been concluded in the year 1986 *i.e.*, the Convention on the Law of Treaties to which International Organisations are the Parties. It is desirable that the municipal legislations of the members provide for the personalities of the organisations to secure effective legal recognition of this capacity for municipal purposes.

It is not necessary that all the organisations are attributed to legal personality. An organisation may exist but lacks the organs and objects necessary for legal personality. The British Commonwealth is an association of this kind.[4] Similarly, a multilateral convention may be institutionalized to some extent making provisions for regular conferences, and yet not involve any separate personality.

1. ICJ Reports (1996).
2. Also See *Re* European Road Transport Agreement (Case 22/70) (1991) CMLR 335.
3. *(1988) 3 All ER 257 (Court of Appeal).*
4. *Brownlie, op. cit., p. 650.*

LEGAL FUNCTIONS OF THE ORGANISATIONS

International organisations, are capable of performing many legal functions in the domain of International Law. Some of them are as follows :—

(a) Treaty making powers

Treaty making powers of the international organisations depend upon the constitutions of the different organisations. Although such a power is not given expressly in the treaties by which they are created, the power vests in them impliedly by the interpretation of the provisions of the constitution. For instance, Article 104 of the Charter of the United Nations obligates each Member of the United Nations to accord to the Organisation within its territory "such legal capacity as may be necessary for the exercise of its functions". The meaning of the above provisions was elaborated by the Convention on the Privileges and Immunities of the United Nations of 1946 as follows : "The United Nations shall possess juridical personality. It shall have the capacity (a) to contract; (b) to acquire and dispose of immovable and movable property; (c) to institute legal proceedings."

It is to be noted that the United Nations has concluded a number of treaties, both with member States[1] and non-member States[2] and with other international organisations. Further, the U.N. Charter specifically authorizes the Organisation to conclude agreements with Member States on the provisions of military contingents (Article 43), and with specialized agencies bringing them into relationship with the United Nations (Article 63). Articles 77 and 105(3) have been interpreted as authorizing the conclusion of trusteeship agreements and conventions on privileges and immunities with member States respectively. Agreements concluded between States and international organisations or between international organisations are regulated by the Convention on the Law of Treaties to which International Organisations are Parties adopted on March 21, 1986. The Convention has been adopted in respect to treaties concluded between States and international organisations or between international organisations because such treaties may have different procedure and form, and may have special rules than to treaties which are concluded by the States.

It may be noted that the United Nations and other organisations have concluded Headquarters agreements with the States and agreements on co-operation with other organisations, although the constituent instrument contains no express authority for these types of agreements. These agreements are international treaties. In the Advisory Opinion delivered on April 26, 1988, the International Court of Justice stated that the Head-quarters Agreement concluded between the United States of America and the United Nations in 1947 "is a treaty in force binding the parties thereto."[3] The Agreement came into force in accordance with its terms on November 21, 1947 by exchange of letters

1. For instance, the Agreement between the United Nations and the United States of America regarding the Headquarters of the United Nations.
2. For instance, the Agreement with Switzerland (when it was not a member of the United Nations) concerning the Privileges and Immunities of the United Nations.
3. *See* the Advisory opinion on Applicability of the Obligation to Arbitrate Under Section 21 of the United Nations Headquarters Agreement of June 23, 1947, Para 7.

between the Secretary-General and the United States Permanent Representative. The Agreement was registered with the United Nations Secretariat, in accordance with Article 102 of the Charter of the United Nations Organisation.

(b) Privileges and Immunities

International organisations require a certain minimum freedom in order to perform their functions smoothly and effectively and legal security for their assets, Headquarters and other establishments and for their personnel and representatives of member States accredited to the organisations. Their representatives therefore get privileges and immunities. Some organisations expressly lay down privileges and immunities which may be provided to their representatives. For instance, Article 105 of the U.N. Charter provides that "the Organisation shall enjoy in the territory of each of its members such privileges and immunities as are necessary for the fulfilment of its purposes, and further, representatives of the Members of the United Nations and officials of the Organisation shall similarly enjoy such privileges and immunities as are necessary for independent exercise of their functions in connection with the Organisation'. Article 105 also authorizes the General Assembly to make recommendations with a view to determining the details of the privileges and immunities to be enjoyed by the Organisation, as well as by the representatives and officials, or to propose conventions for this purpose. In line with this latter provision, the Assembly approved, in February 1946, the General Convention on the Privileges and Immunities of the United Nations and proposed it for accession by each member of the United Nations. The Convention gives a detailed enumeration of the privileges and immunities to the representatives of the United Nations. It provided for the special privileges, including immunity from arrest, inviolability of documents, and freedoms from alien's registration for representatives of member States on organs and conferences of the United Nations. The Convention further provided special privileges for certain United Nations officials of high rank, including the status of diplomatic envoys for the Secretary-General and Assistant Secretaries-General, and special immunities for other officials, for example, from legal process for acts performed or words spoken in their official capacity, from taxation, and from national service obligations.

The question of privileges and immunities is governed by the Vienna Convention on the Representative of States in Their Relations with International Organisations of a Universal Character adopted in 1975. The privileges and immunities have been modelled on the provisions of the Vienna Convention in Diplomatic Relations of 1961 which provides the privileges and immunities to diplomatic agents.

The advisory opinion given by the International Court of Justice on April 29, 1999 in Differences Relating to Immunity From Legal Process of a Special Rapporteur of the Commission of Human Rights is worth mentioning.

Differences relating to Immunity from Legal Process of a Special Rapporteur of the Commission of Human Rights

The Chairman of the Human Rights Commission appointed Mr. Cumaraswamy as the Special Rapporteur on the Independence and Impartiality of the Judiciary, Jurors and Assessors and the Independence of Lawyers in Malaysia in 1994. In the course of the performance of his mission, he gave an interview which was published in the article in the November 1995 issue of International Commercial Litigations. The article gave a critical appraisal of the Malaysian judicial system in relation to a number of court decisions. The article also quoted that various Malaysian lawyers were interviewed who expressed their concern that, as a result of these decisions, foreign investors and manufacturers might loose the confidence they had always had in the integrity of the Malaysian Court. On December 18, 1995, two commercial firms and their legal counsels addressed letters to Mr. Cumarswamy in which they maintained that they were deferred by his statements in the article. They informed him that they had no choice but to issue defamation proceedings against him. In view of the foregoing letters, the Secretariat of the United Nations issued a Note Verbale to the permanent Mission of Malaysia in Geneva requesting that the competent Malaysian authorities be advised, and they in turn advice the Malaysian court, of the special Rapporteur's immunity from legal process. On December 12, 1996, the two commercial firms issued a writ of summons and statement of claim against Mr. Cumarswamy in the High Court of Kaula Lumpur. They claimed damage for slander and libel. The Special Rapporteur informed the Commission of the law suits that had been initiated against him.

The High Court of Kaula Lumpur did not pass upon Cumaraswamy's immunity in *limine litis*, but held that it had jurisdiction to hear the case before it on the merits including making a determination of whether Cumaraswamy was entitled to any immunity. This decision was upheld by both the Court of Appeal and the Federal Court of Malaysia. However, the hearings of the case was stayed on the instance of the Government of Malaysia.

In the meantime, the Economic and Social Council asked for the advisory opinion of the International Court of Justice after it was so authorized by the General Assembly. The Court gave the advisory opinion on April 29, 1999 wherein it stated that Cumaraswamy must be regarded as an expert on mission and that such experts enjoy the privileges and immunities as an agent of the Organisation. The Court further stated that Cumaraswamy is entitled to immunity from legal process of every kind because in speaking the words, quoted in the article in International Commercial Litigations, he was acting in the course of the performance of his mission as Special Rapporteur of the Commission.

U.N. Inspectors in Gulf Crisis.—In the Gulf crisis, when 45 U.N. inspectors visited Iraq for the on-site inspection of its nuclear weapons capabilities in September 1991 in accordance with the Security Council Resolution No. 687 (1991) of April 3, 1991, they were detained for four days by the Iraqi authorities and were forced to camp out in a bus and six vehicles outside the Iraqi Atomic Energy Commission after having obtained what was described as 'top secret' documentation on Iraq's nuclear weapon programme. They were not allowed to take documents along with them. Iraqi troops forcibly seized those papers and demanded the inspectors turn over a video tape they made and documents they collected at the time of search. The above action was condemned by the Security Council[1] and by a number of countries as well. The action was a violation of the provisions of the Convention on the Privileges and Immunities of the United Nations as the inspectors being the representatives of the United Nations were immune from detention as well as arrest. Later, they were freed by Iraq.

The General Assembly, on November 21, 1947 also approved a Convention on the Privileges and Immunities of the Specialized Agencies which provided similar privileges and immunities as contained in the Convention on Privileges and Immunities of the United Nations.[2] In addition to their separate draft annexes to each specialized agency, agreements contain special provisions for privileges and immunities which needed to be made in view of the particular nature of each specialized agency. It is to be noted that in those organisations where constitution do not provide for immunities and privileges expressly, some further arrangements are required to be made therein in order to avoid confusion which may arise in future.

It is submitted that the municipal legislatures of the States are required to give effect to the Convention on the Privileges and Immunities of the United Nations and those of the Specialized Agencies so that their representatives may be accorded privileges and immunities as provided in the Conventions. India in order to give effect to the Convention on the Privileges and Immunities of the United Nations enacted the United Nations (Privileges and Immunities) Act 1947. The Act enabled similar privileges and immunities to be enjoyed by other international organisations and their representatives and officials as well.

(c) Capacity to make International Claims

The capacity to espouse claims depends on the existence of legal personality and in the interpretation of the constituent instrument in light of the purposes and functions of the particular organisations. United Nations can claim the compensation is clear from the Advisory opinion of the International Court of Justice in Reparation case whose facts are as follows. On September 17, 1948, Count Bernadotte, a Swedish national was killed, allegedly by a private gang of terrorists, in the new city of Jerusalum. The new city was then in Israeli possession. Count Bernadotte was the Chief United Nations Truce Negotiator in the area. In the course of deciding what action to take in respect of his death, the United Nations General Assembly sought the advice of the ICJ. The Court held that the United Nations was a legal person with a capacity to bring claims against both members and non-member States for direct injuries to the Organisation.[3] The Court held that :

> ".....It cannot be doubted that the Organisation has the capacity to bring an international claim against one of its Members which has caused injury to it by a breach of its international obligations towards it. It is clear that the Organisation has the capacity to bring to claim for this

1. *See* Security Council Resolution 707 (1991).
2. Also *See* Agreement on the Privileges and Immunities of the International Atomic Energy Agency of July 1, 1959.
3. *See* Security Council Resolution 707 (1991).

damage."[1]

In the light of the opinion of the ICJ, the General Assembly authorized the Secretary-General to seek reparation from Israel in connection with the death of Count Bernadotte. In 1950, Israel paid the sum requested by the Secretary-General as reparation for the damages borne by the United Nations.

(d) Functional Protection

Some international organisations have a legal capacity to perform certain functions in the territory of each contracting party. For instance, International Civil Aviation Organisation enjoys in the territory of each contracting party such legal capacity as may be necessary for the performance of its functions *i.e.*, damage caused to the interests of the Organisation itself, to its administrative machinery, to its property and assets, and to interests of which it is the guardian. As far as protection under the United Nations Charter is concerned, it is to be noted that the Charter does not provide it expressly. However, in the Reparation case it was stated : Under International Law, the Organisation must be deemed to have those powers which, though not expressly provided in the Charter, are conferred upon it by necessary implication as being essential to the performance of its duties. The Court further said that in order that the agent may perform his duties satisfactorily, he must feel that protection is assured to him by the Organisation, and that he may count on it. To ensure the independence of the agent, and, consequently, the independent action of the Organisation itself, it is essential that in performing his duties he need not have to rely on any other protection than that of the Organisation. However, this is subject to a condition, that is all legal personality is compatible with the Constitution and laws of the State concerned.

(e) Responsibility of International Organisations

International organisations being a subject of International Law and having legal personality distinct from that of member States are responsible, like States, for internationally wrongful acts. In the event of a violation of International Law by its organs international responsibility is entailed Thus, as in the case of States, international responsibility may arise when breach of an obligation under International Law occurs in relation to that activity. Draft Articles of International Law Commission on Responsibility of International Organisations under Article 1 laid down that every internationally wrongful act of an international organisation entails the international responsibility of that organisation. International Court of Justice in its advisory opinion on the interpretation of the Agreement of 25th March, 1931 between WHO and Egypt stated that international organisations are :

> bound by any obligation incumbent upon them under general rules of international law, under their Constitutions or under international agreement to which they are parties.[2]

An international obligation may be owed by an international organisation to the international community as a whole or to one or several States (whether

1. ICJ Reports (1949) p. 179 at pp. 184-85, 187.
2. ICJ Reports 1980 p 73.

members or non-members) or another international organisation or to any other subject of International Law.

A number of treaties concerning the exploration and use of outer space have laid down that international organisation and its member States are liable for damage caused by activities carried out by that international organisation in outer space. Such treaties, for instance, are Treaty on Principles Governing the Activities of States in the Exploration and Use of Outer Space, including the Moon and Celestial Bodies (1966); Agreement on the Rescue of Astronauts, the Return of Astronauts, and the Return of objects Launched into Outer-Space (1968); and Convention on International Liability for Damage Caused by Space Objects (1972).

It is to be noted that the law on international responsibility of international organisations is not well settled. The main reason for this is that practice concerning responsibility of international organisations has developed only over a relatively recent period. International Law Commission has therefore concluded in its fifty-second session (2000) that the topic of Responsibility of International Organisations is appropriate for codification. The Commission in the year 2011 adopted the Draft Articles on the Responsibility of International Organisations and submitted to the General Assembly. Law on question of responsibility of member States for conduct that is attributed to an international organisation and many other questions are likely to be settled when the Draft Articles of the Commission takes the shape of law.

On the status and legal functions of international organisations advisory opinion given by the International Court of Justice in Reparation for Injuries Suffered in the Service of the United Nations is relevant.

Reparation for Injuries Suffered[1]

During 1947 and 1948 a number of persons serving on Commissions established by the United Nations were killed or injured while fulfilling their official duties in various parts of the world. Of these, the most important was Count Bernadotte who was murdered on September 17, 1948 while carrying out his duties as United Nations Mediator in Palestine.

On December 3, 1948, the General Assembly by Resolution 258(iii) adopted at its 169th Plenary Meeting decided to ask the International Court of Justice for an advisory opinion on two questions :

(I) In the event of an agent of the United Nations in the performance of his duties suffering injury in circumstances involving the responsibility of a State, has the United Nations, as an organisation, the capacity to bring an international claim against the responsible *de jure* or *de facto* government with a view to obtaining the reparation due in respect of the damage caused (a) to the United Nations (b) to the victim or to persons entitled through him.

(II) In the event of an affirmative reply on point I(b), how is action by the United Nations to be reconciled with such rights as may be possessed by the State of which the victim is a national?

1. ICJ Reports 1949, p. 174.

The Court observed that Question I, relates to the 'capacity to bring an international claim'. In the opinion of the Court, the Organisation was intended to exercise and enjoy, and is in fact exercising and enjoying functions and rights which can only be explained on the basis of the possession of a large measure of international personality and the capacity to operate on an international plane. It is at present the supreme type of international organisation, and it could not carry out the intentions of its founders if it was devoid of international functions to it, with the attendant duties and responsibilities, have clothe it with the competence required to enable those functions to be effectively discharged.

Accordingly, the Court concluded 'that the Organisation is an international person'. That is not the same thing as saying that it is a State, which it certainly is not, or that its legal personality and rights and duties are the same as those of a State. Still less is it the same thing as saying that it is a 'super State', what that expression may mean. It does not even imply that all the rights and duties must be upon the international plane. What it does mean is that it is a subject of International Law and capable of possessing international rights and duties, and that it has capacity to maintain its rights by bringing international claims.

The Court further observed that it cannot be doubted that the Organisation has the capacity to bring an international claim against one of its members which has caused injury to it by a breach of its international obligations towards it.

As to question I(b) the court stated that the Organisation has the capacity to bring a claim on the international plane, to negotiate to conclude a special agreement and to prosecute a claim before an international tribunal.

The Court concluded that in the case of a breach of the obligations entered into by the Members, the Organisation has the capacity to claim adequate reparation, it is authorized to include the damage suffered by the victim or by persons entitled through him.

International Organisations and Development of International Law

International organisations are the subjects of International Law by having rights and duties and having capacity to maintain its rights by international claim. These organisations have brought the various nations—big and small together in an international forum where their problems are discussed and where they evolve global policies for States to implement. These organisations have contributed immensely to the growth of international law for the benefit of entire international community. Many rules of international law which are in existence on the basis of extensive State practice or procedure have been codified such as laws relating to diplomatic and consular relations, treaties, succession to treaties. These codified rules are more precise and adequate in comparison to customary rules. Codification has been done mainly by the International Law Commission.

General Assembly and the Specialized Agencies of the United Nations have also formulated a number of conventions which have proved to be effective in the development of international law. In addition to the codification of existing rules, many rules have also been codified on those subjects which have not yet been regulated by international law. Thus, a number of new rules have come within the domain of international law. A few rules which hitherto were the part of private international law have become the rules of international law. Thus, international law has not only been developed but also expanded.

International Law has developed considerably through the resolutions of the General Assembly. Although resolutions adopted by the Assembly are not binding on member States and therefore they do not possess legal character. Consequently, they do not create legal obligations on its members. However, if a resolution is adopted unanimously or by two-third majority of the members and if the same resolution finds reflections in many other subsequent resolutions, it must not be lightly weighted. The International Court of Justice in the advisory opinion given on the Legality of the Threat or Use by a State of Nuclear Weapons in Armed Conflict[1] stated that the Court notes that General Assembly resolutions, even if they are not binding may sometimes have normative value. They can, in certain circumstances, provide evidence important for establishing the existence of a rule or the emergence of an *opinio juris*. Rosalyn Higgius has rightly stated that resolutions with similar contents repeated through time voted for by overwhelming majority giving rise to a general *opinio juris* have created the norm in question.

Many resolutions adopted by the Assembly provide basis for the progressive development of law. Instances of some of the principles that have acquired the status of customary rules of international law through the adoption of the resolutions by the General Assembly are prohibiting the use or threat of force in international relations, non-intervention, right of self-defence, self-determination, and to prohibit to organise, assist, foment, finance, incite or tolerate subversive, terrorist or armed activities in another State. Further, many resolutions are referred to as law making resolutions such as the Universal Declaration of Human Rights, (1948), Declaration on the Prohibition on the Use of Nuclear Weapons for War Purposes (1961); the Declaration on the Granting of Independence to Colonial Countries and Peoples (1960), the Declaration on Permanent Sovereignty over Natural Resources (1962), the Declaration of Legal Principles Governing Activities of States in Exploration and Use of Outer Space (1963), the Declaration on Principles of International Law concerning Friendly Relations and Corporation Among States in accordance with the Charter of the United Nations (1970) and the Resolution Defining Aggression (1974).

International Court of Justice, a principal organ of the United Nations has also played a significant role in the development of international law by its pronouncements. It interpreted and applied the existing rules in such a way so as to resolve issues affecting the life of nations. For instance, it has put to an end to a long standing controversy which had aroused considerable interest in the maritime States of the World. It has condemned decolonisation and reaffirmed the principle of self-determination. The Court has also made new rules which hitherto were non-existent. International organisations including International Court of Justice have potency to develop international law. It may be a good source of development of more laws in future because laws made by them are in common interest of all the States of international community.

1. ICJ Reports (1996).

It may be stated that the activities of the United Nations, its specialized agencies and subsidiary bodies have bearing upon all the institutions of International Law. It would not be inappropriate to say that presently international organisations have become an integral part of International Law. International Law has developed immensely through the development of international organisations.

Evolution of International Organisations

In the ancient and medieval period direct relations between States remained the basic feature of international relations. Bilateral treaties and the diplomatic contacts were the primary means to establish relations with other States. Diplomatic relations in due course of time became more widespread and expanded in political and economic relations. In the ancient India one can find the practice of sending *doots* from one *rajya* to another *rajya*. However, neither the practice was uniform nor they were sent to other States permanently. Diplomatic agents were sent temporarily to other States for some specific purpose and they used to come back to their own State when the purpose was fulfilled.

In the ancient period a variety of Leagues were formed for conducting the international relations, in addition to diplomatic contacts, for the purposes of defences, religious worship and for trade. In China, as early as in 681 B.C., a few small States, threatened by external danger, had formed a League for mutual defence. The Greek city States also developed the League system. They formed the Amphictyonic League which was originally formed by twelve neighbouring tribes for safeguarding the temple of Delphi. Later, the function of the League expanded to create international unity and avoiding war. Achaean League of the Hellenese consisting of nearly seventy member States who enjoyed full autonomy is an another example of the League system. Treaties of alliances and the League system was the first step towards the creation of international organisations.

The present day growth of international organisations owes to a great extent the conferences and meetings that took place in seventeenth and eighteenth centuries to regulate the inter-State relations. Although these conferences were not international organisations, the joining of many States therein signalled the opening of a new era in international relations. International conferences were used to be held normally on the call of European States in the above period in the aftermath of a war to reach an agreement on territorial changes and adjustments which resulted from war to prepare a peace treaty sanctioning the new situations. Instances of such conferences were Westphalia (1648) and Utrecht (1713).

Peace of Westphalia (First European Congress) (1648)

In the closing phases of the bloody and destructive Thirty Year's War (1618-48) victorious and vanquished nations met for over three years at Osnabruck and Munster (in the German province Westphalia). The Chief participants in the conference were Sweden, France and the States of German Empire. After the protracted negotiations treaties were signed on October 24, 1648 which recognised the independence of Holland and Switzerland.

Individual German States, 332 in number, continued under a confederation with the Emperor as a head and were empowered to conclude treaties with one another and with foreign Powers. They became practically sovereign in their foreign relations as well as absolute rulers within their own domain.

The Peace of Westaphalia which is also referred to as the First European Congress was a notable milestone in the development of international organisations. It was attended by practically every European States and wherein all the aspects concerning the interest in Europe were discussed.

Peace of Utrecht (1713)

The Peace of Utrecht ended the war of the Spanish succession. A number of treaties were concluded amongst the participating States. A treaty was concluded between France and England wherein it was provided that the port and fortifications of Dunkirk should be destroyed and never be rebuilt. French complied with this provision but at the same time began building an even larger port at Mardyck, a league of Dunkirk. Great Britain protested against it on the ground that France, in so acting has violated the reasonable, although not the literal sense of the Peace of Utrecht. France in the end recognised this interpretation and discontinued the building of the new port. By the Treaty, Hudson Bay territory, Acadity, St. kills and Newfoundland were ceded to England. By a commercial treaty England and France granted each other most-favoured nations treatment. By a treaty with the Netherlands, France agreed to surrender to Austria the Spanish Netherlands still in French hands. A commercial treaty between France and Netherland was also signed.

The informal pattern of conferences and consultations amongst the States was a significant feature of seventeenth and eighteenth century diplomacy. Conferences were convened for a specific purpose and they came to end once the subject matter was agreed upon and embodied in an international agreement. International conferences used to be held normally on the call of the European States in the aftermath of a war to reach an agreement on territorial changes and adjustments which resulted from war and to prepare a peace treaty sanctioning the new situation.

International Organisations in Nineteenth Century

Nineteenth Century saw the beginning of the movement towards interdependence and international cooperation. The result was that international conferences acquired new dimensions and they extended their scope beyond that of peace settlement conferences and meetings began to be held in increasing frequency. Congress of Vienna held in 1814-1815 at Vienna is one of the most important international conferences of the European States in the Nineteenth Century.

Congress of Vienna (1815)

The Congress of Vienna was hosted by Francis I of Austria. It met from September 1814 to June 1815 after the defeat of Napoleon I. The Conference was called primarily to remake Europe.

The Final Act of the Vienna Congress was signed on June 19, 1815 by Great Britain, Austria, France, Portugal, Prussia, Russia, Spain and Sweden-Norway.

The Final Act stated four points of immense importance which were firstly, the recognition of the permanent neutralisation of Switzerland (Article 118 No. 11); secondly, free navigation on so-called international rivers (Articles 108-117); thirdly, abolition of the negro slave trade (Article 118 No. 15) and fourthly, the different classes of diplomatic envoys (Article 118 No. 17). The Congress classified diplomatic agents in three categories, *viz,* Ambassadors, Ministers plenipotentiary and Envoys Extraordinary and Charges d' Affairs.[1]

The Congress of Vienna may be regarded as a significant turning point as it was the first systematic attempt to regulate international affairs by means of regular international conferences. The result of the conferences was the emergence of a number of international administrative agencies and public international unions in the latter half of the nineteenth and the early twentieth centuries. These were permanent agencies dealing with non-political technical international activities. Examples of the administrative unions are the Universal Telegraphic Union (1865), International Bureau of Telegraphic Administration (1868), Universal Postal Union (1875), International Bureau of Weights and Measures (1875), International Bureau of Industrial Property (1886).

These administrative unions contributed greatly to the concept of international organisations—a most important factor, namely the institutional element. The motive of their creation was not any idealistic theory of international relations but the compelling force of circumstances. When the States came closer to each other these agencies sorted out the common problems at the international level. The creation of these administrative unions was indeed the first step on the road to an organised international community.

Periodic conferences continued to be held in Europe in the nineteenth century. The Paris Conference of 1856 and the Berlin Conference of 1871 dealt with the problems of Balkans. The Berlin Conference of 1884-85 imposed some order upon the scramble for Africa that had begun to develop.

International Conference on Red Cross (1864)

An international conference attended by delegates of 16 States was held in Geneva which adopted the Geneva Convention of 1864 for the Amelioration of the Conditions of the Wounded and Sick of Armies in the Field—the first multilateral agreement on the Red cross. Signatory States committed themselves to take care for the wounded at war, whether enemy or friend. The Convention thus provided for the neutrality of the personnel of the medical services of civilians who voluntarily assisted them and an international emblem to mark personnel and supplies. In honour of Dunant's nationality, a Red Cross on white back-ground, the Swiss flag with colours reversed was chosen as its symbol.[2]

The worldwide structure of the Red Cross and Red Crescent consists of (a) the International Committee of the Red Cross Founded in 1863, composed of 25 Swiss citizens; (b) the League of Red Cross and Red Crescent Societies founded

1. Later, in the Congress of Aix-la-Chapalle of 1818 a fourth class of diplomatic agents was added *i.e.* Ministers Resident.
2. Henry Dunant—A Swiss humanitarian urged the formation of voluntary aid societies for relief to war victims. A Swiss welfare agency actively seconded Dunant's suggestion and the result was that the international conference was convened.

in 1919, a federation of national societies for mutual help, cooperation and programme development, especially in time of peace and (c) the National Red Cross and Red Crescent Societies.

Hague Peace Conferences

With the Hague Conferences (1899 and 1907), an important threshold was crossed on the way to international institutionalization. These Conferences which were meant to take place every seven years were convened in time of peace and enjoyed nearly universal participation of the then recognised States. Unlike the great-power conferences of the 19th century, the Hague Conferences established rules that were designed to regulate the international system and to remove the causes of crisis and war. And whereas the Great Power conferences had been designed to achieve settlements immediately after wars and crisis, the Hague conferences were preventive and regulatory in nature.

The Hague Conference of 1899, the so called Peace Conference at the Hague was convened on the personal initiative of the Czar Nicholas II of Russia and Queen Wilhelmina of the Netherlands. The Conference met from May 18 to July 29, 1899 and 26 nations took part in the Conference. The Conference resulted in the adoption of three important conventions. Firstly, the Convention for the Pacific Settlement of International Disputes; secondly, the Convention with respect to the Laws and Customs of War on Land, and thirdly, the Convention concerning the Adaptation of Maritime Warfare. These conventions may be called Codes. In addition to them, three declarations of minor value were also adopted by the Peace Conference. One prohibited the use of asphyxiating gases, another prohibited the use of expanding bullets (dumdums), and another prohibited the discharges of projectiles or explosives from balloons.

The Second Hague Peace Conference of 1907 though first proposed by U.S. President Roosevelt was officially convened by Nicholes II. The Conference met from June 15 to October 18, 1907 and was attended by the representatives of 44 States, produced thirteen conventions. While the three conventions, namely, that for the Pacific Settlement of International Disputes, that concerning the Laws and Customs of War on Land, and that concerning the adaptation of the principles of the Geneva Convention to Maritime Warfare took the place of three corresponding conventions of the First Hague Peace Conference, the other ten conventions were entirely new. They laid down rules for the conduct of war on land and naval warfare. For instance, the Second Convention laid down many limitations regarding use of force for enforcing contractual obligations. Third Convention laid down that hostilities shall not be commenced without previous and explicit warning. The Fourth Convention laid down the Regulations Respecting the Laws and Customs of War on Land. By the Fifth Convention the rights and duties of the neutral powers were protected. Sixth Convention regulated the status of the enemy merchant ships. Seventh Convention laid down that no merchant ship shall be converted into a warship unless it is placed directly under the authority and control of the authority, whose flag it flied. Ninth Convention laid down that the belligerents are prohibited from bombarding undefendent ports, towns, villages, dwellings or other buildings by the naval forces. Bombardment of places of worship, art, science, hospital, charitable institutions and historical monuments were also prohibited. Twelveth Convention provided for the creation of an International Prize court to act as a Court of appeal from the national tribunal of the belligerent powers. Apart from the conventions on the limitation of the employment of force for the recovery of contract debts and the opening of hostilities, they were devoted to the regulations of rules of warfare and neutrality in war on land and sea.[1]

The Third Peace Conference was to be held at Hague in 1915, but it could not be covened due to commencement of the First World War.

In addition to the above, London Naval Conference of 1908-1909 undertook the more difficult task of the codification of the "generally recognized principles of International Law" in respect to maritime war, but here the conflict of interest was irreconcilable.[2] When war actually came, only the Hague codes consisting of humanitarian provisions survived, and even these could not stand the strain of new instruments of warfare.

International Organisations in Twentieth Century

The twentieth century witnessed alround development of international organisations. After the traumatic experience of World War I the League of Nations[3] was established in 1920 by the Paris Peace treaty after the First World War with the object of achieving international peace and security and to promote international cooperation. However, it became inactive since 1939 and was finally dissolved in 1946. International Labour Organisation (ILO)[4] and the Permanent Court of International Justice (PCIJ) were originally connected with the League but enjoyed a high degree of independence. The League structure also contained three so-called technical organisations which were : Economic and Financial Organisation, the Communications and Transit Organisation and the Health Organisation.

Permanent Court of International Justice (PCIJ)

The World Court, the popular name of the PCIJ was established pursuant to Article 14 of the Covenant of the League of Nations which provided that the Council of the League shall formulate and submit to the members of the League of adoption plans for the establishment of a Permanent Court of International Justice. The Council of the League accordingly appointed an Advisory Committee of Jurists in February 1918 and charged them with the duty of preparing a draft scheme for the establishment of a Court. The draft with some important amendments was approved by the Assembly on December 3, 1920. The Court had a Statute which was an independent document but it was linked to the League by Article 14 of the Covenant. The Statute was accepted by a Protocol of signature dated December 16, 1920 and subject to ratification, it entered into force on September 2, 1921. The seat of the Court was at Hague.

The Court was empowered to render judgments in disputes between States which were voluntarily submitted to it and give advisory opinion on any matter

1. Oppenheim, International Law, Vol. I, Ninth Edition (1992), p. 99.
2. Fenwick, 'International Law', p. 100.
3. *See* Chapter, 'League of Nations'.
4. Part XIII of the Treaty of Versailles contained the Constitution of the International Labour Organisation. For detail see Chapter 'Specialized Agencies".

referred to it by the Council or Assembly of the League. Its function, thus, was judicial rather than purely arbitral and diplomatic. The Court had originally 11 judges and 4 deputy judges but in 1931, its composition was changed to 15 regular judges. Judges were elected for a nine year term by the Council and the Assembly concurrently. The Court in the course of its existence rendered some 20 judgments and 27 advisory opinions. An important judgment was that which affirmed Danish sovereignty over the North coast of Greenland and disallowed Norway's claim (Legal Status of Eastern Greenland). A notable advisory opinion of the Court declared that the proposed customs of Union of Germany and Austria would violate Austria's pledge to remain independent.

The working of the Court was interrupted after the German occupation of the Netherlands in 1940 and in April 1945, a Committee of Jurists, set up by the sponsoring powers of the Conference of the United Nations at San Francisco, prepared a report as a result of which it was decided that PCIJ should cease to exist and a new Court—International Court of Justice should be set up to take its place. The PCIJ held its final session in October 1945 and in January 1946 all the judges tendered their resignation. In April 1946 the Final Assembly of the League of Nations dissolved the Court.

The Second World War had created horror in the minds of the people. It brought ruthless destruction. People everywhere assumed that some kind of World organisation should be established. After a long and heated deliberations the organisation which emerged was, the United Nations Organisation.[1] The Permanent Court of International Justice was abolished in 1946. A new Court—International Court of Justice, which was an integral part of the Charter of the United Nations, was established in 1946. The Court functions in accordance with the Statute which is based on the Statute of the Permanent Court of International Justice.[2]

In addition to the general organisation of international society as represented by the League of Nations and thereafter the United Nations, the needs of international co-operation have led to the emergence of specialized organisations of States endowed with separate organs of their own. They laid down their constitutions and their objects and also the composition of their organs. Some of these organisations conducted their activities in close cooperation with one another and the United Nations. They are called specialized agencies of the United Nations.[3] At present, there are seventeen such specialized agencies. Three of them : the Universal Postal Union, the International Telecommunication Union and the International Labour Organisation are considerably older than the United Nations itself.

Other important organisations include the functional organisations which are not specialized agencies but still have some affiliation with the United Nationsc[4] are the United Nations Children's Fund (UNICEF) of 1946 at New York; the Office of the United Nations High Commissioner for Refugees of 1951 at Geneva; the International Atomic Energy Agency of 1957 at Vienna, the

1. *See* Chapter, United Nations Organisation.
2. *See* Chapter, International Court of Justice.
3. *See* Chapter, "Specialized Agencies'.
4. See Chapter 'Other Related Organisations of the United Nations'.

United Nations Development Programme (UNDP) of 1966 at New York formed by consolidating the Expanded Programme of Technical Assistance (EPTA) of 1950 at New York and the Special Fund of 1959 at New York.

The specialized agencies and the U.N. affiliated functional agencies have a greater role to play in fostering international co-operation and in improving the life conditions of the people of the World. There is hardly any phase of international life that does not come within purview of these organisations.

Chapter 2

League of Nations

In the beginning of the twentieth century, outstanding conferences that took place were the Hague Peace Conferences of 1899 and 1907. They were mainly related to the development of International Law. However, they were also of significance in the evolution of international organisations.[1] Experiences and experiments of these conferences along with the conferences of preceding century on the one hand and the devastating effects of the First World War on the other hand, led some individuals in England and in America to propose the scheme of a League for the avoidance of war in future. In June 1915, 'The League to Enforce Peace' was founded under the leadership of former President Taft in 1915. After a long and bitter deliberations, the League of Nations Commission of the Peace Conference accepted the joint draft presented by America and England. The Draft was given the final shape by the Commission, and the Covenant of the League of Nations was adopted by the Conference on April 28, 1919. The Covenant consisting of 26 Articles was a part of the Treaty of Versailles of 1919.[2] The League of Nations was established on January 10, 1920.

Preamble of the Covenant

The Preamble of the Covenant laid down the objectives for the creation of the League which were to promote international cooperation and to achieve international peace and security. These objectives shall be obtained by the acceptance of obligations not to resort to war; by the prescription of open, just and honourable relations between nations, by the firm establishment of the understandings of international law as the actual rule of conduct among Governments, and by the maintenance of justice and a scrupulous respect for all obligations in the dealings of organized peoples with one another. Preamble also stated that the High Contracting Parties agree to this Covenant of the League of Nations'.

---

1. Palmer and Perkins lays down that the Hague Conferences of 1899 and 1907 may be said to have represented a transitional step from *ad hoc* conferences and specialized international organisations towards the League of Nations, the first great experiment of an organisation open to all States without a special purpose and character (International Relations p. 320.)
2. The Treaty of Versailles was signed at the end of World War I by the Allied and Associated Powers and by Germany in the Hall of Mirros in the Palace of Versailles (France) on June 28, 1919 which came into force on January 10, 1920. Earlier, the Treaty was negotiated and drafted during the Paris Peace Conference in 1919 which was dominated by the national leaders known as the 'Big Four'—Woodrow Wilson of the United States, Clemenceau of France, Lloyd George of Britain and Vittorio Orlands of Italy. Germany was not included in the consultations.

Membership of the League

There were two kinds of members of the League of Nations. Article 1 of the Covenant, provided that it shall consist of original members and subsequent members, *i.e.*, such members who were to be admitted later. Original members of the League were those States whose names were enumerated in the Annex to the Covenant either as 'Signatories of the Treaty of Peace' or as 'States invited to accede to the Covenant', which did in fact accede without reservation to the Covenant on or before March 20, 1920. The Annex mentioned the names of thirty two States. Out of them, three failed to ratify the Covenant. They were Ecaudor, the Hedjaz and the U.S.A.. Thirteen States were invited to accede to the Covenant and they acceded to it. Thus, forty-two States became the original members of the League. Provisions for the subsequent members were laid down under para 2 of Article 1 which provided that : Any fully self-governing State, Dominion or colony not named in the Annex may become a Member of the League if its admission is agreed to by two-thirds of the Assembly provided that it shall give effective guarantees of its sincere intention to observe its international obligations, and shall accept such regulations as may be prescribed by the League in regard to its military, naval, and air force and armaments. Twenty-one States were admitted in the League as subsequent members. Applications for admission made by Armenia, Azerbaidjan, Georgia, Liechtenstein and Ukraine were refused in 1920.

Membership of the League could be terminated in three ways. Firstly, by voluntary withdrawal from the League after having given two year's notice of its intention to do so provided all its international obligations and all its obligations under the Covenant have been fulfilled at the time of its withdrawal (Article 1 para 3). Secondly, by expulsion *i.e.* any member of the League may be expelled from the League if it has violated the Covenant of the League by a vote of the Council concurred in by the representatives of all the other members of the League represented thereon (Article 16, para 4). Thirdly, by expressing its dissent from amendments (Article 26 para 2).

It is to be noted that the provisions regarding the withdrawal of membership from the League proved detrimental to the interests of the League. In the beginning, there were sixty two members in the League, but in due course of time, the membership was reduced to thirty two. Even some powerful States withdrew from the League. Germany which joined the League in 1926 left it in 1933, Japan left the League after having condemned for its intervention in Manchuria, Italy withdrew from the League in 1937 after its conquest of Ethiopia. U.S.S.R. was expelled from the membership of the League for the violations of Article 16 when it committed aggression on Finland in December 1939.

Organs of the League

The League had two principal organs : the Assembly and the Council, assisted by the permanent Secretariat.

(a) The Assembly

The Assembly was represented by all the members of the League. According to Article 3 each member of the League could send not more than three representatives to the Assembly, but they all had one vote. The Assembly met at least once a year, and more frequently, if required. In practice, the Assembly used to meet annually in September in Geneva. The Assembly could also meet in special sessions. It held many special sessions; important among them was that of March 19, 1926, when Germany applied for membership. The Assembly had six regular standing committees-constitutional and legal, technical organisations, reduction of armaments, budgetary, social and humanitarian and political.

The functions of the Assembly were not adequately laid down in the Covenant. It was provided under Article 3 para 3 that the Assembly may deal at its meetings with any matter within the sphere of action of the League or affecting the peace of the World. Of the many functions performed by the Assembly and the Council : (a) some were exclusively reserved for the Assembly, and (b) others were reserved for the Council of the League; (c) others, again, required the cooperation of these two organs; while (d) with regard to others the Assembly's competence was either concurrent with or alternative to that of the Council. Exclusively reserved functions included the admission of new members (Article 1) by a two-thirds majority; election of non-permanent members of the Council (Article 4), apportioning the expenses of the League among the members, appointment of committees by simple majority, supervising the work of the Council and setting of its own procedure. Prevention of war and to find a peaceful solution of international disputes was the matter which could be dealt with either by the Assembly or the Council.

Decision in the Assembly was taken by at least four kinds of votes depending upon the nature of the matter. These were : (a) unanimous vote of all the members of the League represented at the meeting (Article 5); (b) the vote of a simple majority of the members of the League represented at the meeting, which applied to all matters of procedure... including the appointment of committees of investigation (Article 5); (c) a vote of a two-thirds majority, and (d) a majority vote, but including the votes of all the members represented in the Council.

(b) The Council

The Council was the executive organ of the League. Its size depended, in the first instance, upon the provisions of Article 4. The Council consisted of (a) permanent members namely, those Great Powers who were members of the League *i.e.* the United States of America, the British Empire, France, Italy and Japan. The Council could with the approval of the majority of the Assembly, name other permanent members; (b) eleven non-permanent members of whom three were elected each year and for three years. This group could be sub-divided into (a) non-permanent and not re-eligible until the expiry of three years from the conclusion of their terms of office, and (b) non-permanent declared by a majority of two-thirds of the members of the Assembly voting to be immediately re-eligible. (iii) *Ad hoc* representatives.

Permanent members of the Council were the Great Powers *i.e.*, the Principal Allied and Associated Powers—the United States of America, the British Empire, France, Italy and Japan together with four other members of the

League selected by the Assembly from time to time. United States of America did not join the League as the U.S. Senate refused to give its assent and therefore the number was four in 1920 which increased to 5 in 1926 (with the admission of Germany) to six in 1934-35 (with the admission of the USSR) and then declared to 2 at the end of 1939.[1] They were : France and Great Britain. The number of non-permanent members was increased from four to six in 1922, to nine in 1926, to ten in 1933 and finally to eleven in 1936.

The Council was expected to meet atleast once a year at the seat of the League or at such other places as may be decided upon. The Council could also meet in any emergency arising out of war or threat of a war.

Like the Assembly, the Council could deal with any matter within the sphere of action of the League or affecting the World peace (Article 4 para 4). The functions of the Council may be classified as being (a) within the exclusive competence; (b) requiring cooperation with the Assembly; and (c) within the concurrent or alternative competence of the Assembly and the Council.

The Council could take a decision by means of the following kinds of votes : (a) the unanimous vote of all members of the League represented at the meeting (Article 5); (b) the vote of a simple majority of the members of the League represented at the meeting; (c) the vote of all the members of the League excluding the representatives of the parties to a dispute and (d) the vote of a simple majority of all the members of the Council.

Exclusive functions of the Council included the (1) nomination of additional permanent members of the Council; (2) formulating plans for the reduction of armaments; (3) to advise how the evil effects of manufacture of munitions and implements of war by private enterprise can be prevented (4) advising upon the means by which the members of the League were to preserve as against external aggression, the territorial integrity and existing political independence of other members; (5) supervision of the mandate system; minorities treaties and other agreements; (6) to direct the work to the Secretariat, arrange for international conferences, receive reports from the subsidiary organs of the League, determine which reports should be submitted to the Assembly and to deal with disputes among League members. Safeguarding the peace of the World was the primary responsibility of the Council.

Voting in the Assembly and the Council.—Decisions at any meeting of the Assembly or of the Council required the agreement of all the members of the League represented at the meeting except where otherwise expressly provided in the Covenant or by the terms of the Treaty (Article 5 Para 1). All matters of procedure at meetings of the Assembly or of the Council, including the appointment of committees to investigate particular matters, shall be regulated by the Assembly or by the Council and may be decided by a majority of the members of the League represented at the meeting (Article 5 Para 2). Article 5 Para 3 provided that the first meeting of the Council shall be summoned by the President of the United States of America.

---

1. Japan and Germany withdrew from the League in 1935 and Italy in 1939. USSR was expelled from the League for its attack on Finland.

(c) Secretariat

The Secretariat consisted of the Secretary General and such secretaries and staff as may be required (Article 6 Para 1). Para 2 of Article 6 laid down that the first Secretary-General shall be the person whose name was mentioned in the Annex and thereafter the Secretary-General shall be appointed by the Council with the approval of the majority of the Assembly. Accordingly, the First Secretary-General was Sir Eric Drummond of the Great-Britain. He held office term 1920 to 1923. He was succeeded by Joseph Arenol of France.

The secretaries and the staff of the Secretariat were appointed by the Secretary-General with the approval of the Council. Two Deputy Secretary-General and two under-Secretaries were appointed to assist the Secretary-General.

The Secretariat was established in Geneva—the seat of the League. Functions of the Secretariat was to assist all organs of the League by providing services of different kinds, *viz.*, clerical, research, drafting, publication, coordination, registration of treaties, keeping of records, arrangements of meeting etc. It had a staff of seven hundred persons, working through eleven 'Sections' and numerous services and offices.

Mandates of the League of Nations

The system of mandates established by Article 22 of the Covenant of the League was a form of international guardianship to those colonies and territories which "as a consequence of the war have ceased to be under the sovereignty of the States which formerly governed them and which are inhabited by peoples not yet able to stand by themselves under the strenuous conditions of the modern World." Thus,. the mandate was created in the interest of the inhabitants of the territory, and of humanity in general as an international institution with an international object—a sacred trust of civilisation...[1] the international rules regulating the mandate constituted an international status of the territory.....[2] The above implies that amongst others, the principal obligations of the mandatory, including those relating to international supervision, were held not to have been abrogated by the dissolution of the League. The mandate system was thus limited to the territories of Germany and Turkey and did not extend to colonies and territories of Allied and Associated Powers. The principle upon which the system was based was "the well being and development of such peoples from a sacred trust of civilization and that securities for the performance of this trust should be embodied in the Covenant of the League. The tutelage of these peoples was to be entrusted to advanced nations, which by reason of their resources, their experience or their geographical position can best undertake this responsibility and who are wiling to accept it, and that this tutelage should be exercised as mandatories on behalf of the League.

It was provided under Article 22 Para 7 that in every case of mandate, the mandatory shall render to the Council an annual report in reference to the

1. In the South West Africa case (Second Phase) the ICJ held that the principle of the 'sacred trust' was primarily a moral or humanitarian concept. (ICJ Reports (1966) pp. 34-35.
2. ICJ Reports (1950) p. 32.

territory committed to its charge. The degree of authority, control, or administration to be exercised by the mandatory shall, if not previously agreed upon the members of the League be explicitly defined in each case by the Council. (Article 22 Para 8). A Permanent Commission was constituted to receive and examine the annual reports of mandatory and to advise the Council on all matters relating to the observance of the mandates.

Under the mandate system, three distinct groups of territories were placed, *i.e.*, Class A, Class B and Class C. Class A consisted of certain communities which had reached a stage of development at which their existence as independent nations could be provisionally recognized, subject to a temporary regime of administrative assistance from a mandatory State. Syria, Lebanon, Palestine, Iraq and Trans-Jordan were placed under this class. They became independent by the end of 1946 or were expected to become independent by that time. Class B of mandates included certain former colonies of Germany which were administered by the mandatory State under a separate form of government. They included the British Cameroons, British Togoland and Tanganiya under British mandate, the French Camerons and French Togoland under French mandate, and Rwanda Urundi under Belgian mandate. Class C mandates were administered as integral portions of the territories of mandatory State and had no international status whatever. Such territories included South-West Africa assigned to South Africa, Samoa to New Zealand, Nauru to Great Britain, Asutralia and New Zealand jointly; other Pacific Islands south of the equator to Australia; and Pacific Islands north of the equator to Japan. All the territories belonging to class B and C came under the trusteeship system under the United Nations.[1]

Settlement of Disputes

In order to achieve the main objective of maintaining peace and security the Covenant made elaborate provisions for the settlement of disputes between States. The Covenant under Article 12 Para 1 laid down that in the event of a dispute arising between the members of the League they will submit the matter either to arbitration or judicial settlement or to inquiry by the Council. Article 13 Para 1 stated that matters suitable for submission to arbitration or judicial settlement should be in accordance with Article 13 Para 2 which enumerated that such disputes as involving the interpretation of a treaty, questions of international law, questions of facts bearing upon the breach of an international obligation or the reparation to be made for such breach. Members of the League agreed that they will carry out in full good faith any award or decision that may be rendered, and they will not resort to war against a member of the League which complies therewith. In the event of any failure to carry out such an award or decision, the Council shall propose what steps should be taken to give effect thereto.

If any dispute arises between the members of the League and which is not submitted to arbitration or judicial settlement, members agreed that they will submit the matter to the Council. (Article 15 Para 1). Any party to the dispute may effect such submission by giving notice of the existence of the dispute to

1. See Chapter, 'Trusteeship Council'.

the Secretary General, who will make necessary arrangements for a full investigation and consideration thereof. The Council shall endeavour to effect a settlement of disputes, and if such efforts are successful, a statement shall be made public giving such facts and explanations regarding the dispute and the terms of settlement thereof as the Council may deem appropriate. If the dispute is not settled, the Council either unanimously or by a majority shall make and publish a report containing a statement of the facts of dispute and the recommendations which are deemed just and proper in regard thereto.

It was stated in the Covenant that members shall in no case resort to war until three months after the award by the arbitrators or the judicial decision or the report by the Council. Any member which resorted to war in disregard of the above provisions shall *ipso facto* be deemed to have committed an act of war against all members of the League. They also agreed to immediately take action such as severance of all trade or financial relations, the prohibition of all intercourse between their nationals and the nation of the Covenant-breaking State, and the prevention of all financial, commercial or personal intercourse between the nationals of the Covenant breaking State and the nationals of any other State (Article 16 Para 1).

In the event of a dispute arising between a member of the League and a State which is not a member of the League or between non-members of the League, non-members shall be invited to accept the obligations of membership in the League for the purposes of such disputes upon such conditions as the Council may deem just (Article 17 Para 1). If such invitation is accepted, the provisions of Article 12 to 16 shall be applied with such notifications as may be deemed necessary by the Council. The Council, after the invitation being given, shall immediately institue an inquiry into the circumstances of the disputes and recommend such action as may deem best and most effectual in the circumstances (Article 17 Para 2). If a State so invited refuses to accept the obligations of membership in the League for the purposes of such dispute and resorts to war against a member of the League, sanctions laid down under Article 16 shall be applied against a State taking such action. If both the disputant parties are not members, they both shall be invited and if they refuse to accept the obligations of membership in the League for the pupose of such dispute, the Council may take such measures and make such recommendations so as to prevent hostilities and which may result in the settlement of the dispute.

War and Neutrality

The Covenant of the League did not prohibit war and therefore war was generally not illegal. However, notable regulations were made for resorting war. Members of the League agreed that if a dispute arises between them, they shall submit the matter either to arbitration or judicial settlement or to the inquiry by the Council,[1] and they also agreed that in no case war shall be resorted until three months after the award by the arbitrators or by the judicial decision or the report by the Council,[2] The three months time, i.e., 'cooling period' was provided as it was believed that it will be able to prevent the accidental

1. Article 12 (1).
2. Article 12 (2).

outbreak of hostilities. However, war resorted after following the above procedure was not forbidden. If any State resorted to war without following the above procedure it would be deemed, to have committed 'an act of war against all other members of the League,[1] which is tantamount to aggression against the community of States. Such an aggression is a violation of International Law, customary as well as positive, and against the supreme interest of humanity. Such a war was forbidden under the Covenant. Thus, the Covenant did not prohibit the war altogether. It imposed limitations on the members for waging war. It provided for only a partial prohibition of war that hampered the effective functioning of the the League. The limitations laid down were confined only to members of the League.

The League of Nations considerably affected the notion of neutrality . League envisaged two kinds of war. Firstly, those which were resorted to not in disregard of the provisions of the Covenant, *i.e.,* those which were not forbidden, and secondly, war in disregard of the provisions of the Covenant, *i.e.,* forbidden war. As to the first kind of war, it is to be noted that they were legal wars, and in such cases members of the Covenant were left free to maintain their neutrality in the traditional sense of the term. No restriction or prohibition was made by the provisions of the Covenant as to the attitude of neutrality in such war. However, the concept of neutrality was largely affected in that war which was resorted in disregard of the obligations of the Covenant. Such war was regarded as illegal and if it was resorted, it was *ipso facto* deemed to have been committed as an act of war against all other members of the League' in accordance with Article 16 of the Covenant. Since any such war was a matter for the whole World, and all members were required to give assistance to the victims of aggression, no State could adopt an attitude of neutrality. But the analysis of the provisions of the Covenant reveals that even in any such war (which is resorted in disregard of the Covenant) neutrality may be adopted by the States. For instance, non-members of the League such as the United States, and later on, Japan, Germany and Italy could remain neutral in any such war. Further, there was no authority to determine as to whether a State of war exists or not. And so a member State may remain neutral if it decides in a particular war that no Covenant breaking resort to war had taken place. Stone has very rightly said that the rules of neutrality 'remained operative' even after the establishment of the League of Nations in the following ways : (1) as to non-members of the League such as the United States, and later Japan, Germany, and Italy; (2) as to wars not forbidden, *i.e.,* within the gaps in the Covenant; (3) even in a forbidden war, as to particular members who decided in the particular case that no Covenant-breaking resort to war had taken place.[2]

Practice of the States also suggests that the States adopted the attitude of neutrality in those wars which took place after the establishment of the League. Thus, during the Russia-Polish war in 1920 Germany declared its neutrality. In Greco-Turkish war of 1921, the Allied Governments issued a collective declaration of neutrality. In Chaco war between Bolivia and Paraguay, Argentina, Brazil, Chile and Peru declared neutrality in 1933 in spite of the fact

1. Article 16 (1).
2. Stone, 'Legal Controls of International Conflict', Second Impression, (1959) p. 381.

that three of them were members of the League.

Non-Intervention in the Domestic Jurisdiction of a State.

The principle of non-intervention in the domestic jurisdiction was stated under Article 15 Para 8 which lays down that if the dispute between the parties is claimed by one of them and is found by the Council, to arise out of a matter which by international law is solely within the jurisdiction of that party, the Council shall so report and shall make no recommendation as to its settlement. The above implies that the Council was competent to decide the question as to whether the matter out of which the dispute had arisen was solely within the domestic jurisdiction of the party which made the claim, and this act of the Council implied the decision of the dispute.

Registration of Treaties.

Article 18 of the Covenant provided that every treaty or international engagement entered into hereafter by any member of the League shall be forthwith registered with the Secretariat and shall as soon as possible be published by it. No such treaty or international engagement shall be binding until so registered.

The Secretariat of the League performs the functions of publication of treaties in the League of Nations Treaty Series (LNTS).

Disarmament under the League of Nations.

The Covenant stressed the need to reduce national armaments and armed forces by stating under Article 18 Para 1 that the maintenance of peace requires the reduction of national armaments to the lowest point consistent with national safety and the enforcement by common action of international obligations. The Covenant further provided under Article 18 Para 2 that at least in every ten years the Council of the League after taking into account of the geographical situation and circumstances of each State, shall formulate plans for such reduction for the consideration and action of the several governments. Article 18 Para 3 provided that plans shall be subject to reconsideration and revision at least every ten years. It was also laid down under Para 4 of Article 18 that after these plans have been adopted by the several governments, the limits of armaments therein fixed shall not be receded without the concurrence of the Council.

It is to be noted that the above provisions of the Covenant as to disarmament were too ambiguous to serve any useful purpose. Its provisions were further weakened by the fact that the Covenant neither refrained the members from the use of force in their international relations nor it prohibited war altogether. The result was that there was no basis for implementing disarmament measures.

(I) Codification under the League of Nations

The Covenant of the League was the first instrument which handled the problem of codification properly. The Council of the League, in 1924, appointed a Committee of sixteen jurists to report on those questions which were ripe for codification and to report as to how their codification could best be achieved. The Committee, after examining the reports of sub-committees, gave a report in April 1927 wherein it stated that the following seven topics were ripe for codification : (1) Nationality; (ii) Territorial Waters; (iii) Responsibility of States for Damage done in their Territory to the Person or Property of Foreigners; (iv) Diplomatic Privileges and Immunities; (v) Procedure of International Conferences and Procedure for the Conclusion and Drafting of Treaties; (vi) Piracy; and (vii) Exploitation of the Products of the Sea. In 1927, the Report of the Committee was considered by the Assembly of the League and also the Council's observations thereon, and decided that a Conference should be held at the Hague for the purpose of codifying the subjects mentioned aforesaid under (i), (ii) and (iii).

The Hague Conference met in 1930 and adopted conventions on the topic of Nationality which were : (a) a Convention concerning Certain Questions relating to the Conflict of Nationality Laws; (b) a Protocol relating to Military Obligations in certain cases of Double Nationality; (c) a Protocol relating to Certain Cases of Statelessness; and (d) a Special Protocol concerning Statelessness. It is significant to note that these conventions did not receive wide support is clear from the fact that they were ratified only by a few States. On the topics of Territorial Waters and Responsibility of States for the Damage done in their Territories to the Property and Person of Foreigner, no convention could be formulated because of the lack of general agreement. It is to be noted that the Conference fell short of the expectations that had preceded its convening in view of its limited success. No further attempts of codification were made under the League. Perhaps its enthusiasm for codification wilted after the failure of the 1930 Conference.

Collective Security and the League of Nations

Collective security system received legal status for the first time under the Covenant of the League of Nations. The Covenant under Article 10 provided that the members of the League undertake to respect and preserve as against external aggression, the territorial integrity and political independence of all members of the League. In case of any such aggression, the Council shall advise upon the means by which the obligation shall be fulfilled. Further, Article 11 provided that any war or threat of war, whether immediately affecting any of the members of the League is not hereby declared a matter of concern for the whole League and the League shall take any action that may be deemed wise and effectual to safeguard the peace of nations. The Covenant further provided under Article 12 that members of the League agreed to settle disputes between them either through arbitration or judicial settlement or inquiry by the Council. They shall not resort to war until three months after the award by the arbitrators or the judicial decision, or the report by the Council. Article 13 laid down that members agreed that in case of any dispute between members which they considered suitable for submission to arbitration or judicial settlement shall submit the same to arbitration or judicial settlement. If the disputes are not submitted to arbitration or judicial settlement that would be submitted to the Council. The Council was required to make efforts to settle the dispute. Article

16 provided that if any member of the League resorted to war in disregard of the above provisions it shall *ipso facto* be deemed to have committed an act of aggression against all members of the League. In such cases, the Council was to recommend to the several governments concerned that what effective military, naval or air force the members of the League shall severally contribute to the armed forces to be used to protect the Covenant. The above provisions of the Covenant clearly show that the principle of collective security system evolved and the principle of collective responsibility emerged to thwart the act of aggression or illegal use of force.

Introduction of the collective security system under the Covenant was indeed a landmark in the history of international relations. For the first time members agreed to take action against a State which resorted to war violating the provisions of the Covenant. However, the system was not effective and it did not work in actual working mainly because members failed to abide by their solemn obligations which they undertook under the Covenant. For instance, the League could not take any action against Italy when it conquered the Corfu Island of Greek in 1923 and against Japan when it occupied central Manchuria. The collective security system again failed when Japan attacked Ethiopia. These instances go to prove that collective security system was totally ineffective. Most of the member States, especially Great Powers were interested in safeguarding their national interest than the interest of the international community.

Although collective security system was inadequate under the Covenant of the League of Nations a number of efforts were made to strengthen the system in the inter-war period. The Draft Treaty of Mutual Assistance of 1923, Geneva Protocol of 1924, Locarno Pact of 1925 and the Kellogg Briand Pact of 1928 (Pact of Paris) and the Anti War Treaty of Non-Aggression and Conciliation (1933) tried to strengthen the collective security system as envisaged in the Covenant.

Weaknesses of the League of Nations

An evaluation of the twenty-years (1920 to 1940) record of the League of Nations leads one to classify the first decade (1920-1930) as the successful years and the second decade (1930-1940) as the unsuccessful years. The League of Nations proved its value by settling the Swedish-Finish dispute over the Aaland Islands (1920-21), guaranteeing the security of Albania (1921), rescuing Austria from political and economic disaster (1922), setting the division of Upper-Silesia (1922) and preventing the outbreak of war in the Balkans between Greece and Bulgaria (1925). The above shows that during the first decade, the League's functioning was quite successful. However, in the second decade the League failed miserably in maintaining peace. Some of the instances where the League failed were the Japanese occupation of Manchuria, the Italian occupation of Ethiopia, the Chaco war (conflict between Bolivia and Paraguay), the Spanish Civil War and the Soviet attack on Finland.

By the end of 1939, it became evident that the League has become powerless to prevent the outbreak of war. It became least effective during World War II. The final League Assembly (Twenty-first) was held at Geneva on April 8, 1946 which was attended by 34 delegates. On April 19, 1946 the delegates approved a motion wherein it was declared that with effect from this day, following the close of the present session of the Assembly, the League of Nations shall cease to exist except for the sole purpose of the liquidation of its affairs.

League failed because it suffered from a number of defects which are as follows :

(1) The League failed to attain universality of membership. It consisted mostly of European nation-States. Thus it did not represent the entire World community. Only sixtythree States were admitted to the League and therefore it was not an effective organisation to maintain World peace.

(2) League did not forbid the war completely. War could be resorted by a State after the completion of the formalities as provided in the Covenant. The Covenant laid down that if any dispute arose, that will be settled either through arbitration or by judicial settlement. If the dispute was not resolved through these means, parties could resort to war after the lapse of three months from the date of the decision of the arbitration or of judicial settlement.

(3) One of the great powers—U.S.A. did not become the member of the League because of non-ratification of the Treaty by the Senate. The absence of U.S.A. from the League made even England less enthusiastic.

(4) Powers for the enforcement of the decision was not centralized. The enforcement depended upon the decision of the bulk of the members of the League. Thus, the consent of all members was essential which could not be attained. China in 1932, Abyssinia in 1935 appealed for collective action, but no action could be taken to fulfil the obligation.

(5) Functions of the Council and the Assembly were not clearly demarcated.

(6) Members were not bound by the decisions of the Council.

(7) There was no provision which could prevent the States from the withdrawal from the League of Nations. The result was that the number of members which was initially 62 reduced to 32. Even the powerful States like Japan and Germany which joined the League in 1926 left it in 1933. Italy also withdrew from the League. The League became weak and totally ineffective due to the withdrawal of these States.

(8) There was no provision in the League to deal with the act of aggression effectively. Moreover, forces were also not available to the Council to take action against the culprit State.

(9) The League maintained a distinction between 'Great Powers' and other States. The so-called Great Powers were given permanent seats in the Council whereas the other members could only be its members for a fixed term. The selfish interests of the nations, especially of the Great Powers was supreme. They failed to maintain international peace and security because they failed to support with sufficient vigour especially in Manchurian and Ethiopian cases. As a result of the attitude of major Powers the small. nations lost faith in the

effectiveness of the League to save them from any aggression. The principle of the collective security enshrined in the Covenant was not applied in actual practice.

It is true that the League failed to fulfil its primary object of maintaining international peace and security because of the dominance of national interests of the members; its achievement in social and economic fields reveal that it was the first organisation which spread the idea of international cooperation. It provided for the first time a principle of collective security against the culprit State in an international conflict.

Chapter 3

United Nations Organisation

The failure of the League of Nations on the one hand and the horror and ruthless destruction caused by the Second World War on the other hand disturbed many minds especially in Allied countries.[1] They expressed the desire to establish peace to prevent recurrence of the tragedy of another World War even when the War was in progress. In order to achieve it, frantic efforts to create an international organisation had begun as early as in 1941. Deliberations became intense after the termination of the War which resulted in the creation of the United Nations Organisation on October 24, 1945. The United Nations was therefore founded in the ashes of a war that brought untold sorrow to mankind. A brief account of the important events leading to the establishment of the United Nations are as follows.

Declaration of St. James Palace (1941) :

On June 12, 1941, the representatives of the Great Britain, Canada, Australia, New Zealand and the Union of South Africa, and of the exiled governments of Belgium, Czechoslovakia, Greece, Luxembourg, the Netherlands, Norway, Poland, Yugoslavia and General de Gaulle of France, met at the ancient St. James Palace and signed a Declaration, commonly known as London Declaration, which *inter alia* stated : 'The only true basis of enduring peace is the willing cooperation of free people in a world in which, relieved of the menace of aggression, all may enjoy economic and social security. It is our intention to work together, and with other free peoples, both in war and peace, to this end'. This was the first step towards the creation of a world organisation.

Atlantic Charter (1941) :

The meeting of the American President Roosevelt and the British Prime Minister Churchill, in August 1941 'somewhere at sea' was another step. The meeting resulted in the issue of a joint declaration destined to be known in history, as the Atlantic Charter of August 14, 1941. The Charter was neither a treaty between the two Powers nor was it a final and formal expression of peace aims. It was only an affirmation of certain common principles in the national policies of their respective countries on which they based their hopes for a better

---

1. Allied Powers, also called allies, are those nations who allied in opposition to the Central Powers (Germany, Austria-Hungry and Turkey) in World War I or to the Axis Powers (Germany, Italy and Japan) in World War II.

   In World War II the chief Allied Powers were Great Britain, France, the Soviet Union, the United States and China.

future for the world. Of the eight points of the Atlantic Charter, two bear directly on world organisation. Other points of the Charter affirmed the basic principles of international justice ; no aggrandizement ; no territorial changes without the freely expressed wishes of the people concerned ; the right of every people to choose his own form of government, and equal access to raw materials for all nations. Support for the principles of the Atlantic Charter and a pledge of cooperation to the utmost in giving effect to them, came from a meeting of ten governments in London shortly after Churchill returned from his ocean rendezvous.

United Nations Declaration (1942) :

The next important event took place on Ist January 1942 when President Roosevelt of America, Prime Minister Churchill of Britain, Maxim Litinov of USSR, and T.V. Soong of China signed a short document which later came to be known as the United Nations Declaration. The term United Nations was suggested by President Roosevelt. The next day the representatives of twenty-two other nations added their signatures. Later on, twenty-one States also adhered to this Declaration. The complete alliance was effected in the Declaration in the light of the principles of the Atlantic Charter which stated in the first clause of the United Nations Declaration that the signatory nations had 'subscribed to a common programme of purposes and principles embodied in the Joint Declaration of the President of the United States of America and the Prime Minister of the United Kingdom of Great Britain and Northern Ireland dated August 14, 1941 known as the Atlantic Charter.'

Moscow Declaration (1943) :

Thus by 1943, all the principal Allied Nations were committed to outright victory and, therefore, an attempt to create a world in which "men in all lands may live out their lives in freedom from fear and want." But the basis for a world organisation had yet to be defined. Such a definition came at the meeting of the Foreign Ministers of Great Britain, the United States and the Soviet Union in October 1943. On October 30, the Moscow Declaration was signed by them along with the Chinese Ambassador to the Soviet Union, which under Clause 4 proclaimed that 'they recognize the necessity of establishing at the earliest practicable date a general international organisation, based on the principle of the sovereign equality of all peace-loving States, and open to membership by all such States, large and small, for the maintenance of international peace and security.' The Moscow Declaration was important in the sense that it stressed for the need for an international organisation and it also stated some basic principles and objects, such as the principle of sovereign equality of all peace-loving States and the maintenance of international peace and security.

Tehran Declaration (1943) :

On December 1, 1943, Roosevelt, Stalin and Churchill met at Tehran (Iran) declared that they had worked out concerted plans for final victory. As to peace, the Declaration read : We are sure that our concord will win an enduring peace. We recognize fully the supreme responsibility resting upon us and all the United Nations to make a peace which will command the goodwill of the overwhelming masses of the peoples of the world and banish the scourage and terror of war for many generations.

Dumbarton Oaks Conference (1944) :

In order to prepare the blue print of the principles laid down in Atlantic Charter and the Moscow and Tehran Declarations, the representatives of Great Britan, USSR, China and the United States met at a private mansion at Dumbarton Oaks in Washington D.C. The discussions completed on October 7, 1944 and a proposal for the structure of the World organisation was submitted by the four Powers to all the United Nations Governments, and to the people of all countries, for their study and discussion. According to the Dumbarton Oak proposals, the organisation to be known as the United Nations shall have four principal bodies. They shall be General Assembly, Security Council, the International Court of Justice and a Secretariat. An Economic and Social Council, working under the authority of the General Assembly was also provided for. The essence of the plan was that responsibility for preventing future war should be conferred upon to the Security Council. However, the method of voting in the Security Council was left open for the future discussion.

Yalta Conference (1945) :

The question of voting procedure in the Security Council was taken up at the Yalta in the Crimea where Churchill, Roosevelt and Stalin, together with their Foreign Ministers and Chiefs of Staffs, met in the Conference on February 11, 1945. The Conference announced that the question has been resolved. The agreement provided that all decisions on question of procedure should be taken by a majority of seven votes and that decisions on other questions should be taken by a like majority with the added requirement of unanimity of the permanent members. It was provided, however, that a party to a dispute should abstain from voting in certain matters.

At the end of the Conference, it was announced that the three Governments had agreed to call a conference of the United Nations to meet at San Francisco on April 25, 1945 to prepare the Charter of such an Organisation, along the lines proposed in the informal conversations at Dumberton Oaks. Later on, the Government of China also agreed to become a sponsor of the conference. The Provisional Government of France, however, declared to become one of the sponsoring Governments.

San Francisco Conference (1945) :

San Francisco Conference, officially known as the United Nations Conference on International Organisation (UNCIO) consisting of delegates of fifty nations[1] met on April 25, 1945 to discuss the proposals made by the States on the Dumbarton Oaks Conference, the Yalta Conference and the amendments proposed by various Governments. The delegates, at San Francisco met for two months in full session and in small committees prepared the draft of the United

1. Out of 50 original members, 17 were from Europe, North America and Oceania, 20 were from Latin American countries, 9 from Asia and 4 from Africa.
India was a founding member of the United Nations. It participated in the UNCIO but its views were not the views of India.

Nations Charter having 111 Articles of the Charter. They deliberated hard for over two months and in the end they produced the United Nations Charter and Statute of the International Court of Justice.

The right of each of the 'big five' to exercise a veto on an action taken by the Security Council prescribed long and heated debate. However, this and other vital issues were resolved only because every nation was determined to set up, if not the perfect international organisation, at least the best that could possibly be made. The last session on the Conference was held on June 25, 1945 where the Charter was passed unanimously and was signed by all the fifty representatives on June 26, 1945. Poland, a signatory of the United Nations Declaration, whose Government was announced on June 26, 1945 signed the Charter on October 15, 1945. Thus, the Charter was signed by fifty-one States.

The United Nations did not come into existence at the time of signing of the Charter. In many countries, the Charter was required to be approved by their Congresses or Parliaments. It was therefore provided that the Charter would come into force when the Governments of China, France, Great Britain, the Soviet Union and the United States and a majority of the other signatory States shall ratify it and shall deposit notification to this effect with the States Department of the United States. The United Nations came into existence on October 24, 1945 upon ratification of the Charter by twenty-nine of the signatories including the five permanent members of the Security Council. It is to be noted that the name of the Organisation 'United Nations' was taken from the Declaration of the United Nations and adopted in tribute to the memory of Roosevelt who suggested it.

Preamble of the United Nations :

The preamble of the United Nations is preceded by the words 'Charter of the United Nations'.[1] It indicated the title of that legal instrument and the name of the Organisation constituted by it.[2] The Charter is a multilateral treaty, *albeit* a treaty having certain special characteristics.[3] The term 'Charter' was regarded more appropriate designation of the Constitution of international community than the Covenant, the name given to the Statute of the League of Nations. The term 'Charter' refers to the contents of the Treaty whereas the term Covenant refers to the contract form of the contents.[4]

The Preamble is a part of the Charter. Consequently it has the same legal validity, *i.e.*, the same binding force as the other parts of the Charter. There appears to be no ground for treating the Preamble less important from the legal point of view than the other parts of the Charter. The Preamble introduces the Charter and sets forth the declared common intentions for the creation of the United Nations.

The Preamble of the U.N. Charter has set forth the basic aims of the United Nations which are : (a) to save succeeding generations from the scourage of

1. For the text of the Charter of the United Nations Organisation *see* Appendix 1.
2. Kelsen, 'The Law of the United Nations' (1950) p. 3.
3. *See* Certain Expenses of the United Nations (Article 17, paragraph 2, of the Charter), ICJ Report, 1962, p. 157.
4. Kelsen, op. cit., p. 3.

war ; (b) to re-affirm faith in fundamental human rights ; (c) to establish justice and respect for international obligations ; and (d) to promote social progress and better standard of life. The Preamble also affirms that in order to achieve these ends, the peoples of the United Nations are determined to practice tolerance, to live in peace as good neighbours, to unite to maintain peace and security, to ensure that armed forces shall not be used except in the common interest, and to employ international machinery for the social and economic betterment of all peoples.

The United Nations Organisation is not a super national organisation like a federal government. That has never been the case and can never be as long as States continue to cling to the undiluted concept of national sovereignty. The reality is that the U.N. is an association of independent States and can only do what its members are prepared to have it to do. It is an organisation for co-operation among States voluntarily created by them to achieve certain common ends by their united strength. The Charter is primarily a multilateral Treaty and its binding force is based on the consent of States and can only do what its members are prepared to have it do. However, the Preamble does not use the expression 'High Contracting Parties' which is usually inserted in international treaties. Instead, the Preamble refers the expression 'We the people of the United Nations' like the Constitution of the United States and of the Netherlands. The Preamble also lays down that the Governments of these people have agreed to the present Charter. It is significant to note that the phrase 'the peoples of the United Nations' was inserted to indicate that the United Nations was an organisation of the people, but since all the people cannot participate in its conferences or meetings, therefore they are represented by their Governments. Moreover, by inserting this phrase, the United Nations gave more importance to the people than to the States. However, the wording appears to be defective because Governments are not always the representatives of the peoples. They are the representatives of the States, and therefore, the United Nations is not an organisation of the people but of the States. The drafters of the Charter thus have failed to make the United Nations as an Organisation of the people, which they had perhaps desired.

PURPOSES OF THE UNITED NATIONS :

The purposes for which the United Nations was established are laid down in Article I of the Charter. They are as follows :—

(1) To Maintain International Peace and Security :

The urgent and fundamental need at the time of the creation of the United Nations was the freedom from war and from fear of war, and therefore, Article I, Para 1 of the Charter provided that the primary purpose of the United Nations shall be 'to maintain international peace and security', and to take effective collective measures........for the suppression of....... breaches of the peace. In order to achieve the above purpose, the Organisation shall prevent or remove threat to the peace, breach of the peace or acts of aggression by taking effective collective measures. This very purpose of the United Nations has been characterised by Kelsen as 'World Peace', because the action taken by it is not confined to the relations among the member States only. This very purpose of the United Nations is fulfilled primarily by the Security Council. The primary responsibility has been conferred upon to the Council by the members in order to ensure 'prompt and effective action' and therefore, they agreed that in carrying out the duties under this responsibility the Security Council acts on their behalf. In discharging these duties the Council is required to act in accordance with the purposes and principles of the United Nations.

(2) To Develop Friendly Relations among Nations :

In order to prevent clashes between nations, it was thought essential to develop friendship among nations, i.e., friendship based on respect for the principles of the equal rights and the equal rights of self-determination of peoples. This task and the taking of other measures to strengthen universal peace has therefore been made a purpose of the United Nations.

Self-Determination : At the end of the World War II, almost one quarter of the world's population—more than 750 million people lived in dependent territories. In order to liberate them, it was thought necessary that on the one hand new rules and principles capable of facilitating the liberation of the oppressed people should be framed, and on the other hand, reactionary and colonist rules of International Law should be abolished. When the United Nations was established, the principle of self-determination was invoked within it to end colonialism. The Charter under Article 1, Para 2 laid down that to develop friendly relations among nations based on the principle of equal rights and self-determination of peoples......shall be one of its purposes. Article 55 of the Charter reiterated the same principle. The notion of self-determination has also been incorporated in Chapter XI of the U.N. Charter which deals with Declaration regarding Non-self-governing Territories and in Chapter XII which deals with International Trusteeship System. The principle was later on reaffirmed in a number of resolutions adopted by the General Assembly. The most important amongst them is the Declaration on the Granting of Independence to Colonial Countries and Peoples, adopted on December 14, 1960.[1] The International Court of Justice in the Case Concerning East Timor (*Portugal* v. *Australia*) has also observed that the principle of self-determination of peoples has been recognized by the United Nations Charter and in the jurisprudence of the Court ; it is one of the essential principles of contemporary international law.[2]

Although self-determination has been recognised as an established principle of International Law, meaning of the term has not been made clear neither in the Charter nor in the resolution adopted by the General Assembly. Article 1, Para 2 of the Charter uses the term 'self-determination of peoples' which may mean self-determination for one of the elements of the State, i.e., the population and not of the State. But precisely it is not so. Article 1, Para 2 refers to the relations among States, and therefore the term 'peoples' too means States

1. General Assembly Resolution 1514 (XV). Also see the Declaration on Permanent Sovereignty over Natural Resources adopted by the General Assembly on December 14, 1962 by a Resolution XVII.
2. ICJ Reports, 1995, pp. 90, 102.

since only States have equal rights according to general International Law. Self-determination of peoples used in Article 1, Para 2 means only sovereignty of States.[1] Thus, in the general sense, self-determination involves accession to independent statehood for those people who were subjected to colonial domination or to people who inhabit a non-self-governing territory.

The principle of self-determination has two aspects, viz., external and internal. By virtue of external aspect, the people of a nation determine their international political status themselves either by secession or by formation of an independent State. Internal aspect recognises their right in their economic, social and cultural fields. Declaration on Non-intervention, adopted by General Assembly lays down that every State has an inalienable right to choose its political, economic, social and cultural systems, without interference in any form by another State. Internal aspect also extends to the right of a State to exercise sovereignty over natural resources within its territory. This would include the right of a State to fix the prices of commodities manufactured or tapped within its territory.

The principle of self-determination applies to the colonial peoples. These are the peoples of trust territories and non-self-governing territories. While the trust territories are those which are administered by other States under the supervision of the United Nations, non-self-governing territories are those whose people have not yet attained a full measure of self-government in accordance with Article 73 of the Charter of the United Nations. In 1946, a number of territories under the administration of the member States were placed as not self-governed territories.[2] The principle of self-determination is regarded to be fulfilled for the trust territories either by self-government or independence, and for non-self governing territories, either by emerging as a sovereign and independent State, or free association with an independent State or integration with another State. Thus, the existence of a sovereign and independent State is presumed to satisfy the principle of equal rights and self-determination.

It may be noted that the application of the principle of self-determination in no way extends to sovereign States. Thus, the people of an integral part of a State do not possess the right primarily because it results in secession. The U.N. Declaration on the Granting of Independence to Colonial Countries and Peoples[3] addressed the right of self-determination to territories under colonial possession.

---

1. Kelsen, op. cit., pp. 51-52.
2. Presently, all the trust territories have either become independent States or have associated themselves with the neighbouring States and therefore, the people of such territories possess the right of self-determination. However, as of January 1, 2016 there were still seventeen non-self-governing territories where people are yet to be provided the right of self- determination which are as follows :

American Samoa	Montserrat
Anguilla	New-Caledonia
Bermuda	Pitcairn
British Virgin Islands	St. Helena
Cayman Islands	Tokelau
Falkland Islands (Malvinas)	Turks and Caicos
Gibraltar	U.S. Virgin Islands
Guan	Western Sahara
	French Polynesia.

3. General Assembly Resolution 1514 (XV) dated December 14, 1960.

The International Court of Justice endorsed this view in the *Namibia* case (1970) and in the *Western Sahara* case (1975). In both the cases, the Court found that the declaration of the General Assembly only affirmed the principle of equal rights and self-determination as a policy in relation to trust and non-self governing territories. This principle has also been endorsed by the Court in *East Timor* case.

The Special Committee of 24 on Decolonization formerly known as the Special Committee on the Situation with regard to the Implementation of the Declaration on the Granting of Independence to Colonial Countries and Peoples in its seminar held in May 2001 was charged with bringing to self-government or independence of 16 non-self-governing territories, most of them are small island States. In the year 2004 the General Assembly adopted a resolution wherein it called upon the administering powers to cooperate fully with the special Committee to finalise by the end of 2005 a case by case work programme that would enable people of these territories to exercise their right to self-determination including the option of independence.

During the second-half of the twentieth century, international law of self-determination developed in such a way as to create a right of independence for the people of non-self-governing territories and peoples subject to alien subjugation, domination and exploitation. The right of self-determination is an obligation *ergo omnes.* All states have a legal interest in protecting that right.[1]

In those territories where the right of self-determination to the people has been forcibly deprived, the people of such territories have been conferred the right to struggle to that end. They may also seek and receive help from other countries to achieve it. Forces used by the people of the territories or assistance given by States to the people of such territories would not constitute aggression. Further, the plea of domestic jurisdiction as envisaged under Article 2, Para 7 of the U.N. Charter is not tenable in applying the principle of self-determination. The matter of self-determination has not been regarded by the General Assembly to be exclusively within the competence of a member State. It is a matter of international concern.

(3) To Achieve International Co-operation :

Article 1, Para 3 of the Charter lays down two purposes of the United Nations which are closely related to each other. Firstly, to achieve 'international co-operation' in solving international problems of an economic, social, cultural or humanitarian character, and secondly, 'international co-operation' in promoting and encouraging respect for human rights, and for fundamental freedoms for all without distinction to race, sex, language or religion.

(4) To Make the United Nations an International Forum for Harmonisation :

The fourth purpose of the United Nations was laid down under Article 1 Para 4 of the Charter which States that the United Nations, being the principal

1. East Timor (*Portugal* v. *Australia*) ICJ Reports 1995 p. 102, para 29; Legal Consequences of the Construction of a Wall in the Occupied Palestine. (ICJ Reports 2004 (1) pp. 171-172, para 88.

World Organisation'shall serve as a 'centre for harmonizing the actions of nations in order to achieve these common ends'. Thus, the United Nations is an international forum where World problems—bilateral, regional or global are discussed and it often evolves global policies for States to implement. The greatest advantage of this forum is that it represents the entire international community. However, harmonisation of actions of nations can take place only if the States are willing to accommodate their policies and actions in favour of the will of the World community.

These four purposes are, in the words of a Committee of the San Francisco Conference, 'the cause and object of the Charter to which the member States collectively and severally subscribe'. It is submitted that while there are certain repetitions in the Preamble and the purposes of the United Nations expressed in different languages at both the places, some ideas proclaimed in the Preamble do not find place in any part of the Charter such as 'equal rights of men and women' and 'dignity and worth of the human person' and 'to practice tolerance'. Repetition occurred perhaps because it was difficult to draw a sharp and clear cut distinction between the Preamble, and the purposes of the Unitied Nations.

PRINCIPLES OF THE UNITED NATIONS

Having set forth the agreed purposes, the Charter laid down the basic principles under Article 2 on which the Organisation is founded. These principles are the general obligations which bind each member State and the Organisation as a whole. They are as follows :—

(1) The Principle of Sovereign Equality.—Article 2, Para I of the Charter lays down that the United Nations is based on the 'sovereign equality of all its members'. It implies that all the members of the United Nations are equal irrespective of their size and resources. It may be noted that the principle of sovereign equality is a principle of International Law which the Charter has simply reaffirmed. However, in practice, the principle is not applied absolutely in all the cases. In many cases, the five permanent members of the Security Council have been given special powers wherein they may exercise the right of veto at the time of voting in the Security Council. The right of veto is so vital that a decision cannot be made in spite of voting on it by all the other members. However, this privileged status has been given to them with the consent of all the members, and therefore, it was a sort of compromise between them and other States.

(2) The Principle of the Fulfilment of Obligations.—Article 2, Para 2 of the Charter lays down that all members of the United Nations shall fulfil in good faith the obligations assumed by them in accordance with the Charter. This is also a basic principle of International Law which is known as *pacta sunt servanda*.

(3) The Principle of Peaceful Settlement of International Disputes.—Article 2, Para 3 of the Charter provides that 'all Members shall settle their international disputes by peaceful means and in such a manner that international peace and security, and justice, are not endangered.' The principle of peaceful settlement of dispute was reiterated by 2005 World Summit Outcome by stating that 'we emphasis the obligation of States to settle their disputes by peaceful means in accordance with Chapter VI of the Charter, including, when appropriate, by the use of the International Court of Justice.

(4) The Principle of Non-Use of Force.—The Charter under Article 2, Para 4 stipulates that all members shall refrain in their international relations from the use of force or threat of force against the territorial integrity or political independence of any State, or in any other manner not consistent with the purposes of the United Nations. It is to be noted that the expression 'use of force' as laid down under Para 4 of Article 2 is wider in scope than the expression 'use of armed force'. The former prohibits the use of force of all types, *i.e.*, the armed force as well as other coercive, economic and political measures. The principle therefore lays down that the use of force of all types is unlawful as it constitutes the breach of the principles of the United Nations of 'political independence' and 'territorial integrity'.

The principle of non-use of force is related mainly with one of the purposes of the United Nations, i.e., to maintain international peace and security. It was thought that if the use of force or threat thereof by the States in their international relations shall be prohibited, international peace shall be maintained effectively because use of force or threat thereof by a State is likely to lead to armed conflict, and in that case, 'international peace' is virtually threatened. It may be stated that since the founding of the United Nations, there has been universal acceptance of the rules of International Law as applicable to the use of force. The principle is therefore so important that jurists have referred to it as a 'Universal Norm', a 'Universal International Law', a 'universally recognized principle of International Law' and a 'principle of *jus cogens*'.

Declaration on Non-use of Force (1987) :

When the principle of the non-use of force was being repeatedly violated by the States in all parts of the world, it was felt that an instrument dealing with the principle of the non-use of force should be adopted which would further elaborate the principle and contribute towards an atmosphere of mutual trust between States. In order to draft a Treaty on the non-use of force in international relations and to discuss other issues relating to the principle of non-use of force, a Committee consisting of 35 members known as the 'Special Committee on Enhancing the Effectiveness of the Principle of Non-use of Force in International Relations' was established in 1977 which has been considering these questions. In the Seventh Session, held in 1984, the Committee continued its work with the goal of drafting a World Treaty on the non-use of force in international relations, but due to the divergent views of the States, the Committee was unable to formulate a Treaty. In 1986, the Assembly therefore adopted a resolution[1] wherein it was provided that the Committee shall complete a Draft Declaration on the enhancement of the effectiveness of the principle of non-use of force in international relations, including, as appropriate, recommendations in the peaceful settlement of disputes. Thus, the idea of drafting of a Treaty was dropped and the Committee proceeded to prepare a declaration on the non-use of force in international relations. Accordingly, a Declaration on the non-use of

1. General Assembly Resolution 41/76.

force in international relations was adopted on November 18, 1987. Some of the provisions of the Declaration are :

(1) Every State has the duty to refrain in its international relations from the threat or use of force against the territorial integrity or political independence of any State or in any other manner inconsistent with the United Nations purposes. Such a threat or use of force constituted a violation of International Law and the Charter and entail international responsibility.

(2) States should fulfil their obligations under International Law to refrain from organizing, instigating, assisting or participating in paramilitary, terrorist or subversive acts including acts of mercenaries, in other States or acquiescing in organized activities within their territory towards the commission of such acts.

(3) The principle of refraining from the threat or use of force in international relations is universal in character and binding regardless of each State's political, economic, social or cultural system or relations of alliances.

(4) No consideration of whatever nature may be invoked to warrant resorting to the threat or use of force in violation of the Charter.

(5) All peoples have the right freely to determine, without external interference, their political status and to pursue their economic, social and cultural development.

(6) Neither acquisition nor any occupation of territory resulting from the threat or use of force in contravention of International Law will be recognized as legal acquisition or occupation.

Although it is premature to say as to how far the above principles of the Declaration shall be respected by the States, if the States start following them, international peace will definitely be effectively maintained.[1]

(5) The Principle of Assistance to the United Nations.— Article 2, Para 5 of the Charter lays down two ways by which a State may assist the United Nations. Firstly, no member shall assist any State against which the United Nations is taking 'preventive and enforcement action', and secondly, all the members shall support the Organisation 'in any action' that it takes in accordance with the Charter.

(6) The Principle for Non-Member States.—Article 2, Para 6 of the Charter lays down that the obligations which are to be carried on by the non-members of the United Nations by stating that 'the Organisation shall ensure that States which are not Members of the United Nations act in accordance with these Principles so far as may be necessary to maintain international peace and security'. Thus, the purpose of the United Nations to maintain peace and security is not restricted to the relations among member States only.

---

1. The principle of non-use of force was reiterated by the 2005 World Summit Outcome which stated that we reiterate the obligation of all Member States to refrain in their international relations from the threat or use of force in any manner inconsistent with the Charter of the United Nations.

The principle has been a subject of controversy in the sense that normally treaties do not impose obligations on any State which is not a party to it or which has not given its consent to a treaty. However, the provision was inserted in the Charter because the purpose of the United Nations was not only to maintain peace within the Organisation, but within the whole international community, that is to say, to maintain international peace and security. In order to fulfil this purpose, the Charter imposes directly, obligations not only upon the members of the Organisation, but indirectly, upon the States which are not members of the United Nations. There are jurists who are of the opinion that the Charter cannot impose obligations upon non-members without their consent. For instance Goodrich and Hambro States :

> The Charter does not of course create any legal obligations for States not Members of the Organisation, they are therefore not obligated in a legal sense to act according to the principles of the Charter for any purpose whatsoever.[1] However non-members are also required to act in accordance with the principles laid down under Article 2, Paras 3, 4 and 5 so far as may be necessary where the maintenance of international peace and security is concerned.

However, the Security Council may take enforcement action under Chapter VII against non-members if international peace and security is endangered by their acts. This Article has been invoked on a few occassions by the States. For instance, Poland proposed to take enforcement measures under Article 39 and 41 against Spain in 1946 when it was not a member of the United Nations on the ground that the activities of the Franco regime in Spain have endangered international peace and security.[2] A series of embargoes against South Rhodesia were imposed between 1965 and 1977 when it was not a member of the United Nations. For instance, the Council on November 20, 1965 called upon all States "to do their utmost in order to break all economic relations with Southern Rhodesia including an embargo on oil and petroleum products."[3] In the case concerning Reparation for Injuries Suffered in the Service of the United Nations,[4] the International Court of Justice found that the United Nations was endowed by the Charter with international personality not only in relation to its members but *ergo omnes*. It followed that all States whether members of the United Nations or not, owed their duties as prescribed by general International Law.

A question arises as to what are the differences between a member and a non-member if the latter has to carry out the same obligations which the former is required to follow. It may be stated that there is a difference between the two as to obligations and the rights. There are certain obligations of the members which can hardly be imposed upon non-members. For instances, the obligation to bear the expenses of the Organisation as apportioned by the General Assembly (Articles 17 and 19), the special sanction provided in Article 19 for the

---

1. Leland M. Goodrich and Edvard Hambro, Charter of the United Nations : Commentary and Documents, p. 70.
2. See General Assembly Resolution 32(1) Dated February 9, 1946.
3. *See* Security Council Resolution 217 (1965) of November 20, 1965.
4. ICJ Reports (1949) p. 178 at p. 185.

non-fulfilment of this obligation, suspension of the right of voting in the General Assembly refer to members since the non-members have no such rights. Further, there is a difference between the status of a member and that of a non-member. The latter has all the obligations but not the rights of a member. Non-members have only those rights which the Charter expressly confers upon them, especially the right to bring 'questions' or 'disputes' before the General Assembly or the Security Council according to Article 11(2) and Article 35(2) respectively, and the right to be invited to participate without vote in discussions relating to a dispute under consideration by the Security Council if the non-member is a party to the dispute. The Security Council is authorized to lay down such conditions as it deems just for the participation of a non-member State.

(7) Principle of Non-intervention in Domestic Matters of a State.—Article 2, Para 7 of the Charter lays down that the United Nations shall not intervene in matters which are essentially within the domestic jurisdiction of any State, or compel any member to submit such matters to settlement by the United Nations. However, this general principle shall not prejudice the application of enforcement measures as provided under Chapter VII of the Charter. If in a civil war or in any other situation within a State determined by the competent organ of the United Nations as a threat to international peace the case of intervention on the part of the Organisation is not prohibited according to express provision of Article 2 Para 7 of the Charter.

The principle of non-intervention in the domestic jurisdiction of a State is not a new one. League of Nations under Article 15(8) had laid down that the Council, when exercising the functions in relation to the pacific settlement of disputes, could not proceed with a case if it found that the dispute arose out of a matter which 'by international law is solely within the domestic jurisdiction of a party'.

The same principle has been reaffirmed in the Charter but the provision of the Charter differs from that of the Covenant. Firstly, its scope is not limited to the settlement of disputes. The Charter has imposed a general limitation on the authority of the United Nations by excluding from its jurisdiction matters which are essentially within the domestic jurisdiction of any State but at the same time it makes an important exception to the general rule in favour of the application of enforcement measures under Chapter VII. Secondly, the Charter does not refer to International Law as the determining criterion. Thirdly, it does not exclude only those matters which are 'solely' within the domestic jurisdiction of a State, but all matters which are essentially so.

An important question arises as to what are the matters which may be deemed as 'domestic'. It may be stated that a matter is essentially of domestic concern if it is incapable by its very nature of assuming an international complexion. In other words, if a matter is not likely to have international repercussion, or if it does not affect international peace and security, or if it is not a subject of the U.N. Charter, it may be regarded as domestic matter. However, the organs of the United Nations have certainly not been very consistent or clear as to what they regard as matters essentially within the domestic jurisdiction of a State.[1] It appears that they have accepted the opinion of the Permanent Court of International Justice given in the Tunis-Morocco Nationality Decree case that the question whether a certain matter is domestic or not is essentially relative, and depends upon the development of international relations.[2] It is to be noted that in the modern age of inter-dependence, many matters which on the face are essentially domestic have, in fact, become international and, therefore, no clear cut demarcation can be made between domestic matters and other matters. Perhaps because of this reason the matter is decided by the organs of the United Nations themselves where the question is raised after discussion and vote. Thus a civil war or any other situation which may take place within a State may be interpreted by the competent organs of the United Nations as a threat to international peace and security, and consequently, even in such cases, intervention on the part of the Organisation would not be prohibited according to the express provision of Article 2, Para 7. The practice of the United Nations shows that the main criterion for the determination of the concept of domestic jurisdiction has been the attainment of the aims and purposes of the Organisation. However, the discretionary power of the organs of the United Nations should be taken away otherwise occasions may arise where an internal matter may acquire international status, and thus the restriction implied in the term international peace would become of least importance.

Supremacy of the Obligations :

It is to be noted that all members are under an obligation to act in accordance with the purposes and principles of the Charter. The obligation may be regarded as supreme obligations in the sense that they override all other obligations which are contradictory to them whether accepted by the members either before or after the establishment of the Organisation. The principles laid down in the Charter thus acquire the status of *jus cogens.* The Charter makes a specific mention of the supremacy of the obligations under Article 103 which lays down that 'In the event of a conflict between the obligations of the Members of the United Nations under the present Charter and their obligations under any other international agreement, their obligations under the present Charter shall prevail.'

In the case concerning Questions of Interpretation and Application of the 1971 Montreal Convention arising from the Aerial Incident at Lockerbie (*Libya Arab Jamahiviya* v. *United States of America*) wherein Libya requested to the Court for the indication of provisional measures on March 3, 1992 on the ground that it has fully complied with all the obligations under the Montreal Convention. Later, the Security Council on March 31, 1992 by adopting Resolution—748 (1992) imposed trade embargo against Libya for not co-operating in renunciating the terrorism. The Court observed that Libya is obliged to accept and carry out the decisions of the Security Council in accordance with Article 25 of the Charter. In accordance with Article 103 of the Charter the obligation of the

1. Leland M. Goodrich, 'The United Nations', (1960) p. 78.
2. P.C.I.J., Series B, No. 4, pp. 23-24.

parties in that respect prevail over their obligations under any other international agreement, including the Montreal Convention.[1]

MEMBERSHIP OF THE UNITED NATIONS :

Chapter II of the Charter deals with Membership. The Charter has classified the members into two categories : 'Original Members' and the 'Subsequent Members'.

Original Members

According to Article 3 of the Charter Original Members are the States which signed the United Nations Declaration of January 1, 1942 and signed and ratified the Charter in accordance with Article 110. Fifty States participated in the San Francisco Conference, either from the beginning or following admission by vote of the Conference. Poland, a signatory to the United Nations Declaration did not participate in the San Francisco Conference because at that time it did not have a government recognized by all the sponsoring powers. However, a space was left in the Charter for the signature which its representative affixed on October 15, 1945. Thus these fifty-one States became the Original Members.

It may be stated that all the original members who signed the Charter were not the States in the sense that they did not possess the degree of independence which is required by International Law. For instance, India, Philippine Commonwealth, Byelorussian and the Ukranian Soviet Socialist Republics were not the 'States', and as such they should not have been allowed to become the original members of the United Nations. However, all nations participating in the Dumbarton Oaks Conference were made the original members of the United Nations irrespective of the fact that a few of them were not the 'States'.

Subsequent Members (Admission of a Member)

According to Article 4 of the Charter sbsequent members are those States which are admitted to Membership by a decision of the General Assembly adopted on the recommendation of the Security Council. Wordings of Article 4 give an impression that a member is admitted in the United Nations by the decision of the General Assembly simply on the recommendation of the Security Council, i.e., irrespective of favourable or unfavourable recommendation. But it is not so. General Assembly may admit a member only when the Security Council makes a favourable recommendation. In 1949, the General Assembly resolved to ask the International Court of Justice on the question. Can the admission of a State to Membership in the United Nations, pursuant to Article 4, Paragraph 2, of the Charter, be effected by a decision of the General Assembly when the Security Council has made no recommendation for the admission or of the negative vote of a permanent member upon the resolution. The Court in its Advisory Opinion on the Competence of the General Assembly Regarding Admission of a State to the United Nations[2] was of the opinion that the General Assembly may decide on the admission of new members only on a positive recommendation of the Security Council. Thus a State may be admitted in the

1. ICJ Reports, 1992, p. 3.
2. ICJ Reports (1950) p. 4.

United Nations[1] on two-thirds majority of the General Assembly, but it must be preceded by the affirmative vote of nine members of the Security Council including the concurring votes of the permanent members. The admission of a State as a member in the United Nations is therefore a matter which is decided by both the organs, i.e., by the Security Council and the General Assembly in spite of the wordings of Article 4 paragraph 2, according to which only the General Assembly seems to be authorised to decide upon the admission of new members. If the Security Council is not in favour of the admission of an applicant State, it need not make any recommendation at all. In such cases, the General Assembly is not in a position to take a decision by which the applicant State is admitted to membership. It is also to be noted that the Assembly is not bound to accept the recommendations of the Council. It may refuse to admit a State to membership though recommended by the Council. But the Assembly can decide to admit a State only if it has been 'recommended'. Hence, the favourable recommendation of the Council must precede the decision of the Assembly.

Article 4, Para 1 of the Charter lays down the conditions which a State is required to fulfil in order to become a member of the United Nations. They are : firstly, membership is open to 'peace-loving State', and secondly, to those States which 'accept the obligations' contained in the Charter, and thirdly, to those which are 'able and, willing to carry out the obligations contained in the Charter.' In this connection the reference of the advisory opinion of the International Court of Justice on Admission of a State to Membership in the United Nations is relevant. During 1946 and 1947 a number of States applied for admission, most of whom had their applications vetoed by the USSR, and therefore no State could be admitted in the United Nations. The General Assembly decided on November 7, 1947 to request an advisory opinion from the Court on the legality of such conditions.

The Court in its advisory opinion on Conditions of Admission of State to Membership in the United Nations delivered in 1948[2] laid down five conditions which a new applicant must fulfil for becoming a member of the United Nations. They are (a) it must be a State ; (b) it must be peace-loving ; (c) it must accept the obligations of the Charter, (d) it must be able to carry out these obligations ; and (e) it must be willing to do so. Although the conditions for the admission of a member have been clearly laid down, it is difficult to determine whether an applicant State is a 'peace loving' or whether it is able and willing to carry out its international obligations. It is to be noted that a State must be a 'peace-loving State' has never been implemented. These are such matters which are decided by each member of the Security Council and of the General Assembly not only on merits alone. Political considerations are sometimes involved therein. During the Cold war period the Soviet Union blocked all American supported applicants and the United States replied in the same way. The first breakthrough occured in 1956 when a package deal resulted in the admission of both American and Soviet sponsored applicants. Further, delayed admission of Bangladesh and Vietnam is an ample proof of the involvement of

1. ICJ Reports (1948) p. 4.
2. ICJ Reports (1948) P. 4.

international politics in the admission of a member.

Indian Membership in the United Nations :

India was an original member of the United Nations. The Charter was signed by India on June 26, 1945 and was ratified on October 30, 1945. When India and Pakistan became new Dominions on August 15, 1947, the latter was to apply for membership as a new member in accordance with the Schedule appended to the Indian Independence (International Arrangements) Order, 1947. India was to continue the membership of the United Nations according to the above Order. The Order was therefore communicated to the United Nations on August 27, 1947 through a letter. When the question of membership of these two Dominions was placed before the Secretariat of the United Nations the Assistant Secretary General for Legal Affairs was asked for his opinion who advised that it would.... appropriate for the Secretary-General to suggest to Government of India; that in view of the change in sovereignty, it would be desirable to have new credentials issued to the Indian representatives by the Head of the Government or the Foreign Minister of the new Dominion of India. India continued the membership of the United Nations after completing the above formalities which it is submitted were not required to be undergone. It appears that new credentials were required to be issued to the Indian representatives by the Head of the Government or by the Foreign Minister perhaps because there was no precedent for such situations in the United Nations. This was a typical case which had come before the United Nations for the first time. However, the First Committee referred the following question to the Sixth Committee for advice in future cases :—

> What are legal rules to which, in the future a State or States entering into international life through the division of a Member State of the United Nations should be subjected?

Chinese Representation in the United Nations :

Chinese representation in the United Nations remained for a long time in a confusing state. The Republic of China was an Original Member of the United Nations and was a permanent member of the Security Council. At that time, Chiang Kai Shek was the head of the State. In 1949, his Government was overthrown by the Communist over the main land of China. Chiang Kai Shek fled to Formosa, which is popularly known as Taiwan, and established his Nationalist Government over there. However, it continued to represent the Republic of China in the United Nations. Since 1950, the matter relating to Chinese representation in the United Nations has been discussed in the General Assembly from time to time, because Communist regime in the main land of China has been claiming representation in the United Nations. Chiang Kai Shek continued the representation because of the pressure of the United States and other Western countries. In 1971, after the Kissinger's visit to China, and later, when the relations between the United States and the Republic of China became cordial, the United States advocated for its representation in the United Nations. The General Assembly in 1971 adopted a resolution wherein it was resolved that the representatives of the Government of People's Republic of China are the only lawful representatives of China in the United Nations. Accordingly, on October 25, 1971, the People's Republic of China was admitted in the United Nations and the representatives of Chaing Kai Shek were expelled from the United Nations.[1] Since then, People's Republic of China has occupied one of the permanent seats of the Security Council.

Russian Membership in the United Nations :

When the Soviet Union was dismembered into 12 independent States in 1991, all the successor States except Russia and those which were already members were required to apply afresh in order to become members of the United Nations. As to the membership of Russia it was said that Russia being the successor of the Soviet Union is not required to apply for new membership. Russia therefore continued the membership of the USSR in the United Nations. The above was supported by the decision of the Council of Heads of State of the Commonwealth of Independent States on December 21, 1991 and Russia continued the membership of the USSR in the United Nations including permanent membership of the Security Council and other international organisations.[2]

The total number of the members of the United Nations has gone up to 193. South Sudan which become an independent State on July 9, 2011 after having seceded from Sudan was admitted to the United Nations on July 14, 2011 by the General Assembly on the recommendation of the Security Council[3] as 193rd member State. Thus, the Organisation is represented by the overwhelming majority of the States of the World. It is indeed an important step towards the goal of universality of membership—a goal that it has embraced since its inception.

Suspension of a Member :

Article 5 of the Charter provides that a member may be suspended from the United Nations. According to it a member may be suspended from exercising its rights and privileges of Membership if the Security Council has been taking preventive or enforcement action against it. Suspension may be effected by the General Assembly on the recommendation of the Security Council. Suspension of a member being a non-procedural matter requires the affirmative votes of nine members including concurring votes of five permanent members of the Council. The above provision implies that when a member is suspended, it is deprived of all the rights which a member enjoys. For instance,

---

1. Taiwan, with a population of more than 23 million, has launched a bid to join the United Nations every year since 1993, but China and its supporters have managed every time to keep it off the General Assembly agenda.

   In the year 2002, its bid to gain membership in the United Nations was blocked for the 10th consecutive year. It was agreed that the item would not be included on the agenda of the General Assembly.
2. The legality of the succession of the USSR by the Russian Federation is subject to criticism in view of the fact that the membership of the USSR should have been lapsed and it should have been admitted to membership in the same way as the other newly independent republics. However, Russian Federation continued the membership because it still remains one of the largest States in the world.
3. Recommendation was made by the Security Council on July 13, 2011.

it ceases from representing in the General Assembly and the three Councils, it ceases from electing as a member of these Councils, and it cannot be invited to participate in the discussions of the Security Council under Articles 31, 32 and 34 to bring to the attention of the Security Council, or of the General Assembly and other situations under Article 35, Para 1 of the Charter. It is to be noted that a suspended member remains a member and has to fulfil all the obligations of membership. Suspension from the exercise of the membership does not mean that it has become a non-member. Hence, suspension from the exercise of the membership rights may at least temporarily place the member concerned in a position worst than that of a non-member because it cannot exercise those rights which are available to the non-members. The rights and privileges of a member may be restored to by the Security Council without reference to General Assembly.

No member has been so far suspended from the Membership of the United Nations. However, in 1974, the Assembly suspended South-Africa for its Apartheid policy from participation in the work of its Twenty-ninth session. South Africa lost its voting rights in the Assembly but it retained the UN Membership.

Expulsion of a Member :

Article 6 of the Charter lays down provisions regarding expulsion of a member from the United Nations by stating that if a member persistently violates the principles of the Charter, it may be expelled from the Organisation by the General Assembly on the recommendation of the Security Council. Expulsion from the Organisation is an enforcement action in so far as it is an action taken against the will of the State concerned. Expulsion is enforced upon a member in contrast to voluntary withdrawal. It being a non-procedural matter, requires the affirmative votes of nine members including the concurring votes of the permanent members of the Security Council. The decision of the General Assembly requires, in conformity with Article 18, Para 2, a two-third majority of the members present and voting. Both decisions are necessary to bring about the expulsion of a member. No member has been so far expelled from the Organisation. Once a member is expelled from the Organisation, it acquires the same position as to that of a non-member. Thus, after expulsion, it may exercise all those rights which a non-member has. It appears strange that while a suspended member cannot enjoy the rights of a non-member, an expelled member may exercise all such rights. Hence, the effect of expulsion is not as rigorous as that of suspension.

On October 30, 1974, the Security Council discussed and voted upon a resolution recommending the immediate expulsion of South Africa from the membership of the United Nations. But the resolution failed because of the veto exercised by the three permanent members of the Council.

Yugoslavia's Membership in the United Nations :

When the Socialist Federal Republic of Yugoslavia lost a considerable portion of its territory following secession of Croatia, Slovania, Macedonia, Bosnia and Herzegovina, the Security Council on September 19, 1992 declared that 'the State formerely known as the Socialist Federal Republic of Yugoslavia has ceased to exist' and that 'the Federal Republic of Yugoslavia (Serbia and Montenegro) cannot continue automatically the membership of the former Socialist Republic of Yugoslavia in the United Nations.[1] The General Assembly acting on the recommendation of the Security Council on September 22, 1992 adopted a resolution[2] that the Federal Republic of Yugoslavia consisting of Serbia and Montenegro cannot automatically continue the membership of the former Socialist Federal Republic of Yugoslavia in the United Nations, and it should apply for membership in the United Nations and shall not participate in the Assembly's work. The letter addressed to the Permanent Representatives of Bosnia and Herzegovina and Croatia dated September 29, 1992 from Under Secretary-General, the Legal Counsel of the United Nations stated that while the above-mentioned General Assembly resolution neither terminated nor suspended Yugoslavia's membership in the Organisation, it cannot automatically continue the membership of the former Yugoslavia in the United Nations. The Legal Counsel expressed the view that the admission of a new Yugoslavia to membership in the United Nations in accordance with Article 4 of the Charter of the United Nations, would terminate the situation that had been enacted by the resolution of the General Assembly. Since no further development has occurred in this regard, it is deemed that its membership has been discontinued. Yugoslavia was also prevented from participating in the work of the Economic and Social Council. Later, Yugoslavia was granted the membership of the United Nations on its request on November 1, 2000 by the General Assembly in the name of Federal Republic of Yugoslavia.[3] When Montenegro announced its independence in 2006, Serbia continued the membership of Yugoslavia.

The decision to disallow Yugoslavia from participating in the U.N. debate is the first case in the history of the United Nations. It is to be noted that the decision of the Assembly was not consistent with the practice of the United Nations. If action could be taken against Yugoslavia for having lost a considerable portion of the territory, there is perhaps no reason for having not taken an action in a similar case that occured in 1990 with the dismemberment of the U.S.S.R. Why Russia was allowed to continue the membership of the U.S.S.R. when a considerable portion of its territory was lost due to its dismemberment ?[4]

Withdrawal From the Organisation :

Membership of the United Nations may be terminated against the will of the member by expulsion in conformity with Article 6 of the Charter. But the Charter does not contain any provision for those contingencies where a member

1. Security Council Resolution 777 (1992).
2. General Assembly Resolution 47/1, Dated September 22, 1992.
3. A/55/12, Dated November 1, 2000.
4. In a letter of December 24, 1991, Boris Yeltsin, the President of the Russian Federation informed the Secretary-General that the membership of the Soviet Union in the Security Council and all other United Nations organs was being continued by the Russian Federation with the support of the eleven member countries of the Commonwealth of Independent States.

wishes to withdraw itself from the Organisation voluntarily. The Covenant of the League of Nations had made a provision for the withdrawal of a member. It could be done by a member either by giving a two years' notice, or if any amendment was opposed by a member, or was not otherwise acceptable to it, it could mean that the particular member has ceased to be a member of the League of Nations. But the Charter has not made any such provision. During the debate at San Francisco Conference, the Committee was of the view that the Charter should not make any express provision either to permit or to prohibit withdrawal from the Organisation. The Committee deems that the 'highest duty' of the States, which will become members is to continue their co-operation within the Organisation for the preservation of international peace and security. If however a member because of 'exceptional circumstances' wants to withdraw from the Organisation, and wishes that the burden of maintaining international peace and security should be left to other members, it is not the purpose of the Organisation to compel that member to continue its cooperation in the Organisation. The above view may mean that withdrawal from the Organisation may be possible in 'exceptional circumstances'. Although it is difficult to lay down as to what are the exceptional cases, following may be given by way of examples, that is, when the Organisation has become unable to maintain peace, or when it could do so only at the expense of law and justice, or when a member's rights and obligations as such have been changed by the amendment in the Charter to which it has not concurred ; and when an amendment duly accepted by the necessary majority in the Assembly or in the General Conference fails to secure the ratification necessary to bring such amendment into effect.

Although a member has not been given, under the provision of the Charter, a right to withdraw from the Organisation, withdrawal from the Organisation is a sovereign right of a State, and as such, it may be exercised by its members as and when they desire. In the 9th Plenary Session of the Conference, on June 25, 1945, the Soviet delegate declared that 'the opinion of the Soviet delegation is that it is wrong to condemn beforehand the grounds on which any State might find it necessary to exercise its right of withdrawal from the Organisation. Such a right is an expression of State sovereignty and should not be reviled, in advance, by the International Organisation'. According to the opinion of the delegation of the Soviet Union, the right of withdrawal is a consequence of the principle of democracy as well as of the principle of sovereignty. The view appears to be sound because the Charter is a treaty and no State can be compelled to remain a party to it against its wishes. However, if the Security Council considers that the withdrawal of a member would constitute threat to the international peace and security, it may according to Article 39 recommend to the member to forbear from withdrawing, and in case of non-compliance with the recommendation, it may take enforcement measures against that State. Thus, the Security Council may compel the State to remain a member of the Organisation.

Indonesia :

In the past, on one occasion the question of withdrawal from the membership arose. On January 20, 1965, Indonesia informed the

Secretary-General that it had decided to withdraw from the United Nations as from January 1, 1965 "at this stage and under the present circumstances". It took the decision because Malaysia was elected as a member of the Security Council. However, on September 19, 1966, Indonesia announced its decision to resume full cooperation with the United Nations and to resume participation in its activities starting with the Twenty-first Session of the General Assembly. On September 28, 1966, the General Assembly took note of this decision and the President invited representatives of Indonesia to take seat in the Assembly. The President of the General Assembly at the 1420th Plenary Session stated that : It would therefore appear that the Government of Indonesia considers that its recent absence from the Organisation was based not upon a withdrawal from the United Nations but upon a cessation of cooperation.[1] Thus, Indonesia resumed its seat. It was not a case of withdrawal because had it withdrawn from the Organisation, its admission would have been possible only after completing the procedure which is adopted for a State seeking a Membership of the United Nations as laid down under Article 4 of the Charter.

Observer and Permanent Observer Status :

Those States which are not members of the United Nations may participate in the deliberations of the General Assembly without vote when they are granted 'Observer Status'. Observer status may be granted by the General Assembly by adopting a resolution. There are no provisions for it in the U.N. Charter. When a State having observer status is given a right to participate in all the future meetings of the General Assembly, the status is referred to as 'permanent observer'. According to the practice of the United Nations, permanent observers and the officials from their missions may attend the opening session of the General Assembly, its principal committees and other U.N. bodies. They can distribute documents and materials issued by their governments, obtain documents from U.N. bodies published by the U.N. Secretariat and enjoy other rights and privileges.

Presently, there are two permanent non-member observer States in the United Nations : the Holy See and Palestine.[2] The Holy See was granted permanent observer status on April 6, 1964 and Palestine Liberation Organisation was so designated in 2012,[3] following an application for full

1. GAOR (Provisional), A/PV, 1420, dated September 28, 1966.
2. South Korea (since 1949), Morocco (since 1956), North Korea (since 1973) and Switzerland (since 1946), Austria, Italy, Japan, Federal Republic of Germany, Bhutan, Democratic Republic of Korea and German Democratic Republic were also permanent observers until they became members of the United Nations.
3. See General Assembly Resolution 67/19 dated November 29, 2012. Palestine as an observer was conferred on July 7, 1998 to additional rights and privileges within the United Nations and its conferences. Under the enhanced arrangements, Palestine was granted the right to participate in the General Assembly's general debate and was included in the list of speakers at any meeting of the plenary. It was also granted the right to reply, the right to raise points of order related to the proceedings on Palestinian and Middle East issues. Palestine will also have the right to co-sponsor draft resolutions and decisions on Palestinian and Middle East issues. The General Assembly's decision applies not only to its own work but also to international conferences convened by the United Nations and conferences of the United Nations itself.

membership in 2012 which failed to secure Security Council approval. Both have been given invitation to participate as observers in all the sessions and the work of the General Assembly and to maintain permanent observer mission at Headquarters. Many intergovernmental organisations[1] and a few non-governmental organisations.[2] have also been granted observer status. Some of them maintain a permanent office in the United Nations Headquarters in New York City.

The Charter of the United Nations does not contain any provision relating to observer and permanent observer status. This status therefore is determined purely by practice. But presently, the legal status of the permanent observers has been elaborated by the Convention on the Representative of States in their Relations with International Organisations of a Universal Character of 1975. The Convention laid down the rules as to the establishment and size of missions, inviolability of their premises, personal immunity, freedom of movement for mission members and their families, credentials of delegates, composition and size of delegations, obligations of host States and of sending State, observer delegations entry and transit mission.

SELF DEFENCE.

The term self-preservation was used by the proponents of the Natural School as the right of a State to prevent the imminent danger. The essential characteristic of the right of self-preservation was the unrestricted freedom it gave to a State to act contrary to any norm of International Law and thus to violate any right of another State, if such action was deemed necessary for its own preservation. Hall says that in the last resort almost the whole of the duties of States are subordinated to the right of self-preservation.[3] Practically, there was no limit on the action which a State could take in self-preservation. Instances of such actions were the rupture of diplomatic relations, retortion, reprisals, intervention, embargo, boycott, blockade and the use of force. States themselves were the arbitrators in taking actions. However, with the idea of centralization and collective security system, the freedom allowed to an individual State to exercise the right of self-preservation has become restricted. The Covenant of the League of Nations reserved to the members the right of self-preservation in all cases in which the League was proved unable to settle the dispute.

The Charter of the United Nations has drastically curtailed the freedom of the States to exercise the right of self-preservation. The Charter uses the expression 'self-defence' under Article 51 instead of self-preservation. The former is 'narrower yet firmer basis of one form of self-preservation'.[4] The Charter recognizes self-defence as an 'inherent' right of the States. It follows that

1. Names of some of intergovernmental organisations are African Union, Asian Development Bank, Association of South Asian Nations, Commonwealth of Independent States, International Sea Bed Authority, Organisation of American States, and South Asian Association for Regional Organisation (SAARC)
2. International Committee of the Red Cross, International Federation of Red Cross and Red Crescent Societies, Inter-Parliamentary Union, International Criminal Court, International Olympic Committee, Sovereign Military Order of Malta.
3. International Law, Vol. I, p. 332.
4. Hyde, 'International Law', Chiefly as Interpreted and Applied by the United States, Second Edition, Vol. I, p. 248.

the right of self-defence flows from the natural law rather than by positive International Law. However, the right has to be exercised strictly in accordance with the provisions of the Charter.

A State has a right to take action in self-defence, if it has been attacked by the armed forces. Article 51 *inter alia* says : 'if an armed attack occurs against a member of the United Nations'. It implies that the attack through armed forces is a pre-condition for exercising the right of self-defence. International Court of Justice in the advisory opinion given in Legal Consequences of the Construction of a Wall in the Occupied Palestinian Territory concluded that Article 51 recognises the existence of an inherent right of self-defence in the case of armed attack by one State against another State.[1] Armed attack may take place either by the regular armed forces or by armed bands, groups, irregulars or mercenaries. However, in latter case, right of self-defence would be deemed to have been exercised only if it is of such gravity as may amount to armed attack. In the case concerning Military and Para-Military Activities in and Against Nicaragua, the International Court of Justice observed :

> An armed attack must be understood as including not merely action by regular armed forces across an international border, but also the sending by or on behalf of a State of armed bands, groups, irregulars or mercenaries, which carry out acts of armed force against another State of such gravity as to amount to an actual armed attack conducted by regular forces, or "its substantial involvement therein."[2]

If a State has been attacked by the above means, it can take measures in self-defence to thwart the attack. But some writers[3] have interpreted the expression 'armed attack' differently by stating that, in order to exercise the right of self-defence it is not necessary that a State should have been attacked with the armed forces. They assert that Article 51 allows anticipatory self-defence, that is a pre-emptive strike, once a State is certain that another State is about to attack it militarily. In other words, military preparation by neighbouring States or threat of imminent attack allows another State to take action in self-defence. The rationale behind the doctrine of anticipatory self-defence, stressed by those who advocate it, lies that in the age of missiles and nuclear weapons it is self-defeating to contend that a State should wait the attack by another country when it fully knows that the attack is certain to take place. They also argue that Article 51 did not suppress the pre-existing international rule on anticipatory self-defence. But the above arguments do not appear to be convincing. The text and drafting history of Article 51 makes it clear that the provision did not allow a State to exercise the right of self-defence in the case of anticipatory attack. Further, Article 51 has wiped out all pre-existing laws, and did not leave any room for self-defence except when it

---

1. ICJ Reports 2004(1) para 139.
2. ICJ Reports (1986), pp. 103-104.
3. *See* Stone 'Aggression and World Order', (1958), pp. 43-44 ; Bowett, 'Self-Defence in International Law' (1958), p. 187.

has been attacked with the armed forces.[1] Thus extension of the exercise of self-defence to the anticipatory attack is in no way justifiable.

Article 51 States that armed attack should occur 'against a member of the United Nations' which may be understood to mean member States of the United Nations. A State which is a member of the United Nations, has a right to take action in self-defence if armed attack occurs on it. But a State being a juristic person cannot be attacked. Attack may take place in the territory of the State, which is one of the attributes of the statehood. Thus, attack in the territory of a State is regarded as the attack on the State. But the territory of a State is not the only essential attribute of statehood. People of the State is equally important characteristic of the statehood, and therefore, if the people of a State, whether residing within the State or outside the State, are attacked with armed forces, the attack should be deemed to an attack on the State and the right of self-defence can be justifiably exercised. States' right to exercise the right of self-defence would have been limited to armed attack on the territory only had Article 51 used the terms 'against the territory of a member of the United Nations.' Although armed attack on the people of a State gives a State a right of self-defence, it can be exercised only when the necessity of self-defence is instant, overwhelming and 'no choice of means and moment of deliberation' has been left. Further, action taken in self-defence should be proportionate, i.e., it should not be unreasonable or excessive.[2]

The conditions of proportionately and necessity apply to Article 51 of the United Nations Charter and they therefore do not permit a State to use the nuclear weapons in self-defence if armed attack has occurred against it. The right of self-defence warrants only those measures which are proportionate to the armed attack and necessary to respond to it.[3] Further, the use of nuclear weapons which itself is unlawful does not become lawful on the ground that it is being used in self-defence. The International Court of Justice had an occasion to deal the issue of the legality of the use of nuclear weapons in the advisory opinion given to the General Assembly on the Legality of the Threat or Use by a State of Nuclear Weapons but it failed to respond to this question by stating that

> the Court cannot conclude definitively whether the threat or use of nuclear weapons would be lawful or unlawful in an extreme circumstances of self-defence, in which the very survival of the State would be at stake.[4]

Measures taken by the States in self-defence are required to be

1. Declaration on the Enhancement of the Effectiveness of the Principle of Refraining from the threat or use of force in International Relations adopted by the General Assembly in 1988 has clearly stipulated that States have the inherent right of individual or collective self-defence, if an armed attack occurs as set forth in the Charter of the United Nations.
2. *See* Chapter 'Intervention'.
3. International Court of Justice in the case Concerning Military and Paramilitary Activities in and Against Nicaragua stated that there is a specific rule whereby self-defence would warrant only measures which are proportional to the armed attack and necessary to respond to it, a rule well established in customary International Law (ICJ Reports, 1986, p. 94 para 176).
4. ICJ Reports, 1996.

'immediately reported to the Security Council'. This is an obligation imposed by Article 51 for a State which exercises the right of self-defence. The above Article also further stipulates that the right of self-defence may be exercised by a member until the Security Council has taken the measures to maintain international peace and security. Measures which the Security Council may take are provided under Article 42 which includes demonstrations, blockade and other operations by air, sea or land forces of members of the United Nations', as the Council thinks "necessary to maintain international peace and security". The above implies that self-defence must come to an end as soon as the Security Council steps in and takes over the task of putting an end to the aggression. If the Security Council fails to take any action, self-defence must cease as soon as its purpose, that is, to repel the armed attack, has been achieved.

Use of force in self-defence, subsequent to armed attack, implies an armed contention between the two States. Although such a contention may not be termed war for its prohibition under the U.N. Charter, it amounts to non-war armed conflict or hostilities. Rules of war are required to be followed by the aggressor as well as by the State exercising the right of self-defence. Further, those States which wish to remain neutral in such a non-war armed conflict may lawfully do so.

UNITED STATES ATTACK ON AFGHANISTAN (2001)

United States bombed in Afghanistan with lethal ordanance after its World Trade Center in New York and Pentagon in Washington were struck by hijacked planes on September 11, 2001 where more than 6000 people lost their lives and thousands of persons suffered dreadful injuries. Although perpetrators of the above inhuman act could not be identified with certainty when the attack started, United States claimed that the Saudi born Osama Bin Laden is the prime suspect, who is hiding in Afghanistan. Taliban regime in Afghanistan refused to extradite him to the United States for trial.

The U.S. Ambassador to the United Nations John Negeroponte claimed that the attack on Afghanistan is in conformity with Article 51 of the U.N. Charter.[1] It is true that right to take action in self defence may be exercised by a State if it has been attacked by the armed forces. The term 'armed attack' as used under Article 51 includes armed attack either by the regular armed forces or by armed bands, groups, irregulars or mercenaries.[2] In the latter case the right of self-defence could be exercised only if it is of such gravity as may amount to armed attack.

The attack was made by the United States without having any authority from the Security Council. The Council no doubt adopted a resolution unanimously on September 12, 2001[3] wherein it called terrorism a threat to international peace and security but did not invoke Chapter VII of the U.N. Charter under which punitive measures are envisaged. It made no reference to

1. Siddharth Vardarajan, 'An Ignoble War', Times of India, October 15, 2001.
2. Military and Para Military Activities in and Against Nicaragua, ICJ Reports, 1986, pp. 103-104.
3. Security Council Resolution 1368, dated September 12, 2001.

Afghanistan asking Taliban to hand over Osama Bin Laden. The Council also adopted a resolution unanimously on September 28, 2001 with steps and strategies to combat international terrorism.[1] Again, reference to Afghanistan for extradition of Osama Bin Laden was not made.

Though the U.S. has the right to defend itself against an armed attack from another country, the right is not absolute and unfettered. The United States attacked in Afghanistan in self-defence without having any evidence that the terrorists who struck on September 11 were sent 'by or on behalf of Afghanistan'. A State can use the force in self-defence against a State which has attacked with armed forces. The wordings of Article 51 of the U.N. Charter and the judgment of the International Court of Justice in Military and Para-Military Activities in and Against Nicaragua has expressly laid down this criterion for the exercise of the right of self-defence. The right of self defence can be exercised against a State whose attack has been established beyond doubts.

The right of self defence can be exercised after giving respect to the principles of 'necessity and proportionately'. The principle of necessity requires a State to prove that the attack was done after all avenues for a peaceful solution were exhausted. The necessity of self-defence should be instant, overwhelming and no choice of means or moments of deliberations has been left. In the instant case, no doubt, an appeal was made to Taliban regime to hand over Osama Bin Laden for trial but no other peaceful measures were taken to get him extradited. In order to bring the perpetrators of the crime to justice, the United States should have sought a tightening of United Nations sanctions against Taliban pending further action. Attack on a large part of the territory of Afghanistan resulting in death of hundreds of civilian persons and the American representative's statement before the Security Council that U.S. action in Afghanistan and the likelihood of its extending to 'other organisations and States for the act of September 11 incident is against the principle of proportionately.

International terrorism no doubt is a heinous crime. It should be curbed with all efforts. United States' efforts by initiating 'War Against Terrorism' is commendable. However, its attack against Afghanistan falls short of the requirements which the right of self-defence demands.

REGIONAL ARRANGEMENTS :

Regional arrangements may be created for the maintenance of international peace and security or for the promotion of human rights or for performing economic, social, cultural and educational activities.[2] The League of Nations under Article 21 had made a provision for the regional arrangement when it stated that 'Nothing in the Covenant shall be deemed to affect the validity of international engagements, such as the treaties of arbitration or regional understanding like the Monroe Doctrine, for securing the maintenance of peace.' Due importance was given to the regional arrangements when the United Nations was established. Chapter VIII of the Charter,[3] is devoted exclusively to

1. Security Council Resolution 1373 dated September 28, 2001.
2. For details *see* Chapter 'Regional Organisations'.
3. The Chapter comprises of Articles 52 to 54.

regional arrangements, though it does not define the term regional arrangements.

Regional arrangements could be made by the States for dealing with matters 'relating to the maintenance of international peace and security' as per Article 52(1) of the Charter. Thus, regional arrangements should have the same purpose as that of the Charter. Moreover, the 'activities' of such arrangements are required to be consistent with the purposes and principles of the United Nations. The members of the United Nations entering into such arrangements shall make every effort to achieve pacific settlement of local disputes through such regional arrangements before referring them to the Security Council. Article 52(3) of the Charter States that the Security Council shall encourage the development of pacific settlement of local disputes through such regional arrangements either on the initiative of the States concerned or by reference from the Security Council. The above provisions imply that the obligations undertaken by the members under the Charter are the supreme and they cannot be contradicted by the members before or after the establishment of the Organisation. It is so perhaps because the principles contained in the Charter have acquired the status of *jus cogens*. Their supremacy is well recognized under Article 103 of the Charter. Regional arrangements, being treaties, are required to be registered with the Secretariat of the United Nations in accordance with Article 102 of the Charter and published by it.

Functions of the Regional Organizations :

The Charter confers certain functions upon regional organizations which are as follows :

(1) Pacific Settlement of Disputes :

Settlement of disputes by peaceful means is one of the principles of the United Nations. Article 33, Para 1 of the Charter lays down the various modes of peaceful means which the parties to any dispute, the continuance of which is likely to endanger international peace and security, may adopt in finding a solution. 'Resort to regional agencies or arrangement' is one of them which has been expressly mentioned therein. It implies that one of the functions of the regional organizations is to settle the disputes of the members by peaceful means. Article 52, Para 2 of the Charter expressly lays down this very function of the regional organizations when it says that 'the members of the United Nations entering into such arrangements or constituting such agencies shall make every effort to achieve pacific settlement of local disputes through such regional arrangements or by such regional agencies before referring them to the Security Council'. Further, Para 3 of Article 52 States that the Security Council shall encourage the development of pacific settlement of local disputes through regional arrangements, and initiative for the settlement of disputes through them shall be taken either by the 'States concerned' or by reference from the Security Council.

(2) Enforcement Action :

Regional organizations may also take enforcement action in accordance with the provisions of Article 53 of the Charter which lays down that the

Security Council, shall, where appropriate, utilise such regional arrangements or agencies for the enforcement action under its authority. The enforcement action may be taken to maintain or restore peace within the regional community, against a party to the regional arrangement which is guilty of a threat to the peace, breach of the peace in relation to another party to this arrangement. The regional organizations may take enforcement action even without the authorization of the Security Council. But, such actions are permissible only in three cases. Firstly, enforcement action as a measure against any enemy State provided for pursuant to Article 107. This Article permits action in relation to any enemy State taken or authorised as a result of the Second World War by the Governments having responsibility for such action. Secondly, enforcement action provided for in regional arrangement directed against renewal of aggressive policy on the part of any enemy State until such time as the Organization may, on the request of the governments concerned, be charged with the responsibility for preventing further aggression by such a State, and thirdly, enforcement action in the exercise of collective self-defence under Article 51 of the Charter. This case is not mentioned under Article 53. However, Article 51 provides that 'Nothing in the present Charter shall impair the inherent right of........collective self-defence.......' The right of collective self-defence implies the right of using force organised by the regional arrangements. However, the right of collective self-defence may be exercised until the Security Council has taken measures necessary to maintain international peace and security. If the regional arrangements take any enforcement action for the maintenance of peace and security it has an obligation in accordance with Article 54 of the Charter to inform the Security Council at all times.

SANCTIONS

Rules of legal system are binding upon the subjects to whom it is addressed. If rules are violated or obligations contained therein are not observed by the subjects, enacted specific penalty which is imposed in order to enforce obedience to a law is called sanction. Penalty imposed under international legal system is referred to as international sanction. International Law has been regarded as a legal system in the true sense. The Governments of the different States are of the opinion that its rules are legally binding on them. A question arises as to what sanctions International Law provides to those States which violate the rules.

Sanctions in the modern International Law are quite different from those which existed in the classical International Law. The latter provided the sanction generally in the form of war and reprisals. War waged by its own armed forces was the supreme sanction of International Law. However, at present, war as well as reprisals in most of the cases have become unlawful. Sanctions applied by the aggrieved State are required to be lawful and they must conform to the provisions of the U.N. Charter.

The Charter of the United Nations does not use the term sanction. However, if the provisions of the Charter are not observed by the members it can apply economic, financial, military and political measures as against a State which are as follows :—

(1) Expulsion from the Organisation.—Article 6 of the Charter provides that a member of the United Nations which has persistently violated the principles contained in the Charter may be expelled from the Organisation by the General Assembly on the recommendation of the Security Council.[1]

(2) Suspension from the Exercise of the Rights of Membership.—Article 5 of the Charter provides that a member of the United Nations against which preventive or enforcement action has been taken by the Security Council may be suspended from the exercise of the rights and privileges of membership by the General Assembly on the recommendation of the Security Council. By rights means benefits which a State has in its capacity as Member of the United Nations. Such rights, for instance, are representation in the General Assembly and the three other Councils, to be elected member of these Councils; to be invited to participate in the discussion of the Security Council under Articles 31, 32 and 44; to bring the attention of the Security Council or the General Assembly disputes and other situations under Article 35 Para (1).

The main purpose of this measure is to prevent a member which is not expelled but against which enforcement action is in operation from exercising the rights of a member.

(3) Suspension of the Right of Voting in the General Assembly.—Article 19 of the Charter provides that a member of the United Nations which is in arrears in the payment of its financial contributions to the Organisation shall have no vote in the General Assembly if the amount of its arrears equals or exceeds the amount of contributions due from it for the proceeding two years.

It is an obligation of a member to bear the expenses of the Organisation as apportioned by the General Assembly. In case such if an obligation is not fulfilled it may be suspended from the right to vote in the General Assembly. It implies that such a State may lose the right to vote in the General Assembly but may still exercise all the other rights of membership such as right to participate in the deliberations of the General Assembly, the right to be elected member of the Security Council and if it is a member of the Security Council to vote in the Security Council.

(4) Sanction for Non-compliance with a Judgment of the International Court of Justice.—Article 94 Para (1) of the Charter provides that each member of the United Nations undertakes to comply with the decision of the International Court of Justice in any case to which it is a party. That means that each member shall comply with the decision of the Court. Non-compliance with the decision of the Court constitutes a violation of an obligation.[2]

(5) Sanction for Non-registration of Treaties.—A treaty concluded by the State is required to be registered with the Secretary-General of the United Nations, after it has come into force in accordance with Article 102 of the Charter. The Secretariat, after registration publishes it in the United Nations Treaty Series (UNTS). Article 102 Para 1 of the Charter provides that if treaties are not registered no party to any such treaty or international agreement may invoke before any organ of the United Nations.

1. For Detail see 'Membership' in this Chapter.
2. For Detail See Chapter, 'International Court of Justice'.

(6) Enforcement Measures.—If the Security Council determines, under Article 39, the existence of any threat to the peace, breach of the peace or act of aggression it may make recommendation or decide what measures shall be taken in accordance with Article 41 and 42 to maintain or restore international peace and security. It may apply economic and financial sanction against a State under Article 41 and military sanction under Article 42 which include use of air, sea or land forces as may be necessary to maintain or restore international peace and security.[1]

Although the Charter provides for economic and financial sanctions under Article 41 and military sanctions under Article 41 it does not mention political sanctions expressly by name. However, appeal to a State to do or not to do certain acts, suspension of an exercise of the rights and privileges of the membership of the United Nations,[2] and expulsion from the membership of the Organisation or from the specialised agencies thereof may be called political sanction.[3] Political measures are applied mainly to hurt the prestige of a State. Public opinion becomes adverse with the application of political sanction. Perhaps, it was the World public opinion which forced the United Kingdom and France to pull out their troops from the Suez Canal in 1956. Sanction of public opinion, no doubt is attached to the principles of purely moral obligation; its importance at the present day International Law cannot be denied.

Besides the United Nations, specialised agencies of the United Nations such as ILO, ICAO, WHO, IPO and ITO have also been authorised to take action in accordance with the provisions of their constitutions against a State which fails to perform the obligations contained therein. For instance, Constitution of the International Labour Organisation lays down a procedure for dealing with complaints regarding a failure by a member State to secure the effective observance of an International Labour Convention binding it. If any State violates the procedure, matter may be referred to a Commission of Enquiry, or if necessary, to the International Court of Justice. Further, if a member State fails to carry out the recommendations of the Commission or the decision of the International Court of Justice, the Governing Body of the ILO may recommend action to the International Labour Conference in order to secure compliance with the recommendations.

Above are the sanctions which international legal system provides against a State which fails to observe its obligations. However, they are not effective because there is no political sovereign authority above the sovereign State. Brierly has correctly stated that "sanctions which it possesses are not systematic or centrally directed, and that accordingly they are precarious in their operation.[4] No doubt, the Security Council has been empowered to take action against the culprit State, but in the past its whole sanctioning competence was paralysed due to rivalry between States belonging to Eastern and Western blocs resulting into the exercise of the 'veto' power by the permanent members. However, with the end of the cold war, prospects of the sanctioning authority

1. For Detail see Chapter 'Security Council'.
2. *See*, Article 5.
3. *See* Article 6.
4. The 'Law of Nations', Sixth Edition, p. 10.

of the Security Council have greatly enhanced.

AMENDMENTS

In the San Francisco Conference, an effort was made to harmonise the view points of all the delegates. Great powers and small, those who stressed caution and 'realism', and those who felt that a time had come for an even higher development of international organization—all have to make concessions in order to secure agreement, the Charter therefore represents the maximum agreement available at the time it was written. However, when the Charter was framed, the founder members realised that in due course of time occasion may arise for the possible changes or modifications in the Charter. Chapter XVIII therefore provided the methods by which the Charter may be amended. Two different procedures have been provided for the amendment of the Charter. They are : ordinary procedure and extraordinary procedure.

(1) Ordinary Procedure :

The ordinary procedure is laid down under Article 108 of the Charter which provides that the General Assembly may amend any provision of the Charter by a two-thirds vote of its members. Amendment so made will come into force when they are ratified by at least two-thirds of the Member States including all the five permanent members of the Security Council.

The above implies that all members of the United Nations with the exception of the permanent members have surrendered their sovereignty to the extent of the amendment in the sense that they are required to accept those amendments in the Charter to which they have opposed or to say to which they have not given their consent.

(2) Extraordinary Procedure :

The extraordinary procedure is laid down under Article 109 of the Charter. According to it, a General Conference of the Members of the United Nations for the purpose of reviewing the Charter may be held, if two-thirds of the members of the General Assembly vote for it and by a vote of any nine members in the Security Council. Each Member of the United Nations shall have one vote in the Conference. Any alteration of the present Charter so recommended by the Conference shall take place when it has been ratified by two-thirds of the members of the United Nations including all the permanent members of the Security Council. Article 109 further provides under Para 3 that if such a Conference had not been held earlier, then the proposal to summon it would be automatically placed on the agenda of the tenth Annual Session of the General Assembly in 1955. Accordingly, the General Assembly in November 1955 decided in principle to hold a conference to review the Charter. It appointed a Committee composed of all the members of the United Nations and directed it to report to the Assembly at its twelfth session on the question of fixing an appropriate time and place for the conference. After considering the report of the Committee, the Assembly in 1957 decided to keep the Committee in being and requested it to report with recommendations to the Assembly not later than at its Fourteenth Session.

It is to be noted that although two different procedures have been laid down for the amendment of the Charter, there is hardly any essential difference between the two. The General Conference referred to in Article 109 is composed in the same way as the General Assembly referred to in Article 108. Each member is represented, and has one vote. The text of the amendment is to be adopted by the General Conference in the same way as by the General Assembly, namely, by a two-thirds vote of the members of the respective bodies. It is significant to note that two-thirds vote of its members means two-thirds of all its members and not, as in other important decisions, by two-thirds of the members present and voting. Further, the alterations recommended by the General Conference come into force under the same conditions as the amendment adopted by the General Assembly, namely, by ratification on the part of the two-thirds of the members of the United Nations. The amendment adopted by both the procedures come into force for all members, i.e., for those members as well which through their representatives voted against the amendment in the Assembly or in the conference or did not ratify it.

Amendments in the Charter :

The following amendments have been made in the Charter since its coming into force :—

(1) Amendments Adopted in 1963 :

Amendments to Articles 23, 27 and 61 were approved by the General Assembly on December 17, 1963. It came into force on August 31, 1965. The amendment to Article 23 expanded the number of the non-permanent members of the Security Council from six to ten. The amended Article 27 provides that decisions of the Security Council on procedural matters shall be made by an affirmative vote of nine members (formerly seven) and on all other matters by an affirmative vote of nine members (formerly seven) including the concurring votes of the five permanent members. The amendment to Article 61 enlarged the Membership of the Economic and Social Council from eighteen to twenty-seven members.

(2) Amendment Adopted in 1965 :

The General Assembly adopted on December 20, 1965, an amendment to Article 109 of the Charter which came into force on June 12, 1968. According to the amendment, the General Conference of Member States for the purpose of reviewing the Charter may be held at a date and place to be fixed by a two-thirds vote of members of the General Assembly and by a vote of nine members (formerly seven) of the Security Council.

(3) Amendment Adopted in 1971 :

The General Assembly adopted on 20th December, 1971 an amendment to Article 61 which came into force on September 24, 1973. According to amendment, the membership of the Economic and Social Council was enlarged from 27 to 54.

It is significant to note that all the three amendments were adopted through the ordinary procedure. It is submitted that presently, some of the Articles of the Charter are required to be reviewed because majority of the member States had not taken part in the creation of the Organisation at the San Francisco Conference, and that its structure was insufficient for exerting their influence in its activities. The Charter must be adopted to changes which had taken place since 1945. The Charter is required to incorporate into it new legal concepts which are, at present, the integral parts of private International Law. Revision is also called for in order to change the Economic and Social Council which must adjust to the important place that economic and social problems have assumed in a world in search of a new order in these fields. Further, development of science and technology constitutes the chief source of progress for mankind and therefore the Charter is required to be amended so that a Council for Science and Technology may be established as a principal organ of the United Nations.

Review of the Charter :

In 1974, the *Ad hoc* Committee established for the review of the Charter[1] was reconvened in 1975 as a Special Committee on the Charter of the United Nations and on the Strengthening of the Role of the Organisation which was requested to examine the proposals which had been made, or would be made, with a view to according priority to consideration of areas on which general agreement was possible.

The Special Committee has met annually since 1976 to consider the peaceful settlement of disputes, the rationalization of existing United Nations procedure and the maintenance of international peace and security. Among the Committee's achievement are : (a) the Manila Declaration on the Peaceful Settlement of Disputes (1982) ; (b) Declaration on the Prevention and Removal of Disputes and Situations Which May Threaten International Peace and Security (1988) ; (c) the Declaration on the Enhancement of Co-operation between the United Nations and the Regional Arrangements or Agencies in the Maintenance of International Peace and Security (1994); and (d) the Declaration on Fact Finding by the United Nations in the Field of the Maintenance of International Peace and Security (1991).

In 1995 the Committee recommended to the General Assembly the adoption of a resolution[2] which would recognise that the 'enemy State' clauses used in the Charter under Articles 53, 77 and 107 have become obsolete and expressed its intention to initiate the procedure set out in Article 108 to amend the Charter to delete the 'enemy State' clauses. This was the first occasion when the Special Committee recommended for the amendment of the Charter, though on many occasions it had earlier discussed regarding amendments.

LEGAL STATUS OF THE UNITED NATIONS :

Although it might be looking artificial in saying that the United Nations is a contractual arrangement between certain States, it is a truth which cannot be denied. In spite of this being a fact, the United Nations possesses a distinct legal personality. The International Court of Justice in an Advisory Opinion on

1. General Assembly Resolution 3349 (XXI) December 17, 1974.
2. General Assembly in 1994 by adopting a resolution 49/58 had asked the Committee to recommend the most appropriate legal action to be taken on this issue.

Reparation for Injuries Suffered in the Service of the United Nations[1] considered the judicial nature of the United Nations. The Court was of the opinion that the States which set it up had the power, in conformity with International Law, to bring into being an entity possessing objective international personality.

The United Nations has a distinct legal personality. It is a subject of International Law inasmuch as it is capable of possessing international rights and duties. It therefore can perform international transactions. But it should not be understood that it has unrestricted legal capacity under International Law to do so. The United Nations possesses only those special capacities which have been conferred to it by particular provisions of the Charter. These provisions clearly show that the United Nations possesses juridical personality in the field of International Law as well as in the field of the national laws of the member States. The following points clarify the above proposition :—

(a) Juridical Personality under International Law :

Certain provisions of the Charter have authorized the United Nations to enter into international agreements with the member States and with other international organizations which are as follows :—

(1) Article 26 of the Charter provides that the Security Council shall formulate plans to be submitted to the members of the United Nations for the establishment of a system for the regulation of armaments. When these plans are accepted by the members and when they are submitted, a treaty is established between the United Nations represented by the Security Council, and the member State concerned.[2]

(2) Article 43, Paragraph 3 authorizes the Security Council to conclude on behalf of the United Nations with members or groups of members the agreements governing the numbers and types of forces to be made available to the Security Council, 'their degree of readiness and general location, and the nature of the facilities and assistance to be provided'. Although these agreements are concluded between the Security Council and members or with the groups of members, the Security Council is not a juridical person, and therefore the agreements are deemed to have been concluded by the United Nations through the Security Council.[3]

(3) Article 57, Para 1 provides that the specialized agencies shall be brought into relationship with the United Nations, and Article 63, Para 1 authorizes the Economic and Social Council to enter into agreements with any of the agencies defining the terms on which the agency concerned shall be brought into relationship with the United Nations subject to the approval by the General Assembly. These agreements are treaties concluded between the United Nations represented by the Economic and Social Council and the General Assembly with the international organizations whose agencies are

1. ICJ Reports (1949) p. 174.
2. Kelsen, op. cit., p. 330.
3. Kelsen, op. cit., p. 331.

brought into relationship with the United Nations by these agreements.[1]

(4) Articles 75, 77 and 79 provide for so-called trusteeship agreements by which certain territories may be placed under the trusteeship system of the United Nations. These trusteeship agreements are treaties concluded by the United Nations and the States competent to dispose of these territories.[2]

In addition to above, the United Nations has entered into international agreements not authorized by any provisions of the Charter. For instance, the Interim Agreement on the Privileges and Immunities of the United Nations concluded with the Swiss Federal Council and the Headquarters Agreement signed on June 26, 1947 with the United States of America. The above treaties clearly show that the United Nations possesess juridical personality in International Law.

(b) Juridical Personality under National Laws of the Members :

The United Nations possesses juridical personality in the field of the national laws of the Members is clear from the following provisions of the Charter :—

(1) Article 104 of the Charter provides that 'the Organisation shall enjoy in the territory of each of its Members such legal capacity as may be necessary for the exercise of its functions and the fulfilment of its purposes.' Thus, the Organisation is capable of performing the juridical acts required to put its capacities into operation. For instance, the Organisation must be able, in its own name, to contract, to hold movable and immovable property and to appear in courts. The Convention on the Privileges and Immunities of the United Nations adopted by the General Assembly in 1946[3] provided under Article 1, Section 1 that the United Nations shall possess juridical personality. It shall have the capacity to (a) to contract ; (b) to acquire and dispose of movable and immovable property and (c) to institute legal proceeding.

(2) Article 105 of the Charter provides that the Organization shall enjoy in the territory of each of its Members, such privileges and immunities as are necessary for the fulfilment of its purposes. Para 2 of the above Article provides that the representatives of the members of the United Nations and officials of the Organisation shall similarly enjoy such privileges and immunities as are necessary for the independent exercise of their functions in connection with the Organisation.

The Convention on Privileges and Immunities of 1946 deals with the privileges and immunities referred to in Article 105 paragraph 1 and 2 and also with the legal capacity to be granted to the Organisation under Article 104. Some of the privileges and immunities are as follows :

---

1. *Ibid* pp. 331-332.
2. *Ibid* p. 332.
3. General Assembly Resolution (Doc. A/64, pp. 25).

(1) The United Nations, its property and assets wherever located by whomsoever held shall enjoy immunity from every form of legal process unless it has expressely waived its immunity (Article 2 Section 2).

(2) The premises of the United Nations shall be inviolable. The property and assets of the United Nations shall be immune from search, requisition, confiscation, expropriation and any other other form of interference (Article 2 Section 3).

(3) The archives of the United Nations and in general all documents belonging to it or held by it shall be inviolable wherever located (Article 2 Section 4).

(4) The United Nations, its assets, income and other property shall be exempt from all direct taxes and from customs duties and prohibition and restrictions on imports and exports in respect of articles imported or exported by the United Nations for its official use (Article 2 Section 7).

(5) Representatives of Members to the principal and subsidiary organs of the United Nations and to conferences convened by the United Nations shall while exercising their functions and during their journey to and from the place of meeting enjoy the following privileges and immunities :

  (a) immunity from personal arrest or detention and from seizure of their personal baggage and immunity from legal process of every kind in respect of words spoken or written and all acts done by them in their capacity as representatives.

  (b) inviolability for all papers and documents;

  (c) the right to use codes and to receiver papers or correspondence by couriers or in sealed bags;

  (d) exemption in respect of themselves and their spouses from immigration restrictions, alien registration or national service obligations in the State they are visiting;

  (e) the same facilities in respect of currency or exchange restrictions as are accorded to representatives of foreign governments on temporary official missions;

  (f) the same immunities and facilities in respect of their luggage as are accorded to diplomatic envoys; and

  (g) such other privileges and immunities and facilities as diplomatic envoys enjoy except that they shall have no right to claim exemption from customs duties on goods imported or from excise duties or sales taxes.

In order to give the above privileges and immunities to the United Nations and their representatives States have enacted laws in their domestic legislation.

Indian Position—Enactment of the Convention on the Privileges and Immunities Act of 1947

In order to give effect to the Convention on the Privileges and Immunities of the United Nations, India enacted the United Nations (Privileges and Immunities) Act of 1947.[1] Section 11 of the Act provided that the representatives or members to the principal and subsidiary organs of the United Nations and to conferences convened by the United Nations, shall, while exercising their functions and during their journey to and from the place of meeting, enjoy the following privileges and immunities ;

(a) immunity from personal arrest or detention and from seizure of their personal baggage, and, in respect of words spoken or written and all acts done by them in their capacity as representatives, immunity from legal process of every kind ;

(b) inviolability for all papers and documents ;

(c) the right to use codes and to receive papers or correspondence by courier or in sealed bags ;

(d) exemption in respect of themselves and their spouses from immigration, restrictions, aliens, registration or national service obligations in the State they are visiting or through which they are passing in the exercising of their functions ;

(e) the same facilities in respect of currency or exchange restrictions as are accorded to representatives of foreign governments on temporary official missions ;

(f) the same immunities and facilities in respect of their personal baggage as are accorded to diplomatic envoys ; and also

(g) such other privileges, immunities and facilities not inconsistent with the foregoing as diplomatic envoys enjoy, except that they shall have no right to claim exemption from customs duties on goods imported (otherwise than as part of their personal baggage) or from excise duties or sales taxes.

Section 12 of the Act further provides that the representatives of Members to the Principal and subsidiary organs of the United Nations and to conferences convened by the United Nations, complete freedom of speech and independence in the discharge of their duties, the immunity from legal process in respect of words spoken or written and all acts done by them in discharging their duties shall continue to be accorded, notwithstanding that the persons concerned are no longer the representatives of members. However privileges and immunities accorded under Sections 11 and 12 will not apply as between a representative and the authorities of the State of which he is a national or of which he is or has been the representative.

Headquarters Agreement

Headquarters Agreement between the United Nations and United States of America was signed on June 26, 1947 at Lake Success. The Agreement came into

1. Act No. XLVI of 1947.

force on November 21, 1947 by exchange of letters between the Secretary General and the United States permanent representative. The Agreement provided that the seat of the Organisation shall be called Headquarters district. According to section (a) of Article 3 of the Agreement the Headquarters district shall be under the control and authority of the United Nations. But the control and authority to be exercised by the United Nations under the Agreement is very restricted. The district remains under the laws and judicial jurisdiction of the United States. Thus, the federal, State and local laws of the United States shall apply within the Headquarters district. Federal, State and local courts of the United States shall have jurisdiction over acts done and transactions taking place in the Headquarters district. (Article 3, Section 7). The above courts when dealing with cases shall take into account the regulations enacted by the United Nations.

The United Nations is authorized to exercise a limited legislative power. Section 8 provides that the United Nations shall have the power to make regulations, operative within the Headquarters district for the purpose of establishing therein conditions in all respects necessary for the full execution of its functions. No federal, State or local laws or regulations of the United States which is inconsistent with a regulation of the United Nations shall be applicable within the Headquarters district. Any dispute between the United Nations and the United States as to whether a regulation of the United Nations is authorized or as to whether federal, State or local law or regulation is inconsistent with regulation of the United Nations shall be promptly settled in accordance with Section 21. Pending such settlement the regulation of the United Nations shall apply and the federal, State or local law or regulation shall be inapplicable in the Headquarters district. The above shall not prevent the reasonable application of fire protection regulations of the appropriate American authorities.

The United Nations has no sovereignty over the territory called the Headquarters district. The legal relationship concerned in ownership under the law of the United States. The Headquarters Agreement confers upon the Secretary General a limited authority in the field of police. The police force placed at the disposal of the Secretary General is not a police force of the United Nations. It remains a police force of the United States which authorises the Secretary General to dispose of it for definite purposes and under definite conditions.

The authority competent to settle the dispute between the United Nations and the United States of America is the arbitral tribunal consisting of three arbitrators one to be named by the Secretary of State of the United States and another by the Secretary General of the United Nations and the third to be chosen by the two, or, if they fail to agree upon a third, then by the President of the International Court of Justice. The Secretary General of the United Nations may ask the General Assembly to request to the International Court of Justice for an advisory opinion on any legal question.

Palestine Liberation Organisation (PLO) Case.—Palestine Liberation Organisation (PLO) was granted observer status in the United Nations since 1974. Later, the U.S. Government ordered the closure of the observer mission of the Palestine Liberation Organisation (PLO) and prohibited its activities within the United States after it found that the PLO is a terrorist organisation in view of the Anti-Terrorism Act enacted in 1987. The Order of the United States was inconsistent with the U.N. Headquarters Agreement which the United States had entered into with the United Nations in June 1947 regarding the Headquarters of the United Nations wherein it was provided that the United States as a host country must permit Governments accredited to the World body to stay and work in the United Nations. The General Assembly, on March 23, 1988, by adopting a resolution called the United States' Anti Terrorism Act inconsistent with the Headquarters Agreement and contrary to legal obligations under the Agreement. However, the U.S. Government was still insisting for the closure of the Mission. When the dispute was not settled, the General Assembly referred the following question to the International Court of Justice for its advisory opinion : Is the United States of America, as a party to the Agreement between the United Nations and the United States of America regarding the Headquarters of the United Nations under an obligation to enter into arbitration in accordance with Section 21 of the agreement?

The Court observed that the Headquarters Agreement being a treaty in force is binding on the parties thereto. Since there is a dispute regarding the above Agreement United States is under an obligation, in accordance with Section 21 of that Agreement, to enter into arbitration for the settlement of the dispute between itself and the United Nations.

Comparison Between the League of Nations and the United Nations

League of Nations and the United Nations were the two leading international organisations of the twentieth century. Both the organisations were created for general purposes and were open to all the States of the international community. The idea for the creation of the United Nations came before its framers because of the horror and ruthless destruction caused by the Second World War which had brought innumerable sufferings to humanity and also because of the failure of the League of Nations. The League had ceased to function during the Second World War. The League, no doubt, had a number of weaknesses. The framers of the United Nations learned a lot from the experiences and actual practice of the League. The Charter contained the idea and methods of the League with changes which were deemed necessary in the light of the past experiences. It has incorporated many provisions of the Covenant in different language which were helpful in fulfilling the purposes of the United Nations and discarded those which were detrimental to its purposes.

The Charter is an improved and larger treaty than the League. However, both the organisations were similar in certain respect. For instance, firstly, both were voluntary organisations whose units were mainly sovereign States; secondly, both were global in scope in the sense that both were open to all the States of international community; thirdly, main purpose of both the organisations was the maintenance of international peace and security; fourthly, structure of both the organisations included the Assembly, the Council and the Secretariat, and fifthly, there are certain common points as far as the administration of non-self-governing territories under the United Nations Trusteeship system and the Mandate system of the League. However, both the organisations have many differences :—

(1) League of Nations had three principal organs *i.e.*, Assembly, Council and the Secretariat but the United Nations has six principal organs! General Assembly, Security Council, Economic and Social Council, Trusteeship Council, Secretariat and the International Court of Justice.

(2) Activities of the United Nations are wider than the League. While the purpose of the League was the maintenance of international peace and security by preventing war, the purposes of the United Nations included international cooperation in economic, social, cultural and humanitarian fields in addition to maintenance of international peace and security.

(3) League of Nations operated only in political fields but the United Nations has been dealing in many other activities such as problems relating to human rights, environment, refugees, women, child and migrant workers.

(4) While in the League of Nations the Council was governed by the unanimity rule except in procedural matters, the United Nations take decisions on the basis of majority vote. Thus it is possible under the United Nations that a decision taken by the Security Council is binding on a member without its express consent.

(5) Under the League a member could withdraw itself from the League by giving two years notice or if any amendment was not acceptable to any member of the League that could mean that it has ceased to be a member of the League. But the Charter has not made any provision for the withdrawal of a State from the membership of the United Nations. However, a State may withdraw from the Organisation only in exceptional circumstances such as when the Organisation has failed to maintain international peace and security or when a member's rights and obligations have been changed by the amendment in the Charter to which it has not concurred.

(6) The Covenant of the League did not concede to the right of individual or collective self defence. The Charter of the United Nations specifically provided under Article 51 for the right of self defence and collective self-defence if an armed attack occurs against a member of the United Nations until the Security Council has taken the measures necessary to maintain international peace and security.

(7) The Covenant of the League did not lay down any provision for the regional arrangements or agencies. The UN Charter gives recognition to regional arrangements for the maintenance of international peace and security.

(8) International Court of Justice is a principal judicial organ of the United Nations. The Court carry out its functions according to the Statute which is an integral pant of the Charter. The Statute of the Parmanent Court of International Justice was an independent document. The Court was not an organ of the League but was linked to the League by Article 14 of the Covenant.

(9) Mandate system under the League and the Trusteeship system under

the Charter for the administration of non-self-governing territories had certain common points but Chapter XI under the Charter, 'Declaration regarding Non-self-governing Territories' is an innovation. It states principles which are binding upon all States engaged in the administration of non-self-governing territories and such States have been given an obligation to transmit reports to the Secretary-General of the United Nations.

It may be stated that the central core of both the organisations are the same. However, the United Nations as compared to the League of Nations is more effective in fulfilling its purposes. It is so because it learned a lot from the experiences and actual practices of the League. The framers of the Charter had a base before them. They took the ideas from the League and therefore they did not find much difficulty in the preparation of the Charter for the governance of the international community. It would not be inappropriate to state that the United Nations is the brain child of the League of Nations.

Declaration on the Occasion of the 50th Anniversary of the United Nations

In 1995, the United Nations celebrated its Fiftieth Anniversary. A Preparatory Committee for the Fiftieth Anniversary of the United Nations was established which in its 32nd meeting held on October 21, 1995 adopted the Draft Declaration[1] and decided to forward it to the General Assembly with the recommendation that it be adopted by the General Assembly at its Special Commemorative Meeting as the Declaration on the Occasion of the Fiftieth Anniversary of the United Nations. The Declaration was later on adopted by the General Assembly.

The Declaration reaffirmed the purposes and principles of the Charter of the United Nations ; expressed the gratitude to all men and women who have made the United Nations possible to work and serve its ideals, particularly those who have given their lives during service to the United Nations. The Declaration also stated that we are determined that the United Nations of the future will work with renewed vigour and effectiveness in promoting peace, development, equality and justice and understanding among the peoples of the World. The Declaration also committed to give to the twenty-first century a United Nations equipped, financed and structured to serve effectively the peoples in whose name it was established.

The Declaration was divided into five sections relating to Peace, Development, Equality, Justice and Reforms in the United Nations to meet the challanges of the 21st Century. In order to be able to respond effectively to the challanges of the future and the expectations of the United Nations held by the people around the world, the Declaration stated that it is essential that the United Nations itself be reformed and modernized. The work of the General Assembly, the universal organ of the States members of the United Nations, should be revitalized. The Security Council should be expanded. The role of the Economic and Social Council should be stengthened to enable it to carry out effectively, in the modern age, the tasks, it has been assigned with respect to the

1. *See* Doc A/AC. 240/1995/CRP 11/Rev 1.

well-being and standards of life of all people. The Secretariat of the United Nations system must improve significantly their effeciency and effectiveness in administering and managing the resources allocated to them.

The Declaration may not receive greater consideration at the hands of the powerful nations than the original U.N. Charter, yet in some respects it is a meaningful document. Unlike the Charter formulated by the victorious powers and endorsed by their forty-eight allies, the Declaration has been finalised by 185 nations representating the entire humanity.

2005 World Summit Outcome

The World leaders—Heads of State and Government met at United Nations Headquarters in New York from September 14 to 16, 2005 and adopted a document at the end of the Summit known as 2005 World Summit Outcome. The Outcome document contains a number of global issues on which the leaders agreed to take action. Following are the main features of the Outcome document :—

(1) Strong commitment was made by all governments, in donor and developing nations alike to achieve the Millennium Development Goals by 2015 which have been agreed at the major United Nations Conferences and summits including the Millennium Summit.

(2) Commitment was made to eradicate poverty and promote sustained economic growth, sustainable development and global prosperity for all.

(3) Terrorism was condemned in all its forms and manifestations, committed by whomever, whenever and for whatever purposes as it constitutes one of the most serious threats to international peace and security. Strong push was made to reach an agreement on and conclude a comprehensive convention on international terrorism within a year.

(4) Decision was made to create a Peace-building Commission as an intergovernmental advisory body to advise on and propose integrated strategies for post-conflict peace-building and recovery.

(5) It was agreed that there is a collective international responsibility to protect population from genocide, war crimes, ethnic cleansing and crimes against humanity.

(6) Obligation of States to settle their disputes by peaceful means in accordance with Chapter VI of the Charter was emphasized.

(7) Serious challenge posed by climate change was recognised. It was committed to take action through the U.N. Framework Convention on Climate Change. It was agreed to provide assistance to those most vulnerable, like small island developing States.

(8) It was agreed to establish a U.N. Human Rights Council. The Council will be responsible for promoting universal respect for the protection of all human rights and fundamental freedoms for all without distinction of any kind and in a fair and equal manner.

(9) It was agreed to reform the Security Council as an essential element

of overall effort to reform the United Nations in order to make it more broadly representative, efficient and transparent.

(10) It was agreed to wind-up the Trusteeship Council as it no longer meets and has no remaining functions.

(11) It was agreed that the term enemy States be deleted in Articles 53, 77 and 107 of the Charter.

(12) Security Council was requested to consider the composition, mandate and working methods of the Military Staff Committee.

The above proposals made in the Outcome document were indeed laudable but their implementation appears to be difficult due to diversion of views of the member States. No positive step has been taken for the deletion of the term enemy State from the Charter; Trusteeship Council has not been wound up; the Security Council has not been reformed, and the comprehensive Convention on international terrorism has not be concluded. It may be noted that the above can be achieved only when there is a strong political will of all the member States to make the international society peaceful and tension free.

ACHIEVEMENTS OF THE UNITED NATIONS :

The United Nations has been in existence since last more than seventy years. A question arises that has it managed tc achieve the goals for which it was established ? To assess the achievements of the United Nations is not an easy task in the sense that while on some occasions its failures are clearly visible for one or the other reasons but on many other occasions, it has done commendable job. However, achievements may be generalised which are as follows :

(1) Avoidance of the Third World War.—The United Nations has resolved many conflicts and disputes which otherwise would have been transformed into the World war. Conflicts have been either compromised, postponed or otherwise prevented from leading to serious international crisis. Further, it has been playing a vital role in maintaining World peace by deploying peace-keeping operations and also by taking enforcement action. Since 1945, the United Nations has negotiated 172 peaceful settlements that have ended regional conflicts.

(2) Promotion and Protection of Human Rights.—The United Nations has given attention and importance to the protection of human rights and fundamental freedoms. The Universal Declaration of Human Rights of 1948 and the two International Covenants on Civil and Political Rights and International Covenant on Economic, Social and Cultural Rights have not only set the standards for the treatment of human beings by their States, it has universalised them. Individuals have been given a rights to make complaints as to their violation of rights before international forums under the Protocols adopted under the above Covenants and also under a number of other treaties. It is the United Nations which has led States to accept, through the recognition of human rights, the fact that the States are meant for the service of the human beings.

(3) Decolonisation.—The United Nations has done a rewardable job by liberating most of the dependent territories and colonies and thus providing the right of self-determination to their people. Further, all the trust territories placed under the Trusteeship system have become independent. The Organisation' contribution towards the end of apartheid regime in South Africa is another are where its contribution is praiseworthy. It shows that the United Nation recognises the dignity of human beings.

(4) Universalisation.—The increase in the number of members of the United Nations from 51 to 193 shows that it has achieved near universalization No association or organisation in the history has ever achieved as wide acceptance as the United Nations.

(5) Conclusion of Conventions & Treaties.—Over 300 multilateral treaties and conventions have been concluded under the auspices of the United Nations covering the entire area which are possibly within the reach of the human beings. Outer-space, moon, antarctica, and deep sea are some of the areas which have come under the umbrella of treaty regime. Further, conclusion of a number of conventions under the auspices of the United Nations to improve the quality of human beings is a glorious achievement of the United Nations.

(6) Thinking for the Third Generation.—The United Nations activities are not confined only to the present generation. It has done a comendable job in providing the fundamental rights to the third generation by concluding conventions dealing with the protection of nature and environment. Further, multilateral treaties on arms limitation, disarmament and nuclear test-ban are also relevant to save the third generation from the scourage of war.

(7) Economic, Social and Cultural Development.—One of the outstanding achievements of the United Nations has been in the promotion of the economic, social and cultural development of the poorest and most disadvantaged of the world's peoples. Eradication of poverty, child survival and development, illiteracy, unemployment, population control, health and medical care and food are some of the areas which have been covered by a number of Specialized Agencies of the United Nations.

(8) Respect for International Law.—The settlement of many disputes in accordance with international law[1] by the International Court of Justice, a principal organ of the United Nations and codification of international law have been a major achievements of the United Nations.

In addition to the above, democratisation of States, efforts against illicit production, sale, demand, traffic and distribution of narcotics, strengthening capacity for preventive action and early warning, promotion of peace and development are the other areas which go to prove that the United Nations has become indispensable, and, therefore, it must be preserved. It has made incalculable contributions to the causes of peace, justice and human dignity. Member States are required to co-operate with the United Nations to make it more effective and they must demonstrate that they are willing to empower the United Nations to act on their behalf. They have to prove that the United Nations which was seen as an Organisation of 'good intentions' in reality is an Organisation of 'good results'.

The United Nations provides an apparatus. It is likely to function the way member-States want it to function, and therefore the United Nation's role and

1. *See* Chapter 'International Court of Justice'.

achievements rest on the contribution of individual States. Member States in calculating their national interests are required to give due weight to the value of a just and stable World order. As long as States lack the political will to make it a powerful Organization, it cannot achieve the desired goals. They are required to put the necessary resources at the disposal of the United Nations and should be prepared to accept limitations when it comes to their own freedom to act. However, reforms are required to be made in those areas where it has shown to be faulty, inefficient or out of tune with current conditions so that it may become more effective in confronting mankind's global problems in the present century.

Nobel Peace Prize to the United Nations and its Organisations and Individuals.—The United Nations, and its organisations have been awarded the Nobel Prize for their excellent services from time to time since its inception which are : (1) Office of the United Nations High Commissioner for Refugees, for its assistance to refugees in 1954; (2) United Nations Children's Fund (UNICEF) for its work in helping save lives of the World's children in 1965; (3) International Labour Organisation (ILO) for its progress in establishing worker's rights and protection in 1969; (4) Office of the United Nations High Commissioner for Refugees for its assistance to Asian refugees in 1981; (5) United Nations Peace-keeping Forces for its peace-keeping operations in 1988; (6) United Nations and its Secretary-General Kofi Annan for their work in promoting global harmony in 2001; (7) International Atomic Energy Agency in 2005 and (8) Inter-governmental Panel of Climate Change (IPCC). Albert Arnold (Al) Gore Jr. in 2007 and Organisation for the Prohibition of Chemical Weapons (OPCW) in 2013.

In addition to the above on a few occasions individuals attached to the United Nations have also been awarded Nobel Peace Prize. They are : (1) Cordell Hull, (U.S.A.) Ex-Secretary of State, for his leadership in establishing the United Nations in 1945 ; (2) Lord John Boyd Orr, (United Kingdom) first Director-General of the Food and Agriculture Organisation (FAO) in 1949 ; (3) Ralph Bunche, (U.S.A.), U.N. Mediator in Palestine for his leadership in the armistice agreement signed in 1949 by Israel, Egypt, Jordon, Lebanon and Syria in 1950 ; (4) Lester Pearson (Canada), President of the Seventh Session of the U.N. General Assembly for a lifetime work for peace and for leading U.N. efforts to resolve the Suez Canal crisis ; (5) Dag Hammarskjold (Sweden), Secretary-General of the United Nations for his work in helping settle the Congo crisis ; (6) Sean Mac Bride (Ireland), U.N. Commissioner for Namibia office of the United Nations High Commissioner for Refugees for its assistance to European refugees.

Reforms in the UN Charter

The United Nations Charter emerged from the deliberations of the San Francisco Conference which met in 1945 to discuss the proposals made by the States in the Dumbarton Oaks Conference and in the Yalta Conference. Many vital issues in the above conferences were discussed and resolved but at the same time a series of compromises were made by many States because every State was determined to set up, if not the perfect international organisation, at least the best that could possibly be made. The Charter therefore represents the maximum agreement available at the time it was written However, the framers of the Charter were themselves aware that the Charter is not a perfect treaty and in due course of time occasion may arise for the possible changes or modification in the Charter and therefore sufficient flexibility was made therein so that it may develop according to changing conditions. Consequently, the Charter made a provision for its amendments in Chapter XVIII comprising Articles 108 and 109.

The United Nations was established in 1945. It has been in existence since last more than 75 years. A number of changes have occurred since then due to emergence of a large number of independent States which hitherto were colonies of the metropolitan States. They all have become members of United Nations. They accepted the provisions of the Charter as it is. They did not take part in the deliberations in the San Francisco Conference and had no role in the creation of the United Nations.

After becoming independent and members of the United Nations they have their own aspirations which are required to be incorporated in the Charter by making amendments. Emergence of these States from colonies to independence and other developments have necessitated to make reforms in the Charter of the United Nations. Some areas where reforms are desirable are as follows :

(1) The composition of the Security Council is presently limited to fifteen members. It is required to be expanded in view of a number of quantitative and qualitative changes that have taken place in the international community. Presently, the number of members of the United Nations is 193 and out of them 54 members are from Africa and more than one-third of Security council debates deal with them but it does not look equitable that the Council does not have any permanent member from this Continent. Security Council is required to be expanded and at the time of expansion some key issues are required to be taken into consideration such as categories of members; regional representation and the size of an enlarged Council. Relationship of the Council with the General Assembly also needs reconsideration.

(2) General Assembly consists of all the members of the United Nations. It is merely a deliberative body which is authorized to make recommendations only. Reform is required to be made to shift some powers of the Security Council in relation to maintenance of international peace and security to the General Assembly at least for peace-keeping.

(3) Trusteeship Council has ceased to meet since 1994 as its objective has been fully attained. The 2005 World Summit Outcome had recommended that 'the Trusteeship Council no longer meets and has no remaining functions, we should delete Chapter XIII of the Charter and references to the Council in Chapter XII.' But no step has been taken to delete its provisions in the Charter. Amendment is required to be made to delete the provisions of the Council as it is no longer

relevant.

(4) 'Enemy State' clauses laid down under Articles 53, 77 and 107 of th Charter contain special provisions relating to the member of the Axe in World War II (Germany and Japan etc.). These provisions hav become obsolete and therefore they are required to be deleted. Th Special Committee on the Charter of the United Nations and on th Strengthening of the Role of the Organisation in 1995 ha recommended to the General Assembly to initiate the procedure fc making amendment in the Charter to delete the enemy State claus but no action has been taken to implement the recommendation.

(5) Economic and social problems and violations of human rights hav assumed high dimensions especially in undeveloped States. Revisic is called for in order to change the functioning of the Economic ar Social Council so that it may give due importance to these States.

(6) Development of science and technology constitutes the chief sour of progress for mankind and therefore the Charter is required to l amended so that a Council for science and technology is establishe as a principal organ of the United Nations.

(7) International organisations which are the subjects of Internation Law are required to be allowed to become parties to the Internation Court of Justice alongwith individuals. The Charter is required incorporate into it new legal concepts which are at present tl integral parts of private International Law.

(8) States are reluctant to submit their disputes to the International Cou of Justice by not accepting the compulsory jurisdiction of the Cou In order to make the Court effective it is desirable that the membe should agree to submit their legal disputes to it. The Gener Assembly and the Security Council are required to encourage Stat to ensure that they submit their disputes to the Court.

(9) The United Nations administration (usually called the UN Secretaria is required to be more transparent, more accountable and mo efficient.

(10) Presently, the problem arising from pollution of human environme due to industrialisation, urbanisation, over population and pover has assumed great dimensions throughout the World. The Unite Nations Environment Programme (UNEP) handles the proble relating to environment but its functioning is painfully slow. It shou be replaced by a new and powerful organisation *i.e.*, United Natio Environment Organisation (UNEO) on the line of the World Heal Organisation.

The Charter of the United Nations in order to meet the challenges of th present time is required to be amended. Reforms in the structure of the Unite Nations and its working system is desirably to be made so that all the memb States may participate in all the decisions of the Organisation. The principle sovereign equality of member States and the democratization of the Unite Nations system as a whole should be followed. It may be stated that reforn may be made by making amendments in the Charter.

However, it is a difficult task to make amendments in the Charter as it has to be adopted by the two thirds vote of the members in the General Assembly and to be ratified by at least two-thirds of the Member States including all the five permanent members of the Security Council. The above implies that any reform in the Charter of the United Nations is subject to veto and it is indeed a difficult task to crack the hard nut.

Organs of the United Nations :

The United Nations is an association of States but like other organisations it carries out its functions through organs composed of individuals which in most cases act as representatives of member States. The Charter, apart from establishing the Organisation itself, has created a number of organs for the purpose of carrying out the aims of the Organisation. Chapter III of the Charter comprising of Articles 7 and 8 describe about the organs of the United Nations. Article 7 provides that organs may be of two kinds, *i.e.*, principal organs and subsidiary organs. Principal organs are those whose names are mentioned in the Charter under Article 7. They are : General Assembly, Security Council, Economic and Social Council, Trusteeship Council, International Court of Justice and Secretariat.

In order to co-ordinate the activities of all the organs of the United Nations, it is desirable that the Heads of all the organs meet from time to time in order to fulfil the purposes and principles of the United Nations. In the history of the United Nations, for the first time, heads of all the six principal organs met on October 28, 1998. They discussed current international developments and trends, as well as organising efforts aimed at international reforms. It was an indeed positive step towards the fulfilment of the objectives of the United Nations.

The subsidiary organs are those which may be established in future in accordance with the provisions of the Charter. The Charter authorized the General Assembly under Article 22 and the Security Council under Article 29 to establish subsidiary organs for the performance of their functions. Although Article 68 authorises the ECOSOC to set up Commissions and the Trusteeship Council Rules of Procedure permit the establishment of Committees they are not the subsidiary organs of the United Nations, may be, because the General Assembly and the Security Council have equal status under the Charter. Both the ECOSOC and the Trusteeship Council perform functions under the authority of the General Assembly.

United Nations System.—The United Nations System is referred to all those organisations of the United Nations which have been established by the Charter of the United Nations. It consists of six principal organs of the United Nations, i.e., the General Assembly, Security Council, Economic and Social Council, Trusteeship Council, International Court of Justice and the Secretariat and the specialized agencies[1] and the related organisations.[2] The System also

1. See Chapter 10.
2. See Chapter 11.

includes the subsidiary organs and bodies,[1] separately administered funds and programmes,[2] research and training institutes.[3]

United Nations Emblem.—The General Assembly of the United Nations approved the emblem of the United Nations for its official seal through a Resolution 92(1) adopted on December 7, 1946. The use of the emblem is restricted and the Assembly recommended that legislation should be passed by members to prevent its use for commercial purposes by means of trade marks or commercial labels as well as the use of the initial letters. Use of the U.N. Emblem is restricted further by the Under Secretary General for Management by issuing administrative instructions on Regulation for the control on documents and publications by stating that when the United Nations participates in organising a conference or meeting convened by an outside body or when the United Nations jointly publishes a publication with an outside body/bodies, the emblem may be used, in combination with the name "United Nations" if the emblems of other participating bodies are so used on the documents of the conferences or meeting or on the publication jointly published with the outside body/bodies.

United Nations Flag.—In Resolution 167(11) the General Assembly adopted on October 20, 1947 in pursuance of which the Secretary-General promulgated a flag code which provided : (a) that the flag of the United Nations shall not be subordinate to any other flag; (b) it shall be flown from all buildings, offices and official residences designated as such by the United Nations; (c) that it shall be used by any unit acting on behalf of the United Nations.

The forces operating in Korea were given the name and the flag of the United Nations by a Resolution of the Security council adopted in 1950. The U.N. Flag was also used for instance, by the U.N. Security Forces in West New Guinea (West Iran); the U.N. forces in the Congo and the U.N. forces in Cyprus and by other peace-keeping operations.

The flag code was amended by the Secretary-General on November 11, 1952 which *inter alia* laid down that the flag shall not be subjected to any indignity. Later, the flag code was again amended by the Secretary-General which replaced the code amended on November 11, 1952. The amended Code laid down the provisions regarding the dimensions of the flag; flag protocol; use of flag; prohibitions on its use and its use on mourning upon the death of a Head of State or Head of Government of a member State.

---

1. See Chapter 12.
2. Instances of funds and programmes are the Office of the United Nations High Commissioner for Refugees (UNHCR) Office of the United Nations Commission for Human Rights (UNCHR), the United Nations Children's Funds (UNICEF), the United Nations Conference on Trade and Development (UNCTAD) and the United Nations Environment Programme (UNEP).
3. Instances of research and training institutes are the United Nations Institute for Disarmament Research (UNIDR), United Nations Institute for Training and Research (UNITAR) and the United Nations Research Institute for Social Development (UNRISD).

Chapter 4
General Assembly

General Assembly is one of the principal organs and the chief deliberative and policy making body of the United Nations. Provisions relating to General Assembly are contained in Chapter IV of the Charter comprising of Articles 9 to 22.

Composition :

Article 9 of the Charter lays down regarding the composition of the General Assembly by stating that the General Assembly shall consist of all the members of the United Nations. Each of them possesses equal status irrespective of its size, power or importance. Each member shall have not more than five representatives in the General Assembly. The appointed representatives may be replaced by the member States. The Charter does not provide for alternates or advisors of the representatives. However, member States may appoint alternates and advisors but they shall not be treated as organs of the United Nations. The credentials of representatives and the names of members of a delegation are required to be submitted to the Secretary-General if possible not less than one week before the date fixed for the opening of the session. The credentials shall be issued either by the Head of the State or Government or by the Minister of Foreign Affairs. One of the five representatives may be appointed as Chairman of the delegation by the member States.

The General Assembly shall have a President elected by the General Assembly for each session. Until the President for the session is elected, the Assembly is presided by the President of the previous session. The General Assembly also elects seven Vice-Presidents who shall hold office until the close of session at which they are elected.

In addition to the members of the United Nations States and non-State entities which have been granted observer status also participate in the General Assembly. They take part in the deliberations but do not have voting rights.

Sessions of the General Assembly

General Assembly meets in regular session, special session and the emergency special session.

Regular Session.—Regular session, also called annual session means one session in a year. The first meeting of the General Assembly with full membership of 51 States was held in London on January 10, 1946. The duration of the regular session is not expressly laid down in the Charter. The Assembly meets each year commencing on the third Tuesday of September to December at the Head Quarters in New York.[1] The above period of the regular session appears to be customary in the sense that it has remained constant. It is to be noted that while the time available to the Assembly has remained constant, both the number of members to be heard and the number of items to be discussed have increased. Therefore, the Assembly resumes in January until all the issues on the agenda are addressed which often is just before the next session starts. Thus, the pressure of work has made the management of time limit all the more important.

Special Session.—Special session of the General Assembly may be called within fifteen days either by the Secretary-General at the request of the Security Council or by a majority of member States or by one member State with the concurrence of a majority of members. The above implies that in convoking the special session of the Assembly, the Secretary-General does not act on his own initiative. He acts only at the request of the Security Council or of a majority of the members. Since the convocation of a special session is a procedural matter the decision of the Security Council may be adopted according to Article 27 paragraph 2 of the Charter, *i.e.*, by the affirmative votes of nine members.

In the past special sessions of the General Assembly have been held on a number of occasions to discuss different topics. By the end of 2020 thirtyone special sessions have been held on different subjects which are : Palestine (1947), Palestine (1948), Tunisia (1961), Financial Situation of the United Nations (1963), South West Africa (Namibia) (1967), Raw Materials and Development (1974), Development and International Economic Co-operation (1975), Financing of the UN Interim Force in Lebanon (1978), Namibia (1978), Disarmament (1978), New International Economic Order (1980) Disarmament (1982), Africa (1982) Namibia (1986), Disarmament (1988), Apartheid (1989), Drug Abuse (1990), International Economic Co-operation (1990) Review and Earth Summits (1997), Countering the World Drug Problem (1998); Population and Development (ICDP) (1999), Small Island Developing States (1999), Women 2000 : Gender Equality, Development and Peace for the 21st Century (2000) and Social Development (2000), Implementation of the outcome of the U.N. Conference on Human Settlement (2001), HIV/AIDS (2001), World Summit for Children (2002), Commemoration of the Sixtieth Anniversary of the Liberation of the Nazi Concentration Camps (2005), Follow up to the Programme of Action of the International Conference on Population and Development (2014) and World Drug Problem (2016) and Response to the Coronavirus Disease (Covid-19) Pandemic (2020).

Emergency Special Session.—Emergency special session may be called within twenty-four hours of the receipt by the Secretary General of a request by the Security Council on the vote of any nine of its members or by a majority of the members of the United Nations. It may be noted that the Charter does not contain any provision for the convocation of the emergency special session. However, such a session may be called in accordance with the General Assembly Resolution 377 (A) V adopted on November 3, 1950 which is commonly known as the Uniting for Peace Resolution. It is to be noted that

1. In December 1988, the General Assembly organised its 29th Session in Geneva in order to hear Yassar Arafat.

emergency special session is called when the Assembly is 'not in session' but presently and for the last many years the Assembly meets 'year around' and only adjourns the mid-September the day before the new session begins. There is no break between sessions other than a day or two. In such a practice need for calling for the emergency special session does not arise.

In the past Emergency Special Sessions of the Assembly have been held on ten occasions by the end of 2014 to discuss the critical issues. They dealt with the following critical situations : Suez Canal (1956); Hungary (1956); Lebanon (1958); Congo (1960); The Middle East (1967); Soviet invasion of Afghanistan (1980); Palestine (1980) and resumed in (1982); Namibia (1981); Occupied Arab Territories, (1982) and Illegal Israeli action in East Jerusalem and rest of the occupied Palestinian Territory (1997). The Tenth Special Session was also resumed in 1998, 1999, 2000, 2001, 2002, 2003, 2007, 2009, 2017 and in 2018.

Voting System :

Each member of the General Assembly has only one vote. Thus, in the Assembly the principle of equality of the members is strictly observed. Decisions on 'important questions' as laid down specifically under Article 18, Para 2 to the Charter such as recommendation with respect of maintenance of international peace and security, election of non-permanent members of the Security Council, election of members of the Trusteeship Council and Economic and Social Council, admission, suspension and expulsion of members, trusteeship questions and budgetary matters are taken by a two-thirds majority of members 'present and voting.' It is to be noted that enumeration of the above matters is not exhaustive in view of the wordings of Article 18 Para 2 which lays down that these questions shall 'include' which may mean that the Charter has referred to only certain matters as important questions. Other questions may also be included in the list of important questions. However, the decision, by which a new category of important questions is added to those enumerated in Paragraph 2, may be made by a two-thirds majority of the members. 'Other questions' are decided by a simple majority of the members 'present and voting.' The Assembly itself, voting by simple majority, may add new categories of questions which are to be decided by a two-thirds majority according to Article 18, Para 3.

Article 18(3) of the Charter uses the phrase 'members present and voting'. The term 'present' may mean as present at the meeting when the vote is taken. The question as to how many members must be present for voting is not mentioned in the Charter. However, Rules 67 and 68 specify that no procedural or substantive decision can be made unless representatives of a majority of the members are present. Thus, 'A majority of the members of the General Assembly shall constitute a quorum'. By the term 'and voting' may mean members casting an affirmative or a negative vote. Rules 86 and 126 lay down that members which abstain from voting are considered as not voting.

Article 19 of the Charter lays down that a member shall have no vote in the General Assembly which is in arrears in the payment of its financial contribution to the Organisation provided the amount of its arrears equals or exceeds the amount of the contributions due from it for the preceding two full years. The General Assembly, may nevertheless permit such a member to vote if it is satisfied that the failure to pay is due to conditions beyond the control of the members.

In 1996, 39 members were debarred from voting in the General Assembly owing more than two years of dues. The United States is the largest debtor to the United Nations, however, it paid most of its 1994 dues and was in danger of losing its vote. Eleven members have requested to the Assembly to restore their voting rights as the failure occured due to special circumstances. Similarly, the Assembly in 2000 released a list of 52 States whose arrears have accumulated equal to or greater than their assessments for the previous two years. These countries will loose their vote in the Assembly until their arrears are brought below the two year level except for 7 States with special exemptions. The Assembly on October 9, 2017 adopted a resolution by which it resolved that failure of the Comoros, Guinea Bissau, Sao-Tome, Principe and Somalia to pay the full minimum amount necessary to avoid the application of Article 19 was due to conditions beyond their control and therefore they were permitted to vote in the Assembly until the end of its seventy-second session.

Functions and Powers :

Functions and Powers of the Assembly are laid down under Articles 10 to 17 of the Charter. For convenience, they may be divided into following categories :

(1) General Functions :

The General Assembly is essentially a deliberative body. It has powers of discussion, investigation, review, supervision and to criticise in relation to the work of the United Nations as a whole and various other organs including the specialized agencies as well as any other matter. Article 10 confers upon the Assembly a very wide power by providing that the Assembly has competence to discuss any question or any matter 'within the scope of the Charter' or relating to the powers and functions of any organ provided for in the Charter. After discussion, the Assembly may make recommendations by adopting resolutions on these questions to the member States or to the Security Council or to both.

Thus, there is hardly any international matter which the General Assembly is not competent to discuss and on which it is not competent to make recommendations. However, the function of discussion is subject to one restriction which is provided under Article 2(7) of the Charter which prohibits intervention in the domestic affairs of the States. Thus, the General Assembly is not authorized to discuss those matters which are essentially within the domestic jurisdiction of any State. Further, as to recommendation, and not to discussion, there is one restriction that is, it shall not make recommendations on any dispute or situation which the Security Council has under consideration, unless the Security Council requests.[1] The purpose of the restriction is to avoid conflicts between the General Assembly and the Security Council. The Secretary General therefore informs the Assembly of any matters concerning international peace and security which are being handled by the Security Council. When the Council has ceased to deal with these matters, the Secretary General informs the Assembly or to the member States if the Assembly is not in session.

(2) Promotion of International Co-operation :

Article 13 of the Charter has conferred to the Assembly specifically to 'initiate studies and make recommendations' for the purposes of the promotion of international co-operation in two different fields. Firstly, the promotion of international co-operation in political fields and encouraging the progressive development of International Law and its codification, and secondly, the promotion of international co-operation in the economic, social, cultural, educational and health fields, and assisting in the realisation of human rights and fundamental freedoms for all without distinction as to race, sex, language, or religion.

(3) Maintenance of International Peace and Security :

Although maintenance of international peace and security is the primary function of the Security Council, the General Assembly being an organ of the United Nations also performs functions in this regard. Reference of a matter before the Assembly may be made by a member State under Article 35(1) of the Charter, by a non-member State under Article 35(2) or by the Security Council under Article 11(2). The Assembly may also take action on its own initiative pursuant to Articles 10 and 14. When a matter is brought before the Assembly, it maintains international peace and security in three ways :—

(a) By Initiating Discussion :

The Assembly according to Article 11, Para 2 of the Charter may discuss any question relating to international peace and security. Discussion on such questions take place when they are brought before the Assembly by any member of the United Nations, or by the Security Council, or by a non-member of the United Nations under Article 35 Para 2 of the Charter.

(b) By Making Recommendations :

The Assembly after discussion, may make recommendations on any question relating to the maintenance of international peace and security to the State or States concerned, or to the Security Council, or to both according to Article 11, Para 2 of the Charter. The Assembly has recommended to settle the dispute in the case of Palestine (Resolution 36/120 of 1981) and Namibia

---

1. According to Kelsen the words, "While the Security Council is exercising........the functions' may be interpreted to mean : while a dispute or situation is still on the agenda of the Council', But it may also be interpreted to mean; while the Security Council is actually exercising the functions; so that when the Council because of the exercise of veto right is reduced to inaction, it should not be considered as 'exercising' its functions. Article 12, Paragraph 1 does not prevent the General Assembly to make a recommendation after the Security Council has made a recommendation on the same case. 'The Law of the United Nations', p. 217.

(Resolution 36/121 of 1981). However, recommendations may not be made by the Assembly on those matters which the Security Council has under consideration, unless the Council so requests. It was observed by the International Court of Justice in its advisory opinion[1] given in the Legal Consequences of the Construction of a Wall in the Occupied Palestinian Territory that a request for an advisory opinion is not a recommendation by the General Assembly with regard to a dispute or situation within the meaning of Article 12.

In addition to the recommendation, the Assembly has been conferred power under Article 11 (Para 3) to call the attention of the Security Council to situations which are likely to endanger international peace and security and where 'action is necessary', if brought before it by a member, a non-member or the Security Council. In such cases the General Assembly is bound to refer the question to the Security Council. However, it is authorized to recommend to the Council to take enforcement action. After the Assembly has decided that 'action' is necessary and has referred the case to the Security Council the latter has to deal with it. Is the Security Council bound to execute the decision of the General Assembly? Since the Charter does not impose upon the Security Council any such obligation, the question must be answered in the negative.[2]

The General Assembly has been empowered under Article 14 of the Charter to recommend measures for the peaceful adjustment of any situation which it deems likely to impair the general welfare or friendly relations among nations including situations resulting from a violation of the provisions of the Charter setting forth the purposes and principles of the United Nations. Thus, the General Assembly may recommend measures for the peaceful adjustment of any situation to whatever persons or authorities it deems it necessary.

(c) By Taking Collective Measures : (Uniting for Peace Resolution) :

Provisions for the collective measures taken by the Assembly are not laid down in the Charter, and, therefore, the Assembly in the beginning was not authorized to take collective measures for the maintenance of international peace and security. However, differences in the ideologies and policies of the 'big powers' led to the mutual conflict and non-co-operation among them. One of the main consequences of such rift was that the 'big powers' could not perform the primary function of maintaining international peace and security effectively which was assigned to them through the Security Council. The result was that the United Nations' main purpose of the maintenance of international peace and security began to break down. It therefore became necessary to find out a solution to achieve the end even when the Security Council fails to do so due to the veto power exercised by the permanent members.

This led to the United States, with the support of France and Great Britain to bring an item 'Uniting for Peace', before the General Assembly in the Fifth Regular Session on November 3, 1950 which was adopted by 52 votes with 5 against and with two abstentions. The Assembly adopted three resolutions under the item 'Uniting for Peace' on November 3, 1950. The first of those,

1. ICJ Reports (2004) (1).
2. Kelsen, Op. cit., p. 205.

Resolution A, is the one which is here referred to as Uniting for Peace Resolution.[1] The Preamble of the resolution reaffirmed the importance of the exercise by the Security Council of its primary responsibility for the maintenance of peace and security. It also stated member States of their obligations or the United Nations of its responsibility under the Charter to maintain international peace and security. The operative part of the Resolution consisted of five sections. Section A provided :

If the Security Council, because of the lack of unanimity of its permanent members, fails to exercise its primary responsibility in the maintenance of peace in a case where there appears to be a threat to the peace, breach of the peace or act of aggression, the Assembly shall consider the matter immediately with a view to making recommendations to members for collective measures, including, in the case of a breach of the peace or an act of aggression, the use of armed force when necessary to maintain international peace and security. If not in session, the Assembly shall meet in emergency special session within twenty-four hours on a request for such a session by the Security Council on a vote of any seven of its members, (seven members should be read as nine members after the amendment which took place in the year 1965) or by a majority of the members of the United Nations.

Section B of the Resolution established a Peace Observation Commission of fourteen Members, including the five permanent members of the Security Council, to observe and report of the situation in areas where peace was threatened. By Section C of the Resolution, Members of the United Nations were invited to survey their resources in order to determine the nature and scope of the assistance they might be in a position to render in support of any recommendations of the Security Council or the General Assembly for the restoration of peace and security. It also recommended members of the United Nations to maintain within their national armed forces elements that could promptly be made available for service as a United Nations unit or units, upon recommendation of the Council or the Assembly. Section D of the Resolution established the Collective Measures Committee of fourteen members to report on methods which might be used collectively to maintain peace. Section E of the resolution is of general nature.

The Uniting for Peace Resolution has thus empowered the General Assembly to take enforcement action including the use of armed forces for the maintenance of international peace and security. Two important points involved in the resolution require special consideration. They are, firstly, the validity of the resolution, and secondly, the practical utility of the resolution.

(i) Validity of the Resolution.—The legal value of the resolution has been questioned on the ground that the enforcement action taken under the resolution is inconsistent with the provisions of the Charter. It has been stated that the primary responsibility for the maintenance of international peace and security vests in the Security Council. The enforcement action may be taken only by the Security Council and not by the General Assembly. The latter can only discuss the matter under Article 11, Para 2, and recommend measures for the

1. General Assembly Resolution 377 (v) November 3, 1950.

peaceful adjustment of a situation. The Assembly is not empowered to take enforcement action because the Charter has not empowered it to use the force. If the Assembly does not have the power to use the force under the Charter, how can it acquire the power by the adoption of a resolution ? Would it not amount to an attempt to amend the Charter, in a way different from that prescribed by Articles 108 and 109 ? It has been argued that the collective measures of the Uniting for Peace Resolution only reflect the breakdown of the original plan not permissible under the Charter.

It is submitted that the above criticism does not appear to be sound in view of the provision of Article 1 of the Charter which lays down the purposes of the United Nations. Paragraph 1 of the above Article provides that one of the purposes of the United Nations is 'to maintain international peace and security', and to that end : it may take 'effective collective measures for the prevention and removal of threats to the peace, and for the suppression of acts of aggression or other breaches of the peace.....' It implies, that the maintenance of international peace and security is the responsibility of the United Nations as a whole. No doubt, primary responsibility has been conferred to the Security Council, the term 'primary' does not mean exclusive responsibility. Other organs especially the General Assembly have also been empowered to fulfil this purpose of the United Nations on a secondary level on the condition that if the Security Council fails to do so. While adopting the resolution this aspect was well considered and, therefore, it clearly stipulated that the Assembly shall take action under the resolution if the Security Council fails to exercise its primary responsibility for the maintenance of international peace and security. Thus the resolution was adopted, on the one hand, to fulfil one of the purposes of the United Nations of maintaining international peace and security, and on the other hand, to check the abuse of power which is exercised by the 'big powers' in the Security Council. The recommendations for the enforcement action and for the use of armed force may be made according to Article 10 which lays down that 'the General Assembly may discuss any questions or any matters within the scope of the present Charter......and may make recommendations to the members of the United Nations'. Recommendations under the Uniting for Peace Resolution may be made by two-thirds majority of members present and voting in accordance with Article 18 Para 2 of the Charter.

(ii) Practical Utility of the Resolution.—It has been stated that because of the limitations which the resolution itself carries, there is hardly any practical utility of it. According to them, firstly, recommendation may be made by the General Assembly when the Security Council fails to exercise the primary responsibility for the maintenance of international peace and security. It implies that the Assembly may make recommendations with respect to disputes or situations with which the Council has not yet dealt or with which it has ceased to deal or as Kelsen says when the Council, because of the exercise of the veto right, is reduced to inaction.[1] It may mean that the Assembly cannot take action when the matter is being discussed by the Council. Secondly, the recommendations of the General Assembly are not legally binding on its members. The members therefore may not give assistance to the Assembly in an

1. Kelsen, Op. cit., p. 217.

enforcement action taken under the resolution. Thus, the assistance provided by the members is optional. Thirdly, the resolution shall be operative, without any regard to the big powers, only on the two-thirds majority of the members. It is difficult to obtain the required majority in view of the rivalry of the big powers. It is to be noted that even if the above majority is obtained, how far any action taken by the smaller powers would be effective, after the failure of the big powers in the Security Council, is a question which is difficult to answer.

The above limitations have, of course, placed the 'Uniting for Peace Resolution' in a difficult situation leading to a limited practical utility. However, in the past, on a few occasions, the resolution was adopted by the Assembly to maintain international peace and security. The resolution was invoked for the first time on November 4, 1956 when the United Kingdom, France and Israel attacked on Egypt consequent upon its nationalisation of the Suez Canal. The action led to the United States to make a call to all the nations to refrain from the use of force or threat of force in Egypt in an emergency meeting of the Security Council. But when the resolution was vetoed by Britain and France on October 31, 1956, Yugoslavia with the support of the United States proposed for an immediate meeting of the General Assembly in accordance with the Uniting for Peace Resolution. United Nations Emergency Force (UNEF) was established in 1956. Similarly, United Nations Operations in Congo (ONUC) was established in 1960. UNEF and ONUC it is submitted, were peace-keeping operations and were not enforcement measures or the collective use of force, as the consent of the territorial State was obtained. International Court of Justice in advisory opinion given in Certain Expenses of the United Nations.[1] observed that UNEF and ONUC are peace-keeping operations and were not enforcement actions within the compass of Chapter VII of the Charter.

In other cases where the Uniting for Peace based sessions took place resulted to the Assembly to take a variety of non-use of force measures such as establishing a Commission of Inquiry (Hungary, 1956); calling for the withdrawal of foreign troops from Jordan and Lebanon (1958); calling for the rescission by Israel of unilateral measures in Jerusalem (1967), providing assistance to East Pakistani refugee (1971); calling for the withdrawal of foreign troops from Afghanistan (1980) and calling of Israel from territories occupied, 1967 (1980).

It is submitted that the practical utility of the resolution depends largely upon the co-operation of the members. With the decline of the Security Council, task for the maintenance of international peace and security has been shifted to the General Assembly and therefore it became the responsibility of all the members to give their full support to the Assembly on issues relating to the maintenance of international peace and security including those where enforcement action under Uniting for Peace Resolution is taken.

However, in practice all the hopes raised at the time of the adoption of the Uniting for Peace Resolution belied because of the difficult procedure. It has of course provided a method whereby disputes may be discussed before the Assembly as an alternative mechanism for the maintenance of international

1. ICJ Report 1962 p. 166.

peace and security but it did not make any effective influence as to the maintenance of peace and security.

(4) Elective Functions :

The Assembly is commonly known as the central body of the United Nations because it elects some or all the members of all the other organs of the United Nations. In this regard the Assembly performs the following functions :

(a) The Assembly elects all the ten non-permanent members of the Security Council.[1] Out of them five members are elected every year in accordance with Article 23, Para 2 when equal number of members retire after completing the term of two years;

(b) The Assembly elects all the fifty-four members of the Economic and Social Council.[2] Out of them eighteen members are elected every year as per Article 61, Para 3;

(c) The Assembly elects some members of the Trusteeship Council.[3]

(d) The Assembly elects fifteen Judges of the International Court of Justice. Judges are elected by a complicated system of parallel voting by the Security Council and the General Assembly independently of each other;

(e) The Secretary-General of the United Nations is also appointed by the General Assembly on the recommendation of the Security Council.[4]

(f) The Assembly elects members for subsidiary organs which may be created by it under Article 22.

It is to be noted that election to any of the three Councils (Security Council, Economic and Social Council and Trusteeship Council), being important questions, requires two-thirds majority in accordance with Article 18(2) of the Charter. Article 10 of the Statute of International Court of Justice provides a different rule for the election of the judges of the Court. Judges are elected when they receive support from an absolute majority of the General Assembly and Security Council simultaneously. Secretary-General is appointed together by the General-Assembly and the Security Council. Since the veto applies, an Assembly majority must find a candidate acceptable to all the five permanent members. At the same time, the permanent members must find a candidate acceptable to the Assembly majority.

Elective functions, indispensible as they are, form a part of the work of the General Assembly. Some authors have called electoral functions of the General Assembly as legal functions of the Assembly.

(5) Functions Relating to Admission, Suspension and Expulsion of Members :

A member is admitted to the United Nations by the Assembly upon the recommendation of the Security Council. The Assembly also cooperates with the

---

1. Article 23, Para 1.
2. Article 61, Para 1.
3. Article 86.
4. Article 97.

Security Council in the suspension of member States against which enforcement action is being taken, and the expulsion of those which have been persistently violating the principles of the Charter.

(6) Financial Functions :

The General Assembly performs important functions relating to the finance of the United Nations. It considers and approves the budget of the Organisation.[1] It decides the share of expenses to be borne by each member.[2] Once the General Assembly decides the share of expenses it becomes the obligation of the members to fulfil it. Non-payment of the dues, according to Judge Schwebel of the International Court of Justice, not only has the gravest effect on the life of the Organisation but trangresses the principles of free consent and good faith... which are the heart of international law and relations. The Assembly also considers and approves the financial and budgetary arrangements with specialized agencies and examines the administrative budgets of these agencies and makes recommendations to them.

(7) Supervisory Functions :

The Assembly supervises the activities of other organs and of the specialized agencies of the Organisation. Thus, it considers annual and special reports of the Security Council.[3] It also considers the reports of the other organs, i.e., of the Economic and Social Council, Trusteeship Council, International Court of Justice and the Secretariat.[4] In addition to the above most subsidiary U.N. bodies report to it either directly or through the Economic and Social Council.

(8) Miscellaneous Functions :

A number of other functions are performed by the Assembly which are as follows :

(a) It may establish such subsidiary organs as it deems necessary for the performance of its functions.[5] Subsidiary bodies of the Assembly have a number of effects. Firstly, they permit the Assembly to do more work. They have more time to go into details of an issue. Secondly, they can be used to channel Assembly debates and decisions in predetermined ways in the sense that they are created with definite mandate. Thirdly, all subsidiary organs affect the timing and form of international discussion on the issues they consider. In the past, the Assembly has established many subsidiary organs which includes the

1. Articles 17, Para 1.
2. Article 17, Para 2. The Assembly in the year 2000, was able to formalize a new scale of assessment for the regular budget of the United Nations for 2001-2003. The new scale, adopted without a vote, would be based on a State's gross national product (GNP) over statistical base periods of three and six years, with a low per capita income adjustment of 80 per cent. The Assembly also established a minimum assessment of 0.01 per cent. The maximum assessment rate would be 22 per cent, reducing the assessment of the U.S.A., the largest contributor by 3 per cent.
3. Article 15, Para 1.
4. Article 15, Para 2.
5. Article 22.

International Law Commission (1947), the United Nations Institute for Training and Research (UNITAR) (1963), the Committee on the Peaceful Uses of Outer-Space (1957), the Special Committee on situation with regard to the Implementation of the Declaration on the Granting of Independence to Colonial Countries and Peoples.

(b) The Assembly by Article 96, Para 2 may authorize other organs of the United Nations and specialized agencies to request for the advisory opinion of the International Court of Justice on legal questions.

(c) The Charter may be amended when it has been adopted by a vote of two-thirds of the members of the Assembly including all permanent members of the Security Council.[1]

Legal and Political Functions

The above functions conferred upon the General Assembly are either legal functions or political functions. Legal functions of the Assembly are those which have legal effects, that is to say, if they constitute obligations, rights or competences such as admission of new members under Article 4 or the participation in the amendment procedure under Article 108. Political functions are those which have no such legal effect such as to 'discuss' any matter within the scope of the Charter (Article 10); to 'consider' principles or reports (Articles 11, 15, 24, 87); to accept or receive reports, recommendations or observations (Articles 15, 62, 64), but this only in order to 'consider' or 'discuss' them. The most important political function of the Assembly is to make 'recommendations' (Articles 10, 11, 13, 14, 58, 64, 105). Such recommendations may be made to the members of the United Nations (Articles 10, 11), to non-member States (Article 11 Para 2), or to the Security Council (Articles 10, 11). Recommendations may also be made in the field of international cooperation (Article 13) and for the peaceful adjustment of any situation which it deems is likely to impair the general welfare or friendly relations among nations.

Exclusive, Common or Joint and Concurrent Functions

Functions of the General Assembly may be divided broadly in three categories,*viz.*, exclusive functions, common or joint functions and concurrent functions.

Exclusive function of the General Assembly may mean the function the effect of which can be brought solely by an act of the Assembly. That is, act of another organ is not necessary and no other organ is competent to exercise the function concerned. Thus, the authorisation to other organs and the specialized agencies to request advisory opinion of the International Court of Justice on legal questions under Article 96 Para 2 is an exclusive function of the General Assembly.[2]

The Assembly has an exclusive functions in the economic, social and

1. Article 108.
2. Kelsen, op. cit., p. 216.

cultural fields[1] and also in the field of non-self-governing[2] and trust territories[3] with the exception of trusteeship over strategic areas which is performed by the Security Council.[4] Further, Article 17 gives the Assembly the power to consider and approve the budget of the Organisation and to apportion its expenses among the members. By the same Article, the Assembly has also been given certain powers with respect to the finance of the Specialized Agencies. The Assembly under Article 105 is the sole authority on the privileges and immunities of the Organisation and its officials and of the representatives of members.

The competence is common or joint if the act of the General Assembly can bring its specific effect only together with the act of other organs. For instance, admission of new members (Article 4), suspension from the exercise of the rights and privileges of membership (Article 5) and expulsion of members (Article 6) may be affected by the General Assembly on the recommendation of the Security Council. In the case of suspension, the rights and privileges may be restored by the Security Council alone. Secretary General of the United Nations is appointed by the General Assembly upon the recommendation of the Security Council. Assembly and the Council are also jointly responsible for the election of the judges of the International court of Justice (Article 4(1) of the statute of the ICJ). The two organs proceed independently of one another to elect the members of the Court. The expression 'by the General Assembly upon the recommendation of the Council is laid down under Article 93(2) which provides that the determination of the conditions on which a State, not a member of the United Nations may become a party to the Court. Further, States which are parties to the statute of the Court but are not members of the United Nations may participate in the election of the judge on the condition laid down by the General Assembly on the recommendation of the Security Council (Article 93(2) of the Charter). Amendment of the Charter is also the joint responsibility of the Assembly and the Council which is laid down under Article 108 of the Charter which provides that amendment shall come into force upon ratification by two-thirds of the members of the United Nations including all the members of the Security Council.

Concurrent function is called to those functions which may be exercised by the General Assembly as well as by the other organs of the United Nations, especially by the Security Council.[5] For instance, functions relating to settlement of dispute and adjustment of other situations may be performed by the General Assembly under Article 11 and 33 and by the Security Council under Articles 34 and 38. Further, enforcement action may be taken by the Security council under Article 41 and 42 and if it fails, by the General Assembly under 'Uniting for Peace' resolution.

1. Article 13(1)(b).
2. See Chapter XI of the Charter.
3. See Article 16 and Chapter XII and XIII of the Charter.
4. See Article 83.
5. *Ibid.*

Effect of the Resolutions of the General Assembly :

While performing some of the above functions, the General Assembly by adopting resolutions make recommendations to the Security Council or to the Secretary General, the Economic and Social Council, the Trusteeship Council as well as to subsidiary organs or to the members, or to non-members of the United Nations. A question arises as to what is the legal effect of its recommendations, or to say, resolutions adopted by it. It has been asserted that the Charter has not conferred to the Assembly any law-making power, and therefore, its decisions, which are given by way of recommendations, do not create any legal obligations on its members irrespective of the fact that they have been adopted unanimously, or by overwhelming votes, or even if the contents of it is a matter of common interest for all the States. Thus, the Assembly, according to this view, is totally incompetent to compel a State to implement its recommendations. At the most, States are said to be only morally bound to give effect to the resolutions. It is to be noted that many problems of the World could not be resolved only because member States did not pay any attention to the recommendations of the General Assembly. Non-enforcement of the resolutions has severely affected many important international issues such as the establishment of a New International Economic Order (NIEO).

It may be stated that the resolutions are the expressions of the will of the international community from voting on it. If a resolution is adopted on a particular aspect unanimously or by two-thirds majority of the members (including States with material capability so that they may not overturn the rules by themselves.[1]) and if the same resolution finds reflection in many other subsequent resolutions, it must not be lightly weighted. Any rule adopted through such a resolution has a tendency to become the customary rule of International Law in the sense that such resolutions fulfil two essential conditions, viz., the generality and the continuity, which are normally required by a rule to become the customary rule of International Law. Through its egalitarian character, its majority basis and its democratic origin, it is submitted, that the resolutions adopted therein present sufficient guarantee as a method for the elaboration of International Law responding to the present day need. The resolutions hold a real attraction especially for the developing countries because of their flexibility, rapidity and the security they give to them. The above argument, howsoever convincing it may be, would not change the character of the resolutions of the Assembly, unless revision is made in the Charter, which, of course, is not a smooth sailing. Revision of the Charter especially on such matters, which directly affects the powers of the 'big five' is rather a difficult task. But the suggestion of the revision of the Charter is neither impractical nor hypothetical. The Secretary-General of the United Nations had once recommended for the revision of the Charter in order to oblige all States to comply with the resolutions of the Assembly. International Law is a dynamic law. It must change according to the needs of the international community. If most of the States of the World are in favour of the change, it should be made in the interest and welfare of the international community.

1. For instance, resolutions laying down rules for conduct in space have little value without both United States and Russia.

Binding Resolutions of the General Assembly

Resolutions of the General Assembly are not legally binding on States but in a few cases the U.N. Charter gives the Assembly binding authority which apply to direct relations with member States. Such areas are as follows :—

(1) Decisions about Participation.—The Assembly decides that which government of a particular State shall participate when two delegations sent by rival regimes of a State arrive for the participation. Since each member State may be represented by only one delegation, the Assembly has to make a choice, a choice with strong political implications. Its decisions in such cases are binding on member States. In 1960, rival delegations appointed respectively by President Kasavubu and Prime Minister Lumumba of the then Republic of the Congo (now Zaire) arrived in New York. The rules provided no way out, since heads of State and heads of government were equally entitled to issue credentials. Most members supported Kasavubu's delegation. In 1962, the Yeman civil war produced rival delegations, one sent by the newly proclaimed republic and the other by the previously ruling monarchical government. The Assembly accepted the republican delegates. The Assembly decisions in the case of Chinese and Cambodia's participation in its activities were also binding.

(2) Apportionment of Assessments among Members.—The General Assembly decisions can commit member States for payments for a variety of UN activities according to Article 17(2) of the Charter which provides that the expenses of the Organization shall be borne by the members as apportioned by the General Assembly.

(3) Approval of Trusteeship Agreements and any Alternations thereto.—Administering States held authority under terms of a trusteeship agreement approved by the General Assembly. This does not apply in the case of territories designated to strategic area.

In addition to above, States may also agree to accept individual Assembly decisions as binding in particular cases. However, its binding authority over member States remains limited. A resolution which is not binding on States may nevertheless have binding force in the internal order of the Organisation. Resolutions of the Assembly conveying instructions to organs which are subordinate to it, the Secretary-General, the Economic and Social Council, and the Trusteeship Council as well as subsidiary organs which it has itself created are mandatory for those to whom they are addressed. Recommendations to the Security Council which is independent to the Assembly are not binding.

Structure of the General Assembly :

The Assembly elects its President and Vice-Presidents for each session, and adopts its own rules of procedure. At each session, the Assembly distributes most agenda items among its six main Committees, on which every member State has the right to be represented. These Committees, which prepare recommendations for approval in plenary meetings of the Assembly are : (i) First Committee (Political and Security, including the regulations of armaments). The Special Political Committee shares the work of the First Committee; (ii) Second Committee (Economic and Financial); (iii) Third Committee (Social, Humanitarian and Cultural); (iv) Fourth Committee (Trusteeship, including,

Non-self Governing Territories); (v) Fifth Committee (Administrative and Budgetary), and (vi) Sixth Committee (Legal).

Change in Names and Number of the Committees.—The General Assembly on August 17, 1993 adopted a resolution[1] wherein it was decided that from the Forty-eighth Session (1993) there would be six Committees instead of seven main Committees. The Special Political Committee and the Decolonisation Committee would be merged and shall be known as the Fourth Committee. It was also decided that the Political and Security Committee (First Committee) would be known as the Disarmament and International Security Committee. After the above change, names of the main Committees are as follows :

1. First Committee (Disarmament and International Security Committee). The Committee is concerned with disarmament and non-proliferation of nuclear weapons and internal security questions.
2. Second Committee (Economic and Financial Committee). The Committee is concerned with economic questions such as economic inequality and poverty. The Committee also deals with environmental degradation.
3. Third Committee (Social, Humanitarian and Cultural Committee). The Committee deals with social and humanitarian issues.
4. Fourth Committee (Special Political and Decolonisation Committee). It deals with a variety of political subjects not dealt with by the First Committee and with decolonisation.
5. Fifth Committee (Administrative and Budgetary Committee). It deals with administration and budget of the United Nations.
6. Sixth Committee (Legal Committee). The Committee deals with international legal matters.

All the above Committees consist of all the members of the General Assembly. Each Committee elects a Chairman and three Vice-Chairmen. The organisation of the work of each session is the responsibility of the General Committee which is composed of the President of the Assembly, the seventeen Vice-Presidents and the Chairman of the six main Committees.

The Credentials Committee, consisting of nine members appointed by the General Assembly on the proposal of the President, reports to the Assembly on the credentials of representatives.

The Assembly is assisted by two Standing Committees—the twelve member Advisory Committee on Administrative and Budgetary questions and the ten-member Committee on Contributions which makes recommendations to the General Assembly on the percentage scale for member's contributions to the United Nations. Members of these two committees are selected on the basis of broad geographical representation, personal qualifications and experiences.

In addition, the Assembly has from time to time, set up a number of subsidiary, *adhoc* and related bodies, dealing with relevant topics.

Commissions

The General Assembly has established Commissions from time to time for

1. General Assembly Resolution 47/233, dated August 17, 1993.

its smooth functioning. Presently, there are six such Commissions which are as follows : Firstly, Disarmament Commission[1] established in 1952. Secondly, International Civil Service Commission[2] established in 1949. Thirdly, a International Law Commission[3] established in 1947. Fourthly, United Nations Commission on International Trade Law (UNCITRAL)[4] established in 1966. Fifthly, United Nations Commission for Palestine[5] established in 1948. Sixthly, United Nations Peace-Building Commission[6] established in 2005.

---

1. General Assembly Resolution 502 (VI).
2. General Assembly Resolution 3357 (XXIX).
3. General Assembly Resolution 174 (II).
4. General Assembly Resolution 2205 (XXI).
5. General Assembly Resolution 194 (III).
6. General Assembly Resolution 60/180 and Security Council Resolution 1645, 2005.

Chapter 5
Security-Council

Security Council is a principal organ of the United Nations.[1] Chapter V of the Charter consisting of Articles 23 to 27 lays down the provisions relating to the Security Council.

Composition :

Members of the Security Council are States. States are represented by the individuals. Thus, the Security Council consists of the representatives of the States which are the members of this body. These representatives are to be appointed by the States, that is to say, by organs of the States competent to make the appointment according to their respective constitutions. These representatives are required to act in conformity with the instructions given to them by the competent organs of the States. Each member of the Council shall have one representative (Article 23 Para 3).

The Council originally consisted of eleven members, but it was enlarged to fifteen members in 1965 in accordance with an amendment to the Charter.[2] Out of fifteen members, five are permanent members. Their names are mentioned under Article 23, Para 1 of the Charter. They are : the Republic of China, France, the Union of Soviet Socialist Republics, the United Kingdom of Great Britain and Northern Ireland, and the United States of America.[3] But later on changes took place in the names of the two permanent members. In 1971, the People's Republic of China replaced the Republic of China, and, in 1991, Russian Federation assumed the seat of the Soviet Union after claiming successor status.[4] But both the above changes have yet to be mentioned in the Charter. Article 23, Para 1 is required to be amended in view of the above changes but no amendment has been made as it was regarded that the change of a State's name is too consequential to merit a Charter amendment.

The other ten members of the Security Council are called non-permanent

1. Article 7 of the Charter. The Council met for the first time on January 17, 1946 wherein it adopted its rules of procedure.
2. The Amendment was approved by the General Assembly on December 17, 1963 which came into force on August 23, 1965.
3. The permanent members were the Great Powers at the time of the creation of the United Nations. They all were the victorious Powers of the Second World War with the exception of China that was granted this status to balance the far-eastern powers of that time, *i.e.,* Japan.
4. The President of the Russian Federation, Boris Yeltsin in a letter dated December 24, 1991 informed the Secretary-General that the membership of the Soviet Union in the Security Council and all other United Nations organs shall be continued by the Russian Federation with the support of the 11 member countries of the Commonwealth of Independent States.

members. They are elected by the General Assembly for a term of two years, but each year election of five members take place when the equal number of members retire after completing the term of two years. The above system was adopted so that there may not be complete renewal of all the non-permanent members. According to the last sentence of Article 23, Para 2, a retiring member is not eligible for immediate re-election, and therefore many States are eligible for the membership of the Council. Each member of the Security Council shall have one representative in the Council at all its meetings.[1] Considerations which are given for the election of non-permanent members are, firstly, the contribution of members of the United Nations to the maintenance of international peace and security and to other purposes of the Organisation, and secondly, the equitable geographical distribution.[2]

The term of the office of non-permanent members of the Council begins on January 1 following their election by the General Assembly and ends on December 31 following the election of their successor.

It is to be noted that the provisions relating to the election of non-permanent members suffer from two defects. Firstly, non-permanent members are elected for a period of two years which is not sufficient enough for a member to acquaint true working of the Council. Most of the representatives take more than a year to get a sense of the working of the Council and by the time they become effective members in true sense, their term expires. Secondly, in practice, the contribution of members to the maintenance of international peace and security has never been taken into account and no mechanism has been worked out to fulfil the purpose. Thus, this clause practically remained a dead letter. However, the equitable geographical distribution has always been considered.

The Charter also provides for the *ad hoc* membership of the Council under Article 31 which lays down the possibility of the participation of any member of the United Nations in the Council which is not a member. Such members may participate in the Council, without having a right to vote, in the discussion of any question brought before the Security Council provided that in the view of the latter, the interest of those members are specially affected. It is to be noted that the requests for the participation by the members is normally not rejected. Perhaps, the only case of rejection was that of the Philippines when it wanted to participate in the discussions in the second phase of the Indonesian question. Further, Article 32 stipulates that any member of the United Nations which is not a member of the Security Council, or any State which is not a member of the United Nations, shall be invited to participate without vote in the discussion before the Council, relating to the dispute to which it is a party. The Council shall lay down the conditions for participation of a State which is not a member of the United Nations. If the question under consideration by the Council relates to the employment of the contingents, which a member not represented in the

1. Article 23 Para 3.
2. Article 23, Para 1. The following plan has been formulated for distributing the ten non-permanent members among geographical regions; five for States representing Africa and Asia, two for States representing Latin America and Caribbean region, and two for States representing Western Europe and other States (this refers to Canada, Australia and New Zealand) and one State representing Eastern Europe.

Council is obliged to make available to it may be invited, if it desires, to participate in the decisions of the Security Council.[1]

Security Council elects a President for presiding its meetings. The Charter instead of providing procedure for the selection of the President, gives freedom to the Council to decide on the methods of selecting its President. President of the Council is selected by rotation on a monthly basis in the English alphabetical order of the names of the Council's members. The Presidency is attached to a member State and not to the individual representative accredited to the Council.

The Security Council is organised in such a way that it may be able to function continuously. Each member of the Security Council shall for this purpose be represented at all times at the seat of the Organisation (Article 28 Para 1). The Council meets generally at Headquarters. However, it may meet elsewhere as well. In 1972, it held a session in Addis Ababa (Ethiopia) and in 1977 in Panama City (Panama).

Expansion of the Membership of the Security Council :

The composition of the Security Council does not accord to the present day reality. The Council's membership presently limited to fifteen gives little voice to the concerns and priorities of many members of the United Nations. A number of quantitative as well as qualitative changes have taken place in the international community since the creation of the United Nations, but no change has occurred in the composition of the Security Council except one that took place in 1963 when the number of permanent members was increased to fifteen from eleven. At that time the total number of members of the United Nations was 113. Presently, the number of members has gone up from 51 to 193. Out of them 53 members are from Africa and more than one-third of Security Council debates deal with them but the Council does not have any member from this Continent. The present size of the Council appears to be disproportionate to the enlarged size and functions of the Organisation. The above proposition is clear from the following chart :

Year	Number of Members of the United Nations	Number of Members of the Security Council	Percentage
1945	51	11	21.56%
1963	113	15	13.27%
2021	193	15	7.77%

The above figures show that it is expedient to expand the membership of the Council so that those parts of the World which are hitherto not represented may get place in the Council in the spirit of democracy. It is desirable that the number of members of the Council is increased to 25 so that the percentage of members of the Council to members of the United Nations may be brought to 1963 level. Heads of the States and the Governments in the 2005 World Summit Outcome supported the early reform of the Security Council 'in order to make it broadly representative'. The changed composition is required to have

1. Article 44.

equitable and fair representation of all the regions of the World.[1]

A number of States including India have made a demand from time to time for the change in the composition of the Council, but it has been negatively responded by the permanent members of the Security Council on the ground that the Council in order to be effective must remain a small body. According to them a larger body would be more unwieldy and would be difficult to manage than the present Council.

In 1993, the matter for the expansion of the membership of the Security Council was discussed by the General Assembly which on December 4 decided by consensus to set up a Working Group on the Question of Equitable Representation on and Increase in the Membership of the Security Council. The first meeting of the Group was held in New York in January, 1994. Wherein according to the informal paper issued by the General Assembly, virtually all member States of the United Nations favoured an increase in the membership of the Security Council with no voices to the contrary. Most States envisaged the total number of seats being increased from 15 to between 19 and 25, although some favoured 31. In 1995, the General Assembly adopted a Declaration on the occasion of the Fiftieth Anniversary of the United Nations which accepted that the Security Council should be expanded in a way that will further strengthen its capacity and effectiveness and enhance its representative character. Although most of the members were in favour of the increase in the number of members of the Security Council, the Working Group could not take any decision in this regard even in its meeting held in January, 2001.

A high level U.N. panel in its report submitted in December, 2004 has made two proposals to expand the membership of the Security Council. The first proposal envisages addition of six new permanent members without veto power : two from Asia, two from Africa, one each from Europe and the Americas. The first proposal also added three new non-permanent members for a term of a two years, in addition to existing ten non-permanent members.[2]

Thus, according to this proposal, the Council shall have a strength of 24 members, *i.e.*, 5 + 6 + 13. The second proposal is for eight seats in a new class of members, who would serve for four years, subject to renewal. They would include two each from Africa, Asia, Europe and the Americas. In addition, one

---

1. African and Latin American Countries do not have any permanent representation in the Council.
2. Later, in 2005 India, Brazil, Germany and Japan—the so called Group of Four (G-4) proposed expanding the Council to 25 seats. Their proposal was for six permanent seats without veto power (All the four members of G-4 and two reserved for Africa and the addition of four non-permanent seats, including one for Africa).
   In September, 2007 a fresh proposal was tables in the U.N. General Assembly by India, Brazil, South Africa and some key African nations (ISBA) for the expansion in both the permanent and non-permanent seats. The fresh resolution urged greater representation of developing countries in the Council. The resolution was similar to that made by the Group of Four (G-4). However, the new proposal did not specify anything in terms of numbers.
   In September, 2008 United Nations member States endorsed India's viewpoint that the General Assembly should begin the Inter-Governmental Negotiations on Expansion of the Security Council. Such a reform has been opposed by the 'uniting for consensus groups' which includes Italy, Spain, Mexico, Colombia, Argentina, Pakistan and South Korea.

non-permanent two years seat shall be added to the existing 10 such members. Thus, the number of members shall be 24, *i.e.*, 5 + 8 + 11.

It appears that even after the above proposals the expansion of the Security Council remains distant. It is evident from the U.N. panel's failure to come up with an unanimous proposal. The panel chose to keep the debate open by suggesting two loose options. The reality is that the existing permanent members are not interested in an expanded Security Council. Expansion of the Council is likely to reduce their existing international role in the Council, and therefore they pretend to support reform of the Council by expanding the membership, reality is that there is very little prospect of any change. China, Russia and the United States have written letters to the U.N's Special Committee in charge of the Inter-Governmental Negotiations (IGN) in July, 2015 that they are not in favour of any large scale reforms in the structure of the Security Council. They are of the view that the prerogative of the present permanent members of the Security Council including the veto power should remain intact. Thus, the whole process of the issue of the expansion of the permanent members of the Security Council has been put in cold storage. However, landmark decision of the General Assembly taken on September 14, 2015 gave some hope on the expansion of the members of the Security Council. In a draft decision submitted by the Assembly President the body decided that it would convene the open-ended Working Group on the Question of Equitable Representation and Increase in the Membership of the Security Council and other Matters related to the Security Council during the 70th session. General Assembly on June 25, 2019 decided that talks shall continue on the reforms of the Security Council. The process of IGN slowed down in 2020 due to the Covid-19 pandemic.

Expansion of the Council is unconceivable without a reconciliation of the permanent members. The opposition has also come from some ordinary members of the United Nations[1] because they have little to gain from a larger permanent membership. It is to be noted that the Council cannot be expanded without the approval of two-thirds of the U.N. members. It is a difficult task, and therefore, chances for the expansion of the Security Council in near future is very remote despite the fact that 2005 World Summit Outcome has adopted that the Security Council should be 'more broadly representative'.

India's case for the Permanent Seat in the Security Council :

A number of statesmen of different countries have been advocating from time to time for the permanent membership of India in the Security Council. India itself has been claiming for the permanent seat of the Council. A question arises as to what are the grounds on which its case may be taken into consideration. The following factors are relevant in this regard :

1. India is the largest democratic system of Government in the world.

2. India has contributed significantly to the United Nations peace-keeping operations. It has played a significant role during the U.N. most elaborate peace-keeping venture in Congo (UNOC) both militarily and

---

1. They have formed a consensus aiming to counter G-4 bids for a permanent seat. This group is led by Italy, Pakistan, Maxico and Argentina.

financially. India also supplied a contingent of troops for the United Nations Emergency Force (UNEF) in the Sinai Peninsula. India has participated in about 25 peace-keeping operations including Somalia, Angola and Rwanda. In Somalia, its seven peace-keepers and three Indian Army doctors were killed.

3. India has an influence among the non-aligned and other developing countries, which constitute the majority of the members of the United Nations. It has also played an important role in the multilateral movements of colonies and newly independent countries that developed into the Non-Aligned Movement.

4. India is the most populous State in the World after China.

5. India has made distinct contribution to the various activities and ethos of the United Nations. It has played an innovative, moderating and pragmatic role on a whole range of issues.

6. India is committed to complete disarmament and non-proliferation of nuclear weapons.

7. India is committed to combat global war on terrorism.

8. India has contributed immensely for the cause of international peace and security especially when it was a member of the Security Council during 1951-52, 1967-68, 1972-73, 1977-78, 1984-85, 1991- 92 and 2011-12. It has been elected again as a non-permanent member of the Council for the term beginning from January 1, 2021.

9. India happens to be the second fastest growing economy of the World making it an ideal destination for foreign investment and future growth.

The combination for all the above factors make India a deserving candidate for the permanent membership of the Security Council. The argument that India is not militarily very strong to become the permanent member of the Security Council is not tenable. The weightage to the military importance has to be disregarded because firstly, this is a premium to armaments and run counter to the ultimate aim of general disarmament; secondly, it is not easy to assess the military capability of the nations, and thirdly, a State may possess sophisticated arms but not in a position to put them effectively to use.

VOTING SYSTEM :

Each member of the Security Council has one vote.[1] Decisions of the Council, on procedural matters are made by an affirmative vote of nine members.[2] On all other matters, which, for convenience, may be referred to as non-procedural matters, decisions are made by an affirmative vote of nine members including the concurring votes of the permanent members.[3] However, for any decision under Chapter VI, and under Para 3 of Article 52, a party to a dispute abstains from voting. The above voting system of the Security Council requires the consideration of the following points :

1. Article 27, Para 1.
2. Article 27, Para 2.
3. Article 27, Para 3.

(a) Procedural and Non-Procedural Matters :

The voting system for the procedural and non-procedural matter is different. It is therefore necessary to distinguish procedural matters from non-procedural matters. The Charter has not laid down as to what shall be the procedural and non-procedural matters. The Joint Statement of the Sponsoring Powers, before the adoption of the Charter, had pointed out an explanation that procedural matters shall include (a) the adoption or alteration of the rules of procedures; (b) determination of the method of selecting its President; (c) its self-organisation for continuous functioning; (d) selection of time and place of the meeting; (e) establishment of such bodies as it may deem necessary for the performance of its functions; (f) invitation to the non-members of the Council in the meetings of the Council during discussions of items specially affecting their interests; and (g) the invitation to a State, which is a party to a dispute to participate in the discussions. But the enumeration, in practice was not treated as exhaustive. Many matters which should have been included in the list were not enumerated under the procedural matters. General Assembly, later on, recommended a list of forty-five matters which should be treated as procedural matters. But the recommendation of the General Assembly was not accepted by the Security Council. In view of this uncertainty, the Council sometimes is faced with a difficult situation at the time of deciding as to whether a matter is procedural or non-procedural. In such cases, the President of the Council determines the procedure of voting. He decides whether a matter is procedural or non-procedural. Thus, whether a matter is procedural or non-procedural is dependent upon the discretion of the President. If he decides that a particular matter is non-procedural, it is decided by a vote of nine members including the concurring votes of the five permanent members of the Council. But if he decides that a matter is procedural, it can be challenged by any permanent member of the Council by giving a vote against the decision of the President. Thus, the matter becomes non-procedural, from procedural, as earlier decided by the President. It implies that in such cases question as to whether a matter is procedural or non-procedural is decided by the affirmative vote of nine members including the concurring votes of the permanent members.

In order to make the Security Council more effective in taking the decision, it must be clarified as to what constitutes a procedural matter as reflected in Article 27 (2) of the Charter. It is suggested that the Council may seek advisory opinion of the International Court of Justice on this issue.

(b) Absence of a Member in the Security Council :

The Charter does not provide any quorum for the meetings of the Security Council. It raises a question as to whether a decision can be taken by the Council when a permanent member remains wilfully absent in the meetings of the Security Council. It may be stated that each member of the Council is required to remain present in all the meetings of the Security Council. In order to make it possible, each member is required to represent 'at all times' at the seat of the Organisation according to Article 28, Para 1. If a member remains absent, its absence shall be deemed as a violation of the member's obligation in carrying out the primary responsibility for the maintenance of international peace and security. It also implies some sort of evasion of responsibility or obligations of a member towards the functioning of the Council. Failure of a member to fulfil the obligations does not mean that the intention of the multilateral agreement could be by-passed. If a member remains absent in a meeting, the Security Council, nevertheless shall be able to take decisions on the procedural matters (decisions on such matters require an affirmative vote of nine members of the Council). The Council would also be able to take decisions on non-procedural matters as well even if a permanent member is absent from the Council and if the absent permanent member is a disputant State. As to non-procedural matters, the Charter does not lay down any provision for such situations. It is clear from the strict interpretation of the Charter as well as from the practice of the Security Council that the Council is able to take decisions on non-procedural matters even if a permanent member remains absent.

The Charter provides that the decisions on non-procedural matters according to Article 27, Para 3 are taken on an affirmative vote of nine members including the concurring votes of the permanent members. The expression 'concurring votes (i.e., by express consent) of the permanent members' should not be interpreted as the concurring votes of all the permanent members. It may mean that a decision may be taken by the Council so long a dissenting vote is not given on a particular decision. Had the Charter used the words "all permanent members", perhaps no decision would have been taken as one finds under Articles 108 and 109. Moreover, since the absence of a member in the Council does not amount to dissenting vote of that member, a valid decision may be taken by the Council on the concurring votes of the remaining permanent members present in the Council.

Concurring votes of the permanent members may mean therefore the permanent members who participate in the meeting. Kelsen has categorically stated that 'in the practice of the Security Council absence of a member, even of a permanent member, does not prevent this from adopting a resolution. Absence of a permanent member is considered to be equivalent to abstention from voting.[1]

In 1950, when the question of Korea was being discussed, the Security Council took a decision[2] by adopting Resolution 82 on June 25, 1950 even when the representative of the Soviet Union was not present in a meeting of the Council. Although, Soviet Union was of the view that the Security Council cannot take a valid decision when a permanent member remains absent, other members of the Council did not accept the argument. Since then, it has been the practice of the Council to take a decision on non-procedural matters even if a permanent member remains absent in a meeting of the Council. It may be noted that the practice of the Security Council is generally accepted is quite consistent with the provisions of Article 27, Para 3. In Namibia case, Judge Nervo stated that "it is generally recognized that the absence of a permanent member from a meeting of the Security Council does not prevent it from taking of decisions

1. Law of United Nations, op. cit., p. 244-245.
2. The Soviet Union had left the Council at the 461st meeting on January 13, 1950 in protest over the presence in the Council of the Nationalist China. Later, the Soviet Union remained absent in two other resolutions concerning Korea.

which are valid even if they relate to questions of substance."[1]

(c) Abstention From Voting in the Security Council :

Abstention from voting is different from those cases where a member remains absent. In the former case, although a member remains present in the Council, but at the time of voting, it does not vote either in favour of the decision or against it. If a member abstains itself from voting in the procedural matters, a valid decision may be taken by the Security Council on a vote of nine members. As far as non-procedural matters is concerned it may be stated that the Charter has not laid down any provision for such contingencies. However, the Council is not prevented from taking a valid decision on non-procedural matters even if a permanent member abstains itself from voting. Presently, it has become an established practice that the abstention of a permanent member does not affect the validity of a resolution. The International Court of Justice in Namibia case also upheld the above practice, despite its apparent inconsistency with the wording of Article 27(3) by stating :

> "...........the proceedings of the Security Council extending over a long period supply abundant evidence that presidential rulings and the positions taken by members of the Council, in particular its permanent members, have consistently and uniformly interpreted the practice of voluntary abstention by a permanent member as not constituting a bar to the adoption of resolutions....." By abstaining, a member does not signify its obligation to the approval of what is being proposed. In order to prevent the adoption of a resolution requiring unanimity of the permanent members, a permanent member has only to cast a negative vote. This procedure followed by the Security Council........has been generally accepted by Members of the United Nations and evidences a general practice of that Organisation.[2]

Abstention is a form of concurrence and therefore abstention from voting by a permanent member in an issue does not mean dissenting vote. If a permanent member abstains from voting, it indicates that the member agrees to the decision of the Security Council without its own vote. Intention of an abstention by a permanent member is to permit the Security Council to act. Abstention is therefore a form of concurrence to the Council action. It permits the Security Council to function without its own vote. Had it been not agreed to the decision, it would have given its dissenting vote. After the amendment to the Charter adopted in 1963, composition of the Security Council has changed which has created the possibility for taking decisions calling for action under Chapter VII even if all the permanent members abstain from voting.

Veto Power :

Article 27, Para 3 stipulates that the decisions on non-procedural matters shall be taken on a vote of nine members of the Council including the concurring votes of the permanent members. It means that no decision can be taken by the Council on such matters if a dissenting vote is given by any

---

1. ICJ Reports (1971) p 116.
2. *Ibid.*, p. 22.

permanent member. It implies that if a permanent member wishes that no decision should be taken by the Council on any particular issue, it has a power to do so by giving dissenting vote. Thus, by giving a dissenting vote a permanent member has a power to block the issue in the Council. In other words, if the concurring vote is withheld by any permanent member the proposal shall be deemed vetoed, *i.e.*, it could not be validly adopted. This power of the permanent members is known as the veto power.[1] A veto may thus be defined as a negative vote cast by a permanent member of the Security Council that has the effect of nullifying the affirmative votes of an adequate majority. Absence of a member nor abstention at the time of voting in the Security Council count as a vote. However, the term 'veto' does not find place in the Charter of the United Nations.

In the San Francisco Conference, the right of each of the 'big five'[2] to exercise a 'veto' on an action by the powerful Security Council provoked long and heated debate. At one stage the conflict of opinion on this question had threatened to break up the Conference. The smaller powers feared that while one of the 'big five' menaced the peace, the Security Council would be powerless to act, in the event of a clash between two Powers, the big five could act arbitrarily. They strove therefore to have the power of the veto reduced. But the great Powers unanimously insisted on this provision as vital, and emphasized that the main responsibility for maintaining world peace would fall most heavily on them. Eventually the smaller powers conceded the point in the interest of the setting up the World Organisation. The veto power was therefore the price given to the 'big five' for the creation of the United Nations.

The veto power was conferred to 'big five' in a good faith because the framers of the Charter had realized that the co-operation of all the big powers is necessary for the maintenance of international peace and security. They had hoped that the big powers, united in war shall remain united in peace. However, the hope for their co-operation was belied soon after the establishment of the United Nations. There developed a 'cold war'[3] between them, and it became apparent that the World is divided into two blocks-East and West. The result of their conflict paralysed the whole functioning of the Security Council. It impaired the efficiency of the Security Council in performing the functions relating to the maintenance of international peace and security, because the 'big five' by exercising the veto power prevented the Council to take

1. Non-permanent members collectively also have a power to block the issue in the Council. If they decide collectively that on a particular issue no decision should be taken by the Council they can give dissenting vote and in such a case the Council shall be unable to take a decision despite the concurrence vote of all the permament members of the Council.
2. Big Powers or Great Powers is not a substantive notion in public international law. There is no formal procedure by which a State is juridically recognised as a Great Power. The factual basis of being a Great Power is a State's political power. This general political power is shaped by a variety of factors, each of which alone would not suffice to identify a Great Power, but which together constitute one. Among the necessary preconditions are a large territory and population, international unity, technological superiority and economic strength.
3. Cold War is called, to a large extent, to an ideological confrontation. While communism is manifestly an ideology, the 'non-communism' or even the 'anti-communism' of the West is negatively ideological.

any decision in this regard. The relations between the 'super powers' were so tense that to achieve the rule of unanimity, which was the cornerstone of the functioning of the United Nations' collective security system, was almost in every case out of question. While the American could not willingly contemplate being called on to use its power against other nations without its own consent; the U.S.S.R. wished to block sanctions action against itself or its allies.[1] The adverse impact was so intense that as early as in 1947 it led to a 'strong movement' for a revision of Article 27, Para 3.[2] However, nothing took place except the consideration of the matter by the Interim Committee of the General Assembly and the submission of its recommendation to the Assembly.[3]

The result is that many international problems could not be resolved by the Council mainly because they are related to the 'big five' or their client States. On many occasions, the Council could not take enforcement action against a State where it was genuinely required to be taken due to the veto power.[4] With the change in the World political scenario, relationship of the permanent members has also changed. This in turn, has changed the attitude of the 'big five' towards the maintenance of international peace and security. It is the unanimity of the big five that led to the adoption of a number of resolutions in relation to Gulf Crisis in 1990 in view to maintain international peace and security. Later, the Council also helped in resolving some other regional conflicts by taking action against many States including Yugoslavia, Libya, Cambodia and Somalia.

After the end of the cold war, veto power was exercised for the first time by the Russian federation on May 11, 1993 on an issue relating to the financing of the United Nations Peace-keeping force in Cyprus (UNIFICYP)[5] and by the United States on May 18, 1995 to block a resolution which would have criticized Israel for the appropriation of East-Jerusalem. Thus, the veto power was not exercised by the permanent members from May 31, 1990 to May 10, 1993.

It is to be noted that the veto power is confined only to those cases where a permanent member gives a dissenting vote in a non-procedural matter. So long the power is not exercised expressly at the time of voting in the Security Council, decisions of the Council are not affected. Thus, even if a permanent member abstains from voting on any issue, or if it remains absent from the meetings of the Council, the Council may take valid decision because neither abstention from voting nor absence in the Security Council amounts to dissenting vote.

---

1. Potter, 'An Introduction to the Study of International Organisations', Fifth Edition, p. 267.
2. *See* Kelsen, op. cit. 277.
3. General Assembly Resolution 117 (II) of November 21, 1947.
4. Since the inception of the Security Council veto has been exercised on 258 occasions.
5. Other cases where veto have been exercised after the end of cold war are by Russian Federation in 1994 on Transit Traffic in Yugoslavia, by U.S.A. in 1995, 1997 and again in 1997 on the issue of Occupied Arab Territories and by China in 1997 in Guatemala issue. Veto power was also exercised on October 14, 2003 on a draft resolution concerning the Construction by Israel of the Wall in the Occupied Palestinian Territory.

Criticism of the Veto Power :

The veto power vested in the hands of the permanent members has been criticized on many grounds. Firstly, it has created a difference between the permanent and non-permanent members of the Security Council and in the entire membership of the United Nations. Secondly, it is an antithesis of the principle of sovereign equality of member States and the democratization of the U.N. system as a whole. Thirdly, the fate of the World has been left just in the hands of five permanent members of the Security Council which is not desirable because their narrow interests are sometime opposed to the interests and wishes of the vast majority of the peoples of the World. Fourthly, it has ruled out the possibility of taking an action against the permanent members. It is a club of the most powerful countries which only take action to champion their own stratagic interests. For instance, the Council took action to protect Kuwait which had substantial oil resources. No action could be taken against the United States when it unjustifiably attacked Iraq in 2003.[1] Fifthly, reason for the grant of veto power to the Great Powers does not appear to be sound in view of the fact that the concept of Great Power is not static. It is a shifting phenomenon. The permanent members of the Security Council were the Great Powers at the time of the creation of the United Nations but they all are not so at the present time. For instance, France and Britain are presently not as powerful as those of Germany and Japan. Further, the former Great Power, the U.S.S.R. has been dismembered and its permanent membership has been succeeded to Russia which is impoverished, much reduced in size and independence of action. Further, the five permanent members created in 1945 no longer reflect the present day global landscape radically transformed by global economic and security realignment.

Although the elimination of the veto power has been advocated by different States from time to time no positive step has been taken to eliminate it.

The So-called 'Double Veto' :

The right of veto may be exercised by the permanent members of the Security Council on two different occasions. Firstly, at the time of deciding the nature of matter, *i.e.*, whether the matter is procedural or non-procedural. If the President of the Council decides that a particular matter is procedural, it becomes non-procedural if the veto power is exercised on the decision of the President. And, secondly, when the Council is taking decision on any non-procedural matter. Thus, a permanent member first asserts that the matter is not a procedural but a non-procedural matter. It therefore makes a matter non-procedural from procedural by exercising the veto power. When a matter becomes non-procedural, it may again exercise the veto power at the time of taking decision on that very matter. The combined effect of the above is that the Council cannot take a decision even on procedural matters if the same has been made non-procedural by the exercise of the right of veto by any permanent member. The exercise of veto power on two different occasions has been referred to as 'double veto'. The right of double veto was exercised in the Spanish case,

---

1. For detail *see* Chapter 'Collective Security'.

Czechoslovak case, and in the Greek case. In the Formosa case and the Laos case it was attempted but not actually exercised.

FUNCTIONS OF THE SECURITY COUNCIL :

Functions of the Security Council may be divided into three broad categories. They are as follows :—

(1) Maintenance of International Peace and Security :

The maintenance of international peace and security is the primary responsibility of the Security Council. The power has been conferred to it under Article 24, Para 1 of the Charter which lays down that 'in order to ensure prompt and effective action by the United Nations, its Members confer on the Council primary responsibility for the maintenance of international peace and security.............'The members also have agreed that the Council shall act on their behalf in carrying out its duties under this responsibility. Article 25 clearly lays down therefore that 'the Members of the United Nations agree to accept and carry out the decisions of the Security Council in accordance with the present Charter'. Thus, the effect of the decisions of the Council is different from that of the General Assembly. While the decisions of the former are binding upon the members, it is not so with the recommendations of the Assembly.

The Security Council is empowered to maintain international peace and security but the powers of the Council in this regard are not absolute. It has to exercise this power with certain limitations. Firstly, Article 24, Para 2 of the Charter lays down that the Council is required to maintain international peace and security in accordance with the purposes and principles of the United Nations, as laid down under Articles 1 and 2 of the Charter respectively. Thus, the powers of the Council to maintain international peace and security are strictly regulated and governed by those fundamental principles which have acquired the status of *jus cogens.* Secondly, the Security Council while maintaining international peace and security is required not to violate general international law unless the Charter allows it to do so. The Council being an organ of the United Nations which is a subject of international law, is under a duty to comply the general principles of international law like other subjects. If the Council uses the armed force against a State for the maintenance of international peace and security it has a duty to comply international humanitarian law in armed conflicts. Further, it has a duty to respect at least those human rights which are specified in the Covenant on Civil and Political Rights from which no derogation is permitted even in time of emergency or armed conflicts.

The Council performs the functions relating to the maintenance of international peace and security in two ways, *i.e.,* by peaceful means and by taking enforcement action.

(a) By Peaceful Means :

Chapter VI of the Charter provides various modes by which the Council settles the disputes which are likely to endanger international peace and security. But a question arises how the Council would come to know about the existence of a dispute ? The Council comes to know about a dispute which is deemed to have threatened international peace and security in following ways :

(1) when any member of the United Nations, whether a party to a dispute or not, brings any dispute before it under Article 35, Para 1, or

(2) when a non-member of the United Nations brings any such dispute under Article 35, Para 2;

(3) when all the disputant parties refer a dispute under Article 38;

(4) when one of the disputant States refer a dispute under Article 37, Para 1;

(5) when the General Assembly calls the attention of the Security Council under Article 11, Para 3 to situations which are likely to endanger international peace and security; and,

(6) when the Secretary-General of the United Nations under Article 99 of the Charter brings to the attention of the Council any matter which in his opinion may threaten the maintenance of international peace and security.

Once a dispute has been brought before the Council by any of the above modes, it considers the nature of the dispute, *i.e.,* whether the dispute is likely to endanger international peace and security. It is significant to note that Chapter VI confers no power on the Council to deal any dispute not endangering international peace and security except for the purpose of determining whether it does or not. Whether a dispute is likely to endanger international peace and security or not is a subjective question and also a non-procedural matter, and therefore its determination is subject to the veto right. Unless this barrier is passed, the Council can only discuss whether a dispute can be discussed and dealt by it or not. If it determines that a dispute might endanger international peace and security, it may take following measures to settle the dispute :—

(i) To Call upon the Parties to Settle the Dispute Peacefully.—The Council shall, when it deems necessary, in accordance with Article 33 Para 2, call upon the parties to settle their dispute by those peaceful means which are mentioned under Article 33, Para 1 which are negotiation, enquiry, mediation, conciliation, arbitration, judicial settlement, resort to regional agencies or arrangements. The enumeration of the above means is not exhaustive. In a conflict between Iran and Iraq it adopted Resolution 475 on September 28, 1980 requesting the parties to refrain from the use of force and to settle their dispute by peaceful means. The parties may settle their dispute by other peaceful means of their own choice as well.

Article 37, Para 1 provides that if the parties to a dispute fail to settle it by the means indicated in Article 33, they shall refer it to the Security Council.

(ii) Investigation of the Dispute.—The Council may, under Article 34, investigate any dispute, or any situation which might lead to international friction or give rise to a dispute, in order to determine whether the continuance of the dispute or situation is likely to endanger the maintenance of international peace and security. The term 'investigation' is a broad term and it includes the power to study the documents submitted, to hear the parties or to collect evidence, and to appoint a Committee or Committees to find facts with the object of coming to a conclusion whether or not it has any jurisdiction in the given dispute.

The task of investigating disputes and situations by the Security Council is performed either through a subsidiary organ or a Commission. In the past, the Council has performed this function on various occasions through various means. For instance, in the Spanish question (1946), the Council established a Sub-committee and instructed it to examine the evidence and to report to the Council in order to enable the Council itself to determine the nature of the dispute. In the Indo-Pakistan question (1948), the Council established an independent Commission for India and Pakistan to investigate the facts.[1] In some other cases, the Council has carried out investigation through a Special Commission. For instance, while dealing with the situation, concerning Western Sahara (1975), the Council requested the Secretary-General to enter into immediate consultations with the parties concerned and to report to the Council on the results of his consultations in order to enable the Council to adopt the appropriate measures. It is to be noted that this kind of work is normally done through the special envoys of the Secretary-General. For instance, Benon Seven acted as the Special Representative of the Secretary-General to investigate Afghan Situation. Cynis Vance was appointed to investigate the situation in South Africa on the backdrop of the Boipatong killings in July 1992. An Independent Investigation Commission (UNIC) was established in 2005 to investigate the assassination of the former Prime Minister Hariri in Beirut on February 14, 2005.[2] In those cases where the Council establishes a subsidiary organ to carry out an investigation, it reserves the right of making the final determination as to the nature of the dispute or situation, as envisaged in Article 34.

(iii) Recommendation for the 'Appropriate Procedures' or Methods of Adjustment.—The Council may recommend to the disputant parties 'appropriate procedures' or methods of adjustment.[3] Although disputant parties themselves are expected to work out methods of pacific settlement and the Security Council may call the procedures listed in Article 33 to their attention, the Council in addition to it, may recommend some specific methods of settlement. The Council is free to utilize any technique or procedure or combination of methods which according to it might prove useful while making recommendations. While making recommendations, the Council should take into consideration any procedure for the settlement of the dispute 'which have already been adopted by the parties'.[4] Further, it should also take into consideration that legal disputes should as a general rule be referred by the parties to the International Court of Justice.[5]

---

1. The Commission was composed of representatives of three members of the United Nations; one member selected by each of the two parties, and the third, designated by the two members so selected.
2. See Security Council Resolution, 1595 dated April 7, 2005. The UNIC was established initially for a period of three months.
3. Article 36, Para 1
4. Article 36, Para 2
5. Article 36 Para 3.

(iv) Recommendation for the Terms of Settlement.—The Council may, under Article 37, if all the parties to any dispute so request, make recommendations to the parties with a view to a specific settlement of the dispute. In the past, the Council has recommended 'specific settlement terms', to the parties in a few cases. For instance, in the *Corfu Channel* Case (1947) it recommended to the United Kingdom and Albania to refer the dispute to the International Court of Justice. On the Palestine Question (1948), it recommended that all the parties concerned take specific measures with a view to the cessation of violence.

It may be stated that under Chapter VI, the Security Council has power only to discuss a dispute which is likely to endanger international peace and security, and thereafter to make recommendations to the disputant parties. The Charter has not conferred to the Council any power to enforce the recommended measures. As such, the recommendation as to terms of settlement may not be enforced under Chapter VI. However, a refusal to comply accompanied by threat of force may be met by preventive and enforcement action under Chapter VII of the Charter. Presently, the situation is more favourable than ever before for peaceful settlement of international disputes, and the Security Council should make it mandatory for States with disputes to settle them peacefully in accordance with Chapter VI with threat of sanctions in case of failure to do so.

(b) By Taking Enforcement Action :

Once the Council has determined that there is a threat to peace or breach of the peace or an act of aggression has been committed, it is empowered to take enforcement action under Chapter VII of the Charter which was recognised by the delegates to the San Francisco Conference as "the teeth of the United Nations". In such cases, the Council performs two important functions.

It determines the existence of threat to the peace, breach of the peace or an act of aggression under Article 39. Although the Council has the legal obligation to determine the existence of any threat to the peace, breach of the peace or an act of aggression, it was a difficult task to perform in view of the fact that the Charter has not defined 'threat to the peace', 'breach of the peace' or 'act of aggression'. The question as to what constitutes threat to the peace or breach of the peace is determined or decided by the Council in each individual case. In the past, the Council on the one hand failed to decide, on a few occasions, that there existed threat to the peace or breach of the peace where the situation in fact demanded it to decide, and on the other hand, it in fact has decided that there existed threat to the peace or breach of the peace where international peace and security was not at all at stake. After the end of the cold war Big Powers have tried to take action against a State by broadening the definition of the phrase "threat to the peace" to encompass situations that the authors of the U.N. Charter never dreamt of. Thus, famine, civil war, coups, the proliferation of weapons destruction, the failure of a State to surrender its citizens for trial in another have all become reasons for the U.N. Security Council to impose sanctions against sovereign States. Whether an act of aggression has been committed by a State was a difficult question to decide in the absence of any guidelines. The Council has therefore complete discretion in the matter to declare any act or series of acts as aggression and to take action accordingly. However, with the formulation of the 'Definition of Aggression'[1] by the General Assembly in 1974, the problem has been resolved to a great extent.

It is to be noted that the Charter does not provide explicitly that on whose initiative the Council shall determine the existence of threat to the peace, breach of peace or an act of aggression. In other words, who shall bring the attention of the Security Council as to existence of threat to the peace, breach of the peace or an act of aggression is not clear. However, the matter may be brought before the Council either by the Secretary-General of the United Nations under Article 99, or by the General Assembly under Article 11, Para 3 of the Charter. Further, each member of the Council along with the President has a right to determine the situation under Article 39. Whether there exists any threat to the peace, breach of the peace or an act of aggression is a non-procedural matter, and therefore, it is decided by a vote of nine members including the concurring votes of the permanent members. Thus, the 'big five' has a right to exercise veto in such decisions.

When the Security Council has determined that threat to the peace, breach of peace or any act of aggression exists, it decides as to what measures are to be taken in accordance with Articles 41 and 42, to maintain or restore international peace and security. It is a discretionary power of the Council which is exercised by a separate vote in which again each 'big five' may prevent action by use of its veto.

It is to be noted that before making the recommendations for measures to be taken under Articles 41 and 42, the Council is empowered to take 'provisional measures' as provided under Article 40 of the Charter to prevent an aggravation of the situation. Under the above Article, the Council may call upon the parties concerned to comply with such provisional measures as it deems necessary or desirable. Such provisional measures shall be without prejudice to the rights, claims, or position of the parties concerned. Provisional measures are executed by the parties concerned. These measures are not listed under Article 40, but among them are included cease-fire, withdrawal of troops from occupied territory, the setting of an interim demarcation line, the establishment of a demilitarized zone, a buffer zone etc. In the past, the Council has, on three occasions, taken decision to take provisional measures. They are : the request for a cease-fire in Kashmir, in 1948-49, request for a cease-fire and the cessation of all hostilities in the Middle East in October 1973 and request for an immediate cease-fire, a cessation of all hostilities on land, at sea and in the air and withdrawal of all forces to the internationally recognized boundaries without delay in conflict between Iran and Iraq in 1987. It is to be noted that failure to comply with provisional measures that the Council may call for may be considered as a breach of the peace. In the Middle East dispute, while ordering a cease-fire declared that the failure of the parties to comply would demonstrate a breach of the peace within a meaning of Article 39, requiring consideration with a view, to further action under Chapter VII.[2]

1. *See* Chapter 'Subsidiary Organs and Bodies of the United Nations'.
2. Goodrich and others, op. cit., p. 298.

(i) Measures Involving Non-Use of Force :

Article 41 lays down that the Security Council may call upon the members of the United Nations to take measures not involving the use of armed force, i.e., measures where the armed forces are not employed. These measures include 'complete or partial interruption of economic relations and of rail, sea, air, postal, telegraphic, radio and other means of communication and the severance of diplomatic relations'.

In order to take measures provided under Article 41, States have made provisions in their municipal laws. For instance, India in 1947 enacted the United Nations (Security Council) Act[1] which provided that if the Security Council calls upon the Central Government to apply any measures not involving the use of armed forces, to give effect to any decision of that Council, the Central Government may, by order published in the Official Gazette, make such provisions (including provisions having extra-territorial operations) as appear to it necessary or expedient for enabling those measures to be effectively applied, and without prejudice to the generality of the foregoing power, provision may be made for the punishment of persons offending against the order.

Measure under Article 41 have been applied in many cases in different names such as economic sanctions, trade sanctions, trade embargo, arms embargo, aerial embargo and diplomatic sanction etc. During the cold-war period the above measures were applied in two cases. Firstly, in connection with the situation in South Africa, the Council in 1977, imposed mandatory 'arms embargo' against the apartheid regime.[2] Secondly, following Southern Rhodesia's unilateral declaration of independence, the Council in 1966 imposed economic sanctions against the White minority regime of that country.[3]

After the end of the Cold War measures under Article 41 have been taken in different names in many cases which includes the following :—

(1) Economic Sanction Against Iraq.—After the Iraq's invasion of Kuwait in 1990, the Council imposed mandatory economic sanction against Iraq.[4]

(2) Arms and Air Embargo Against Libya.—Following the destruction of the two civilian aircrafts—Pan American which exploded over Lockerbie (Scotland) on December 21, 1988, and UTA explosion in Niger on September 19, 1989 and the resultant loss of life, the Security Council on January 31, 1992 adopted a resolution[5] wherein it condemned the Libyan act. The resolution strongly deplored the fact that the Libyan Government has not responded to requests for cooperation in establishing responsibility for these terrorist acts. Libya was urged immediately to give full and effective response to these

1. *See* Act 43 of 1947.
2. *See* Security Council Resolution 418, dated November 4, 1977. The mandatory arms and other restrictions were terminated on May 25, 1994 (*See* Security Council Resolution 919 dated May 25, 1994).
3. *See* Security Council Resolution 232, dated December 16, 1966. The sanctions were lifted on December 21, 1979 (*See* Resolution 460 dated 21 December 1979), as a result of the agreement leading to the independence of Zimbabwe.
4. *See* Security Council Resolutions 661 (1990), dated August 6, 1990. (For detail *see* Chapter 'Collective Security').
5. Security Council Resolution 731 (1992), dated January 31, 1992.

requests so as to contribute to the elimination of international terrorism.

When Libya failed to comply with the above resolution, the Council imposed an aerial embargo against Libya on March 31, 1992.[1] The embargo prevents Libya from receiving arms and related materials of all types. It also prohibited air traffic to or from that country. The arms and aerial embargo came into force from April 15, 1992. The Council also decided to establish a Committee consisting of all the members of the Council to consider and decide on any application by States for approval of flights on grounds of significant humanitarian needs. It was also decided by the Council that the sanction shall be reviewed every 120 days or sooner should the situation so requires. When Libya failed to handover the two suspects involved in the Pan American aircraft despite the aerial embargo imposed against it, more stringent sanctions were imposed against it on November 11, 1993 by the Security Council.[2] The Council by adopting a resolution approved the freezing of Libyan foreign funds and financial resources, banned export to it of equipment and prohibited licensing arrangements for the manufacture or maintenance of such items. The resolution also asked all States to close Libyan Arab Airlines offices within their territories and prohibit any commercial transactions with it. These measures became effective from December 1, 1993.

(3) General and Complete Arms Embargo Against Yugoslavia (Serbia and Montengro).—The former Yugoslavia consisted of six constituent Republics— Bosnia, Herzegovina, Croatia, Macedonia, Slovenia, Serbia and Montengro. Following the internal disorder and crisis, Croatia and Slovenia, and later on Macidonia seceded from Yugoslavia and became independent States. Fighting between Yugoslavia (Serbia and Montengro) and Bosnia and Herzegovina detoriated the situation in the region. The Council acting under Chapter VII of the Charter on September 25, 1991 by adopting a resolution urged parties to end conflict and abide strictly by the cease-fire. The Council also imposed a general and complete embargo on all deliveries of weapons and military equipments.[3]

When the fighting did not stop, the Council on May 15, 1992 adopted resolution 752 wherein it demanded an immediate end to fighting in Bosnia and Herzegovina and to forcible expulsions and attempts to change the entire composition of the population anywhere in the Yugoslavia as well as the immediate cessation of all outside interference. On May 30, 1992 the Council imposed both economic and diplomatic sanctions including a flight ban, and the prevention of the participation in sports and cultural events against Yugoslavia due to its failure to take effective measures to fulfil the requirements of Resolution 752 (1992).[4]

The Council on November 16, 1992 by adopting another resolution widened the existing sanctions against Yugoslavia to include "all inward and

---

1. Security Council Resolution 748 (1992), dated March 31, 1992.
2. Security Council Resolution 883 (1993), dated November 11, 1993.
3. Security Council Resolution 713 (1992), dated September 25, 1991.
4. Security Council Resolution 757 (1992), dated May 30, 1992. The Security Council on January 8, 1992 reaffirmed the arms embargo (*See* Security Council Resolution 723, dated January 8, 1992.)

outward maritime shipping.[1] The Council asked States to act to ensure strict implementation of wide-ranging sanctions already imposed. Again, on April 17, 1993, the Security Council decided to strengthen sanctions against Yugoslavia by adopting a resolution.[2] Tougher sanctions will prevent diversion to Yugoslavia of commodities and products said to be destined for other places and to freeze its funds held in other States" to ensure that they are not made available directly or indirectly to or for the benefit of Yugoslavian authorities.

The Council on September 23, 1994 imposed sanctions against the Bosnian Serbs. Among other actions, the resolution 942 adopted on September 23, 1994 prohibited States from admitting in their territories Bosnian Serbs officials and military officers; prohibited trade with any entity owned or controlled by Bosnian Serb forces, except for relief supplies, and froze Bosnian Serb financial assets held abroad.

The Council on September 23, 1994 by adopting Resolution 943 suspended certain sanctions on Yugoslavia for an initial period of 100 days beginning October 5, 1994, following a report of the Co-Chairman of the International Conference on the former Yugoslavia (ICFY) transmitted by the Secretary-General to the Security Council. Later, the Council adopted Resolution 1021 and 1022 on November 22, 1995 set out the terms of termination of the arms embargo. In accordance with the resolution 1021, March 13, 1996 was the date of termination of all provisions of arms embargo, except those related to heavy weapons, mines, military aircraft and helicopters. The Council also agreed to terminate the remaining provisions of the resolution 1022 indefinitely suspendend the sanctions against Yugoslavia. The sanctions against the Bosnian Serbs were suspended starting on February 27, 1996.

(4) Trade Sanction Against Cambodia.—A peace Treaty to end the 13 year conflict in Cambodia and to prepare for elections was signed in Paris on October 30, 1991. When in some parts of Cambodia controlled by Khmer Rouge, the Paris agreement was not given effect and when they refused to disarm themselves under the terms of the Treaty, and put other obstacles in the way of the United Nations officials to keep the peace processes on schedule, trade sanctions were imposed by the Council against them on October 23, 1991.[3]

(5) Arms Embargo on Liberia.—A complete embargo on the delivery of weapons and military equipment to Liberia was imposed by the Security Council on November 19, 1992[4] after condemning the cease-fire violations and attacks on West-African peace-keeping forces. Under the terms of resolution 788 (1992), the peace-keeping forces of the Economic Community of West-African States (ECOWAS) were exempted from the arms embargo.

(6) Arms Embargo Against Somalia.—Somalia on January 20, 1992 requested the Council to consider the deteriorating human dilemma prevailing in Somalia following the Civil war situation which was worsening day by day. The Council on January 23, 1992 unanimously adopted a resolution by which it decided that States should, for establishing peace and stability in Somalia,

1. Security Council Resolution 787 (1992), dated November 16, 1992.
2. Security Council Resolution 820 (1993), dated April 17, 1993.
3. Security Council Resolution 792 (1992), dated Nov. 30, 1992.
4. Security Council Resolution 788 (1992), dated Nov. 19, 1992.

immediately implement a general and complete embargo on all deliveries of weapons and military equipment to that country until it decided otherwise. The resolution also urged all parties to the conflict to agree to a cease-fire and to promote the process of reconciliation and political settlement in Somalia. Increased humanitarian assistance was asked with a coordinator appointed to oversee the effective delivery of such assistance to the affected Somalia population.

The U.N. arms embargo and the intense negotiations involving the United Nations resulted into the signing of the cease-fire agreement on March 3, 1992 by the Somalia's Interim President Ali Mahdi Mohammad and General Mohammad Farah Aidid, Chairman of the United Somalia Congress (USC)-Leaders of the two factions of the same movement who were for the most part the main parties to the fighting in Mogadishu.

(7) Oil and Arms Embargo in Haiti.—In Haiti the first democratically elected President-Jean Bertrand Aristide was ousted in September 1991 by the military coup. Thereafter violation of human rights began to occur in large scale. When the situation deteriorated in Haiti, a Joint-United Nations and Organisation of American States (OAS) mission was sent to verify Haiti's respect for human rights with the approval of the General Assembly on April 20, 1993. The Joint Mission was called the International Civilian Mission to Haiti. The mission comprised of some 141 members, on June, 1993 reported that numerous human rights violations are being taking place in Haiti.

When the situation did not improve, the Security Council on June 16, 1993 unanimously adopted a resolution[1] by which oil and arms embargo was imposed. Under the resolution, all States were obliged to prevent the use, sale or supply, by their nationals or from their territories or using their flag vessels or aircraft, of petroleum or petroleum products or arms and related material. States were to freeze all funds in the name of the Government of Haiti or of the *de facto* authorities, as well as those controlled directly or indirectly by them. The sanctions entered into force on June 23, 1993.

An agreement to resolve the political crisis was signed by the President Aristide and the Commander-in-Chief of Haiti's Armed Forces Raous Cedras. On July 3, 1993 with the conclusion of the agreement, the sanctions were suspended by the Security Council on August 27, 1993. It was also resolved that the embargo will be lifted permanently if the Secretary-General gives a report that the agreement concluded between the President and the Commander-in-Chief of Armed Forces of Haiti is being implemented. The Security Council on October 13, 1993 considered the report submitted by the Secretary-General wherein he had reported that agreement was not given effect and implemented. The Security Council re-imposed oil and arms embargo under its Resolution 873 (1993). On October 16, 1993 the Council by adopting Resolution 873 (1993) called for strict implementation of the Haitian embargo. The Council warned on October 25, 1993 that it would consider additional measures if the Agreement was not fully implemented.

The Security Council on May 6, 1994 tightened sanction against Haiti's

1. Security Council Resolution 841 (1993), dated June 16, 1993.

military rulers to force them to allow the return of ex-President Aristide and restore democracy. The trade embargo took effect at midnight on May 27, 1994.

Haiti is the first country ever to invite U.N. sanctions because a democratically elected government was unseated by a military coup. It is also the first regime ever to have sanctions suspended and then reimposed for breaching an agreement brokered under international auspices. The Security Council on September 29, 1994 terminated the measures set out in resolutions 941, 873 and 917 following the return of President Jean Bertrand Aristide.[1]

(8) Arms and Oil Embargo Against Angolan Rebel Group.—The Security Council on September 25, 1993 imposed an oil and arms embargo against the territory not controlled by the Government, *i.e.*, on the Angolan Rebel Group.[2] The Council decided that all States should prevent the sale or supply of weapons, ammunition and military equipment, as well as petroleum products to the territory of Angola other than through points of entry named by the Angolan Government. The Council decided that with a view to prohibiting the sale and supply of arms and related material to the National Union for the Total Independence of Angola (UNITA), the embargo would enter into force in ten days unless a cease-fire had been established. A ten day grace period was given with the hope that UNITA will respect the Peace Accord signed in Bicesse (Near Lisbon) Portugal on May 31, 1991.

When the situation did not improve, the Security Council on August 28, 1997 decided,[3] that all States should take 'necessary measures' to restrict the travel of senior officials of the UNITA and adult members of their families and to close UNITA offices with effect from September 30, 1997, unless the Council is informed by the Secretary-General that UNITA had taken concrete and irreversible steps to comply with its demands. It was also decided that States would prohibit the flight of aircraft or their components to UNITA, and the insurance, engineering and servicing of UNITA aircraft. States would also be required to deny permission to any aircraft to take off from or intended to land at a place not included in list to be supplied by the Angolan Government to the Sanctions Committee established by resolution 864 (1993) of September 15, 1993. When the situation continued to deteriorate, the Security Council by adopting a resolution on June 24, 1998, decided to impose prohibiting measures against the UNITA.[4] The Council decided that measures shall come into force from June 25, 1998.

(9) Arms Embargo Against Rwanda.—The Security Council on May 17, 1994 decided that all States shall prevent the sale or supply to Rwanda by their nationals or from their territories or using their flag vessels or aircrafts of arms and related material of all types, including weapons and ammunition, military vehicles and equipment, paramilitary police equipment and spare parts.[5] The Council on August 16, 1995 decided to suspend with immediate effect and until

1. Security Council Resolution 944, dated September 29, 1994.
2. Security Council Resolution 861, dated August 27, 1993.
3. Security Council Resolution 1127 (1997), dated August 28, 1997.
4. Security Council Resolution 1176 (1998), dated June 24, 1998.
5. Security Council Resolution 918, dated May 17, 1994; Also *see* Security Council Resolution 997, dated June 9, 1995.

September, 1996, the arms embargo on the sale and supply of arms and related material to the Government of Rwanda through specified points of entry.[1]

(10) Diplomatic Sanction Against Sudan.—On April 26, 1996, the Security Council by adopting resolution 1054 (1996) imposed diplomatic sanction against Sudan for giving shelter to three Egyptians who were wanted in connection with the assasination attempt on the life of Egyptian President Hosni Mubarak in June 1995. The Council demanded that the Sudan desist from assisting, supporting and facilitating terrorist activities and from giving shelter and sanctuary to terrorist elements. The Council also demanded Sudan to henceforth act with its neighbours and others in full conformity with the Charter of the United Nations and of the Organisation of African Unity. The above demands were originally contained in the Council's resolution 1044 (1996) of January 31, 1996.

The Council decided that if Sudan fails to comply with its demands by May 10, 1996, all States shall significantly reduce the number and level of their staff at Sudanese diplomatic missions and restrict or control the movement within their territory of all remaining staff. In addition, all States were asked to restrict the entry into, or transmit through their territory, of members of the Sudanese Government and of its armed forces. These measures would remain in force until the Security Council determines that Sudan has complied with its demands.

The Council on August 16, 1996 called on all States to deny Sudan registered aircraft permission to take off from land in or overpluse their territories.[2]

(11) Petroleum and Arms Embargo Against Sierra Leone.—After democratically elected Government was toppled on May 25, 1997 in Coup d'etat, the Security Council on August 6, 1997 stated that the military junta should take immediate steps to bring about the unconditional restoration of the democratically elected Government of President Ahmed Tejan Kabbah. When it did not take place, the Security Council, acting under Chapter VII of the U.N. Charter imposed the petroleum and arms embargo on October 8, 1997. The Council also decided that all States should prevent the entry into or transit through their territories of members of the junta or adult members of their families, except for 'verified humanitarian purposes.[3]

Expressing concern at the role played by the illicit diamond trade in fuelling the conflict in Sierra Leone, the Security Council on July 5, 2000 imposed a ban on illicit imports of country's rough diamonds and urged all States to take the necessary measures to prohibit the direct or indirect import of such diamonds to their territory, exempting imports of rough diamonds.

(12) Arms Embargo Against Yugoslavia.—The Security Council by adopting a resolution,[4] on March 31, 1998 imposed an arms embargo on the Federal Republic of Yugoslavia. The Council decided that 'all States shall for the

---

1. Security Council Resolution 1011, dated August 16, 1995.
2. Security Council Resolution 1070 dated August 16, 1996.
3. Security Council Resolution 1132 (1997) dated October 8, 1997.
4. Security Council Resolution 1160 dated March 31, 1998. The sanction was lifted by the Security Council on September 10, 2001.

purposes of fostering peace and stability in Kosovo, prevent the sale and supply to Yugoslavia, including Kosovo, by their nationals or from their territories or using their flag vessels and aircrafts, of arms and related material of all types, such as weapons and ammunition, military vehicles and equipment and spare parts for the aforementioned, and shall prevent arming and training for terrorist activities there. The arms embargo shall extend to the nationals of all States.

The Council established a Committee, consisting of all the members of the Security Council to carry out various functions relating to the arms embargo, namely, to seek informations from all States regarding their actions, to implement the ban and to examine those reports to consider information brought to it by any State concerning violations of the ban and to recommend appropriate measures in response, and to make report periodically to the Council on such alleged violations.

(13) Arms Embargo Against Taliban.—The Security Council by adopting a resolution 1333 (2000) imposed sanctions which included arms embargo covering all types of weapons and related matters, as well as ban on the provision of technical training or advice related to the military activities of armed personnel under Taliban[1] control.[2] On the diplomatic level, States with ties to the Taliban were urged to reduce the number and level of staff at Taliban missions and to restrict the movement of the remaining staff. The sanctions also require freezing of all funds and other financial assets of Bin Laden and individuals associated with him.

The above sanctions were tighter than the restrictions initially imposed in October, 1999 under Resolution 1267 to prompt Bin Laden's handover, following his indictment in the United States for the bombing of two of its embassies in Kenya and Tanzania. The new sanctions went into effect on January 19, 2001 and shall remain in effect for one year. If the demands are not met by that time, the Council may decide to extend the restrictions. However, when the Taliban rule in Afghanistan ended, the Council on January 11, 2002 decided that the sanctions imposed on it 'have lost focus and shall have to be adjusted to new realities.'

The Council by adopting a Resolution on December 20, 2002 decided that sanctions on freezing of funds shall not apply to funds and other financial assets or economic resources that have been determined by States to be "necessary for basic expenses", including payments for foodstuffs, rent or mortgage, medicines and medical treatment, taxes, insurance premiums and public utility charges. Thus, the Council adopted humanitarian exceptions to the earlier sanctions.

(14) Arms Embargo Against North Korea (2006).—North Korea became a party to Non-Proliferation Treaty (NPT) in 1985 but it withdrew from NPT in

1. Taliban emerged in 1994 with many followers who had attended conservative Muslim schools in Pakistan. In a short span of time they rose to power and by 1996 they took the capital Kabul and controlled 90 percent of Afghanistan. It was recognized by Pakistan, Saudi Arabia and the United Arab Emirates and have granted it full diplomatic recognition. However, after the terrorist act committed in the U.S.A. on September 11, 2001, the U.A.E. and Saudi Arabia withdrew the recognition. Later, Pakistan also withdrew the recognition. The Organisation of the Islamic Conference having 56 member nations has refused to admit the regime.
2. Also *see* Security Council Resolution 1390 (2002).

2003. Later, on October 9, 2006 it conducted a test of a nuclear weapon which the Security Council considered that it poses danger to peace and stability in the region and beyond and determined that it has threatened international peace and security. The Council on October 14, 2006 adopted a resolution[1] wherein it was laid down that all members shall prevent the direct or indirect supply, sale or transfer to North Korea, through their territories or by their nationals, or using their flag vessels or aircraft (i) any battle tanks, armoured combat vehicles, large calibre artillery systems, combat aircraft, attack helicopters, warships, missiles or missile systems, or related material including spare parts. The Council also decided that all member States shall prevent the supply of all items, materials, equipments, goods and technology as determined by the Security Council which could contribute to North Korea's nuclear-related, ballistic missile-related or other weapons of mass destruction and luxury goods. It was also laid down in the resolution that all member States shall prohibit the procurement of all these items from North Korea. Member States were required by the resolution to report to the Security Council within thirty days of the adoption of the resolution on the steps they have taken with a view to implementing effectively the above provisions of the resolution. The resolution further stated that sanctions do not apply to financial or other assets or resources that have been determined by relevant States.

The Council by the above resolution also decided to establish, a Committee of the Security Council consisting of all the members of the Council to seek information regarding the actions taken by them to implement effectively the measures imposed by the resolution.

The sanctions were renewed and extended by Resolution 1874 (2009) and Resolution 2087 (2013). The Council on March 7, 2013 adopted Resolution 2094 by which additional sanctions were imposed on North Korea in response to its nuclear test conducted on February 12, 2013. The sanctions required all countries to freeze financial transactions or services that could contribute. North Korea's nuclear or missile programmes. The Resolution also specified some luxury items with North Korea's elite are not allowed to import with the aim to stop the financial institutions dealing with North Korea.

When the fourth nuclear test was conducted by North Korea, Security Council adopted a Resolution 2270 on March 2016 wherein sanctions were further strengthened by banning the export of gold, vanadium, titanium and rare earth metals. The export of coal and iron were also banned with an exception for transactions that were purely for livelihood purposes. Further, the Council adopted Resolution 2321 in November 2016 whereby exports of copper, nickel, zinc and silver were banned. Further sanctions were imposed by the Council on September 17, 2017 by adopting Resolution 2375 wherein all exports of North Korean coal, iron ore, lead, lead are and sea food has been prohibited. The Resolution also imposes new restrictions on North Korea's Foreign Trade Bank and bans the country from increasing the number of workers it sends abroad.

1. Security Council Resolution, 1718 (2006), dated October 14, 2006.

(ii) Measures Involving Use of Armed Force :

If the Security Council considers that measures provided for in Article 41 are not adequate or they have proved to be inadequate, 'it may take such action by air, sea, or land forces as may be necessary to maintain or restore international peace and security' as provided under Article 42. These may include demonstrations, blockade, and other operations by air, sea or land forces of Members of the United Nations. The above implies that the United Nation's system of collective security presupposes the conclusion of military agreements supplementary to the Charter. In the absence of agreements there is no guarantee that the Council will ever be able to apply military sanction.

Special Agreements :

Action under Article 42 could be undertaken by the Security Council only in accordance with special agreements contemplated by Article 43 which provides under Para (1) that all members of the United Nations, in order to contribute to the maintenance of international peace and security, undertake to make available to the Security Council on its call and in accordance with a special agreement or agreements, armed forces, assistance, and facilities, including rights of passage, necessary for the purpose of maintaining international peace and security. Para 2 of the above Article provides that such agreement or agreements shall govern the numbers and types of forces, their degree of readiness and general location, and the nature of the facilities and assistance to be provided. If the Council decides to take action under Article 42 of the Charter, every member shall make available to the Council, according to Article 43, on its call and in accordance with a special agreement or agreements, the armed forces, the assistance, and facilities it requires, including the rights of passage. Thus how much 'strength' each member nation provides, where these forces are made available; how ready they are for action and what other facilities the nations give, are the questions which are to be worked out in special agreements concluded between the Security Council and each Member or group of Members. The recommendation of the Security Council made to the member States under Article 42 becomes an obligation for them which none can shrink. Besides being obligatory, the application of enforcement measures, in order to be effective, must above all be swift. Thus if the Security Council decides to take action, no time is given for further deliberation by the General Assembly. It would have been impossible to conceive of swift and effective action, had the decision of the Council been submitted to ratification by the Assembly, or had the measures applied by the Council been susceptible of revision by the Assembly. Thus, the legal requirements for military action are satisfied once the Council has acted.

However, no such agreement has been entered into as yet. It follows that when the Security Council decides for taking an enforcement measure, it also determines the part to be played by each member country. All or only some members may be required to participate, but every member is to join in mutual assistance.

Military Staff Committee :

Immediate and effective military action on the outbreak of a crisis is impossible without a great deal of previous planning and staff work. The Council was therefore equipped with a Military Staff Committee, a subsidiary organ of the Council, the task of which was to advise and assist it on all military problems. Article 46 provides that 'plans for the application of armed forces shall be made by the Security Council with the assistance of the Military Staff Committee'. The Committee shall consist of the Chiefs of Staff of the permanent members of the Council or their representatives as provided under Article 47, Para 2. The para further lays down that the Committee of Military Experts may invite other member States to be associated with it as and when required. They undertook to make available forces which the Security Council might utilize for the maintenance of international peace and security. The Military staff Committee is responsible for the strategic direction of armed forces placed at the disposal of the Security Council. If needed, the Military Staff Committee can, with the sanction of the Security Council and after consultation with the appropriate regional agencies, establish regional sub-committees.

Functions of the Military Staff Committee are stipulated under Article 47, Para 1 which are : to advise and assist the Council on all the military requirements of the Council, on the employment and command of the armed forces placed at the Council's disposal, and on the regulation of armaments as well as disarmament. The Committee is also responsible for the strategic directions of armed forces placed at the disposal of the Council, but questions relating to the command of such forces are to be worked out subsequently.

The Committee began its work in the month of February 1946 by studying the scope of its functions. On April 30, 1947, it presented a report to the Security Council on General Principles which should govern the organization of the United Nations armed forces.[1] The report set forth the recommendations of the Committee in the form of 41 Articles. On sixteen of these Articles, the Committee had been unable to reach unanimous agreement. The unanimity could not be achieved even on the basic question of the overall strength and composition of the United Nations armed forces. In the atmosphere of the cold war, there was a total absence of the political will for setting up the U.N. collective security system. In July 1948, the Committee informed to the Council that it was not able to make further progress until agreement had been reached in the Council on the agreement principles earlier reported upon.[2] The Council failed to discuss the related problems, and the Committee continued to meet without being able to report any progress on the matter. The result is that the Military Staff Committee went into a state of suspended animation due to the basic differences amongst the members on practically all matters. It was only in the Gulf crisis in 1990 that it was activated on the suggestion of the Soviet President, Makhail Gorbachev who stated that the Committee manage the action taken by the Council against Iraq. However, the Committee played no role in co-ordinating the eventual blockade. Further, Resolution 678 also did not mention the role of the Committee.

In the past, the Council has taken action involving use of force in the

---

1. *See* Doc. 5/336.
2. *See* the Letter of the Chairman of the Military Staff Committee of July 2, 1948 (5 Doc. 5/879).

Korean affair in 1950 and in the Gulf Crisis in 1990. In both the cases, instead of taking action itself, the Council authorized its members to take collective action. Such a course was adopted by the Council in view of its incapability in concluding special agreements with the members for the availability of forces. It is to be noted that the role of the Military Staff Committee is vital in any action which is taken by the Security Council. Boutros Ghali in his Agenda for Peace stated that the Military option envisaged by the Charter was essential to the credibility of the UN as an international organisation. In view of this 2005 World Summit Outcome requested the Security Council to consider the composition, mandate and working methods of the Military Staff Committee. Military Staff Committee is required to be revived and may perform a number of functions to maintain international peace and security such as arms control, coordination of anti-terrorist operations and may engage in military peace-keeping duties.

Joint Action Under Article 106 :

The failure to conclude an special agreement and the suspension of the working of the Military Staff Committee had virtually made the Council impotent to take a collective action against a State. It has neither any force at its disposal to maintain international peace and security, nor any body which could advice and assist on the application of such force.

Framers of the Charter had perhaps visualized the situation that if a sufficient number of special agreements referred to in Article 43 are not concluded, it would be difficult to take 'prompt and affective' action in order to maintain international peace and security, and therefore, a provision was made under Article 106 of the Charter which lays down that pending the coming into force of such special agreements referred to in Article 43 as in the opinion of the Security Council enable it to begin the exercise of its responsibilities under Article 42, the parties to the Four-Nation Declaration, signed at Moscow, on October 30, 1943, and France, shall, in accordance with the provisions of Paragraph 5 of that Declaration, consult with one another and as occasion requires with other Members of the United Nations with a view to such joint action on behalf of the Organization as may be necessary for the purpose of maintaining international peace and security.

The above Article provides for a 'joint-action' of the 'Great Powers'—Permanent members of the Security Council, as long as the Security Council has not expressed the opinion that enough special agreements have been concluded to enable it to begin the exercise of its responsibilities under Article 42. Joint action taken by the Great Powers was an action taken on behalf of the Organization. However such an action by the Great Powers under Article 106 may be taken only when the Security Council has determined for taking the enforcement action under Article 42. The above implies that action under Article 106 will cease to have validity as soon as the sufficient number of special agreements have been concluded. Since not even a single agreement has been concluded as yet, Article 106, which was a transitory provision, is still operative.

(2) Miscellaneous Functions :

Besides performing its main responsibility for maintaining international peace and security, the Council performs a number of other functions which have been conferred to it under the Charter. Such functions are as follows :—

(a) The Council may recommend the Assembly for admission of a State in the United Nations (Article 4, Para 2). The Assembly may admit a member only when the Council gives a favourable recommendation. The Council before making the recommendation satisfies itself as to whether a State which applies for membership is peace-loving and able and willing to carry out the obligations of the Charter.

(b) The Council has been empowered to recommend the Assembly to suspend (Article 5) or expel (Article 6) a member of the United Nations. The suspension of rights and privileges of any member against whom it is taking preventive or enforcement action may be restored by the Council along with the Assembly.

(c) The Council is empowered to control and supervise the strategic areas of the trust territories (Article 83, Para I).

(d) The Council approves the terms of the Trusteeship agreements (Article 83, Para I). The terms of agreements may also be altered or amended by it.

(e) The Council recommends the Assembly for the appointment of the Secretary-General of the United Nations (Article 97).

(f) Amendment in the Charter comes into force for all members of the United Nations when they have been adopted by a vote of two-thirds of members of the General Assembly including all the permanent members of the Security Council (Article 108).

(g) The Security Council encourages the development of pacific settlement of local disputes through such regional arrangements or by such regional agencies either on the initiative of the States concerned or by reference from the Security Council (Article 52, Para 3).

(h) The Security Council may suspend the investigation or prosecution of a case for a period of one year pending before the International Criminal Court.[1]

(i) The Security Council may convoke a special session or an emergency special session of the General Assembly (Article 20). by making a request to the Secretary-General.

(j) The Council may establish subsidiary organs as it deems necessary for the performance of its functions (Article 29). A subsidiary organ may be of one man or a committee or a peace-keeping force. It can be established by the Security Council, or by the President of the Security Council or by the Secretary-General pursuant to the decision of the Security Council. Such organs include : (a) Military Staff Committee; (b) Committee of Experts : (c) Committee on Admission

1. Article 16 of the Rome Statute of the International Criminal Court lays down that : No investigation or prosecution may be commenced or proceeded with under this Statute for a period of twelve months after the Security Council, in a resolution adopted under Chapter VII of the Charter of the United Nations, has requested the Court to that effect, that request may be renewed by the Council under the same condition.

of New Members; (d) Committee of Experts (Mini States); (e) Commission for Conventional Armaments; (f) Atomic Energy Commission; (g) Committee on Council Meeting away from Headquarters; (h) United Nations Compensation Commission (UNCC).[1]

(3) Functions in Relation to International Court of Justice :

The International Court of Justice is the 'principal judicial organ' of the United Nations.[2] The Court performs its functions in accordance with the provisions of the Statute which is an integral part of the Charter.[3] The Security Council has been given a number of functions to perform either by the Charter or by the Statute in relation to the International Court of Justice which are as follows :

(a) The Security Council and the Assembly elect the judges of the Court simultaneously but independently of one another,[4]

(b) The Council is empowered to recommend the General Assembly the conditions on which a State not belonging to the United Nations may become a party to the Statute of the International Court of Justice;[5]

(c) If a party to a case fails to perform the obligations incumbent upon it under a judgment rendered by the Court, Council may, at the appeal of the other party, make recommendations or decide upon measure to be taken to give effect to the judgment.[6]

(d) The Council recommends to the General Assembly the conditions for non-members of the United Nations participating in the election of the judges.

(e) The Council lays down the conditions under which the Court shall be open to non-parties to the Statute;[7]

(f) The Council recommends to the General Assembly conditions for participating of States which are parties to the Statute but not members of the United Nations in the process of amending the Statute of the Court.[8]

The above shows that the Council performs its functions in two ways. While some of them are performed by the Council exclusively, a number of functions are exercised by it concurrently with the General Assembly. Concurrent functions of the Council are referred to joint functions. They are performed by the Council and the Assembly concurrently. Such functions are : (a) admission of new members; (b) suspension from the exercise of the rights and privileges of membership; (c) expulsion of a member; (d) election of the

1. UNCC was established in 1991 to process claims and pay compensation for losses resulting from Iraq's invasion and occupation of Kuwait.
2. Article 92. For detail *See Chapter 'International Court of Justice'.*
3. *Ibid.*
4. Article 8 of the Statute of the Court.
5. Article 93 (2).
6. Article 94.
7. Article 35, Para 2 of the Statute of the Court.
8. Article 69 of the Statute of the Court.

Judges of the International Court of Justice; (e) functions relating to amendment of the Charter; and (f) appointment of the Secretary-General of the United Nations. It implies that the smooth functioning of the Security Council, in many cases, largely depends upon the cordial relationship between the Security Council and the General Assembly.[1] They are the principal organs of the United Nations and are required to coordinate the work to fulfil the objectives of the United Nations.

---

1. The two organs are also connected with each other in many other ways. For instance, the General Assembly considers annual and special reports of the Security Council; the budget of the Security Council is approved by the General Assembly, Further, the primary responsibility for the maintenance of international peace and security rests upon the Security Council, the General Assembly may perform this function under Uniting for Peace Resolution, if the Security Council fails to perform this duty.

Chapter 6

Economic and Social Council

The Preamble of the Charter proclaims that the peoples of the United Nations are determined 'to promote social progress and better standards of life in larger freedom'. Further, Para 3 of Article 1 lays down that it is a primary purpose of the United Nations to achieve international co-operation in solving international problems of an economic, social, cultural or humanitarian character, and to promote and encourage respect for human rights and fundamental freedoms without distinction to race, sex, language or religion. To achieve these ends, the Charter established the Economic and Social Council which is one of the principal organs of the United Nations.

Composition :

Provisions regarding the composition of the Economic and Social Council are laid down in Article 61 of the Charter. The Council consists of fifty-four members which are elected by the General Assembly.[1] One third of the total members, i.e., eighteen members of the Council are elected each year for a term of three years. Retiring members are eligible for immediate re-election. Each member is represented by one representative in the Council.[2] Elections to the Council are held in accordance with the principle of equitable geographical distribution. President of the Council is elected for one year.

The permanent members of the Security Council have no privileged position in the Economic and Social Council. However, they have served continuously as its members. It is submitted that the composition of the ECOSOC should be reformed. Presently, most of the members are from developing countries and therefore the wealthiest countries have not wished to submit to the Council which they do not control and on which none has a guaranteed position. In order to make the ECOSOC more effective it is desirable that the membership of the Council is reduced to twenty-five States (which would make it about the same size as is widely agreed to be appropriate for the Security Council).[3] The wealthiest countries (say, the Group of 8) and a similar number of the most populous countries (China, India, Brazil, Indonesia and Nigeria) could be made standing members, with the remaining members being elected for fixed terms on a regional basis. The above change in the composition

1. Before August 31, 1965, the Council had 18 members. The number was increased to 27 by an amendment in the Charter adopted on December 17, 1963 which came into force on August 31, 1965. Later, an amendment was adopted on December 20, 1973 by which the number of members was increased to 54.
2. Article 61 Para 4.
3. Julian Disney, UN Chronicle, Vol. XXXVII (2000) No. 2, p. 27.

of the ECOSOC requires an amendment in the Charter which of course is a difficult task. However, unless the amendment is made, it is difficult to see much prospect of the United Nations substantially strengthening its influence on international economic policy-making.

Voting System :

Voting in the Council is simple and direct. Each member has one vote. All decisions are taken by a simple majority of those present and voting. The Council invites any member of the United Nations to participate, without vote, in its deliberations on any matter of particular concern to that member.[1] Article 70 lays down that the Council provides arrangements for such participation by specialized agencies.

The Council elects a president and a first and second Vice-president at the start of its first session. These officers are eligible for re-election but they may not hold office after the State, they represent, is no longer a member of the Council.

Powers and Functions :

Regular sessions of the Council are held twice in a year, each one month long, in New York and Geneva. The first session is usually devoted to social and human rights and the second session to economic and developmental matters. In addition to regular session, special session may also be held.

The Council performs concrete tasks in the field of international economic and social co-operation and it carries out functions under the guidance of the General Assembly. The Council performs the following functions :

(1) The Council may make or initiate studies and reports with respect to international economic, social, cultural, educational, health and related matters. It may make recommendations with respect to any such matters to the General Assembly, to the members of the United Nations and to the specialized agencies concerned.[2]

(2) The Council may make recommendations for the purpose of promoting respect for, and observance of human rights and fundamental freedoms for all.[3]

(3) The Council may prepare draft Conventions for submissions to the General Assembly on any subject falling within its competence.[4]

(4) The Council may call, in accordance with the rules prescribed by the United Nations, international conferences on mattes falling within its competence.[5]

(5) The Council may make arrangements with the members of the United Nations to obtain reports on the steps taken to give effect to its recommendations and to the recommendations of the General

1. Article 69.
2. Article 62, Para 1.
3. Article 62, Para 2.
4. Article 62, Para 3.
5. Article 62, Para 4.

Assembly on matters falling within its competence.[1] When these reports are received, it may communicate its observation on these reports to the General Assembly.

(6) 'The Council may also furnish informations to the Security Council and assist the Security Council upon its request.'[2]

(7) The Economic and Social Council shall perform such functions, as fall within its competence in carrying out of the recommendations of the General Assembly.[3]

(8) The Council may, with the approval of the General Assembly, perform services at the request of the members of the United Nations and at the request of specialized agencies.[4]

(9) The Council may perform such other functions as are specified elsewhere in the U.N. Charter or as may be assigned to it by the General Assembly.[5]

The Council is a principal body for coordination, policy review, policy dialogue and recommendations on issues of economic and social development, as well as for implementation of the development goals agreed at the major United Nations summits and conferences. The 2005 World Summit Outcome stated that in order to achieve these objectives, the Council should (a) promote global dialogue and partnership on global policies and trends in the economic, social, environmental and humanitarian fields; (b) hold a biennial high-level Development Cooperation Forum to review trends in international development cooperation; (c) ensure follow-up of the outcomes of the major United Nations Conferences and Summits, including the internationally agreed development goals; (d) support and complement international efforts aimed at addressing humanitarian emergencies, including natural disasters; and (e) play a major role in the overall coordination of funds, programmes and agencies, ensuring coherence among them and avoiding duplication of mandates and activities.

Under the U.N. Charter, the Council's powers are merely recommendatory which are legally not binding upon the members and therefore it has 'sunk to a level of unimportance'. However, one of the greatest achievements of the United Nations has been in the economic and social fields which could be possible with the effective functioning of the Economic and Social Council.

Functions Relating to Specialized Agencies :

Specialized agencies[6] are the several inter-governmental organizations established to deal with specific international problems. The Council stands in special relation to these organizations. The Council is empowered to perform a number of functions in relation to these Agencies which are as follows :

(a) The Council may enter into agreements with these agencies to bring them into relationship with the United Nations. However such

---

1. Article 64.
2. Article 65.
3. Article 66 Para 1.
4. Article 66 Para 3.
5. Article 66 Para 2.
6. For detail *See* Chapter 'Specialized Agencies'.

agreements are required to be approved by the General Assembly.[1]

(b) The Council is empowered to co-ordinate the activities of the specialized agencies through consultation with and recommendations to such agencies and through recommendations to the General Assembly and to the members of the United Nations.[2]

(c) The Council is empowered to obtain regular reports from the specialized agencies. The Council may make arrangements with member States and with specialized agencies to secure reports on steps taken to give effect to its own recommendations or to the recommendations made by the General Assembly on matters falling within the Council's competence[3] and communicate its observations to these reports[4] to the General Assembly.

(d) The Charter provides that the Council may initiate negotiations among the States concerned for any new specialized agencies which may be required for the accomplishment of its social, economic, health and cultural objectives. Responsibility for taking steps to create new specialized agencies is vested in the General Assembly, and under the authority of the Assembly, in the Economic and Social Council. For instance, it was the Council which initiated the arrangements for setting up, for example, the World Health Organization. First of the measures which it took in this connection was to summon an international conference of health authorities.

Thus, by co-ordinating the specialized agencies, by its own deliberations, and through the work of its Commissions and Committees, Economic and Social Council grapples with almost every aspect of human well being. Its task is no less than to guide mankind in constructive international co-operation so that all people may indeed live in greater prosperity and larger freedom.

FUNCTIONAL COMMISSIONS :

The Charter under Article 68 provides that the Economic and Social Council shall set up commissions in economic and social fields and for the promotion of human rights, and such other commissions as may be required for the performance of its functions. Acting under this provision, the Council has established ten functional commissions from time to time which are as follows :—

(1) Commission for Social Development (CSD).—CSD was established in 1946 by the Economic and Social Council to advise and assist on social policies of general character and on other related matters. The Commission consists of 46 members. It meets once a year at the United Nations Headquarters. In the year 1995 the World Summit for Social Development was held in Copenhagen. Since then the Commission has been the key UN body in charge of the follow-up and implementation of the Copenhagen Declaration and Programme of Action. As a result of the Summit, the mandate of the Commission was

1. Article 63, Para 1.
2. Article 63, Para 2.
3. Article 64 Para 1.
4. Article 64 Para 2.

reviewed. Since 1995, the Commission has taken up key social development themes as part of its follow-up to the outcome of the Copenhagen Summit.

(2) Statistical Commission.—The Commission met for the first time in 1947. The statistical activities of the United Nations are carried out under the guidance of the Commission. It also advises the Economic and Social Council and the Secretary-General on the promotion and development of national statistics, the coordination of statistical work and the development of statistical services.

(3) Commission on Population and Development.—Population Commission was established in 1946 by the Economic and Social Council to study and advise on the size and structure of population and changes therein. In 1994 the name of the Population Commission was changed to Commission on Population and Development (CPD). The CPD is composed of 47 members who are elected for a period of four years by the Economic and Social Council. The goal of the CPD is the follow-up to the implementation of the Programme of Action of the International Conference on Population and Development. The Commission shall monitor, review and assess the implementation of the Programme of Action at the regional, national and international levels and advise the Economic and Social Council on issues such as population issues and trends, integrating population and development strategies on population and related development policies and programmes. The United Nations Population Division is the main Secretariat unit which assists the Commission in the compilation and in analysing data on population.

(4) The Commission on Crime Prevention and Criminal Justice.—The Commission was eastablished by the General Assembly on the recommendation of the Economic and Social Council in 1992. The resolution provided the mandate and priorities of the Commission which are : international action to combat national and international crime, including organized crime, economic crime and money laundering; promotion of the role of criminal law in protecting the environment; crime prevention in urban areas, including juvenile crime and violence; and, improving the efficiency and fairness of criminal justice administration system. Aspects of these principal themes are selected for discussion at each annual session.

(5) Commission on the Status of Women.—The Commission was established in 1946 as a mechanism to promote, report on and monitor issues relating to economic, civil, social and education rights of women. During its first session, the Commission declared as one of the guiding principles to raise the status of women, irrespective of nationality, race, language or religion; to equality with men in all fields of human enterprise and to eliminate all discrimination against women in the provisions of statutory law, in legal maxims of rules, or in interpretation of customary law. The Bureau of the Commission plays an important role in gaining proper preparation for, and in making sure that the annual sessions of the Commission are successful. The Commission was helpful in adopting the Convention on the Elimination of All Forms of Discrimination Against Women (1979). The Commission also made efforts to prepare a Convention of Nationality of Married Women adopted by the General Assembly in 1957.

(6) Commission on Narcotic Drugs.—Commission was established in 1946. It consists of 53 members who serve for four year term. The Commission has power to influence drug control policy by advising other bodies and deciding how various substances will be controlled. It also assists in exercising powers of supervision over the application of intentional Conventions and agreements dealing with narcotic drugs such as Single Convention on Narcotic Drugs, Convention on Psychotropic Substances and the United Nations Convention Against Illicit Traffic in Narcotic Drugs and Psychotropic Substances.

(7) Commission on Human Rights.—The Economic and Social Council (ECOSOC), appointed the Commission on Human Rights[1] which was approved by the General Assembly on February 12, 1946. Functions and composition of the Commission were outlined in a resolution[2] adopted by the Economic and Social Council. The Commission was composed of 18 members who were elected by ECOSOC. In 1962, the membership was increased to 21, and in 1996 to 32. Since 1990, the Commission has 53 member Governments. The Commission met annually in Geneva for six weeks beginning in March. The Commission may also meet between annual sessions to deal with urgent human rights situations. Such special sessions have taken place five times by the end of 2004.[3] The Commission reports to ECOSOC which, in turn, reports to the General Assembly.

The Commission, as determined by its terms of reference, was directed to prepare recommendations and reports on the following items :

1. on international bill of rights;
2. international declarations and Conventions on civil liberties, the status of women, freedom of information and similar matters;
3. the protection of minorities;
4. the prevention of discrimination on grounds of race, sex, language or religion.

The Commission was empowered to carry out studies, make recommendations and draft new international treaties. In addition, it could investigate allegations of human rights violations an could take action when presented with evidence of large scale violations. It was also empowered to establish sub-commissions.

The Commission began its work in January, 1947 under the Chairmanship of Mrs. Franklin D. Roosevelt. In its First Session, the Commission on Human Rights established the Sub-Commission on Prevention of Discrimination and

1. The establishment of a Commission on Human Rights was recommended in 1945 by the Preparatory Commission of the United Nations in order to deal with those human rights issues which could not be resolved during the original drafting of the U.N. Charter.
2. Resolution 1/5 of February 16, 1946.
3. Twice in 1992 during the crisis in the former Yugoslavia, in 1994 over the atrocities in Rwanda, in 1999 to discuss the East Timor situation and in 2000 concerning violation of Palestinians's human rights by Israel.

Protection of Minorities, a body of independent experts.[1] The Commission in the same Session appointed a Committee which is known as Drafting Committee for the preparation of the draft of an International Bill of Rights. It drafted the Universal Declaration of Human Rights which was adopted by the General Assembly on December 10, 1948. Since then the Commission concentrated its efforts on standard setting. Using the Declaration as the basis, the Commission prepared International Covenant on Civil and Political Rights and International Covenant on Economic, Social and Cultural Rights in 1966. In 1967, the Commission was authorised by the Economic and Social Council to start to deal with violations of human rights. For, instance in 1967, the Commission set up an *ad hoc* Working Group of experts on South Africa and has since established Working Groups on Chile; Situations revealing a consistent Pattern of Gross Violations on Human Rights; Disappearances and the Right to Development.

The Commission has set up an elaborate machinery and procedures, country oriented or thematic to monitor compliance by States with international human rights law and to investigate alleged violations of human rights. It is done mainly by despatching fact-finding missions to countries in all parts of the World whether they are rich or poor, developing or developed countries. For instance, in 1994 the Special Rapporteur on Religious Intolerance visited China and the Special Rapporteur on Contemporary Forms of Racism visited the United States of America. During 1970s and 1980s these implementation and fact-finding machinery and procedures became the focus of the Commission's attention.

The Commission in 1990s has increasingly turned its attention to provide with advisory services and technical assistance to the needy States so that they may overcome the obstacles in securing the enjoyment of human rights by all. At the same time, more, emphasis has been put on the promotion of economic, social and cultural rights, including he right to development and the right to an adequate standard of living. The Human Rights Commission was replaced in March, 2006 by the Human Rights Council.[2]

(8) Commission on Sustainable Development (CSD).—CSD was established in 1992 by the resolution of the General Assembly implementing a recommendation made in Chapter 38 of Agenda 21 of the United Nations Conference on Environment and Development (known as Earth Summit) of 1992. CSD was to review the urgent fulfilment of all Rio Commitments concerning concrete measures from the transfer of environmentally sound technologies to developing countries. The twelfth session of the CSD held in 1993 was an organisational session which focussed on establishing priorities and

1. In 1999 the Economic and Social Council changed its title from the Sub-Commission on Prevention of Minorities to the Sub-Commission on the Promotion and Protection of Human Rights. The Sub-Commission, a main subsidiary body of the Commission of Human Rights was composed of 26 experts whose responsibility was to undertake studies and make recommendations to the Commission concerning the prevention of discrimination of any kind relating to human rights and fundamental freedoms and protection of racial, national, religious and linguistic minorities. It has established seven working groups that investigate specific human rights including concerning minorities, transnational corporations, administration of justice and anti-terrorism.
2. For detail *See* H.O. Agarwal, 'Human Rights', Chapter, 'United Nations and Human Rights', Edition 17th (2021).

an agenda for the second ten-year cycle of the Commission.

(9) The Commission on Science and Technology for Development (CSTD).—CSTD which replaced the Intergovernmental Committee on Science and Technology for Development and its Advisory Committee met for the first time in 1993. CSTD was established to provide the General Assembly and the Economic and Social Council with high level advice on relevant issues through analysis and appropriate policy recommendations or options. The Commission Consists of 43 members who are elected by the Economic and Social Council for a term of four years.

(10) United Nations Forum on Forests.—Forum on Forests was established by the Economic and Social Council in 2000 to promote the management, conservation and sustainable development of all types of forests and to strengthen long-term political commitments to this end based on the Rio Declaration and the Forests Principles. Main functions of the Forum on Forests are to facilitate implementation of forest-related agreements and foster a common understanding on sustainable forest management, to provide for continued policy development and dialogue among governments, international organisations and major groups; and to foster international cooperation.

The above Commissions are composed of experts chosen on the basis of personal qualifications so that they may provide the best technical advice. Thus, these Commissions are the expert investigative bodies, on matters falling within their competence. These Commissions submit reports to the Council which then decides on further action.

REGIONAL COMMISSIONS :

Although the Charter has not made any provision for the creation of the regional commissions, the Economic and Social Council has established such commissions as its subsidiary organs. The main aim of their creation is to assist in raising the level of economic activity in their respective regions and to maintain and strengthen the economic relations of the countries in each region both among themselves and with other countries of the World.

These commissions undertake research and advise the Economic and Social Council on problems of a regional nature. They are empowered to make recommendations directly to member governments and to the specialized agencies on matters falling within their competence. But no action can be taken by the commissions in respect of any country without the agreement of the government of that country. The commissions make an annual report on their activities which are submitted to the Council. The commissions adopt their own rules and procedures including the methods of selecting their chairman. The Secretariat of the commissions are integral parts of the United Nations Secretariat as a whole. Each commission is headed by the Executive Secretary who holds the rank of under-secretary of the United Nations.

The Council has established five regional commissions on the initiative of the General Assembly to assist it in the performance of its functions which are as follows :

(1) Economic Commission for Europe (ECE).—The ECE was established by the Economic and Social Council in March 1947 "to initiate and participate in measures for facilitating concerned action for the economic reconstruction of Europe, for raising the level of European economic activity and for maintaining and strengthening the economic relations of the European Countries both among themselves and with other countries of the World. The ECE was also to provide governments with economic, technological and statistical analysis and information.

Presently, its major aim is to promote pan-European economic integration by bringing together 56 States of the European Union (EU), non-EU Western and Eastern Europe, South East Europe and Commonwealth of Independent States (CIS) and North America by dialogue. To this end, it provides analysis, policy advice and assistance to governments. It also sets out norms, standards and conventions to facilitate international cooperation.

The Headquarters of the ECE is situated at Geneva. It holds one public session each year. Closed meetings of its subsidiary organs are held throughout the year. The permanent committees of the Commission operate in many sections including agriculture, coal, electric power, gas and development of trade, housing and planning.

(2) Economic and Social Commission for Asia and Pacific (ESCAP).— The Economic Commission for Asia and the Far East (ECAFE) established by the Economic and Social Council in March 1947 was renamed in 1974 as ESCAP to reflect an equal concern for economic growth and social progress and to clarify the geographical scope.

It has membership of sixty-two governments and is the largest United Nations body serving the Asia-Pacific region. ESCAP carries out work in a number of areas including statistics, trade and development, transport, environment and sustainable development and social development.

The purposes and scope of action of the Commission are set out in its terms of reference which includes to initiate and participate in measures for facilitating concerted action to raise the level of economic activity of Asian and Pacific Asian Countries (for maintaining and strengthening the economic relations of the countries of those areas both among themselves and with other countries) to make or sponsor investigations and studies of economic and technical problems and to assist the Economic and Social Council in discharging its functions within the region in connection with any economic problems, including problems in the field of technical assistance.

The Headquarters of the ESCAP are in Bangkok. The work of the Commission is conducted through its annual sessions and through meetings of the main committees and subsidiary bodies.

The most important achievement of the ESCAP is the establishment of the Asian Development Bank in 1966 with Headquarters in Manila.

(3) Economic Commission for Latin America and Caribbean (ECLAC).— The Economic Commission for Latin America (ECLA) was set up in February 1948 with the aim of helping Latin American governments, promote the economic development of their countries. The promotion of region's social development including the improvement of the standard of living of their peoples was included among its primary objectives. In 1983, ECLA incorporated the Caribbean region into its name becoming ECLAC. Headquarters of ECLAC are situated in Santiago (Chile).

(4) Economic Commission for Africa (ECA).—ECA was established on April 29, 1958 by a unanimous decision of the Economic and Social Council. The tasks assigned to ECA were (a) to promote and facilitate concerted actions for the economic and social development of Africa; (b) to maintain and strengthen the economic relations of African countries and territories; (c) to undertake or sponsor investigations, research and studies of economic and technological problems and development; (d) to collect, evaluate and disseminate economic, technological and statistical information, and (e) to assist in the formulation and development of coordinated policies in promoting economic and technological development in the region.

The Headquarters of ECA are situated in Addis-Abbaba. The ECA has sub-regional organisations known as Multinational Programming and Operational Centres.

(5) Economic and Social Commission for Western Asia (ESCWA).—ESCWA was established in 1973 and has met annually since 1974. ESCWA was earlier Headquartered in Beirut. However civil strife and conflict in Lebanon led it to relocate to Amman (Jordan) but returned to Beirut in 1997. It comprises fourteen Arab countries. The main objectives of ESCWA are : to support economic and social development in the countries of the region to promote cooperation between the countries of the region; to encourage, interaction between member countries and promote the exchange of experience, best practice and lessons learnt and to achieve regional integration between member countries.

These commissions are composed of countries within the areas and of certain other countries with special interest. These commissions undertake research and advise the Council on problems of a regional nature and make recommendations to member governments admitted in an advisory capacity and specialized agencies on matters falling within their competence. These commissions have proved to be most successful organs of the United Nations in promoting co-operation in the economic fields.

Standing Committees, Expert Bodies and Programmes

Economic and Social Council has established a number of standing committees and expert bodies and runs many programmes on a variety of subjects. Sanding Committees include Committee for Programme and Coordination; Committee on Non-Governmental Organisations; Committee on Negotiations with Inter-Governmental Agencies and Commission on Human Settlement. Expert bodies established by the Council cover a vide range of subjects such as Committee on Crime Prevention and Control, Committee on Development and Planning, Committee on Experts on the Transport of Dangerous Goods. The Council runs a variety of programmes including the Environment Programme and the Drug Control Programme and has established a number of other bodies such as the Office of the UN Commissioner for Refugees and the UN Conference on Trade and Development.

Chapter 7
Trusteeship Council

In international relation for the first time mandate system was introduced under the League of Nations to improve the well-being of the peoples of the colonies and dependent territories. However, the system came to an end with the dissolution of the League. When the United Nations was established the mandate system was introduced in the name of the trusteeship system, and therefore trusteeship system may be called the successor of mandate system. While the principles of the two are essentially the same, they differ in organisation and functions. Further, the scope of the trusteeship system is wider than the mandate system.

Trusteeship system applies to those territories which have been placed under the authority of the United Nations for their administration and supervision. Such territories are called trust territories. They are administered by an authority called administering authority of the trust territory. Such authority may be one or more States or the Organisation itself. The United Nations supervises the administration of such territories through the General Assembly and the Security Council; both are assisted by a special organ, the Trusteeship Council. The trusteeship system therefore involves three elements : (a) a territory placed under the trusteeship system called trust territory; (b) an administering authority and (c) the United Nations for the supervision of such territories

Objectives of the Trusteeship System

Article 76 of the U.N. Charter lays down the following objectives of the trusteeship system—

(a) the furtherance of international peace and security;

(b) the promotion of the political, economic, social and educational advancement of the inhabitants of the trust territories, and their progressive development towards self-government or independence.

(c) The encouragement of respect for human rights and for fundamental freedoms for all without distinction as to race, sex, language, or religion, and the recognition of the interdependence of the people of the world.

(d) The ensuring of equal treatment in social, economic and commercial matters for all members of the United Nations and their nationals, and the equal treatment for the latter in the administration of justice.

Territories to be placed under Trusteeship System

Article 77 of the Charter provides that the trusteeship system shall apply to such territories in the following categories as may be placed thereunder by means of trusteeship agreements :—

(a) territories now held under mandate;

(b) territories which may be detached from enemy States as a result of the Second World War; and

(c) territories voluntarily placed under the system by States responsible for their administration.

Trusteeship system applies to above territories but the Charter does not impose upon the members an obligation to place certain territories under the trusteeship system. Such a territory may be placed voluntarily by the State which is entitled a right to place the territory under trusteeship only by agreement called trusteeship agreement. The trusteeship agreement concluded between the power which is entitled to dispose of the territory and the power under whose administration the territory is to be placed is required to be approved by the Organisation through the Security Council or the General Assembly.

Kinds of Trusteeship

There are two kinds of trusteeship, firstly, trusteeship with respect to areas designated in the trusteeship agreement as strategic area (Article 82 and 83), and secondly, trusteeship agreement with respect to areas not designated as strategic. Designation of area as strategic may be a part or all of the trust territory in the trusteeship agreement itself. The terms of the agreement for strategic area is approved by the Security Council and all functions relating to such territories are performed by the Council. The Council shall avail the assistance of the Trusteeship Council while performing these functions of the United Nations under the trusteeship system relating to political, economic, social and educational matters (Article 83, Para 3). The basic objectives set forth under Article 76 of the trusteeship system shall apply to the people of the strategic areas.

Differences between a strategic trust territory and non-strategic territories are laid down in the Charter itself which are :—

(1) The supervision of the administration of non-strategic areas is carried on by the General Assembly (Article 85) whereas the supervision of the administration of strategic areas is carried on by the Security Council (Article 83).

(2) In the non-strategic areas the assistance of the Trusteeship Council is obligatory in the performance of all functions of the Organisation, its assistance in strategic areas is obligatory only in the performance of the functions relating to political, economic, social and educational matters.

(3) Only in relation to non-strategic areas the competence of the Organisation to take measures such as to consider reports submitted by the administering authority [Article 87 Clause (a)] and to tak

action in conformity with the terms of agreement [Article 87 clause (d)] is obligatory.

Trusteeship Council :

Trusteeship Council has been set up for the detailed work of supervision of the trust territories. Chapter XIII of the Charter deals with the composition, voting system, procedure and functions and powers of the Trusteeship Council which is a principal organ of the United Nations.

Composition :

The Trusteeship Council is composed of the following members of the United Nations : (a) Those members administering trust territories; (b) Such permanent members of the Security Council as do not administer trust territories; and (c) States elected by the General Assembly for a period of three years. In this category as many States are to be elected as is necessary to ensure that the total number of members of the Trusteeship Council is equally divided between those members of the United Nations which administer trust territories and those which do not. Each member of the Trusteeship Council has to designate a specially qualified person to represent it therein.[1]

Voting System and Procedure :

Each member of the Council has one vote.[2] Decisions of the Trusteeship Council are made by a majority of members present and voting.[3] The Trusteeship Council adopts its own rules of procedure, including the method of selecting its President. The Council is required to meet in accordance with its rules, including provisions for convening of meetings on the request of a majority of its members. The Trusteeship Council must when appropriate, avail itself, of the assistance of the Economic and Social Council and of the specialized agencies in regard to matters with which they are respectively concerned.

Functions and Powers :

The Trusteeship Council, under the authority of the General Assembly, performs the following functions as conferred to it by Article 87 of the Charter :

(1) It may consider reports submitted by the administering authority. These reports are prepared on the basis of a questionnaire on the political, economic, social and educational advancement of the inhabitants drawn up by the Trusteeship Council.

(2) It may accept petitions and examine them in consultation with the administering authority.

(3) The Council may provide for periodic visits to the trust territories at times agreed upon with the administering authority.

(4) The Council may take other actions, along with the above, in conformity with the terms of trusteeship agreements.

1. Article 86, Para 2.
2. Article 89.
3. Article 89 Para 2.

Termination of the Status of Trusteeship

The Charter contains no express provision concerning the termination of the status of trusteeship. However, Article 76 Clause (b) may be interpreted to refer indirectly to it which says that when the basic objective of the trusteeship system to promote the development of the inhabitants of the trust territories towards self-government or independence is achieved, the trusteeship system is terminated as soon as the people of the trust territory have reached the political status of self-government or independence.

ACHIEVEMENTS OF THE TRUSTEESHIP COUNCIL :

Under the Mandate system sixteen territories were placed which were classified in three categories, i.e., Class A, Class B and Class C mandate. Syria, Lebanon, Palestine, Iraq and Trans-jordan were Class A mandate. They had either become independent by the end of 1946 or were expected to become independent, and therefore, they did not become trust territories under the trusteeship system. The other 11 mandate territories belonging to class B and C were eligible for the trusteeship and agreements were required to be entered into between the appropriate organ of the United Nations (the General Assembly or in the case of strategic areas, the Security Council) and the administering authority. By the year 1947, all the mandated territories belonging to class B and C came under the trusteeship system for which agreements were made by the General Assembly excepting the Pacific mandated territories which were designated as strategic areas, and therefore agreement was concluded between the administering authority and the Security Council. South West Africa, a territory mandated in Class C was the only territory in respect of which the administering authority, South Africa refused to place it under the Trusteeship System.[1] In addition to the above territories, Somaliland became a trust territory in 1950. Thus in total 11 territories were placed under the trusteeship system.

The Trusteeship Council has done a remarkable work. Of the 11 territories placed under the trusteeship system, all have attained the objectives of the system either by becoming independent States or by associating themselves with the neighbouring States.

Palau—an entity of the trust territory of Pacific Island, was the last such territory whose trusteeship agreement was terminated by the Security Council on November 10, 1994,[2] in the light of the entry into force on October 1, 1994 of a Compact of Free Association between Palau and the Administering Authority—the United States.[3]

Suspension of the Operation of the Trusteeship Council.

With the termination of the Trusteeship Agreement for Palau the objectives of the Trusteeship Council have been fully attained. The Council formally

1. For detail *See* Independence of Namibia in this Chapter.
2. Security Council Resolution 956 (1944) dated November 10, 1994.
3. The Security Council expressed satisfaction in the resolution adopted on November 10, 1994 that the people of Palau had freely exercised their right to self-determination approving the new status agreement in a plebiscite observed by a Trusteeship Council Mission.

suspended its operations after nearly half a century. By a resolution adopted on November 10, 1994, the Council amended its rules of procedure to drop the obligation to meet annually and agreed to meet as occasion required by its decisions or the decision of the President, or at the request of a majority of its members or the General Assembly or the Security Council.

The Trusteeship Council has not met since then. The Secretary General of the United Nations had recommended to the Assembly in 1995 to proceed with steps to eliminate the Council by making amendments in the Charter. But no step was taken. The 2005 World Summit Outcome reiterated 'that the Trusteeship Council no longer meets and has no remaining functions, we should delete Chapter XIII of the Charter and references to the Council in Chapter XII.'

Independence of Namibia :

The territory of Namibia, earlier known as South East Africa was occupied by Germany in the 1884-90 period. During the First World War, following German's defeat, it became a League of Nations mandate on his Bratainic Majesty, to be exercised on his behalf by the Union of South Africa. South Africa, as a mandatory power, fulfilled its obligations by submitting the required annual reports to the Permanent Mandate Commission. When the United Nations was established, International Trusteeship System was created for all the territories which were held under the mandate system. However, the system for the administration and supervision of such territories, as may be placed thereunder was to take place by subsequent individual agreements. In 1946, General Assembly recommended Trusteeship status for South West Africa and invited South Africa to propose agreement. South Africa did not approve the change (from mandate to trusteeship) and proposed to annex South West Africa. In 1947, South Africa submitted the required reports on South West Africa for consideration by Trusteeship Council, however, in the year 1949, it informed to the United Nations that it will no longer transmit the information on South West Africa. Refusal to bring the territory under the Trusteeship system and non-submission of the report on the territory posed a problem for the United Nations. Illegal occupation of the territory by South Africa continued. Conditions of black Namibian further deteriorated when South Africa accelerated the process of racial separation. They were required by law to confine themselves to non-white homeland. Rich lands were declared to be reserved exclusively for whites. In order to make Namibia (South West Africa) independent, United Nations took a number of steps. All its activities to achieve the end may be divided broadly in four stages, i.e., negotiation, assumption of the responsibility for direct administration of the territory, making settlement plan and the implementation of the plan.

In the first instance, General Assembly United Nations asked for the advisory opinion of the International Court of Justice in 1949 on the status of the territory and the obligations of South Africa. The Court in the Advisory Opinion given in 1950[1] found that South West Africa remained under international mandate and that South Africa was not competent to modify that status except with the consent of the United Nations; that South Africa

1. ICJ Reports (1950) p. 128.

continued to have international obligations, including the obligations to submit annual reports. The Court observed that the supervisory functions which were performed by the League of Nations shall be exercised by the United Nations. Two supplementary Advisory Opinions, given in 1955 and 1956, on Admissibility of Hearings of Petitions by the Committee on South West Africa dealt with the method of voting in the Assembly and the hearing of petitions.[1] In 1970, the Court, on Legal Consequences for Status of the Continued Presence of South Africa in Namibia (South West Africa),[2] asked by the General Assembly, was of the opinion that the continued presence of South Africa in Namibia is illegal and it is under an obligation to withdraw its administration from Namibia and put to an end to its occupation of the territory. The Court also held that members of the United Nations are obliged to recognize the illegality of South Africa's presence in Namibia, and refrain from assisting that regime.

Since 1950, the General Assembly sought by negotiation to reach agreement with South Africa on the implementation of the Court's 1950 Advisory Opinion. However, no agreement was reached. South African Government did not accept the Advisory Opinion and was unwilling to accept any form of United Nations supervision over the territory's administration. Further efforts at negotiations from 1957 to 1959, to reach basis for an agreement which could continue to accord on international status to the territory or to have the territory placed under the trusteeship system also failed to produce a solution acceptable both to the General Assembly and to South Africa.

In 1965, thirty-five African States requested that the question of South West Africa be considered as "a matter of priority" by the Assembly. On the recommendation of a sub-committee of the Special Committee on Decolonization, General Assembly in 1966 terminated South Africa's mandate over the territory on the ground that South Africa had failed to fulfil its obligations thereunder. The Assembly also decided that the territory would come under the direct responsibility of the United Nations. Thus, the United Nations assumed responsibility for administering South West Africa. A fourteen member *Ad hoc* Committee for South West Africa was established to recommend practical means for administering the territory. In 1967, the General Assembly established an eleven member United Nations Council for South West Africa to administer the territory until independence. In 1969, Security Council calls on South Africa to withdraw from Namibia saying that its establishment of bantustan destroyed national unity and territorial integrity and that the amendment of South West Africa Bill violated Assembly resolutions. South Africa replied that it did not intend to leave the territory. Security Council and General Assembly also uphold the opinion that the presence of South Africa in Namibia is illegal.

Security Council's efforts to take action against South Africa under Chapter VII of the Charter started in 1975. In 1975 and 1976, the proposed arms embargo on South Africa was vetoed by France, United Kingdom and United States. However, in 1977, the Council unanimously voted to impose a mandatory arms embargo against South Africa, the first time in the history of the United Nations,

1. ICJ Reports (1956) p. 23.
2. ICJ Reports (1970) p. 16.

such action has been taken against a member State under Chapter VII of the U.N. Charter. In 1978, the five Western countries (Canada, France, Germany, United Kingdom and U.S.A.) proposed for settling the Namibian question which was accepted by South Africa and South West Africa People's Organization (SWAPO)—the authentic representative of the Namibian peoples. The proposals call for the appointment of a Special Representative, to ensure establishment of conditions for free and fair elections, release of all Namibian political prisoners and return of all refugees; cessation of hostilities by all parties. The Council also decided to establish United Nations Transition Assistance Group (UNTAG) in Namibia to assist in implementing the settlement plan.

When South Africa decided to hold unilateral elections in Namibia in 1978, the Security Council and the Assembly condemned the decision, and declared the result null and void. The foreign ministers of Western 'Contract Group' declared that the unilateral elections by South Africa cannot be reconciled with the terms of the proposed settlement endorsed by the Council. Resolution of the Council could not be implemented in spite of the repealed insistence from time to time by a number of States in the meetings of the General Assembly and the Security Council. In 1983, the International Conference in support of the struggle of the Namibian People for Independence held in Paris also recommended for taking measures for securing the early implementation of the United Nation's Plan. The main reason for non-implementation of the plan was the linkage of Namibian's independence to the withdrawal of Cuban troops from Angola. The Council rejected the linkage. This obstacle delayed the independence of Namibia. It was only in the year 1988, after an intense negotiation, Angola, Cuba and South Africa signed agreements on the withdrawal of Cuban troops from Angola and the achievement of peace in South Western Africa. The way to Namibia's independence was therefore finally cleared.

Implementation of the U.N. Plan for the independence of Namibia, the third phase, began in 1989, after the obstacles of the withdrawal of Cuban troops from Angola was removed. On January 16, 1989, the Security Council adopted a resolution which provided that April 1, 1989 will be the starting date of the implementation of the U.N. Plan. The resolution also called on South Africa to reduce immediately and substantially the existing police forces in Namibia in order to achieve reasonable balance between those forces and UNTAG.

The main task of the UNTAG was the supervision of free and fair elections of Namibian citizens to a Constituent Assembly which is to draft a Constitution for the new nation—The last step before independence. UNTAG was composed of about 8000 strong contingent from 109 States. Elections in Namibia were held under the supervision of UNTAG in November 1989 in which SWAPO won 41 seats in the 72 member Constituent Assembly. The Assembly drew up a Constitution providing for an executive President for Namibia and multi-party democratic set up. On April 23, 1990, Namibia became independent and on the same date it became a member of the United Nations.

Non-Self-Governing Territories Not Placed Under the Trusteeship System

At the time of the adoption of the Charter there were number of territories whose peoples have not yet attained a full measure of self-government. These people lived in dependent territories which are normally referred to as colonies and were not included in the trusteeship system. In order to liberate them so that these territories may attain a full measure of self-government, provisions have been there in the Charter in Chapter XI entitled Declaration Regarding Non-self-Governing Territories comprising Articles 73 and 74.

Article 73 of the Charter imposes obligations on States which assume responsibilities for the administrations of such territories to promote to the utmost the well-being of the inhabitants of these territories. To that end they accept certain specific obligations, including the obligation to develop self-government and to assist the inhabitants in the progressive development of free institutions and to further international peace and security. They also have an obligation to promote constructive measures of development the encourage research and to cooperate to the practical achievement of the social, economic and scientific purposes.

The most important obligation as laid down under Article 73 clause (e) is to transmit regularly to the Secretary-General for information purposes. However, the obligation to transmit information is subject to many restrictions. Firstly, the Charter does not provide as to what shall be done with the information the Secretary General receives from the Members. Secondly, the obligation to transit information is only of technical nature and relates only to 'economic, social and educational conditions' in the territories concerned. The above implies that the administering governments are not obliged to transmit information relating to the political conditions of the territories under their jurisdiction. Thirdly, the security and constitutional consideration will be taken while transmitting information.

The General Assembly, as early as in 1946 declaring itself keenly aware of the problems and political aspirations of the peoples who have not yet attained a full measure of self-government drew attention to the fact that obligations under Chapter XI of the Charter were in force. In response Australia, Belgium, Denmark, France, the Netherlands, New Zealand, the United Kingdom and the United States enumerated seventy-four territories on which they would transmit information. Those territories varied in size and political status. The territories enumerated by the United Kingdom included colonies and protectorates.

Although thirty non-self governing territories attained self-government or independence by the end of 1960, there was a growing concern among members of the United Nations that the progress in this regard is too slow. This led to the General Assembly to adopt a Declaration on the Granting of Independence to Colonial Countries and Peoples[1] in the year 1960. The Declaration solemnly proclaims the necessity of bringing colonialism to a speedy and unconditional end in all its forms and manifestations.

In accordance with the provisions of the Declaration, the General Assembly decided to establish a Committee to make recommendation on the progress. The Committee known as Special Committee on the Situation with Regard to Implementation of the Declaration on the Granting of Independence to Colonial

1. General Assembly Resolution 1514 (XV) dated December 14, 1960.

Countries and Peoples consisting of 24 members was established which began work in 1962.

The Special Committee has been trying hard to end the colonialism and to provide right to self-determination to the peoples of non-self-governing territories. However, there are still seventeen non-self-governing territories where people have yet to be provided the right of self-determination which are as follows :—

American Samoa	Montserrat
Anguilla	New-Caledonia
Bermuda	Pitcairn
British Virgin Islands	St. Helena
Cayman Islands	Tokelau
Falkland Islands (Malvinas)	Turks and Caicos
Gibraltar	U.S. Virgin Islands
Guan	Western Sahara.
	French Polynesia.

The Special Committee in the year 2001 was charged with bringing to self-government or independence to the above non-self-governing territories, most of them are small island states. In the year 2004, the General Assembly adopted a resolution wherein it called upon the administering powers to cooperate-fully with the Special Committee to finalise by the end of 2005 a case by case work programme that would enable people of these territories to exercise their right to self-determination. However, peoples of these territories have yet to exercise the right of self-determination.

Chapter 8
The Secretariat

The Secretariat is a principal organ of the United Nations. The provisions regarding the Secretariat are laid down under Chapter XV of the Charter.

COMPOSITION :

Article 97 of the Charter provides that the Secretariat shall comprise of Secretary-General and such staff as the Organisation may require. The above implies that the Secretariat is the office comprised of the Secretary-General and the members of its Staff. Although Secretary-General is also a member of the Secretariat's staff, he has been mentioned separately because he is the Chief Administrative Officer of the Organisation.

Secretariat's staff may be divided broadly into three categories. Firstly, Senior Administrative Officials such as the Secretary-General and his deputies; secondly, international officials of the specialists class; and thirdly, technical persons such as secretaries, typists and courier etc. The system of the appointment of the Secretary-General and of other members of the Secretariat is different.

APPOINTMENT OF THE SECRETARY-GENERAL :

According to Article 97 of the Charter the Secretary-General of the United Nations shall be the Chief Administrative Officer of the Organization. He is appointed by the General Assembly upon the recommendation of the Security Council. If the Security Council is unable to make a recommendation because of the lack of unanimity among the permanent members, the Assembly cannot make new appointment but simply continue the Secretary-General in office whose term has expired. If the office of the Secretary-General remains vacant, great practical difficulties for the organisation may arise. However, the Charter did not lay down the procedure for appointing the Secretary-General. The procedure was specified by Rule 48 of the Provisional Rules of Procedure of the Security Council which laid down that any recommendation to the General Assembly regarding the appointment of the Secretary General shall be discussed and decided at a private meeting. The relevant decision of the Council is made by an affirmative note of nine members including the concurring votes of the permanent members. The decision takes the form of a resolution recommending to the Assembly the name of a person to be appointed Secretary-General. The resolution, thereafter is transmitted to the Assembly through a letter from the President of the Council. The General Assembly which considers the recommendation, vote upon it by secret ballot in private meeting in accordance with Rule 141, Chapter XV of the Rules of Procedure of the General Assembly. Since the question for the appointment of the Secretary-General has not been specified under Article 18 of the Charter as important question, he is appointed by a majority of the members present and voting otherwise known as simple majority. The phrase 'present and voting' means members casting an affirmative or negative vote. It implies that those members who abstain from voting are considered as not voting. The recommendation of the Security Council is made to the General Assembly by a vote of nine members including the concurring votes of the permanent members.

Although the Charter has laid down the method of the appointment of the Secretary-General, it is silent on the term of his office. In 1946, the General Assembly adopted a resolution which governs the term of appointment. It provided that the Secretary-General should be appointed for five years and that the appointment be open to renewal at the end of that time "for a further five years term." However, both the Assembly and the Council were left free to modify the term in the future. Since no modification has been made, 1946 resolution of the General Assembly still governs the term of appointment. It is important to note that the post of the Secretary-General is most distinguished in the United Nations. But for such an important post the Charter does not specify any qualification for the candidate. The appointment is made on the basis of political considerations involving both the Security Council and the General Assembly. By tradition, the post is given to a national belonging to States other than the permanent members of the Security Council and, that too, on rotation among major geographical regions.

Trigve Lie of Norway was the first Secretary-General of the United Nations. He was succeeded by Dag Hammarskjold of Sweden. U Thant of Burma succeeded him as the third Secretary-General of the United Nations. He was succeeded by Kurt Waldheim of Austria. Zavier Perez De Cuellar of Peru became the fifth Secretary-General who took up the charge of his post on January 1, 1982. In October, 1986, he was unanimously elected for another term beginning from January, 1987 for a period of five years. After the expiry of his term on December 31, 1991, Boutros Ghali was elected as the Secretary-General from January, 1992. After the completion of the term Boutros Ghali could not be re-elected for the second term due to the veto power exercised by the United States. Kofi Annan of Ghana was elected the seventh Secretary-General who took up the charge of his post from January 1, 1997. He was unanimously appointed by the General Assembly for a second five years term as the Secretary-General of the United Nations on the recommendation of the Security Council. Kofi Annan was appointed for a five years term beginning January 1, 2002 and ending on December 31, 2006. After the expiry of the term Ban Ki-Moon of South Korea assumed the office of the Secretary-General of the United Nations on January 1, 2007. He was appointed to a second term beginning from January 1, 2012 to 31st December, 2016. After the expiry of his term Antonio Guterres of Portugal was appointed the Secretary-General by the General Assembly for a period of five years. He assumed office on January, 2017.

The above appointments make it clear that the Secretary-General is a person who is more than an administrator. All the above appointees have had experience in foreign affairs in general and they have conducted multilateral negotiations. In other words, the person appointed as the Secretary-General should be a diplomat.

The Secretary General is a true international civil servant. He needs to be perceived to be both impartial and accountable only to the U.N. Charter and member States. His impartiality must remain untainted by any feeling of indebtedness to governments which may have supported his appointment. Further, he is required neither to seek nor receive instructions from the government or external authority. Trigve Lie was not liked by the Soviet bloc on Korean issue. Soviet Russia doubted about his independence and impartiality.

Functions of the Secretary-General :

The Secretary-General, the head of the Secretariat performs a variety of functions as conferred to him by the Charter. They are as follows—

(1) The Secretary General acts in that capacity at all meetings of the General Assembly, Security Council, Economic and Social Council and Trusteeship Council, and shall perform such other functions as are entrusted to him by these organs.[1]

(2) The Secretary-General in accordance with Article 98 of the Charter performs such other functions as are entrusted to him by the General Assembly, the Security Council, Economic and Social Council and Trusteeship Council. The above Article has given to the Secretary-General a variety of powers to perform.

The Secretary-General Dag Hammarskjold invoked Article 98 of the U.N. Charter to justify his visit to Beijing in 1956 to negotiate over American-Korean War prisoners with Chou En Lai, the Prime Minister of the People's Republic of China (PRC was not allowed to take up its seat in the United Nations by that time). The Secretary-General secured general approval for what became known as the "Peking Formula". In February 1998, members of the Security Council expressed their "complete confidence" in the Secretary General's ability to find the ways and means of resolving the crisis relating to the United Nations weapons inspections in Iraq. The Secretary General Kofi Annan visited Iraq and signed an agreement with Iraqi Deputy Prime Minister Tariq Aziz which was aimed at achieving a diplomatic solution regarding the weapons inspections. The agreement was endorsed by the Security Council on March 2, 1998.[2]

(3) The Secretary-General is required to make an annual report to the General Assembly on the work of the Organization[3]

(4) He with the consent of the Security Council, notifies the General Assembly of matters relating to the maintenance of peace and security which are being dealt with by the Security Council[4] and shall similarly notifies the Assembly or the members of the United Nations if the General Assembly is not in session, when the Council has ceased to deal with matters relating to maintenance of international peace and security.[5]

(5) He may bring to the attention of the Security Council any matter which in his opinion may threaten the maintenance of international peace and

1. Article 98.
2. Security Council Resolution 1154, dated March 2, 1998.
3. *Ibid.*
4. Article 12, Para 2.
5. Article 12, Para 2.

security.[1] (Article 99) It may be noted that Article 99 does not impose upon the Secretary-General an obligation to bring to the attention of the Security Council any matter which in his opinion may threaten international peace and security. The function laid down under Article 99 is exercised at the discretion of the Secretary-General.The right to call a meeting of the Security Council under Article 99 has only rarely been expressly invoked. During the Korean armed conflict, the Secretary-General Lie later claimed that he had invoked Article 99 on that occasion. In the past on three occasions Article 99 has been explicitly invoked-over the Congo problem in 1960, the United States embassy personnel held hostage in Iran in 1979 and the Lebenon situation in 1989. In all the three cases, a formal meeting of the Security Council followed the Secretary-General's initiative. In some other cases, the power under Article 99 has been exercised in an implied fashion, in a sense that the formal meeting of the Security Council was not insisted. It was left for the consideration of the Security Council at the discretion of its members. Situations in Laos (1959), East Pakistan (1971), Cyprus (1974) and Iran-Iraq (1980) were some of the instances in this regard.

(6) The Secretary-General convokes Special Session or the Emergency Special Session of the General Assembly at the request of majority of member States or of the Security Council,[2]

(7) The declaration regarding non-self governing territories specifies that members who have responsibilities for the administration of territories where peoples have not yet attained a full self-government should transmit regularly to the Secretary-General, for 'information purposes', statistical and other information of a technical nature on the economic, social and educational conditions in the territories.[3]

(8) The Secretary-General at the instance of the Security Council and/or the General Assembly may perform the task of negotiation, good offices and mediation. In the past, Secretary-Generals have performed these functions with varying degrees of effectiveness.

(9) The Secretary-General remained always an important source of aid and advice to the Security Council and to the General Assembly in finalising plans for the deployment of a peace-keeping mission in a troubled region. Once the peace-keeping mission is established, the Secretary General becomes responsible for the executive command/control of these peace operations, of course within the overall political authority of the Security Council. On a few occasions the Secretary General acted without the prior authorisation from the U.N. Organ. For instance, U Thant sent observer teams to Yeman in (1963) and India and Pakistan in (1965) and later informed the Council about the action taken.

(10) The Secretary General registers and publishes every treaty and every international agreement entered into by any member of the United Nations submitted to it for this purpose.

---

1. Article 99.
2. Article 20.
3. Article 73.

Functions of the Secretary-General in Relation to International Court of Justice :

International Court of Justice is a principal judicial organ of the United Nations. The Court carry out its functions according to the Statute which is an integral part of the Charter. Statute provides many functions which are to be performed by the Secretary-General. They are as follows—

(1) The Secretary-General has several functions in respect of the election of Judges of the International Court of Justice which are as follows : (a) He makes a request for nominations from national groups.[1] (b) He prepares, and submits a list to the General Assembly and the Security Council of these nominations.[2] (c) When a Judge resigns, the President of the Court notifies the Secretary-General and this notification makes the place vacant according to Article 13, Para 4 of the Statute of the Court. It is then for the Secretary-General to make arrangements for the election of a new judge.[3] (d) Formal notification of the dismissal of a Judge by unanimous vote of the other Judges has to be made to the Secretary General.[4]

(2) Declaration by State parties to the Statute of the International Court accepting its compulsory jurisdiction are to be deposited with the Secretary-General in accordance with Article 36, Para 4 of the Statute. The Secretary-General transmits copies thereof to the parties to the Statute and to the Registrar of the Court.

(3) The Court notifies, through the Secretary-General, to the members of the United Nations of cases filed.[5]

(4) Before the Court delivers an advisory opinion, it should give notice to the Secretary-General.[6]

(5) When the Court proposes amendments to its Statute, it has to do so by a written communication to the Secretary-General.[7]

The enumeration gives a picture of the Secretariat which under its Secretary-General keeps the machinery of the United Nations functioning. The immense amount of preparatory work from the drafting of research documents, surveying a problem to the arrangements for the convenience of the delegates, falls upon the Secretariat, and when the decisions have been taken, it is the function of the Secretariat to help in implementing them by continuous administrative action.

Appointment of Deputy Secretary-General.

The Secretary-General in December 1977 created a post of Deputy Secretary-General to assist him in managing the operations of the Secretariat. The post of the Deputy Secretary-General shall be an integral part of the office

1. Article 4, Para 2 of the Statute.
2. Article 7 of the Statute.
3. Article 14 of the Statute.
4. Article 18, Para 2 of the Statute.
5. Article 40, Para 3 of the Statute.
6. Article 67 of the Statute.
7. Article 70 of the Statute.

of the Secretary-General. The Deputy will be appointed by the Secretary-General following consultations with member States for a term not to exceed that of the Secretary-General. The Deputy will support the Secretary-General in ensuring coherence of activities and programmes and in elevating the profile and leadership of the United Nations in the economic and social spheres, and as a leading center for development policy and development assistance. Following shall be other functions of the Deputy Secretary-General :

1. The Deputy Secretary-General will act for the Secretary-General at United Nations Headquarters in his or her absence.
2. The Deputy Secretary-General will represent the Head of the United Nations at conferences, official functions and ceremonial occasions.
3. The Deputy Secretary-General shall also undertake other assignments as determined by the Secretary-General.

Louise Frechette of Canada was appointed by the Secretary-General Kofi Annan on January 12, 1998 the first person to hold the post of Deputy Secretary-General. Asha Rose Migiro of Tanzania was appointed the Deputy Secretary-General by the Secretary-General Ban Ki-Moon in 2007.

Appointment of Other Members of the Secretariat.—It is evident that the Secretary-General is not able to perform all the functions conferred upon him by the Charter personally. He needs deputies and assistants. As to the assistants the Charter provides for a staff of the Secretariat which according to Article 101 Para (1) shall be appointed by the Secretary-General under regulations established by the General Assembly. The staff permanently assigned to the Economic and Social Council, Trusteeship Council, and as required to other organs of the United Nations shall form a part of the Secretariat according to Article 101 Para (2). Para (3) of the above Article provides that the paramount consideration in the employment of the staff and in the determination of the conditions of service shall be the necessity of securing the highest standards of efficiency, competence, and integrity. Due regard shall be paid to the importance of recruiting the staff on as wide as geographical basis as possible.

Legal Status of the Members of the Secretariat.—In order to enable the members of the Secretariat to perform their functions independently Article 100 Para (1) of the Charter provides that in the performance of their duties the Secretary-General and the staff shall not seek or receive instructions from any government or from any authority external to the Organisation. They shall refrain from any action which might reflect on their position as international officials responsible only to the Organisation. Article 100 Para (2) lays down that each member of the United Nations undertakes to respect the exclusively international character of the responsibilities of the Secretary-General and the staff and not to seek to inference them in the discharge of their responsibilities.

Chapter 9

International Court of Justice

One of the purposes of the United Nations is to "bring about by peaceful means, and in conformity with the principles of justice and International Law, adjustment or settlement of international disputes or situations which might lead to a breach of the peace." In order to achieve the above purpose, it was essential to establish a judicial arm of the Organization. At San Francisco Conference it was therefore decided to establish a Court which was named the International Court of Justice. The Court carry out its functions according to the Statute which is an integral part of the Charter.[1] It may mean that the provisions of the Statute may be considered as the provisions of the Charter. Although the Statute of the Court does not lay down expressly the objectives or the functions for which it has been established its main objectives are firstly, to settle international disputes or situations, which are submitted to it by the States, in accordance with the principles of justice and international law, and secondly, to render advisory opinion on legal questions to any body which has been authorised in accordance with the Charter of the United Nations.

The Seat of the Court.—Article 22 of the Statute lays down that the seat of the Court shall be established at the Hague. The Permanent Court of International Justice had laid down similar provision. But the Statute of the ICJ stipulates an additional provision : 'This however shall not prevent the Court from sitting and exercising its functions elsewhere whenever the Court considers it desirable. The above provision obliges all the parties to the Statute to permit the Court to sit and exercise its functions on their territories whenever the Court adopts a decision to this effect. The decision of the Court is to be adopted, in accordance with Article 55 of the Statute, by a majority of the judges present. If the Court decides to sit and exercise its functions 'elsewhere' the seat of the Court, as determined by the Statute is not changed. The seat of the Court remains at the Hague. Thus, the Hague must be considered to be the permanent seat of the Court but the Court may establish its temporary seat elsewhere.

The Court as Principal Judicial Organ of the United Nations

The Charter of the United Nations under Article 92 lays down that the International Court of Justice shall be the principal judicial organ of the United Nations. If the term 'judicial organ' means 'tribunal', the International Court of Justice is not only the 'principal' organ but it is the only judicial organ of the United Nations, atleast the only tribunal established by the Charter as an organ of the United Nations. The Security Council and the General Assembly are, no

1. For the text of the Statute see Appendix II.

doubt, also competent to sattle disputes, but they are only quasi-judicial organs of the United Nations. However, the Security Council under Article 29 of the Charter is empowered to establish a tribunal as a subsidiary organ for the performance of its functions, and if it establishes such a tribunal for the settlement of the disputes, the International Court of justice shall cease to be the only judicial organ of the United Nations. But as long as such a tribunal is not established, the Court is the only judicial organ of the United Nations to which the members are authorized to submit their disputes.[1]

Successor to the Permanent Court of International Justice (PCIJ) :

The Council of the League of Nations in February 1918 appointed an Advisory Committee of Jurists to prepare a draft scheme for the establishment of a Court. The draft with some important amendments was approved by the Assembly on December 3, 1920. The Court named as Permanent Court of International Justice (PCIJ) had a Statute which was an independent document but was linked to the League of Nations by Article 14 of the Covenant. It was accepted by a Protocol of Signature on December 16, 1920 subject to ratification. The Statute entered into force on September 2, 1921.[2]

The Court was a permanent body composed of fifteen members : eleven judges and four deputy-judges to be elected by the Assembly and the Council of the League. Only States or members of the League could be parties before the Court. The Court had jurisdiction to decide those cases which the parties referred to it and matters specially provided for in treaties and Conventions in force. Jurisdiction of the Court was not compulsory, but Article 36 of the Statute contained an optional clause by which States could declare that they recognised 'as compulsory *ipso facto* and without special agreement, in relation to any other Member or State accepting the same obligation.

The Court functioned from January 30, 1922 to February 26, 1940. The first sitting of the Court was held on February 15, 1922 with the Dutch jurist Loder as President. The PCIJ became the primary global institution for judicial settlement and obtained adherence from some fifty States but not from the Soviet Union or the United States of America. Before its work was interrupted by World War II, the Court rendered 29 judgments in contentious cases and delivered 27 advisory opinions. In April 1945, a Committee of Jurists, set up by the Sponsoring Powers of the United Nations at San Francisco prepared a report, as a result of which it was decided that the PCIJ should cease to exist and a new Court— International Court of Justice should be set up to take its place. The PCIJ held its final session in October 1945 and on January 30, 1946 all its judges tendered their resignations. The final Assembly of the League of Nations dissolved the Court on April 18, 1946.

The International Court of Justice may be looked upon as the successor to

---

1. Although the Security Council in the past has established a few tribunals such as International Criminal Tribunal for Yugoslavia (ICTY), International Criminal Tribunal for Rwanda, Special Court in Sierra Leone, Special Tribunal in Lebanon and Special Tribunal in Cambodia, they are not the tribunals where members of the Court can submit their disputes.
2. The Statute was amended on September 24, 1929. Amended Statute entered into force on February 1, 1936.

the Permanent Court of International Justice. The Statute of the ICJ is an almost literal copy of the Permanent Court of International Justice. Article 92 of the Charter expressly lays down that the Statute of the International Court of Justice is based upon the Statute of the Permanent Court of International Justice. The provisions of the Statute of the present Court are therefore similar to that of the Statute of the Permanent Court of International Justice except for a few changes, most of which are purely formal. Furthermore, when the new Court met, it adopted the Rules of the Court of its predecessor without any substantial change.[1] Succession is also evident from Article 36, Para 5 of the Statute of the new Court which says that the declarations made by the States under Article 36 of the Statute of the Permanent Court of International Justice and which are still in force shall be valid between the parties to the present Statute for the acceptance of the compulsory jurisdiction of the International Court of Justice for the period which they still have to run. The new Court is the successor of the Permanent Court of International Justice is further clear when it is looked from the point of view of the continuity of the Court. The seat of the new Court is the same, *i.e.*, at the Peace Palace in the Hague, which was also the seat of the Permanent Court of International Justice. The new Court was inaugurated on the same date, *i.e.*, on April 18, 1946, on which the Permanent Court ceased to function on paper through a resolution adopted by the Assembly of the League of Nations.[2] The retiring President of the Permanent Court, Judge Gerrero became the first President of the new Court.

However, there are some notable distinguishing points between the old and the new Court. Firstly, the Statute of the new Court is an integral part of the United Nations' Charter, the Statute of the Permanent Court of International Justice was not so of the League of Nations. Secondly, provisions in the Statute of the International Court of Justice regarding the election of five judges at an interval of three years by the General Assembly and the Security Council are different from the Statute of the Permanent Court of International Justice. Thirdly, the present Court is to form chambers for dealing with particular cases instead of the provisions in Articles 26 and 27 of the Statute of the Permanent Court of International Justice. Fourthly, Articles 69 and 70 of the present Statute dealing with the Amendment to the Statute are quite new.

COMPOSITION OF THE COURT :

The Court consists of fifteen judges (called as Members of the Court) according to Article 3, Para 1 of the Statute. However, two of them may not be nationals of the same State. The judges of the Court are to be elected by the

1. On May 10, 1972 certain amendments were adopted. Later, on April 14, 1978 the Court adopted a completely revised set of Rules which came into force on July 1, 1978. Rules of the Court were amended again which came into force on April 14, 2005.
2. Members of the International Court of Justice for the first time were elected on February 6, 1946 at the first session of the General Assembly held in London. They met for the first time at the Hague on April 3, 1946. The new Court elected its President, its Vice-President and its Registrar on April 6, and held its inaugurai Session on April 18, 1946. The first case entered in the general list of the Court was of Corfu Channel : *United Kingdom* v. *Albania*, submitted on May 22, 1947.

General Assembly and by the Security Council independently,[1] but simultaneously. Those candidates who obtain an absolute majority of votes in the Assembly and in the Council are considered as elected. In electing the judges, the permanent members of the Security Council have no right of veto; (Article 10 para 1) but the States represented in the Security Council have double vote since they are also the members of the General Assembly.

Judges are elected by these two organs of the United Nations from a list of persons nominated by the national groups in the Permanent Court of Arbitration[2] established by the Hague Convention of 1907. In case, members of the United Nations are not represented in the Permanent Court of Arbitration, candidates shall be nominated by the national groups appointed for this purpose by their government under the same conditions as those prescribed for members of the Permanent Court of Arbitration by Article 44 of the Convention of the Hague of 1907 for the pacific settlement of international disputes.[3] A list of all the persons so nominated is prepared by the Secretary-General[4] which is submitted by him to the General Assembly and the Security Council.[5] Non-members of the United Nations, which are parties to the Statute, also participate in the election of the judges. The conditions for their participation in election are laid down by the General Assembly upon recommendation of the Security Council.[6]

The judges of the Court are required to be independent. Article 20 of the Statute lays down that the judges, before taking up their duties, are required to make a solemn declaration in open Court that they will exercise their powers impartially and conscientiously.[7] They should be the persons of high moral character. Judges of the Court may not exercise any political or administrative function or engage in any other occupation of a professional nature (Article 16, Para 1). They are required to possess the qualifications required in their respective countries for the appointment to the highest judicial offices.[8] They may also be the jurisconsults of recognized competence in International Law.[9] Besides the above qualifications, the electors are also required to bear in mind at the time of every election that in the body as a whole the main forms of

1. Article 8.
2. Article 4, Para 1.
3. Article 4, Para 2.
4. Article 7, Para 1.
5. Article 7, Para 2.
6. Article 4, Para 3.
7. The provisions of the Statute in order to assure certain impartiality and independence of the decisions of the Court are laid down under Article 16 which stipulates under Para 1 that 'no member of the Court may exercise any political or administrative function, or engage in any other occupation of a professional nature. Para (2) lays down that any doubt on this point shall be settled by the decision of the Court. Article 17 further provides under Para (1) that 'No member of the Court may act as agent, counsel, or advocate in any case. Para (2) stipulates that 'No member may participate in the decision of any case in which he has provisionally taken part as agent, counsel, or advocate for one of the parties, or as a member of a national or international Court, or of a commission of enquiry, or in any other capacity.'
8. Article 2.
9. *Ibid.*

civilization and of the principal legal systems of the World is well represented.[1] In order to fulfil this condition judges are appointed from different regions of the World, *i.e.*, three from Africa, two from Latin America, three from Asia, five from Eastern Europe and other States including States from Northern America and Oceanic and two from Eastern Europe. The judges are elected for a period of nine years.[2] However, the terms of five judges elected at the first election expired at the end of three years and the terms of another five judges expired at the end of six years.[3] The judges whose term expired at the above mentioned initial periods of three and six years were chosen by a lot to be drawn by the Secretary-General immediately after the first election was completed.[4] The result of the above provision is that five judges retire in every three years. The retiring judges are eligible for re- election.[5]

No member of the Court can be dismissed unless in the unanimous opinion of the other members, he has ceased to fulfil the required conditions.[6] The conditions which a member is required to fulfil are laid down under Articles 16 and 17 of the Statute which are : firstly, no member may exercise any political or administrative function, or engage in any other occupation of a professional nature;[7] secondly, no member of the Court may act as agent, counsel or advocate in any case,[8] and thirdly, no member may participate in the decision of any case in which he has previously taken part as agent, counsel or advocate for one of the parties.[9] It is to be noted that no member of the Court has yet been dismissed. The quorum of the Court is fixed at nine judges.[10]

When a member of the Court gives a resignation, his vacancy is filled by the General Assembly and the Security Council for the remainder period from the nationals of that very State. When Sir Robert Jennings of the United Kingdom gave resignation he was replaced by Mrs. Rosalyn Higgins of the same State for the remaining period, *i.e.*, upto February 2000. Mrs. Rosalyn Higgins was the first Lady Judge of the International Court of Justice.

President of the Court :

The Court elects its President and Vice-president for a period of three years.[11] They may be re-elected after the expiry of the term.[12] Article 32 of the Rules of the Court says that 'If the President of the Court is a national of one of the parties in a case he shall not exercise the functions of the Presidency in respect of that particular case. In such cases Vice-president of the Court proceeds the case. When a case was submitted by Libya against the United Kingdom in 1992, before the International Court of Justice, the President of the Court Sir

1. Article 9.
2. Article 13, Para 1.
3. *Ibid.*
4. Article 13, Para 2.
5. Article 13, Para 1.
6. Article 18, Para 1.
7. Article 16, Para 1.
8. Article 17, Para 1.
9. Article 17, Para 2.
10. Article 25, Para 3.
11. Article 25 Para 3.
12. *Ibid.*

Robert Jennings, a British national precluded from presiding the case. The case was presided by the Vice-president of the Court, Judge Shigeru Ode.

The President, if the Court is not sitting, has a power under Article 74, Para 4 of the Rules of the Court to call upon the parties in a case to act in such a way as will enable any order the Court may make on this request to have its appropriate effect. When India approached the Court in May 2017 to put on hold the execution of Kulbhushan Jadhav, the retired Indian Navy Officer who was convicted of espionage charges by a Pakistani Military Court, the President Ronny Abraham wrote to the Pakistan government that 'In my capacity as President of the Court, and exercising the powers conferred upon me under Article 74, para 4 of the Rules of the Court, I call upon your excellency's government, pending the Court's decision on the request for the indication of the provisional manners, to act in such a way as will enable any order the Court may make on this request to have its appropriate effects.

Chamber :

The Court may from time to time form chambers composed of three or more judges as the Court may determine for dealing with particular categories of cases such as labour cases and cases relating to transit and communications.[1] In July 1993 the Court decided to form a Special Seven Member Chamber for deciding environmental matters in view of recent developments in the environmental law. Earlier, the Court had considered forming an *ad hoc* Chamber to deal with environmental matters, but it has decided to deal with environmental cases through a Special Chamber.[2] Since the Court did not receive more environmental disputes the Special Chamber for environmental matters was closed in 2008.

In addition to the above, the Court may at any time form a Chamber for dealing with a particular case. The number of judges to constitute such a chamber is determined by the Court with the approval of the parties.[3] In the Gulf of Maine case between United States and Canada,[4] the Court was asked, by the parties that a Special Chamber of the Court be constituted to set the boundary of their continental shelf and fishery zones in the Gulf. This was the first time that the Court was asked to constitute a Special Chamber to settle a dispute. The Court decided to agree to the request to constitute the Special Chamber and it held elections for the Judges on January 15, 1982. Similarly, in the case of Frontier Dispute between Burkina *Faso* and Mali,[5] a Special Chamber of five judges was constituted by the Court on April 3, 1985, on the request of the parties to deal with the case.

Special Chambers were also constituted in the case between El Salvador and Hondorus, the case Concerning Electronica Sicula S.P.A. (SLSI)[6] and in 1992 in Land, Island and Maritime Frontier Dispute (El Salvador/Hondurus/

1. Article 26, Para 1.
2. ICJ Reports (1989) p. 15.
3. Article 26, Para 2.
4. ICJ Reports (1984) p. 246.
5. ICJ Reports (1985) p. 6.
6. ICJ Reports (1989) p. 15.

Nicaragua intervening case).

Ad hoc Judges :

Besides the judges, the Statute of the ICJ lays down the provision regarding the appointment of *ad hoc* judges. Article 31, Para 2 of the Statute provides that in cases where a party has no national judge on the Court, it may appoint a person to sit as a judge adhoc for the purpose of the case. *Ad hoc* judges are not permanent judges of the Court, and sit only in the particular case for which they are appointed. They take part in the decision on terms of complete equality with the other judges of the Court. It is to be noted that the system for the appointment of *ad hoc* Judges is not adequate, in the sense that they are not independent. On a few occasions they have been appointed and they have invariably given judgments in favour of their own States. For instance, in the case concerning the Aerial incident of August 10, 1999 (*Pakistan* v. *India*)[1] While Judge *ad hoc* Pirzada, appointed by Pakistan gave judgment in favour of his country, Judge *ad hoc* Jeevan Reddy, appointed by India gave judgment in favour of India. It is also possible to appoint *ad hoc* Judges in advisory proceedings. Article 68 of the Statute provides that in the exercise of its advisory functions, the Court shall further be "guided by the provisions of the present Statute which apply in contentious cases to the extent to which it recognizes them to be applicable."

The Court may also invite assessors to sit with it for the consideration of a particular case. Unlike the judges *ad hoc*, assessors are not entitled to vote. Assessors are chosen by the Court itself and not by the parties. The Court may also entrust any individual or organization that it may select with the task of carrying out an inquiry or giving an expert opinion.

Criticism :

It is to be noted that the provisions regarding composition of the Court suffer from a number of defects which are as follows :

(1) Although judges are required to possess the 'recognized competence in International Law', and they therefore are the experts of general principles of International Law, sometimes they are not able to resolve the specific issues adequately because of the lack of special competence. For instance, to resolve an issue relating to the law of the sea and law relating to environment, special competence in law of the sea or environmental law is needed, but the 'special competence' factor has not been regarded necessary at the time of the appointment of the judges. Further, in the past not a single judge possessed any formal qualification or special training in Islamic legal jurisprudence or African traditional laws. An examination of the composition of the Court in the recent past picking out all the judges from the developing States would lead to the discovery that practically all these judges were trained in European Laws or in the seats of Western legal education. Thus, their legal view point *prima facie* has been Euro-centric and Western orientated.[2]

---

1. The Case was decided by the International Court of Justice on June 21, 2000.
2. Gbenga Oduntan, 'Africa before the International Court : The Generational Gap in International Adjudication and Arbitration', IJIL Vol. 44 (2004) p. 734.

(2) The Court as a whole is required to have the representation of the main forms of civilization and the principal legal systems of the World. Since all the Great Powers represent a main form of civilization and one of the principal legal systems of the world, they have a political claim for the representation in the Court. Nationals of the four Great Powers U.S.A., U.S.S.R. (later Russian Federation) U.K. were always elected as judges of the Court.[1] Thus, nationality has always been a factor in electing the judges which is certainly not in harmony with the principle that the judges shall be elected 'regardless of their nationality.'

(3) Electors are required to bear in mind that 'in the body as a whole, the representation of the main forms of civilization and of the principal legal systems of the World is well represented'. This provision has not been followed in practice. The Court does not have representation of all the geographical regions of the World community.

(4) The number of judges in the Court is required to be fifteen. It is to be noted that since 1945, when the Statute was drafted, the number of members of the United Nations was 51. At present, it has gone to 193. With the emergence of a large number of States to independence which hitherto were colonies, and because of other new circumstances, increase in the number of the judges has become necessary. However, the Court still has the same number of judges.

(5) The judges are elected for a period of nine years and after completing the term, they are eligible for re-election. The above provision has resulted a judge to remain in the Court for fairly a long time. The system has affected the independence and impartiality of the judges. The general proposition is that judges elected for lifetime or with a certain age limit are normally regarded as more independent than judges for whom consideration of re-election might be a factor.

(6) The system of appointing the *ad hoc* judges is also a matter of criticism. The appointment of the judges of the nationality of each of the parties to a case is inconsistent with the principle of *nemo debet esse judex in propria causa* which means no one ought to be a judge in his own cause.

(7) Judges of the Court are required not to engage themselves in any other occupation of a professional nature. However, an investigation report published by Canada-based International Institute for Sustainable Development (ISSD) reported that many judges worked as arbitrators during their tenure despite the prohibition specifically laid down in the Statute of ICJ. Sir Cristopher Greenwood who lost the election in 2017 was found to have worked according

---

1. However, in November, 2017 U.K. suffered a humiliating blow when it will not have a judge in the Court for the first time in the history of the Court. Dalveer Bhandari of India defeated Sir Cristopher Greenwood of the United Kingdom nominee. Judge Bhandari received 183 votes out of 193 votes in the General Assembly and secured all the 15 votes in the Security Council after separate and simultaneous elections after Sir Cristopher Greenwood withdrew his nomination.

Justice Bhandari is the fourth Indian who was appointed the Judge in the ICJ. Other Indians who have held the post of Judges in the ICJ are B.N. Rao (1952-53); Justice Nagendra Singh (1973-1982). He was again appointed as a judge for the next term of nine years but he died in 1988. Justice R.S. Pathak became the judge of the ICJ for the remaining period (1989-91).

to the report as an arbitrator in atleast nine investment arbitration cases during his tenure. Judges are required to devote full time in the Court and strictly adhere to the provisions of the statute.

ACCESS TO THE COURT :

The following may have access to the Court—

(1) States :

Article 34 of the Statute lays down that 'Only States may be parties in cases before the Court'. It implies that it is not necessary that the States should be sovereign and independent in order to become parties to the Court. India was a party to the Statute before it became independent.[1] Similarly, San-Marino was a party to the Court, in spite of the fact that it was a not-fully-independent State. The meaning of Article 34 of the Statute is that only disputes between the States shall be decided by the Court. Thus, disputes between a State and an individual and between a State and a community of States, especially a dispute between a State and the United Nations, or disputes between international communities are excluded from the jurisdiction of the Court. Following States may become parties to the Court :

(a) Members of the United Nations.

The Charter of the United Nations under Article 93(1) provides that all members of the United Nations are *ipso facto* parties to the Statute of the Court which means that they all have automatic access to the Court.

(b) Non-member of the United Nations.

Article 93, Para 2 of the Charter provides that non-members of the United Nations may also become parties to the Statute. They could do so only on conditions to be determined in each case by the General Assembly on the recommendation of the Security Council. At the request of Switzerland—the first such State to ask to become a party to the Statute—the Assembly adopted a resolution defining the conditions which are as follows. Firstly, acceptance of the provisions of the Statute of the Court; secondly, acceptance of the obligations under Article 94, Para 1 of the Charter relating to compliance with the decision of the Court; and thirdly, an undertaking to contribute to the expenses of the Court, such equitable amount, as may be, assessed by the Assembly after consultation with the Swiss Government. Switzerland was the first country which is not a member of the United Nations but became a party to the Statute on July 28, 1948. Later on, Liechtenstein became a party on March 29, 1950 on similar conditions. San-Marino and Japan also became parties to the Court on February 18, 1954 and April 2, 1954 respectively on identical conditions. Although conditions are determined in 'each' case separately, in all the above cases they were identical. Japan in 1956, Liechtenstein in 1990, San-Marino in 1992, Nauru in 1992 and Switzerland in 2002 became members of the United Nations and hence at present there is no non-member of the United Nations who is a party to the Statute.

---

1. For detail See H.O. Agarwal, 'Some Observations on the Jurisdiction of the International Court of Justice' published in 'International Court in Transition'. Edited by R.P. Dhokalia and B.C. Nirmal, p. 285.

(c) Non-parties to the Statute.

The Court is also 'open to other States' which are not parties to its Statute in accordance with Article 35, Para 2 of the Statute of the Court. Such States may become a party on conditions laid down by the Security Council in a resolution of October 15, 1946 which are firstly, those States which have deposited with the Registrar of the Court a declaration by which they accept the Court's jurisdiction in accordance with the Charter of the United Nations and with the terms and subject to the conditions of the Statute and rules of the Court; and secondly, undertake to comply in good-faith with the decision or decisions of the Court; and thirdly, accept all the obligations of a member of the United Nations under Article 94 of the Charter. Such a declaration may be either particular or general. A particular declaration is one accepting the Court's jurisdiction in respect of a particular dispute or disputes which have already arisen. A general declaration is one accepting the jurisdiction in respect of all disputes, or of a particular class or classes of disputes, which have already arisen or which may arise in the future. Such declarations were filed in the past by several States which have since become members of the United Nations.

It is to be noted that there is hardly any essential difference between the conditions on which the Court shall be open to States which are not parties to the Statute and the conditions on which a State which is not a member of the United Nations become a party to the Statute. However, there is a difference of procedure between the two. While a State which is not a member of the United Nations may become a party to a Statute on the conditions which are determined by the Security Council together with the General Assembly whereas under Article 35, Paragraph 2 of the Statute, the conditions are determined by the Security Council exclusively. Further, conditions are determined in 'each' case separately in cases of those States, which are not members of the United Nations whereas the Court is open to those States not parties to the Statute on the conditions laid down not only for a single State, but as a general rule applicable to any State.

(2) International Organizations :

According to the wordings of Article 34, Para (1) of the Statute, international organizations do not have access to the Court. They, including the United Nations, of which the Court is the 'principal judicial organ', are barred from appearing before it as parties, even when they are in a legal situation similar to that of States such as that of being a claimant for direct or indirect injury against a State. Originally, the purpose of Article 34, Para 1 was to exclude individuals from bringing claims against States before the Permanent Court of International Justice. However, when a proposal was made to the 1929 Committee of Jurists that Article 34 be amended so that the League of Nations might be a party before the Court, President Anzilotti expressed the view that if the League possessed a collective personality in International Law, Article 34 would not exclude it from appearing before the Court'. Thus, according to Anzilotti, fulfilment of the condition, i.e., the possession of an international personality by the international organisation is necessary before they could appear before the Court. Presently, the international personality of the United

Nations has been unequivocally recognized by the Advisory opinion in the Reparation case,[1] and therefore, it should have a right to bring claims before the Court. However, presently, international organizations do not have access to the Court in contentious cases. However, they may seek advisory opinion of the Court on any legal questions. Although the United Nations cannot do so, its organs may seek advisory opinion of the Court on any legal question. While General Assembly and the Security Council may request the Court to give an advisory opinion on any legal question in accordance with Article 96, Para 1 of the Charter, other Organs of the United Nations may seek the advisory opinion on legal questions arising within the scope of their activities which may at any time be so authorized by the General Assembly. Specialized agencies of the United Nations may also seek advisory opinion of the Court if authorized by the General Assembly in accordance with Article 96, Para 2 of the Charter.[2]

(3) Individuals :

Individuals have no access to the Court. Neither the Statute nor the Rules of the Court permit the individuals to file petitions in the Court. It has, therefore, always refused to entertain the petitions and requests which have often been addressed to it by individuals. However, where the cause of the individual is sponsored by the State against another State, the Court may hear the cases. In the past, the Court decided five cases including the cases of Haya de la Torre[3] and Nottebohm[4] on the initiative of their States. In 2017, the Court decided the case of an Indian, Kulbhushan Jadhav which was filed by India against Pakistan.[5] In such cases what is then involved is a dispute between States. Individual by himself has no *locus standi* before the Court.

Criticism :

Article 34 of the Statute which says that only 'States may be parties in cases before the Court' does not conform to the present day development of International Law. International organizations have been playing a significant and growing role in international relations. They do possess legal personality by virtue of having rights and duties under International Law. In the Reparation case, the Court came to the conclusion that the United Nations Organization is an international person. In the opinion of the Court, the Organization was intended to exercise and enjoy, and in fact exercising and enjoying functions and rights which can only be explained on the basis of the possession of a legal measure of international personality and the capacity to operate upon an international plane.[6] In 1954, Institute of International Law had adopted a resolution wherein it stated that "It is a matter of urgency to widen the term of Article 34 of the Statute so as to grant access to the Court to international Organizations of States of which at least a majority are members of the United

---

1. See Chapter, 'Concept of International Organisations'.
2. See A/64/Add 1, p. 183. The text of the resolution of General Assembly was suggested by the Committee of Experts of the Security Council.
3. ICJ Reports (1951) p. 71.
4. ICJ Reports (1955) p. 4.
5. See Illegal Detention of Kulbhushan Jadhav by Pakistan (*India* v. *Pakistan*).
6. ICJ Reports (1949) pp. 178-179.

Nations and parties to the Statute of the Court."[1] Similarly, the International Law Association also proposed that Article 34 of the Statute of the Court should be amended to give the United Nations and specialized agencies direct access to the Court in contentious cases.[2] But no change has been made as yet and they are not eligible to become a party in cases before the Court. They should be given direct access in contentious cases. Further, individuals who have been given rights under International Law, do not have access to the Court, in case their rights are violated. The fact that no private individual has access to the Court seems to be inconsistent with the fact that the Charter of the United Nations contain provisions whose purpose is to protect the individuals against the State.[3] Access to the Court is imminent to individuals especially in cases of violation of human rights which at present has become a matter of international concern. But at present, there is complete absence of any firm move for the extension of the jurisdiction of the Court to the individuals. Further, a number of international organizations, other than specialized agencies should also be made eligible for at least seeking advisory opinion of the Court since they all possess international personality.

JURISDICTION OF THE COURT :

The Statute of the Court under Article 36 para 1 lays down that the jurisdiction of the Court comprises all cases to which the parties refer to it. The above may mean that the parties may bring before the Court any dispute whether it is a legal dispute or a non-legal, *i.e.* political dispute. But the Court does not decide all the disputes. If the parties submit their dispute to the Court for a settlement the Court decides the dispute only when the dispute is a legal dispute, *i.e.*, where the parties to the dispute base their respective claims and contentions on grounds recognized by International Law. In the case Concerning Border and Transborder Armed Action (*Nicaragua* v. *Honduras*) the Court stated that the Court is only concerned with cases involving a legal dispute, in the sense of a dispute capable of being settled by the application of principles and rules of International Law.[4] It is so because, perhaps the judicial procedure provided by the Court is not suitable for the political disputes.

If in any legal dispute political aspects are present, the Court as a judicial organ cannot concern itself with the political motivation. It was observed by the International Court of Justice in an advisory opinion given in Legality of the Threat or Use of Nuclear Weapons[5] that the fact of legal question also has political aspects does not suffice to deprive it of its character as a 'legal question' and to deprive the Court of a competence expressly conferred on it by its Statute; and the Court cannot refuse to admit the legal character of a question which invites it to discharge an essentially judicial task. Thus, International Law is not concerned with all the disputes of the States, and therefore, meaning of

1. AJIL Vol. 49 (1955) p. 15.
2. See 47th Report (1956) at VIII.
3. Kelsen, op. cit., p. 484.
4. I.C.J. Reports 1988 p. 69 at p. 91.
5. I.C.J. Report (1996) (1) p. 234 para 13. Also see Advisory Opinion of the Court given in Legal Consequences of the Construction of a Wall in Occupied Territory (Advisory Opinion was given on July 9, 2004).

the term 'dispute' should be taken in a restricted sense. However, when there is a dispute between two States on the question as to whether a particular dispute is or is not a legal dispute, the dispute is settled by the decision of the Court in accordance with Article 36, para 6 of the Statute which says that in the event of a dispute as to whether the Court has jurisdiction, the matter shall be settled by the decision of the Court.

Jurisdiction of the Court may be divided, broadly, in two categories, i.e., contentious jurisdiction and advisory jurisdiction.

(1) Contentious jurisdiction :

It is one of the fundamental principles of International Law that "no State can, without its consent, be compelled to submit its disputes with other States either to mediation or to arbitration, or to any kind of pacific settlement".[1] Consent is the basis of jurisdiction of an International tribunal and therefore it is not possible to summon any State against its will to submit to the jurisdiction of the Court. Thus, the Court is forbidden by its Statute and jurisprudence from exercising its jurisdiction in a case in which the parties have not given their consent. This results from Article 36 Para (1) of the Statute which provides that the jurisdiction of the Court comprises all cases where the parties refer to it and all matters specially provided for in the Charter of the United Nations or in treaties and Conventions in force. The consent is not required to be given in any particular form. In certain cases the Court may infer it from the conduct of the parties. The consent of a State to the jurisdiction of the Court may also be established by means of acts subsequent to the initiation of preceedings, which is referred to as the doctrine of *forum prorogatum*. The Court cannot proceed to adjudicate a dispute merely because one State files a case against another; the other party too, the defendant State, has to agree that the Court should try the case.

If one State submits a case and the other State makes an objection to the jurisdiction of the Court, a dispute as to the jurisdiction of the Court is deemed to have arisen.[2] A dispute relating to the jurisdiction is decided by the Court itself in accordance with Para 6 of Article 36 of the Statute which lays down that in the event of a dispute as to whether the Court has jurisdiction, the matter shall be settled by the decision of the Court.

When the Court decides a case, on the basis of the consent of the disputant parties, jurisdiction of the Court is called contentious jurisdiction. States parties to the Court may give their consent, firstly, either in advance by signing various treaties and Conventions, or secondly, by the conclusion of a special agreement, or thirdly, by accepting the compulsory jurisdiction clause. While the first is

1. Eastern Carelia Case PCIJ Series B No. 5 p. 27; Also See Peace Treaties Case, ICJ Reports (1952) p. 103; Monetary Gold Removal from Rome in 1943 (ICJ Reports 1954 p. 32). In the Legality of Use of Force (Yugoslavia v. Belgium), Judge Oda stated that 'the consent of each State to accept such an obligation was deemed to be absolutely necessary' (Judgment was delivered by the International Court of Justice on June 2, 1999).
2. See Interpretation of Peace Treaties case, I.C.J. Reports (1950), p. 65; East Timor case, I.C.J. Reports (1995), p. 90; Genocide (*Bosnia and Herzegovina* v. *Yugoslovakia* case, I.C.J. Reports (1996), para 29.

called voluntary jurisdiction, second and third are referred to *ad hoc* jurisdiction and compulsory jurisdiction respectively.

(a) Voluntary Jurisdiction :

If the parties to a treaty or Convention in force stipulate in that document that dispute under it shall be referred to the Court, the jurisdiction of the Court is established. In such cases the consent of the parties to the jurisdiction of the Court is given in advance, i.e., at the time of the conclusion of the treaty or Convention. Such type of consent is different from those where consent is given after the occurrence of the dispute. In voluntary jurisdiction consent is given before the occurrence of the dispute. This jurisdiction has been termed voluntary inasmuch as the parties on their own sweet will and accord decide to refer to the Court any dispute which may arise under the treaty or Convention. Several treaties and Conventions which are still in force provide that disputes under them shall be referred to the Permanent Court of Justice, shall apply to the present Court in accordance with Article 37 of the Statute. In these matters, therefore, the Court has automatic jurisdiction.

The General Assembly in 1947 adopted a resolution wherein it called upon the States to encourage the insertion of a clause in their treaties or Conventions for referring disputes arising thereunder to the Court. While many States such as Sweden, Finland and Norway in a number of treaties have complied with the request of the General Assembly, the practice is not followed by a large number of States. It is to be noted that only about 130 multilateral and 180 bilateral treaties involving at least sixty-four States contain clauses relating to the jurisdiction of the Court in contentious proceedings. It is in the interest of States themselves to insert such a clause in their treaties or Conventions they make, so that their disputes relating to the document may be decided by the International Court of Justice.

(b) *Ad hoc* Jurisdiction

When the disputant parties themselves refer the dispute to the Court, there is no question about the Court's right to take up the case. This jurisdiction of the Court is known as *ad hoc* jurisdiction inasmuch as in such cases parties give their consent after the occurrence of the dispute by the notification of a 'special agreement' concluded for that purpose by the two States.

The consent may be given by the disputant parties themselves or on the recommendation of the Security Council in accordance with Article 36, Para 3 of the Charter. In the Asylum case of Haya de la Torre, where Colombia and Peru were involved, the dispute was submitted to the Court by the parties themselves. Similarly, Botswana and Namibia concluded a Special Agreement on February 15, 1996 for the submission to the Court of the dispute existing between them concerning the boundry around Kasikili/Sedudu Island and the Legal status of that Island. The Corfu Channel case is an example where the Security Council recommended to the parties—United Kingdom and Albania, to refer the case to the Court. Consequently, the United Kingdom filed the application with the Court. Although Albania resented the unilateral application by the United Kingdom, and also disputed the jurisdiction of the Court, it was decided that Albania had given consent (tacit) to the jurisdiction of the Court on the basis of the doctrine of *forum proprogatum.*[1] By this doctrine, the Court has jurisdiction where the parties have given their consent by separate acts expressly or impliedly accepting it, one of those acts being the making of a unilateral application under Article 40(1) of the Court's Statute.

(c) Compulsory Jurisdiction :

At San Francisco Conference it was argued that the time had come when the Court should be given compulsory jurisdiction, i.e., all members of the United Nations should bind themselves in advance to the Court's having the right to consider legal disputes between them. This would have meant that if one party to the Statute of the Court filed a case against another party to the Statute, the Court would automatically and, without reference to the other party, have the right to try the case. This proposal was rejected because some of the delegates feared that such a provision might make the Statute totally unacceptable to their countries. Instead, the Statute of the Court provided that it would be optional for the States to recognize the compulsory jurisdiction of the Court. The compulsory jurisdiction of the Court may be recognized by the States in two ways :—

(a) By Making Declarations for the Recognition of the Jurisdiction of the Court.—The Statute under Article 36, Para 2 provides that it is open to a State party to the Statute to declare at any time that it recognizes, in relation to other States which are parties, and which have accepted the same obligation, the jurisdiction of the Court in all legal disputes concerning the interpretation of a treaty; any question of International Law; the existence of any fact which, if established, would constitute a breach of an international obligation; the nature or extent of the representation to be made for the breach of an international obligation. In the Case Concerning the Right of Passage over Indian Territory it was stated by the Court that : "by the deposit of its Declaration of Acceptance with the Secretary-General, the accepting State becomes a party to the system of the optional clause in relation to the other declarant States, with all the rights and obligations deriving from Article 36. The contractual relation between the Parties and the compulsory jurisdiction of the Court resulting therefrom are established, *ipso facto* and without special agreement,' by the fact of the making of the declaration...For it is on that very day that the consensual bond, which is the basis of the optional clause, comes into being between the States concerned.[2] The Permanent Court of Justice had a similar provision, the 'optional clause' as it is called, for accepting compulsory jurisdiction.

In Legality of Use of Force (*Yugoslavia* v. *Belgium*) case[3], Judge Oda has very rightly observed that :

1. The institution of *forum prorogatum* was introduced into the procedure by the Court's practice in the Rights of Minorities in Polish Upper Silesia case (P.C.I.J. Series A, No. 5, p. 27 (1925) in which Poland had first raised objections to jurisdictions in its second written pleadings (its rejoinder) after having argued the Case on its merits in its first written pleading (its counter-memorial) the Court said : "And there seems to be no doubt that the consent of a State to the submission of a dispute to the Court may not only result from an express declaration, but may also be referred from acts conclusively establishing it.
2. ICJ Reports 1957, page 146.
3. The Judgment of the International Court of Justice was delivered on June 2, 1999.

"The 'optional clause' in effect plays a double role : one positive in that it may occasion enable a unilateral application to succeed, and the other negative, in that it may sometimes result in respondent being brought to the Court against its will".

The Court decides the case on the basis of the optional clause declaration. However, in order for the Court to have jurisdiction on the basis of optional clause declarations, there must exist a 'legal dispute' between the parties. In Territorial and Maritime Dispute (*Nicaragua* v. *Colombia*),[1] the Court found that there is no extant legal dispute between the parties on the question of sovereignty over the three islands (San Andues, Providencia and Santa Catalina) and therefore the Court cannot have jurisdiction over this question on the basis of the optional clause declarations.

(b) By the Declarations made under the Statute of the Permanent Court of International Justice.—The Statute of the present Court provides under Article 36, Para 5 that such of those declarations made under Article 36 of the Statute of the Permanent Court of International Justice and which were in force when the Statute was signed shall be deemed, as between parties to the present Statute, to be binding with respect to the new Court. They would be binding, of course, only for the unexpired period, and they would be subject to such other terms and conditions as the declarations had stipulated. Thus, the declaration as to the acceptance of the compulsory jurisdiction of the Court shall be deemed to have been made by those States which had accepted the compulsory jurisdiction of the Permanent Court of International Justice for the unexpired period.[2] In the case concerning Military and Paramilitary Activities in and Against Nicaragua between Nicaragua and the United States of America, the Court decided in 1984 that it has jurisdiction to decide the case on the basis of the declaration made by Nicaragua on September 24, 1929 wherein it recognized the compulsory jurisdiction of the Permanent Court of International Justice, which it claimed continues in force although objected by the United States of America. Such jurisdiction is also called transferred jurisdiction. The Court may decide a case under transferred jurisdiction when the treaty or Convention is in force between the litigating States and when all the parties to the dispute have become parties to the new Statute.

The declaration for the acceptance of compulsory jurisdiction of the Court is deposited by a State with the Secretary-General of the United Nations, who transmits copies thereof to the parties to the Statute and to the Registrar of the Court. The declaration may be made with or without conditions or reservations. The Statute of the Court under Article 36, Para 3 refers the conditions. They are : firstly, condition of 'reciprocity' on the part of several or certain States, and secondly, the condition for a 'certain time.'

Past practice of the States show that compulsory jurisdiction of the Court has not been accepted by many States is clear from the following chart :—

1. Judgment was delivered on December 13, 2007.
2. Declarations of the six countries—Dominican Republic, Haiti, Luxemburg, Nicaragua, Panama and Uruguay have not expired by the end of 2013.

Year	States accepting compulsory jurisdiction	States parties to the Statute	Percentage
1945	23	51	45%
1950	35	61	57.37%
1960	39	85	45.88%
1970	46	129	35.65%
1980	47	157	29.93%
1990	53	162	32.71%
2000	63	190	33.15%
2021	74	193	38.34%

The above figures suggest that presently only 38.34% States parties to the Statute have accepted the compulsory jurisdiction of the Court. Further, permanent members of the Security Council are not enthusiastic in accepting the compulsory jurisdiction of the Court. China withdrew in 1972 when People's Republic of China replaced the Nationalist Chiang Kai Shek Government as the legal representative of the Chinese people in the United Nations. France terminated its declaration in 1973 and U.S.A. withdrew its declaration on October 8, 1985 when it lost the case against Nicaragua. U.S.S.R. never accepted the compulsory jurisdiction. After disintegration of the U.S.S.R. Russian Federation did not accept the compulsory jurisdiction of the Court. U.K. is the only permanent member which has accepted the compulsory jurisdiction of the Court on July 5, 2004. Moreover, those States which have made the declarations accepting the compulsory jurisdiction of the Court have made a number of reservations. In addition to the conditions of 'reciprocity' and time limit as provided in the Statute States have also put a number of other conditions. For instance, reservation as to domestic jurisdiction is most controversial. A few States have reserved for themselves to decide which questions are of a domestic character and which were international for the purpose of determining jurisdiction of the Court. The number of States accepting the compulsory jurisdiction of the Court, and the reservations which the States have made at the time of making the declaration, have considerably reduced the competence of the Court to decide a number of important disputes of the States. If the jurisdiction of the Court has to be made meaningful, it is desirable that the States accept the compulsory jurisdiction of the Court with minimum of reservations.

The declaration once made by the States accepting the compulsory jurisdiction of the Court can be withdrawn by the States. The effect of the withdrawal is that other States, which have already accepted the jurisdiction of the Court, have been deprived of the right they had to bring proceedings before it, against the withdrawing State. However, the withdrawal cannot be effective without allowing a reasonable period to elapse. In the case concerning Military and Paramilitary Activities in and Against Nicaragua, the International Court of Justice stated that the right of immediate termination of declaration with indefinite duration is far from established. It appears from the requirements of good faith that the withdrawal of declaration requires a reasonable time to lapse.

The Court, however, did not specify that what would be the reasonable time.[1]

The above three sources of jurisdiction were clearly indicated by Judge Hackworth in the *Anglo-Iranian Oil* case when he stated that from the principle of consent "........it necessarily follows that unless a State by special agreement, by treaty or Convention or by a declaration made under the optional clause of Article 36, Para 2 of the Statute occupied jurisdiction, the Court is without jurisdiction."[2] It is to be noted that in the above cases, stage at which consent is given is different. While in the *ad hoc* jurisdiction, consent is given *ad hoc*, in cases of voluntary and compulsory jurisdiction, consent is given *ante ad hoc.*

Indian Declaration :

India accepted the compulsory jurisdiction of the Court by making a declaration on September 18, 2019.[3] This declaration has revoked and replaced the earlier declaration made on September 14, 1959. The declaration made in 2019 contains a number of reservations. Firstly, it reserves the right either to amend or terminate the declaration at any time, by means of a written notification addressed to the Secretary-General of the United Nations. Amendments or termination shall be effective from the moment of such notification. It means that the acceptance of the compulsory jurisdiction of the Court can be withdrawn at any time by giving notice. Secondly, 'condition of reciprocity' has been laid down. Thirdly, the jurisdiction of the Court extends to all disputes other than (a) disputes in regard to which the parties to the dispute have agreed or shall agree to have recourse to some other method or methods of settlement; (b) disputes with the Government of any State which is or has been a member of the Commonwealth of Nations; (c) disputes in regard to matters which are essentially within the domestic jurisdiction of the Republic of India; (d) disputes relating to or connected facts or situations of hostilities, armed conflicts, individual or collective actions taken in self-defence; (e) disputes with regard to which any other party to a dispute has accepted the compulsory jurisdiction of the Court exclusively for or in relation to the purpose of such disputes; (f) disputes where the jurisdiction of the Court is or may be founded on the basis of a treaty concluded under the auspices of the League of Nations, unless the Government of India specially agree to jurisdiction in each case; (g) disputes concerning the interpretation or application of a multilateral treaty unless all the parties to the treaty are also parties to the case before the Court or Government of India specially agree to the jurisdiction; (h) the disputes with the Government of any State with which, India has no diplomatic relations or which has not been recognized by the Government of India; (i) disputes with non-sovereign States or territories; (j) disputes with India relating to (i) the status of its territory or the modification of its frontiers or any other matter

1. Judgment dated November 26, 1984, para 63. Also see Case Concerning Land and Maritime Boundary between Cameroon and Nigeria, International Court of Justice, Judgment delivered on June 11, 1998.
2. ICJ Reports (1952) p. 139.
3. For the text of the Declaration *See* IJIL Vol. 14 (1974) p. 450. Earlier, (British) India had submitted its declaration in 1940 accepting the compulsory jurisdiction of the Permanent Court of International Justice with some reservations. India after its independence revised this declaration in 1956. In 1959, it further revised the declaration which has been revoked by the declaration of 1974.

concerning boundaries; (ii) the territorial sea, the continental shelf and margin, the exclusive economic zone, and other zones of national maritime jurisdiction; (iii) the condition and status of its islands, bays and gulfs; (iv) the air space superjacent to its land and the maritime territory; and (v) the determination and delimitation of its maritime boundaries; (k) disputes prior to the date of the declaration. The above reservations in the declaration accepting the compulsory jurisdiction of the Court reveal that hardly any dispute can be brought before the Court. If States would make similar reservations, the jurisdiction of the Court would become meaningless.

Aerial Incident of August 10, 1999 (Pakistan v. India)

Pakistan on September 21, 1999 instituted proceedings before the Court against India in respect of a dispute concerning the destruction of a Pakistani aircraft, Atlantique on August 10, 1999. In its application, Pakistan contended that the unarmed aircraft of the Pakistan navy was on a routine training mission with 16 personnel on board when while flying over Pakistan air space it was fired upon with air to air missiles by Indian air force planes, without warning, resulting in the death of all the persons.

Pakistan maintains that the above act constituted breaches of the obligation to refrain from the threat or use of force under Article 2 Para 4 of the Charter of the United Nations and of the provisions of the Agreement of April 6, 1991 between Pakistan and India on Prevention of Air space violations and of the obligations under customary international law not to use force against another State and not to violate the sovereignty of another State. Pakistan therefore requested the Court to judge and declare that the acts of India constituted breaches of these various obligations for which India bears exclusive legal responsibility and that India is under an obligation to make reparations to Pakistan for the loss of the aircraft and as compensation to the heirs of those killed.

India on November, 2, 1999 stated that it has preliminary objections to the assumption of jurisdiction by the Court.

The Court on June 21, 2000 decided that it does not have jurisdiction to adjudicate the case brought by Pakistan. The decision which was adopted by a vote of 14 to 2 was based partly on the parties declarations of acceptance of compulsory jurisdiction of the Court and reservations attached to them. One of the reservations in India's declaration indicated that it would consider disputes with any State 'which is or has been' a member of the Commonwealth of Nations excluded from the Court's jurisdiction. As Pakistan is a member of the Commonwealth, the Court could not adjudicate the case. The Court, however stressed that the fact that it did not have jurisdiction did not mean that an act was in conformity with international law and reminded the parties that despite its lack of jurisdiction, they were still obliged to settle their dispute peacefully.

Appearance of the Parties before the Court :

In all the cases where States have given their consent for the decision by the Court, the parties are required to appear and defend the case when their case is being decided by the Court. However, if one of the parties does not appear before the Court, or fails to defend its case, it does not mean that the Court is unable to act. If one of the parties remains absent, the other party may, according to Article 53, call upon the Court to decide in favour of its claim. The Court must before doing so satisfy itself, not only that it has jurisdiction 'but also that the claim is well founded in fact and law'. Thus, the Court has a jurisdiction to investigate on its own initiative any preliminary question of admissibility or jurisdiction that may arise even if one party fails to appear before the Court provided the claim of a party is well founded in fact and law.

In the case of the United States Diplomatic and Consular Staff in Tehran[1] (*United States of America* v. *Iran*), when the United States instituted proceedings against Iran in a case arising out of the situation at its Embassy in Tehran, Iran expressed in a letter to the Court that the Court could not and should not take cognizance of the case. At the time of public hearing at the Court,[2] Iran did not take part in the proceedings. It neither filed pleadings nor it represented at the hearing, and no submissions were therefore presented on its behalf. The Court expressed regret that Iran did not appear before it to put forward its arguments. The absence of Iran from the proceedings brought into operation to Article 53 of the Statute. The Court was satisfied that the allegations of facts on which the United States based its claim were well founded, and decided the case accordingly. Similarly, when Nicaragua filed a case Against the United States concerning Military and Paramilitary Activities in and Against Nicaragua, the Court decided[3] that it had jurisdiction to decide the case. The United States on January 18, 1985 informed to the Registrar of the Court that it has decided not to participate in further proceedings of the Court initiated by Nicaragua. The decision of the Court regarding jurisdiction, according to it was contrary to law and fact and the proceedings are a misuse of the Court for political purposes. However, when Nicaragua informed to the President of the Court on January 22, 1985 that his government maintained its application and availed itself of the rights provided for under Article 53 of the Statute, the Court decided the case even in the absence of the United States, when it was satisfied that the claim of Nicaragua was well founded in 'fact and law'.

When one of the parties fails to appear before the Court or fails to defend its case, the Court usually expresses regret, in view of the fact that such a decision has a negative impact on the sound administration of justice.[4] In the case concerning Military and Paramilitary Activities in and Against Nicaragua,[5] the Court regrets even more deeply the decision of the United States not to participate in the proceedings of the case because this decision was made after the United States had participated fully in the proceedings on the request for provisional measures and the proceedings on jurisdiction and admissibility. It is to be noted that non-participation of a party in the proceedings at any stage of the case cannot, in any circumstances, affect the validity of the judgment. A State which decides not to appear remains a party to the case, and is bound by the

1. ICJ Reports (1979) p. 21.
2. ICJ Reports (1980) p. 3.
3. See *Nicaragua* v. *United States of America*, ICJ Reports (1984), Paras 27 to 29.
4. *See* Nuclear Tests Case ICJ Reports (1974) p. 257; Aegean Sea Continental Shelf Case, ICJ Reports (1978) p. 7.
5. op. cit., Para 27.

judgment of the Court in accordance with Article 59 of the Statute.

(2) Advisory Jurisdiction :

According to Article 65 of the Statute, the Court may give an advisory opinion on any 'legal question' to any body which has been authorized in accordance with the Charter of the United Nations or in accordance with the Statute. The Charter under Article 96, Para 1 lays down that the Security Council and the General Assembly may request to the Court to give an advisory opinion on any legal question. In addition to them, other organs of the United Nations and specialized agencies may also request for an advisory opinion on 'legal questions' arising within the scope of their activities if so authorized by the General Assembly. It may be noted that the above bodies may seek the advisory opinion only on legal questions. But there is a difference in the seeking of advisory opinion of the Court by the General Assembly and the Security Council, and by the other organs of the United Nations. While the former may seek advisory opinion on any 'legal question', latter can do so only on such 'legal questions' which arise within the scope of their activities.

It is to be noted that the Court will give advisory opinion even if a question bears legal as well as political character. In the Legal Consequences of the Construction of a Wall in the Occupied Palestinian Territory,[1] it was contended that the question posed before the Court for the advisory opinion is of political character, and therefore it has no jurisdiction. The Court did not accept the view by stating that the fact that a legal question also has political aspects, does not suffice to deprive it of its character as a 'legal question' and to deprive the Court of a competence expressly conferred on it by its Statute, and the Court cannot refuse to admit the legal character of a question which invites it to discharge an essentially judicial task.[2]

Discretionary Power to give Advisory Opinion :

It is to be noted that the power to give the advisory opinion conferred upon to the Court is discretionary. Article 65(1) of the Statute of the Court clearly states that 'the Court may give an advisory opinion'.[3] The use of the expression "may" denotes that the Court is not obliged to give an opinion, and can decline to do so, even where it would unquestionably have the right to comply with the request for an opinion. However, in principle the Court does not refuse such a request provided the opinion is sought appropriately from the organ or organization on any legal question. In the case of Reservations to the Genocide Convention the Court stated that "A reply to a request for an opinion should not, in principle, be refused".[4] However, the Court may decline to give an opinion, in the following cases :—

(1) Where the opinion given by the Court is likely to amount as a

---

1. The Judgment was delivered by the Court on July, 9, 2004.
2. Legality of the Threat or Use of Nuclear Weapons, ICJ Reports 1996 (1) p. 234 para 13.
3. Article 65, Para 1 of the Statute of the Court says that the Court may give an advisory opinion on any legal question at the request of whatever body may be authorized by or in accordance with the Charter of the United Nations to make such a request.
4. ICJ Reports (1951) p. 19.

decision of the Court in a contentious case. In Eastern Carelia case[1] the Permanent Court of International Justice declined to give an opinion on the ground that answering the question would be "substantially equivalent to deciding the dispute between the parties."[2]

(2) Where the Court considers that even on legal questions the opinion is likely to raise serious political issues. In the Certain Expenses case[3] the Court stated that "even if the question is a legal one, which the Court is undoubtedly competent to answer, it may nonetheless decline to do so" on 'compelling reasons'. One of such reasons is that the opinion given by the Court may have far reaching political implications.

(3) Where the Court does not have adequate information on the issue on which the opinion has been sought.

(4) If the Court considers that it lacks jurisdiction to give advisory opinion on a particular question. In the case concerning the Legality of the Use by a State of Nuclear Weapons in Armed conflict,[4] the Court refused to give the advisory opinion to the World Health Organisation, on the ground that the request for an advisory opinion submitted by the WHO does not relate to a question which arises "within the scope of (the) activities" of that Organisation. The Court observed that 'an essential condition of founding its jurisdiction in the present case is absent and that it cannot, accordingly, give the opinion requested'.

Although the Court may decline to give an advisory opinion on the basis of 'proprietary' it has to be cautious in doing so. The Court in principle does not decline to give an advisory opinion. It refuses only on 'compelling reasons'.[5] If the Court adopts the practice of not to give the opinion without any convincing reasons even on legal questions, its image is likely to be lowered down. It is to be noted that in the history of the International Court of Justice there has been no refusal to act upon a request for advisory opinion. The Court for the first time refused to give advisory opinion to the WHO in the case concerning the Legality of the Use by a State of Nuclear Weapons in Armed Conflict. It is relevant to mention the case in detail which is as follows :

---

1. PCIJ Series B, No. 5.
2. *Ibid.*, p. 29.
3. ICJ Reports (1962) at p. 155.
4. ICJ Reports, 1996.
5. In the Advisory Opinion given by the Court in Legal Consequences of the Separation of the Chago Archipelago from Mauritius in 1965 the Court elaborated the words compelling reasons on which it may decline to give the advisory opinion which are firstly, advisory proceedings are not suitable for determination of complex and disputed factual issues; secondly, the Court's response would not assist the General Assembly in the performance of its functions; thirdly, it would be inappropriate for the Court to re-examine a question already settled by the Arbitral Tribunal and fourthly, the question asked is related to pending bilateral dispute between two States (See Para 67 of the Advisory Opinion given in February 2019).

Advisory Opinion requested by the World Health Organisation (WHO) (1996)

World Health Organisation (WHO) on August 27, 1993 asked to the Court for the advisory opinion on the question "In view of the health and environmental effects, would the use of nuclear weapons by a State in war or other armed conflict be a breach of its obligations under International Law including the WHO Constitution ?"

The Court gave the advisory opinion on July 6, 1996. First of all, it considered that there are three conditions which must be satisfied in order to found the jurisdiction of the Court when a request for an advisory opinion is submitted to it by a specialized agency. Firstly, the agency requesting the opinion must be duly authorized under the Charter; secondly, the opinion requested must be on a legal question; and thirdly, the question must be one arising within the scope of the activities of the requesting agency.

The Court was of the opinion that the first two conditions had been met. With regard to the third, the Court found that according to the Constitution of the WHO, it is authorized to deal with the effects on health of the use of nuclear weapons, or of any other hazardous activity, and to take preventive measures aimed at protecting the health of population in the event of such weapons being used or such activities engaged in. The question put to the Court in the present case relates not to the effects of the use of nuclear weapons on health, but to the legality of the use of such weapons in view of their health and environmental effects. The Court pointed out that the Constitution of the WHO does not expressly refer to the legality of any activity hazardous to health and none of the functions of its dependant upon the legality of the situations upon which it must act. The Court observed that the question put to it in the present case relates not to the effects of the use of nuclear weapons on health, but to the legality of the use of such weapons in view of their health and environmental effects. The Court pointed out that whatever those effects might be, the competence of the WHO to deal with them is not dependent on the legality of the acts that caused them. In view of the Court, therefore, the question is not being capable of being considered as arising "within the scope of the activities of the WHO". The Court pointed out that international organisations are subjects of the International Law which do not, unlike States, possess a general competence. International Organisations are governed by the principle of 'speciality', that is to say, they are invested by the States which create them with powers, the limits of which are a function of the common interests whose promotion those States entrust to them. The Court is of the opinion, however, that to ascribe to the WHO the competence to address the legality of the use of nuclear weapons—even in view of their health and environment effects—would be tantamount to disregarding the principle of speciality.

The Court therefore concluded that the responsibilities of the World Health Organisation are necessarily, restricted to the sphere of public 'health', and that there is no doubt that question concerning the use of force, the regulations of armaments and disarmament do not come within the scope of the WHO, and therefore, the request for an advisory opinion by the WHO does not relate to a question which arises within the scope of activities of that Organisation. The request for an advisory opinion was therefore dismissed.

Nature of the Advisory Opinion :

The purpose of the advisory opinion is not to settle at least directly disputes between States, but to offer the legal advice to the organs and institutions requesting the opinion, and therefore, the opinion given by the Court is referred to as 'legal advice', it does not have any binding force, primarily because the objective of procedure contained in Articles 65-68 of the Statute of the Court is purely advisory. In the Peace Treaties case,[1] it was stated by the Court that the opinion is only of an advisory character and 'as such it has no binding force'. But if the organisation and other party, in a special agreement, assume the obligation to consider the advisory opinion of the Court as binding the provision of the Statute may be eluded. For instance, the General Convention on Privileges and Immunities of the United Nations lays down under section 30 that '......If a difference arises between the United Nations on the one hand and a member on the other hand, a request shall be made for an advisory opinion on any legal question involved in accordance with Article 96 of the Charter and Article 65 of the Statute of the Court. The opinion given by the Court shall be accepted as decisive by the parties.[2] The above may mean that the advisory opinion given by the Court shall be binding upon the parties. The opinion of the Court even in the absence of any special agreement is regarded as an authoritative statement of International Law as it comes from the highest judicial authority. The opinion of the Court is cited by the Court itself in the subsequent cases and also by the publicists and writers of International Law. Further, provisions of many instruments, other than the Charter and the Statute, characterize the opinion requested the Court as a 'decision' in relation to the dispute at issue; that is they confer binding force on the opinion for the parties to the dispute. Examples of such provisions may be found in some of the Headquarters Agreements between these organizations and the States on whose territory they carry out their activities;[3] general Conventions on the Privileges and Immunities of the United Nations, the Specialized Agencies and the International Atomic Energy Agency.[4]

The above implies that the Court's advisory opinions are to be regarded as

1. See Interpretation of Peace Treaties, ICJ Reports (1950) p. 71; Also see Advisory Opinion on the Reservations to the Convention on Genocide, ICJ Reports, 1951, p. 20; Certain expenses of the United Nations, op. cit., p. 168.
2. Also see Section 21 of the Headquarters Agreement between the United Nations and the United States of America of June 26, 1947.
3. Agreement between United Nations and Chile Regulating Conditions for the Operation of the Headquarters of the United Nations Economic Commission for Latin America of 1953 (Article XI, Sec. 21); Agreement between United Nations and Thiland Relating to the Headquarters of the Economic Commission for Asia and the Far East of 1954 (Article XIII, Sec 26); Agreement establishing a radio-isotope center in Cairo of 1967 (Article XVI, Sec. 39) between Egypt and International Atomic Energy Center.
4. *See* Article VIII Sec. 30 of the Convention on the Privileges and Immunities of the United Nations of 1946; Article XI, Section 33 of the Convention on the Privileges and Immunities of the Specialized Agencies of 1947 and Article X, Sec. 34 of the Agreement on the Privileges and Immunities of the International Atomic Energy Agency of 1959.

inherently capable of pertaining, of the nature of a judicial decision.[1] They often contribute to the clarification and development of International Law and thereby to the strengthening of peaceful relations between States.

LAW APPLIED BY THE COURT :

The Statute under Article 38, Part 1 lays down that the disputes which are submitted to it are decided 'in accordance with International Law'. The expression 'International Law' is elaborated under the Statute in the same para of Article 38 which says that the Court shall apply (a) international Conventions whether general or particular, as recognized by the contesting States ; (b) international custom, as evidence of a general practice accepted as law ; (c) the general principles of law recognized by civilized nations ; (d) judicial decisions and the teachings of the most highly qualified publicists of the various nations, as subsidiary means for the determination of rules of law. Further, Article 38, Para 2 of the Statute lays down that the Court has a power to decide a case *ex aequo et bono*, if the parties agree thereto. The principle *ex aequo et bono* is a principle which is recognized in some legal systems as a part of positive law. According to the phrase, the Court may decide the dispute equitably and not strictly according to law. But this principle shall be applied by the Court only when consent of the parties is acquired as to its application i.e., if the parties agree thereto. Although, so far no case has been decided by the Court on this principle, in a few cases, one of the contesting States wanted the application of this principle.

The procedure followed by the Court in contentious cases is defined in the Statute, and in the Rules of Court adopted on April 14, 1978. The proceedings include a written phase, in which the parties file and exchange pleadings, and an oral phase consisting of public hearings at which agents and counsel address the Court. After the oral proceedings, the Court deliberates in camera and then delivers its judgment at a public sitting. As the Court has two official languages (English and French) everything written or said in one is translated into the other.

It is submitted that provisions relating to law which the Court applies, suffer from many defects. For instance, the Court applies customary rules of International Law, but what are the customary rules is a question which is difficult to answer. If one party in a case before the Court seeks solution on the basis of the existing customary law, and the other party objects to it, it becomes difficult for the Court to find a solution. This led to the conclusion that, to some extent, there exists subjectivity which is not desirable. Further, United Nations law, which is being practised by the States in their international relations did not find place under Article 38 of the Statute. Resolutions and declarations of the General Assembly and of the Security Council, particularly those which are referred to as 'law making' must find place under Article 38(1), at least as subsidiary means for the determination of the rules of law, ahead of judicial decisions and the teaching of the publicists.

---

1. *See* Roberts Ago, 'Binding Advisory Opinions of the International Court of Justice', AJIL 85 (1991) p. 439.

JUDGMENT OF THE COURT :

It is one of the most important functions of the Court to resolve the dispute placed before it. The obligation to decide the case was referred to by the Court in the Libya/Malta (Application for Permission to Intervene) case wherein it was noted by the Court that it was the duty of the Court 'to give the fullest decision it may in the circumstances of each case.[1] The decision of the Court according to Article 59 of the Statute is binding 'between the parties and in respect of that particular case'. Thus, the judgment of the Court is binding to the contesting parties only, and therefore it does not create precedence for the subsequent cases. However, in subsequent cases, it is difficult for the Court to ignore the earlier judgment of the Court. Judgment of the Court, in subsequent cases is respected. If the judgment is not unanimous, the Court decides the case on the majority of the judges present.[2] In the event of an equality of votes, the President or the judge who acts in his place exercises casting vote.[3]

The judgment of the Court is final and without appeal.[4] The jugement shall state the reasons on which it is based.[5] It shall contain the names of the judges who have taken part in the decision.[6] If the judgment does not represent in whole or in part the unanimous opinion of the judges, any judge shall be entitled to deliver a separate opinion.[7] The judgment is signed by the President and by the Registrar. It is read in open Court after having been given due notice to the agents.[8]

After the Court has given a judgment, the only procedure available to a party is to make a request for an interpretation of the judgment in the event of dispute as to its meaning or scope. Subject of a request for interpretation of the judgment rendered by it may be either on preliminary objections or on the merits of the dispute.[9] Further, judgment once rendered by the Court may be revised on an application for revision.[10] In the Case Concerning the Continental Shelf between Tunisia and Libya, Tunisia applied to the Court on July 27, 1984 for the revision and interpretation of the 1982 Judgment of the Court. The Court on December 10, 1985 rendered an unanimous decision wherein it found inadmissible the request for revision of its judgment.[11] However, it found admissible the request for interpretation of the judgment related to the most

1. I.C.J. Reports (1984) pp. 3, at p. 25. Also see Judge Weeramantry's Dissenting Opinion in the East Timor case. (I.C.J. Reports, (1995), pp. 90, 158.)
2. Article 55 Para 1.
3. Article 55 Para 2.
4. Article 60.
5. Article 56 Para 1.
6. Article 56 Para 2.
7. Article 57.
8. Article 58.
9. See the Request for Interpretation of judgment on 11 June, 1998 in the case concerning the Land and Maritime Boundary between Cameroon and Nigeria (Cameroon and Nigeria), Preliminary Objections (Nigeria and Camroon). In the above case the Court, for the first time, was called upon to rule on a request for interpretation of a judgment on preliminary objections. On March 25, 1999, the Court declared inadmissible Nigeria's request for interpretation.
10. Article 61.
11. Continental Shelf (*Tunisia* v. *Libya*) Case ICJ Reports (1985), p. 192.

westernly point of the Gulf of Gabes. It is to be noted that application for revision and interpretation may be given only when it is based upon the discovery of some fact of such a nature as to be a decisive factor, which fact was, when the judgment was given, unknown to the Court and also to the party claiming for revision.

ENFORCEMENT OF THE JUDGMENT :

All the members of the United Nations are required to comply with the decisions of the Court in accordance with Article 94, Para 1 of the Charter. A State party to the Statute but not a member of the United Nations is also required to do so as it is one of the conditions for becoming a party to the Statute which is imposed in accordance with a resolution of the General Assembly. However, the Statute does not contain a provision guaranteeing the execution of the decisions of the Court against a recalcitrant State. If any party to a case before the Court fails to perform its obligations under a judgment of the Court ; the other party may bring the matter before the Security Council in accordance with Article 94, Para 2 of the Charter. The Security Council is empowered by the Charter to 'make recommendations or decide upon measures to be taken to give effect to the judgment'. The above provisions do not impose upon the Security Council the obligation to enforce the judgment of the Court against recalcitrant party. It provides for a procedure of appeal in case of non-compliance with the judgment of the Court. The Security Council has a discretion to choose between two different actions : either to make recommendations, or to decide upon measures to be taken to give effect to the Judgment of the Court.

If the Security Council decides to make recommendations, it may recommend to a party to comply with the judgment of the Court. But in making a recommendation under Article 94, Para 2, the Security Council is not bound to conform with the judgment of the Court with which the party concerned did not comply. The Security Council may recommend a solution of the dispute totally different from that decided by the Court. It may mean that the Council shall enforce its own recommendation instead of enforcing the judgment of the Court. By having recource to the Security Council under Article 94, Para 2, the party places the Court under the control of the Council. Such recourse may have the effect of transforming a legal dispute, decided by the Court in accordance with existing law, into an issue to be settled new by the Council according to political principles. Further, the system for the enforcement of the judgment by the Council is not appreciable because of the voting procedure also. While the party which does not comply with the decision of the Court, if happens to be a member of the Council, is not excluded from voting in the decision by which the Council makes the recommendation for the settlement of the dispute brought before it under Article 94, Para 2, the aggrieved State, whose right under the judgment of the Court has been openly violated, is excluded, from voting, if it is not a member of the Council. Further, if the State which does not comply witn the decision of the Court happens to be a permanent member of the Security Council or its client State, it can prevent, by its veto, any recommendation of the Council not favourable to it.

In case the Security Council decides upon measures to be taken to give effect to the judgment of the Court, it has again a choice between two kinds of action, i.e., measures which may be taken either under Article 41 or 42 of the Charter. But again, decision to this effect may be made by a vote of nine members including the concurring votes of the permanent members. It means the decision of the Council has to cross the barrier of the 'veto'. Hence, the judgment of the Court cannot be enforced against permanent members of the Council or their client States. Further, action under Chapter VII of the Charter can be taken only if international peace and security is endangered.

Nicaragua's Claim for Reparation :

In the case between Nicaragua and the United States of America such a contingency arose. When the Court in 1986 decided that the United States had breached International Law by having mined Nicaraguan waters and by supporting the so-called Contra Guerillas, and therefore it must pay reparation to Nicaragua for causing damages, and later, when Nicaragua brought the matter before the Security Council for the enforcement of the Judgment, it was vetoed by the United States, and thus the Judgment of the Court could not be enforced.[1] The attitude on the part of the United States sets a dangerous precedent in International Law. It has denied the basic mechanism upon which the operation of the International Court of Justice depends.

Although Nicaragua's claim to reparations was pending before the Court, it did not in fact receive it. On September 12, 1991 Nicaragua informed the Court that it has 'decided to renounce all further rights of action based on the case and did not wish to go on with the proceedings and requested that an order be officially made recording the discontinuance of the proceedings and directing the removal of the case from the list. Consequently, the President of the Court made an order recording the discontinuance of the proceedings and directing the removal of the case from the Court's list.

If the Court has to be made meaningful, adequate procedure for enforcing the judgment of the Court has to be found out.

Provisional Measures taken by the Court.—Article 41 (Para 1) of the Statute of the ICJ provides that the Court shall have the power to indicate, if it considers that circumstances so require any provisional measures which ought to be taken to preserve the respective rights of either party. Notice of the measures suggested shall henceforth be given to the parties and to the Security Council, pending the final decision. The power of the Court to indicate provisional measures under the above Article has its object *i.e.*, the preservation of the respective rights of the parties in a case, pending its decision on the merit. Such measures are also taken by the Court mainly to prevent the aggravation of the dispute and to prevent irreparable prejudice to human life on the request of one of the parties. The Court may exercise this power only if it satisfied the

1. *See* the draft resolution of July 31, 1986 put forward by Congo, Ghana, Madagascar, Trinidad and Tobago and UAE (S/18250). The vote in the Council was 11 in favour to 1 against (United States) with 3 abstentions. Again on October 28.1986, a draft resolution was vetoed by the United States. (S/18428)......Earlier the General Assembly on January 3, 1986 adopted a resolution by which it called for full and immediate compliance of the Judgment, Resolution 41/31 of January 3, 1986.

rights asserted by the party, requesting such measures are at least plausible.[1] In the past provisional measures have been taken by the Court in many cases.[2] The Court on May 18, 2017 ordered provisional measures in the Jadhav case (India and Pakistan). Jadhav, an Indian national, a former Naval Officer who was sentenced to death by a Pakistani military court for alleged espionage activities. The Court in its order on Provisional Measures directed Pakistan not to carry out the sentence and report to the Court what steps it had taken to comply with the provisional measures indicated by the Court.

THIRD STATE AND THE DECISION OF THE COURT :

When a third State considers that 'it has an interest of a legal nature which may be affected by the decision in the case, it may submit a request to the Court to be permitted to intervene'. However, the Court is empowered to decide upon the request. It may allow or deny permission to a third State to intervene. In the Continental Shelf (*Libya* v. *Malta*) case,[3] Italy applied for permission to intervene in the proceedings of the case, but the permission was rejected as it was opposed by the contending parties to the case.[4] However, the Court observed that it cannot wholly put aside the question of the legal interest of Italy, and therefore the decision of the Court must be confined to the interest of the parties,[5] and ensured the interest of Italy. In Continental Shelf Case (*Tunisia* v. *Libya*),[6] the Court again rejected the permission to Malta to intervene in the proceedings of the case.

In the case concerning the Land, Island and Maritime Frontier Dispute (El Salvador/Honduras) Nicaragua had shown interest of a legal nature which may be affected by part of the Judgment of the Chamber. The Court decided that Nicaragua is permitted to intervene in the case pursuant to Article 62 of the Statute, to the extent, in the manner and for the purpose set out in the present Judgment, but not further or otherwise.[7]

EVALUATION OF THE COURT :

The Court was established to achieve one of the purposes of the United Nations, i.e., to adjust or settle international disputes or situations which might lead to a breach of the peace. A question arises as to how far the Court has been successful in achieving the object ? It is to be noted that by the end of 2019, 178 contentious cases have been entered in the general list for the consideration of the Court since its inception. A few of them have been removed from the list, and in some cases the Court declared that it could not adjudicate because of the lack of jurisdiction. Besides these, 27 advisory opinions have been delivered by the Court from time to time. One would agree with the view that the number

1. See Application of the International Convention on the Elimination of All Forms of Racial Dissemination (*Qatar* v. *UAE*) ICJ Reports 2018 (II) pp. 421-22.
2. As of 1989, the ICJ had dealt with twelve requests for the indication of provisional measures of protection.
3. ICJ Reports (1984), p. 3.
4. *Ibid* p. 27.
5. *Ibid*, p. 25.
6. ICJ Report (1986) p. 3.
7. Judgment was delivered on September 13, 1990.

of contentious cases and the advisory opinions is not great considering the length of time during which the Court has been functioning. The above figure implies that the States are reluctant to submit the disputes to the Court. This attitude has been adopted by them in two ways. Firstly, States have not made declarations for accepting the compulsory jurisdiction of the Court. They have regarded it political and psychological. Even those States which have deposited declarations in this regard have done so with reservations of their own making. The reservation as to matters essentially within their domestic jurisdiction has been more sweeping and has weakened the Court. Secondly, bilateral treaties containing a clause for the submission of disputes to the Court are only in numbers. States do not include the clause in their treaties. General Assembly in the year 1974 had suggested that States study the possibility of accepting, with as few reservations as possible, the compulsory jurisdiction of the Court, and that the attention of States should be drawn to the advantage of inserting in treaties a clause providing for submission to the Court of disputes arising from the interpretation or application of such treaties. But the suggestion has not changed the attitude of the States.

Main reasons for hesitating to submit the dispute to the Court are, firstly, judges of the Court have not always been impartial. There is a belief prevalent that the Court is not the appropriate place for the settlement of disputes of which the solution is primarily of juridical character. Secondly, procedure of the Court is complicated, time consuming[1] and expensive,[2] and thirdly, States are not prepared to submit a dispute to the Court whose judgments are enforced by the Security Council, a political organ of the United Nations.

It is submitted that the Statute of the Court was drafted in 1945 and it contained most of the provisions of the Statute of the Permanent Court of International Justice which was drafted in 1920. Since then, especially after the Second World War, remarkable advances have been made in virtually every sector of international organizations except in judicial sector. The result is that some of the provisions at present have become obsolete and inadequate in view of the totally changed structure of the world community. Moreover, circumstances under which the Statute was drafted have undergone a drastic change at present. Legal system including law and the Court is required to keep pace with the changed situation and circumstances, and if it does not change as one finds in the case of International Court of Justice, it is bound to collapse. If the functioning of the Court has to be made relevant, drastic reforms and amendments should be made in its composition, jurisdiction, the law which it applies and the procedure for the enforcement of the judgments so that it may fulfil the aspirations of all the States on an equitable basis. Unless and until

1. The Court normally takes about three years' time in deciding the contentious cases, and about two years' time in delivering the advisory opinion. However, in the case concerning Dumitry Mazuln, the advisory opinion was given by the Court within six months' time.
2. A State needs several million dollars to take a case before the Court. Boundary litigation especially those involving maritime territories which are the majority of African international disputes at the ICJ involves exceptionally high open and hidden costs. There would usually be the need for experts on geography, cartography, oceanography, geologists and other specialists in addition to costs of exhibits, memorials and lawyers. (See Gbenga Oduntan, op. cit., p. 738 f.n. 78.

reforms by making amendments are made in the Statute, future of the Court would remain grim.

Creation of a Trust Fund :

In recent past an attempt has been made by the Secretary-General of the United Nations to encourage the parties to bring their cases before the Court. On November 1, 1989 he announced for the establishment of a 'Trust Fund'[1] to provide financial assistance to States for expenses incurred in connection with (i) a dispute submitted to the Court by way of a specified agreement, or (ii) the execution of a judgment of the Court resulting from such special agreement. Its main purpose is to assist parties with cases before the Court who lack funds for legal expertise. Requests for Assistance from the Fund are to be referred to a panel of experts who advise the Secretary-General. The term of references specify that the fund will be financed out of voluntary State contributions. Contributions are also accepted from corporations, foundations, organisations with legal interests. By the year 2002 trust has been utilized only in four cases.

Chad was the first country to receive the assistance under the scheme. Undoubtedly, to provide assistance to States so that they may bring their cases before the Court is a good idea but, it is quite likely that States would still prefer not to bring their cases before the Court rather than to ask for funds, as it may lower the image and dignity of the States.

Since the fund is made available only in those categories of cases which are submitted to the Court by joint agreement of the parties, the dignity factor may not be as relevant as the settlement of a dispute. Other category of cases where financial assistance may be provided are those where one or both the States are unable to bring the case before the Court because of the lack of funds or expertise.

ROLE OF THE COURT IN THE DEVELOPMENT OF INTERNATIONAL LAW :

Decisions of the Court reveal that it has played a significant role in the development of International Law. It has dealt with major questions in conformity with International Law, and made pronouncements thereupon. For instance, it has delivered judgments on disputes concerning land frontiers and maritime boundaries, territorial sovereignty, the non-use of force, non-interference in the internal affairs of States, diplomatic relations, hostage-taking, the right of asylum, nationality, guardianship, rights of passage and economic rights. In addition to the above the Court has given advisory opinions, concerning *inter alia* admission to United Nations membership, reparation for injuries suffered in the service of the United Nations, territorial status of South-West Africa (Namibia) and Western Sahara, expenses of certain United Nations operations, applicability of the United Nations Headquarters Agreement, the status of human rights reapporteurs and the legality of the threat or use of nuclear weapons.

While dealing with the above and other subjects, the Court contributed towards the development of International Law in two directions. Firstly, it

1. For the text of the announcement see IJIL Vol. 29 (1989) p. 508.

interpreted and applied the existing rules in such a way so as to resolve issues affecting the life of nations. For instance, it has put to an end to a long standing controversy which had aroused considerable interest in the maritime States of the World. It has condemned decolonisation and reaffirmed the principle of self-determination as provided under the United Nations' Charter. The Court has stated that the doctrine of non-intervention is to be treated as a sanctified absolute rule of law. Secondly, in those cases where no rule existed in International Law or where the Court was faced with the new situations, it evolved certain new principles. For instance, in the Reparation case it stated that the United Nations Organisation is an international person. The Organisation has been exercising and enjoying functions and rights which can only be explained on the basis of the possession of a large measure of international personality and the capacity to operate upon an international plane. Thus, the Organization can bring claim in respect of injury to the United Nations caused by the injury to the agents. The Court has also dealt and established the rule regarding the conditions of admissions of States to membership and competence of the General Assembly regarding admission of a State to the United Nations.

But the small number of cases that were brought before the Court till eightees invariably indicate that the Court was not fully utilised by the States for settling international disputes and thus one of the purposes of the United Nations i.e., the adjustment or settlement of international disputes or situations which might lead to a breach of the peace, suffered a set back. The Court did not have enough work and had no pending case. But in the recent years the trend has changed especially after the end of the cold war. It is having an unprecedented amount of work. Its dockets are full and it was never so busy in its history. While 10 cases appeared on the Court's list in 1994 and 12 in 1998, it was 25 at the end of 1999—a new record in the annals of international justice. While in 2000, 24 cases were pending before the Court it was 12 in 2005 and 15 in 2017. It is so mainly because of the following reasons—

(1) Change in the Attitude of States :

Attitude of the States towards the submission of the their disputes to the Court has considerably changed. The United States which had withdrawn its declaration accepting the compulsory jurisdiction of the Court and which had refused to appear before the Court in the Nicaragua case decided to appear in the Aerial Incident case[1] involving the international responsibility of the United States for the shooting down of Iran Air Flight 655 by the USS Vincennes in the Parsian Gulf during the Iran-Iraq war, when the United States was taking an active containment role in petrolling gulf waters.[2] Further, Asian and African States which used to distrust the Court, have brought many disputes before the Court.

1. *See* Keith Highet,'The Peace Palace Heats Up : the World Court in Business Again, AJIL Vol. 86 (1991) p. 650.
2. Iran which earlier did not appear in the two cases before the Court—Anglo-Iranian Oil Company cases and US Hostages case, sought the justice through the Court in Aerial Incident case.

(2) Constitution of Special Chamber :

The Court itself revised its rules to enable the States to form chambers of the Court[1] for dealing with particular categories of cases ; for example, labour cases and cases relating to transit and communications. In 1993 the Court decided to form a Special Chamber for deciding the cases relating to environment. Chambers of the Court consists of normally three to four judges as the Court may determine but the judgment of the Chamber is considered as rendered by the Court.[2] The States have on many occasions utilized this procedure for the adjudication of their disputes. For the first time the Court was asked to constitute a Special Chamber by the U.S.A. and Canada in the Gulf of Maine case.[3] The Court decided to agree to the request to constitute the Special Chamber and it held elections for the Judges on January 15, 1982. Similarly, in the case Concerning Frontier Dispute between Burkina Faso and Mali, a Special Chamber of five judges was constituted by the Court on April 3, 1985 on the request of the parties to deal with the case.[4] No doubt all the judges of the Court possess the recognised competence of International Law and they therefore are the experts of general principles of International Law. However, sometimes they are not able to resolve the specific issues adequately because of the lack of special competency. In the Chamber procedure disputes are decided by the experts and the judges who have special competency, which has been welcomed by the parties.

(3) Creation of a Trust Fund :

The announcement of the Secretary-General Javier Perez de Cuellar in the General Assembly on November 1, 1989 that a 'Trust Fund' will be established to assist the parties in settling the dispute through the International Court of Justice has also encouraged the parties to bring their disputes before the Court since many disputes could not be brought before the Court for want of resourse and expertise. It is quite likely that States would still prefer not to bring their cases before the Court rather than to ask for funds, as it may lower the image and dignity of the States. Since, the fund is available mainly in those categories of cases which are submitted to the Court by joint agreement of the parties, the dignity factor may not be as relevant as the settlement of a dispute.[5] Other categories of cases where financial assistance may be given are those where one or both the parties are unable to bring the case before the Court because of the lack of funds or expertise. Chad was the first country to receive the assistance under the scheme.

The Court no doubt possesses the competency and potentiality to develop

1. The Court in 1978 revised its rules by introducing into the Rules of the Court a provision that the President of the Court shall ascertain their views regarding the formation of a Chamber to deal with a particular case.
2. *See* Article 27 of the Statute of the Court.
3. ICJ Reports 1984, p. 246.
4. ICJ Reports 1986, p. 554, Later, the United States and Italy submitted a case Elletronica Sicula, S.P.A. to a Chamber (ICJ Reports 1991, p. 15).
5. However, creation of the Trust Fund has not been very successful due to fund's meagre resources, lack of publicity, lack of regular contribution and because of its strict conditions for eligibility.

International Law further and to settle the disputes of the States, but it would be possible only when the States would bring their disputes to resolve their conflicts. Possession of competency to do something itself is not enough. That has to be shown in the decision where the disputes are brought before it. In the recent past, many Afro-Asian States have submitted their disputes and hence the Court at present is busier than ever in resolving them. The monitor of cases which it has been handling may be more in comparison to earlier years, but the number is too meagre when it is compared to disputes which the States have in their international relations with other States. The success of the Court will continue to be limited as long as States are not willing to submit their disputes to it for decision either by making a declaration for accepting the compulsory jurisdiction of the Court or by inserting a clause in their treaties that any dispute arising under it shall be referred to the Court. In order to prepare the States for doing so, drastic reforms are required to be made by making appropriate amendments[1] in the provisions of the Statute relating to composition, jurisdiction, the law which it applies and in the procedure for the enforcement of the judgments. The Statute of the Court was drafted in 1945 and it contained most of the provisions of the Statute of the Permanent Court of International Justice which was drafted in 1920. Since then, especially after the Second World War, numerable advances have been made virtually in every sector of international organisations except in judicial sector. The result is that some of the provisions at present have become obsolete and inadequate in view of the totally changed structure of the World community. Moreover, circumstances under which the Statute was first drafted have undergone a drastic change at present. Legal system including law and Court is required to keep pace with the changed situation and circumstances. Although the idea of making amendments in the Statute of the Court might appear to be absurd when the World was divided into two powerful blocks, feasibility of such amendments has increased with the end of cold war. As long as it is not done to fulfil the aspirations of all the States on an equitable basis, it would be indeed utopian to call to the International Court of Justice as World Court.

---

1. The Statute of the Court under Article 69 provides for the amendments to the Statute.

Chapter 10

SPECIALIZED AGENCIES

The United Nations has been assigned by the Charter, the general task of promoting progress and international co-operation in economic, social, health, cultural, educational and related matters. However, it was contemplated that these tasks will be mainly fulfilled not by the organs of the United Nations, but by autonomous international organizations established by inter-governmental agreements, outside the United Nations. However, they shall be brought into relationship with the United Nations by concluding agreements with them. Specialized agencies, therefore, are those inter-governmental agreements which have been brought into relationship with the United Nations. Economic and Social Council has been authorized to enter into such agreements which are required to be approved by the General Assembly. These agreements are treaties concluded between the United Nations represented by the Economic and Social Council and the General Assembly on the one hand and the international organisations whose agencies are brought into relationship with the United Nations by these agreements on the other hand. They perform a number of functions in the economic, social, cultural, educational and health fields.

The Charter does not recognise these specialized agencies as organs of the United Nations. However, they may be characterised at least as 'indirect organs',[1] because these agencies established by inter-governmental agreements and having international responsibilities as defined in their basic instruments, have been brought into relationship with the United Nations.[2] The General Assembly and the Economic and Social Council possess a number of rights in relation to specialized agencies. Firstly, the activities of these specialized agencies are 'co-ordinated' by the Economic and Social Council upon recommendations on the part of the Organisation.[3] Secondly, according to Article 17, Para 3, the General Assembly is authorised to 'consider and approve' the financial and budgetary arrangements of these agencies and to examine their administrative budgets with a view to making recommendations to them. These provisions have put the specialized agencies into a special position. They are not the organs of the United Nations yet they have relationship with the United Nations. However, in spite of this relationship, the specialized agencies are independent international organizations. Membership in the United Nations is not an indispensable condition for membership in the specialized agencies. The instruments defining the relationship are the individual agreements between the United Nations and the specialized agencies. There are seventeen specialized

1. Kelsen, 'Law of United Nations', p. 146.
2. Article 57 of the U.N. Charter.
3. Article 58 of the U.N. Charter.

agencies of the United Nations which are as follows :—

(1) International Labour Organisation (ILO) :

ILO was established after the First World War on April 19, 1919 as an autonomous institution by the Treaty of Versailles and was associated with the League of Nations. Its original Constitution formed part of the Treaty of Versailles. On October 9, 1946 the amending instrument was signed at Montreal which is cited as the ILO Instrument of Amendment, 1946. ILO became the first specialized agency associated with the United Nations when the agreement was approved by the General Assembly on December 14, 1946. The ILO has 186 member States : 185 of the 193 U.N. member States and the Cook Islands.

The ILO consists of : (a) International Labour Conference known as General Conference, (b) Governing Body and (c) an International Labour Office (Secretariat). International Labour Conference is the supreme body which meets annually at ILO headquarters in Geneva. Each national delegation is composed of two Government delegates, one employer's delegate and one worker's delegate. The Governing Body (Executive Council) normally meets three or four times in a year at Geneva. It elects the Director-General of the International Labour Office (Secretariat) in Geneva which is composed of the permanent Secretariat and professional staff. The Conference, the Governing Body and the Office make up ILO.

Each member is represented in the General Conference by four delegates of whom two are representatives of the Government, one is of employers and one is of employees. Except for the government representatives, delegates vote as individuals. The General Conference adopts Conventions or recommendations by a two-thirds vote of the members. The main function of the Conference is to lay down the minimum standards of working and living conditions of workers. The Conference holds election of the members of the Governing body. It also approves annual budget of the Organisation. The Conference examines reports from the member States regarding implementation of Conventions and recommendations adopted by the Conference.

The Governing Body which is known as the executive organ of the ILO follows tripartite principle. Half of its members are government representatives and remaining half are equally divided between the employers and workers. The Governing Body consists of 56 members which normally meets three or four times in a year at Geneva. It elects its own chairman and vice-chairman for a period of one year. It also elects the Director-General of the International Labour Office (secretariat).

The International Labour Office is headed by the Director-General and is staffed by experts drawn from different countries of the World. The Office is located at Geneva but its branch offices are in many other countries. The chief responsibility of the Office is to prepare documents and bring out publications. It also makes studies and researches on different problems connected with labour.

The Conference, Governing Body and the Office make up ILO.—The main objectives of the ILO are to examine and consider all international economic and financial policies and measures so that all human beings may pursue both their material well-being and their spiritual development in conditions of freedom and dignity based on economic security and equal opportunity. It also considers all the relevant economic and financial factors and takes decisions and makes recommendations which it considers appropriate.

The functions of the ILO include the development and promotion of standards for national legislation to protect and improve working conditions and standards of living. The ILO also provides technical assistance in social policy and administration and in workforce training and foster cooperative organisations and rural industries. It also compiles labour statistics and conducts research on the social problems of international competition, unemployment and under employment, labour and industrial relations and technical change. The ILO has been working for the development of labour standards and conditions throughout the World since last ninety years. It has drafted scores of Conventions and recommendations, collectively designated as International Labour Code, covering a variety of subjects, such as relating to employment, unemployment, conditions of employment, employment of women and children, vocational training, industrial health and safety, social security, industrial relations, maritime labour, immigration, freedom of association and trade union rights. ILO was awarded the Noble Prize for Peace in 1969 in recognition of its activities.

In the first decade the ILO was primarily concerned with legislative and research efforts with defining and promoting proper minimum standards of labour legislation for adoption of member states. During the Worldwide economic depression of the 1930 the ILO sought ways to combat widespread unemployment. After the Second World War, the ILO addressed itself to new issues such as social problems created by the liberalisation of international trade, the problem of child labour and the relationship between working conditions and the environment.

Efforts of the ILO to protect the rights of children and young persons as an essential prerequisite for social justice has been commendable since its inception. Over the years, the ILO has adopted 12 major Conventions which either prohibit the employment of children or set basic conditions above a certain age when they may be permitted to work in different sectors of employment. ILO in 1990 launched a major global offensive by establishing the International Programme on the Elimination of Child Labour (IPEC). The Programme provides, upon the request of individuals, technical advisory services focusing on the worst abuses; hazardous work, forced labour, street children, girls and the employment of children who are less than 13 years old. The most effective step was taken by the ILO when it adopted on June 17, 1999 in Geneva, a landmark Convention on Worst Forms of Child Labour Convention (ILO Convention No. 182). The Convention came into force on November 19, 2000. The Convention applies to all children under the age of 18, called for countries, debt bondage and child prostitution and also on forced recruitment of children in armed conflict. The Convention also required ratifying countries to provide support for improving children from dangerous labour and ensure access to education or vocational training.

ILO Conventions are juridical instruments similar to treaties. Member

States are required to submit them to the competent legislative authorities to decide whether or not the Convention should be put into effect. Although ILO cannot enforce States to accept its standards, it does keep watch over the way Conventions are applied in the countries which have ratified them. Member States are required to make regular reports to ILO regarding the adaptation of standards and the ways in which the ratified Conventions are put into effect.

In 1969 the ILO received the Nobel Peace Prize for improving fraternity and peace among nations, pursuing decent work and justice for workers and providing technical assistance to other developing nations.

(2) Food and Agriculture Organisation (FAO) :

The FAO came into being on October 16, 1945 at a Conferences on food and Agriculture at Rome convened by the United Nations. Later, it became a specialized agency when the agreement was approved by the General Assembly in December, 1946. At present FAO is the largest of U.N. specialized agencies. As of August, 2013 it had 194 member States. FAO was established with the main objectives : (a) to raise level of nutrition and standard of living; (b) to secure improvements in the efficiency of the production and distribution of all food and agricultural products from farms, forests and fisheries; (c) to provide technical assistance to members that seek assistance; and (d) to eliminate hunger.

FAO works through a Conference, a Council and a Secretariat. The Conference, a supreme body of FAO is convened ones in two years to define FAO's policy and approve its budget. The Council, an executive body, consists of representatives of 49 member States and is elected by the Conference. Members of the Council serve three year rotating terms. The Council acting on behalf of all FAO members, is accountable to the Conference. In the period between Conference sessions, the Council is FAO's leading body. Operations of the Secretariat are managed by the Director-General who is appointed by the Conference and is the head of the Secretariat.

The FAO has performed various activities in different directions. In 1950, it assumed the responsibility for the World Agricultural Census and was instrumental in drafting the International Wheat Agreement, to which most of the major wheat producing countries have adhered. In 1960, it launched a Freedom from Hunger Campaign. In 1963, United Nations and FAO jointly established the World Food Programme (WFP) 'to explore the possibilities of stimulating economic and social development through aid in the form of food.' In 1974 World Food Conference was held in Rome during a period of food shortages in the southern Sahara which prompted the FAO to promote programs relating to World Food security, including helping small farmers to implement low-costs projects to enhance productivity. FAO has also played a major role in the U.N.'s technical assistance work. It has aided in a variety of problems such as animal and plant disease control, storage of grains, conservation and prevention of soil erosion and fishery production and conservation. World Food Day is observed every year on October 16—the day FAO came into existence.

(3) United Nations Educational, Scientific and Cultural Organisation (UNESCO) :

The UNESCO came into being on November 4, 1946 and was brought into relationship with the United Nations when its Constitution was approved by the General Assembly in December, 1946. The purpose of UNESCO as defined in its Constitution, *i.e.*, to contribute to peace and security by promoting collaboration among the nations through education, science and culture in order to further universal respect for justice, for the rule of law, and for the human rights and fundamental freedoms for all. Its permanent headquarters are in Paris (France).

UNESCO works through a General Conference, an Executive Board and a Secretariat. The General Conference, the highest ruling body, composed of representatives of member countries, meets biennially to decide the policy, programme and budget of the Organisation. Each member State can appoint not more than five delegates but has one vote in the General Conference. The General Conference determines the main lines of the work of the Organisation. It considers the annual reports submitted by the members. The General Conference elects the members of the Executive Board and with their consent appoints the Director-General of the Secretariat. The Executive Board, consisting of 58 members elected by the General Conference meets at least twice a year and responsible for supervising the execution of the programme adopted by the General Conference. The members of the Executive Board are elected for a term of three years and are eligible for re-election. The Secretariat, headed by the Director General, carries out the programme. The Director General is appointed by the General Conference on the recommendation of the Executive Board for a period of six years. The nine members of the staff are appointed by the Director-General.

UNESCO's programme has two main aspects : 'permanent activities' of general interest to all member States, such as the exchange of information and documentation, assistance to international non-governmental organizations and the preparation of international Conventions, and 'special activities' designed to deal with specific problems in particular States. This programme is broken down into six main areas of activity : education, natural science, social and human sciences, culture, mass communication and international exchanges.

UNESCO's initial emphasis was on assisting member States in developing their educational programmes at all levels to eliminate illiteracy and to extend free education. UNESCO also seeks to encourage the free exchange of ideas and knowldge by organising confernces and provding clearing house and exchange service. UNESCO's programme also included the elimination of poverty, illiteracy and under-development.

UNESCO's activities was criticised by the United States and other countries for its alleged anti-Western approach to cultural issues and the sustained expansion of its budget. The issue prompted the United States to withdraw from the Organisation in 1984, and the United Kingdom and Singapore withdrew in 1985. However, United Kingdom rejoined UNESCO in 1997 and the United States followed suit in 2003. In November, 2011, Palestine was admitted as a full member of the UNESCO. This brings the total number of UNESCO member States to 195.

(4) World Health Organisation (WHO) :

The creation of a specialized institution in the field of health was proposed at the United Nations Conference on International Organisation at San Francisco in 1945. Later, in 1946, an International Health Conference, convened by the Economic and Social Council was held in New York wherein the Constitution of WHO was drafted and signed. The Constitution came into force on April 7, 1948. Although WHO inherited specific tasks relating to epidemic control, quarantine measures, and drug standardization from the Health Organisation of the League of Nations set up in 1923 and the International Office of Public Health established in 1909, WHO was given a broad mandate under its Constitution. By the end of 2015 WHO had 194 member States, *i.e.,* all the members of the United Nations, Cook Islands and Nive. The objective of WHO is "the attainment by all peoples of the highest possible level of health", Health, as defined in the WHO Constitution is "a state of complete physical, mental and social well being and not merely the absence of disease or infirmity." WHO accordingly performs a wide range of functions.

WHO has three main organs : (1) World Health Assembly, consisting of the delegates of the member States of the Organisation is the supreme body. The Assembly meets annually to determine the policies and programmes of WHO. (2) The Executive Board, comprising of 34 members are elected by the World Health Assembly, for three years term. The Board is a technical and non-political organ which meets at least twice a year to give effect to its decisions. (3) The Secretariat which has regional offices and field staff throughout the World is headed by a Director-General who is appointed by the Assembly. The Headquarters of the WHO is located in Geneva, but the activities of the Organisation have been largely decentralized to six regional organizations.

The work of the WHO may be divided into three categories : (1) It provides a central clearing house and research services. It has established a codified set of international sanitary regulations, for example, designed to standardize quarantine measures without interfering unnecessarily with trade and air travels across national boundaries; (2) It sponsors measures for the control of epidemic and endemic disease by promoting mass campaigns involving nationwide vaccination programmes, instruction on the use of antibiotics and insecticides, assistance in providing pure-water supplies and sanitation systems and health education for people in rural communities; and (3) It encourages efforts to strengthen and expand the public health administrations of member States.

WHO has performed a commendable work in different fields related to international health work. It has given major assistance to many countries in the fight against malaria, tuberculosis, poliomyelitis, veneral diseases, influenza, small pox, leprosy, yaws, trachoma (an eye disease) and many other communicable diseases.

WHO played a crucial role in the prevention and eradication of Covid-19 pandemic which originated from the city of Wuhan (China) in December 2019 and in a very short-time spread all over the World. Most affected countries are

U.S.A., Brazil, U.K., Italy, Spain and India. More than 13 million people have been affected by the Covid virus and more than 1 million people lost their lives in a very short span of time.

WHO declared Covid-19 as a global pandemic.[1] It helped the countries to prepare and respond and set up the Covid-19 Solidarity Response Fund to ensure patients get the care they need. A team was set up to give everyone access to timely, accurate and easy to understand advice. WHO also provided Personal Protective Equipment (PPE) to ensure health professionals who are able to save lives including their own. WHO also provided training to health professionals. It has been helpful in providing guidance, assistance, coordinating research on vaccine, diagnostics and anti-virus.

(5) International Bank for Reconstruction and Development (IBRD) :

IBRD commonly known as the World Bank was founded in 1944 at the UN Monetary and Financial Conference, commonly known as the Bretton Woods Conference[2] which was convened to establish a new, post World War II, international economic system. It came into existence on December 27, 1945 and began its speration in June, 1946. IBRD became a specialized agency in relation with the United Nations on Novermber 15, 1947. The Bank is an international cooperative organisation, associated with the United Nations. However, it is not accountable either to the General Assembly or to the Security Council.

The IBRD is owned by the governments of the member countries. Membership of the IMF is the principal condition for membership of the Bank.

The purposes of the Bank as laid down in Article 1 of the Agreement are :

(1) To assist in the reconstruction and development of the territories of the members, by facilitating the investment of capital for productive purposes, including the restoration of economies destroyed or disrupted by war, the reconversion of productive facilities to peace-time needs, and the encouragement of the development of productive facilities and resources in less developed countries;

(2) To promote private foreign investment by means of guarantees or participation in loans and other instruments made by private investors; and when private capital is not available on reasonable terms, to supplement private investment by providing on suitable conditions, finance for productive purposes out of its own capital funds raised by it and other resources.

(3) To promote the long-range balanced growth of international trade and the maintenance of equilibrium in the balance of payments, by encouraging international investment of the productive resources of members, thereby

1. Security Council unanimously adopted Resolution 2532 on July 1, 2020 wherein it recognised that Covid-19 pandemic 'is likely to endanger international peace and security'. General Assembly also convoked a Special Session in Response to the Coronavirus Disease (Covid-19) Pandemic on December 3-4, 2020.
2. The Conference was held at Bretton Woods from July 1 to July 22, 1944 to make financial arrangements for the post-war World after the expected defeat of Germany and Japan. The Conference was attended by experts representing 44 States. It drew up a project for the International Bank for Reconstruction and Development (IBRD) and a project for the International Monetary Fund (IMF). By December, 1945 the required number of governments had ratified the treaties.

assisting in raising productivity, the standards of living and conditions of labour in their territories.

Main organs of the IBRD are the Board of Governors, Executive Directors and the President. The Board of Governors is composed of representatives from all the member States. This body elects a Chairman every year. The Board of Governors appoints a body consisting of twenty four members called Executive Directors. It carries out the policy matters of the Bank. It meets at least once in a month to approve all loans at the Bank headquarters. The President of the Bank is the Chief Officer of the Bank. He is selected by the Executive Directors. The President is assisted by other members of the staff.

Voting power in the Bank's decision is based on a country's capital subscription which is based in turn on its economic resources. The wealthier and more developed countries constitute the Bank's major shareholders and thus exercise greater power and influence. For example, in the year 2000-01, the United States exercised more than one-sixth of the votes which is more than double to that of Japan which is the second largest contributor. Developing countries hold only a small number of votes. For instance, in the late 1990 approximately 2 percent of the votes were held by 25 African countries combined. Thus the voting system is not democratic. It does not allow the developing countries to raise their voice despite the fact that they are the primary recipients of the World Bank's loans.

The Bank lends funds for the development of economic facilities. By doing so, it promotes the flow of the capital internationally for productive purposes. The Loans may be made to member countries, or to their political sub-divisions, or to private business enterprises in their territories. If the borrower is not a Government, the guarantee of the member government concerned is required. Loans are granted for long term-ten to thirty-five years. The rate of interest charged by the Bank is related to the rate of interest which it would itself have to pay to borrow money at the time the loan is made, and the ability of member countries to raise funds in the capital markets of the world. The Bank's aid is not limited to granting loans. It also provides a wide range of technical assistance services to member countries in a wide variety of ways ranging from full-scale economic surveys of their development potential to regional investigations or advice on particular projects.

The functioning of the Bank depends largely upon its lending capacity. Its lending capacity in recent years has proved to be inadequate to meet the requirements of the developing countries. It is so because of the two main reasons. Firstly, the demand of the loan has considerably increased, and secondly, contributions to the Bank have not been increased by the States. The Bank is also criticised on the ground that the interest rate charged by it, *i.e.*, 8.2 per cent is too high.

The World Bank Group comprises five constituent institutions : the International Bank for Reconstruction and Development (IBRD), the International Development Association (IDA), the International Finance Corporation (IFC), the Multilateral Investment Guaranter Agency (MIGA) and the International Center for Settlement of Investment Disputes (ICSID).

(6) International Finance Corporation (IFC) :

IFC is closely associated with the World Bank, but is a separate legal entity. It was enacted by the Washington Agreement of May 25, 1955 and was established in July 1956. It became a specialized agency in relationship with the United Nations on February 20, 1957.

The main aims of the IFC are to assist in financing private enterprise in its member countries which could contribute to development by making investments without a guarantee of repayment by the member-government concerned; to bring together investment opportunities, domestic and foreign capital, and experienced management; and to stimulate the flow of private capital, democratic and foreign, into productive investment in member countries.

Activities of the IFC are regulated through the Board of Governors and the Board of Directors. The Board of Governors in which all powers of IFC are vested consists of the Governors and alternates of the World Bank who represent countries which are also members of the IFC. The Board of Directors is composed of the Executive Directors of the World Bank who represent countries which are also members of the IFC. The Board of Directors supervises the general operations of the IFC. The President of the World Bank serves *ex-officio* as chairman of the Board of Directors of IFC. The headquarters of the IFC are situated in Washington D.C. Membership in the IFC is open to all States which are members of the World Bank.

The IFC makes its investments in partnership with private investors from the capital exporting country in which the enterprise is located, or both. The IFC charges interest on the loan; rate of interest in each case is a matter of negotiation depending on the risks and other investments. The IFC, after having recognised the important contributions of financial markets to economic development, has created a specialised department that is the focal point of the capital market development activities of the IFC and the World Bank. The Department provides specialised resources for addressing the financial market needs and problems of developing countries. In response to the economic situation, in 1984, the IFC began to expand its operations in a new era assisting in the physical and financial restructuring of existing firms (corporate restructuring). The IFC has further expanded its activities into several other new areas. For instance, it has provided help creating a bonding facility for construction firms operating outside their own country.

The privatisation trend all around the World has greatly increased the role of the IFC. It has provided loan to many enterprises but it has never gained general acceptance in the advanced donor States and therefore in the developing countries for its inadequate availability of the fund.

(7) International Development Association (IDA) :

The IDA was established on September 24, 1960, as an affiliate of the World Bank. The object of the IDA was to promote economic development in the less-developed areas of the world included within its membership by providing long term interest free loans (credit) to their important development requirements. The membership of the IDA is open to all member countries of the World Bank. IDA's Board of Governors and Executive Directors are the same as hold the equivalent position in the Bank, serving ex-officio in IDA.

The bulk of IDA's resources comes from three sources : transfers from the Bank's net earnings; capital subscribed in convertible currencies by the members of the IDA and contributions from IDA's richer members, chiefly the 26 wealthiest countries.

In order to avail credit from the IDA, a country must meet three criteria. Firstly, poverty test, *i.e.*, IDA's assistance is limited to the poorest countries which continue to face severe handicap as excessive dependence on volatile primary products markets, heavy debt servicing burdens and rates of population growth that outweigh the gains of production. Secondly, performance test, *i.e.*, within the range of difficulties of establishing objective standards of performance, these factors serve as the yardstick for an adequate performance test, satisfactory overall economic policies and past success in project execution. Thirdly, project test, *i.e.* the purpose of IDA is to advance soft loans, and not finance soft projects. IDA projects are appraised according to the same standards as that applied to the Bank projects—the test essentially requires that the proposed projects yield financial and economic returns which are adequate to justify the use of source capital.

IDA provides credit (as they are called to distinguish them from Bank loans) for a long term. The credit matures after a period of fifty years, and there is a grace of another ten years. The credit provided by it is interest free. However, IDA charges 3% as service charges on the outstanding credit amount.

(8) International Monetary Fund (IMF) :

International Monetary Fund was established under the Bretton Woods Agreement on December 27, 1945 when representatives of 29 countries whose quotas amounted to 80 per cent of the Fund's resources had deposited their ratification of the Agreement. The IMF became a specialized agency in 1947. Membership in the IMF is open to every country[1] that controls its foreign relations and is able and prepared to fulfil the obligations of membership. By the end of 2015 IMF has 188 member States. Membership of the Fund is a pre-requisite to membership in the World Bank (IBRD) which indicates that there is a close working relationship between the two organisations. Its headquarter is located in Washington D.C. Articles of Agreement of the IMF have been amended by the First Amendment which came into effect in 1969 and by the Second Amendment which came into force on April 1, 1978.

The purposes for the creation of IMF are laid down under Article 1 of the Agreement which are as follows :—

(1) To promote international monetary cooperation through a permanent institution which provides the machinery for consultation and collaboration on international monetary problems.

(2) To facilitate the expansion and balanced growth of international

1. All the members of the IMF are not sovereign States and therefore all of these are not the members of the United Nations. Member countries of the IMF that are not member States of the United Nations for instances are Aruba, Hong Kong, Macau and Kosovo.

trade, and to contribute thereby to the production and maintenance of high levels of employment and real income and to the development of the productive resources of all members as primary objectives of economic policy.

(3) To promote exchange stability, maintain orderly exchange arrangements among members, and to avoid competitive exchange depreciation.

(4) To assist in the establishment of a multilateral system of payments with respect to current transactions between members and in the elimination of foreign exchange restrictions which hamper the growth of world trade.

(5) To give confidence to members by making the general resources of the Fund temporarily available to them under adequate safeguards, thus providing them with opportunity to correct maladjustments in their balance of payments without resorting to measures destructive of national or international prosperity.

(6) In accordance with the above, to shorten the duration and lessen the degree of disequilibrium in the international balances of payments of members.

The Fund shall be guided in all its policies and decisions by the above purposes.

The work of the Fund is carried out through a Board of Governors, an Executive Board (or a Board of Executive Directors), a Managing Director, and Staff. Each member country is represented by a Governor and an Alternate Governor on the Board of Governors, which is the fund's highest authority. The Board of Governors meet once a year. The members of Board whose number is 24 are appointed for a term of five years. Board of Executive Directors exercises the powers delegated to it by the Board of Governors. The Managing Director is appointed by the Executive Directors and he must not be a Governor or an Executive Director. The Managing Director serves as the chairman of the Executive Board and as chief of the operating staff of the Fund, with a five year term of office.

Each member of the fund is assigned a quota. The quota was fixed under the original Articles of Agreement or it is assigned by a four-fifths vote with the consent of the members. Quotas of all fund members are reviewed at intervals of not more than five years. In the past many general increases have been agreed to bring fund quotas in line with the growth of the World economy and need for additional international liquidity.

The voting power of a member in the Fund depends upon the quota of its members. The system is inequitable in the sense that the quota of the developed countries is higher and as such they have more votes than to the votes of developing countries. The result is that the developed countries regulate the entire working of the Fund. They decide the important issues of the Fund according to their own wishes disregarding the interest of the under-developing countries. It is desirable that the voting system is changed so that under-developed countries may participate on equal footing in all phases of decision-making for the formulation of an equitable and durable monetary system.

The IMF is actually a Bank. It enables member countries to convert their currencies into the currencies of all other member countries. According to the provisions of the Fund, a member State can purchase or draw from the Fund foreign currencies in exchange for its own currency up to 125 per cent of its quota. During any one year, however, a country can purchase from the Fund foreign currencies only upto 25 per cent of its quota limit or till the purchasing country's currency with the Fund becomes equal to 200 per cent of its quota. The Fund grants loans of foreign currencies to member countries to correct any disequilibrium in their balance of payments position provided such disequilibrium is only of a temporary nature likely to be removed in the earliest possible period. The IMF may also lend the countries to support the external value to their currencies.

In the past, the IMF has designed many new schemes to help member countries to solve their balance of payments problems. These schemes include : Standby Agreements, Supplementary Financial Stability, Extended Fund Facility, Compensatory Financing Facility and Buffer Stock Facility.

(a) Standby Agreements :

The Fund enters into 'standby arrangements' with a member under which the member may draw upon the Fund's resources upto a specified limit and within an agreed period without any further consideration of the member's position. This is to help a country which tends to relax its exchange control but fears an extraordinary drain from its monetary reserves as a result. The Fund then agrees to stand ready to provide foreign currencies to meet the drain.

(b) Supplementary Financial Stability :

In 1977, the Fund set up the scheme, the purpose of which was to enable the IMF to provide supplementary financing along with its ordinary resources to member countries facing serious payments imbalances that are large in relation to their economies and their Fund quotas. The Fund has borrowing agreements with member countries and monetary authorities to provide supplementary financing.

(c) Extended Fund Facility :

In September 1974, the Fund established an extended fund facility to provide, in certain circumstances, assistance to members to meet their balance of payments deficits for longer periods and in amount larger in relation to quotas that has been the practice under normal credit policies.

(d) Compensatory Financing Facility :

In 1975, the Fund created this facility to help member countries which suffer from temporary shortfalls in export earnings due largely to conditions beyond their control or from an excess in the cost of their cereal imports. The assistance is in addition to that available to members under the Fund's normal credit facilities. In 1982, compensatory financing purchases amounted to SDR 2.6 billion, which is also 35 per cent of the total purchases from the Fund.

(e) Buffer Stock Facility :

In 1969, the scheme was introduced to assist the members in balance of payments need for the purpose of financing the cost of their contributions to buffer stock established under international agreements approved by the Fund. (tin, sugar and natural rubber). Buffer stock facility has so far been used only twice. A total of SDR 30 million was purchased by five members for the Fourth International Tin Agreement. For the 1977 International Sugar Agreement, SDR 74 million was purchased by six members to enable them to meet their international stocking obligations.

By 1969, when the volume of international reserves was found inadequate to the rising demand for international reserves, the Fund decided that the desire of the member countries to increase their international liquidity shall be met through the allocation of Special Drawing Rights to the extent of the gap of SDR from 3 to 3.50 billion per year for the period of 1970 to 1972. The ten leading members of the Fund, after a long process of discussion and negotiation, agreed to create a new system of international reserves known as the Special Drawing Rights (SDR). Under the Scheme introduced on July 28, 1969, each member country was given a proportionate share in the reserve pool of SDR. The share was dependent upon the member's subscription to the Fund. Under the SDR system a member country can use SDR to settle its debts to other member countries. The most radical aspect is that 70 per cent to these new units needs never to be repaid. They are, in fact, newly created money. SDR would serve as additional reserve units. A country running into deficit on its balance of payment need not rush for immediate aid from IMF, or from other sources, or take hasty restrictive action but use its SDR to pay up its deficits. The SDR has greatly helped to solve problem of international liquidity.

(9) International Civil Aviation Organisation (ICAO) :

The International Civil Aviation Conference was held on November 1, 1944 at Chicago to conclude international rules for commercial air traffic rights. The Conference attended by fifty two States adopted a Convention which is known as Chicago Convention on International Civil Aviation.[1] The Convention had three main parts. Part I deals with Air Navigation, Part II is the Constitution of the International Civil Aviation Organisation and Part III deals with International Air Transport. The ICAO, whose constitution was drawn up by the Conference came into force in April when the Convention was ratified by 26 States. Thus, ICAO is a part of the Convention on the International Civil Aviation. ICAO became a specialized agency of the United Nations in 1947. It has its headquarters at Montereal (Canada). By the end of 2011 ICAO had 191 member States.

The main aim of the ICAO which is set forth in the annexes to the Chicago Convention is to facilitate the safety, regularity and efficiency of civil air transport. Other objectives of the ICAO are : to study problems of international civil aviation, to establish international standards and regulations for civil aviation and to foster the development and planning of international air transport.

ICAO operates through an Assembly, a Council and a Secretariat and also through a number of commissions and committees. The Assembly consists of all member States of ICAO. Each of them has one vote. The Council consisting of 33 members are elected by the Assembly for a period of three years. The Council

1. Full name of the Convention is the Convention for the Unification of Certain Rules Regarding International Air Transport.

elects its President, appoints the Secretary General and administers the finances of the Organisation. It carries out the directions of the Assembly. The Council takes the decision on rules relating to air navigation by a vote of two thirds majority. Rules adopted by it are obligatory to all members excepting those that express their disapproval within a specified time. The Council is consisted by an Air Navigation Commission and five Committees.

The principal achievements of ICAO in the legal field are four international air Conventions and a Protocol of Amendment to the Warsaw Convention which has been in existence since 1929. The four Conventions are : (1) Convention on the International Recognition of Rights in Aircraft (1948); (2) Rome Convention on Damage Caused by Foreign Aircraft to their parties on the Surface (1952); (3) The Convention, Supplementary to the Warsaw Convention, for the unification of certain rules for the International Carriage by Air by a person other than the Contracting Parties (1961), and (4) The Convention to provide accident victims potentially unlimited compensation (1977). A Protocol of Amendment to the Warsaw Convention of 1929 concerning the Liability of the Air Carrier to Passengers and Cargo was adopted at the Hague in 1952.

Since the establishment of the ICAO there has been the tremendous growth of air transport. It could not have been possible to handle the growth without the international coordination which is necessary for the development of a unified and efficient network of international air-lines and airports. At present, what is required is that a single Convention is concluded by the ICAO on the lines of the Convention on the Law of the Sea of 1982 to establish international standard in this regard.

(10) Universal Postal Union (UPU) :

The first International Postal Congress adopted the Berne Treaty signed on October 9, 1874. It came into force on July 1, 1875; and formally established the General Postal Union. Name of the Union was changed to the Universal Postal Union by the Second International Postal Congress held in 1878 at Paris. Under an agreement signed at Paris on July 4, 1947, between the UPU and the United Nations, the UPU was recognized by the United Nations as a specialized agency responsible for international postal services. The aim of the UPU is to secure the organisation and improvement of postal services and thus to promote the development of international collaboration in the cultural, social and economic sphere. To this end, the members of UPU form a single postal territory for the reciprocal exchange for correspondence. The principal organs of the UPU are the Universal Postal Congress, the Executive Council, the Consultative Committee for Postal Studies and the International Bureau. The basic activity of the Union is to make provisions for the international postal services carried out by the postal administration of its members.

(11) International Telecommunication Union (ITU) :

The origin of the ITU can be traced to 1865 when the International Telegraph Union was established. In 1906, International Radio Telegraph Union was established to secure cooperation among the members in the field of communication. The two Organisations were merged in 1932 at the

Telecommunication Conference of Madrid and the new organisation was created under the name of International Telecommunication Union (ITU). ITU was reorganised in 1947 and it entered into an agreement with the United Nations in 1948 whereby it was recognised as the specialized agency of the United Nations. Its Headquarters are in Geneva.

The main aim of the ITU is to promote international cooperation in telegraph, telephone and radio services and to foster technical development of these services and to extend their use by the public. In order to achieve the above aims, ITU effects the allocation of the radio frequency spectrum and registration of radio frequency assignments. Since the number of frequencies is limited and it has to allocate them into a large number of States, the ITU performs the function of allocation amongst the members. The International Frequency Registration Board was set up to assign allocation. In addition to the above, ITU also promotes the adoption of measures for ensuring the safety of life through the cooperation of telecommunication services undertakes studies, makes regulations and formulates recommendations and opinions, and collects and publishes information concerning telecommunication matters.

The supreme organ of the ITU is the Plenipotentiary Conference which meets normally every five years. Its main function is to lay down the basic policy of the ITU. Plenipotentiaries in 1983 Conference emphasized the principles of the universality of the Union, rotation and geographical distribution for high level posts both at Conference and Union headquarters.

The Administrative Council, consisting of 43 members of the Union is elected by the Plenipotentiary Conference. It meets annually and coordinates the work of five permanent organs at ITU headquarters which are the General Secretariat, International Frequency Registration Board, International Radio Consultative Committee, International Telegraph and the Telephone Consultative Committee and the Telecommunications Development Bureau.

The two consultative Committees study technical and operating issues in their specific fields. The Telecommunications Development Bureau was set up in 1989 to strengthen technical assistance to developing countries.

(12) World Meteorological Organisation (WMO) :

WMO was established in 1873 as a non-governmental organisation at a Conference held in Utrecht, the Netherland. The Conference of Directors of the national meteorological services in 1947 adopted the World Meteorological Convention thus establishing a new inter-governmental Organisation in 1950. In 1951, the WMO commenced activities, the former Organisation having been dissolved. It became a specialized agency of the United Nations in 1951. WMO has a membership of 191 member States and territories. The main purposes of WMO are : to facilitate international co-operation in the establishment of networks of stations and centres to provide meteorological services and observations; to promote the establishment and maintenance of systems for the rapid exchange of weather information; to promote standardization of meteorological observations and to ensure the uniform publication of observations and statistics; to further the application of meteorology to aviation, shipping, agriculture and training in meteorology.

WMO consists of World Meteorological Congress, consisting of representatives of all members which meet at least every four years and sets general policy and adopts regulations; Executive Committee, comprising of 29 members, meets at least annually and implements general policy; and the Secretariat which serves as the administrative center of the Organisation. There are six regional associates in which members discuss problems peculiar to their regions.

(13) International Maritime Organisation (IMO) :

The Inter-Governmental Maritime Consultative Organisation (IMCO) Convention was drawn up at the United Nations Maritime Conference in 1948. The Convention came into effect on March 17, 1958. On November 14, 1975, certain amendments were made to the Convention on the International Maritime Organisation (IMO) by the IMO Assembly. Amendments came into force on May 22, 1982. They changed the title of the Convention to the Convention on the International Maritime Organisation. As of 2018 the Convention has 174 member States and three associate members.

The aims of IMO are to facilitate co-operation and exchange of information among governments on technical matters affecting shipping and, with special responsibility for the safety of life at sea, to encourage the removal of discriminatory action and of unnecessary restrictions by governments; to consider any matters concerning shipping that might be referred to it by any organ or specialized agency of the United Nations. IMO also drafts international Conventions and agreements and convenes international conferences on shipping matters. It functions in a consultative and advisory capacity. In order to increase the role of developing countries in world shipping, the World Maritime University (WMU) has been established in 1983 under the auspices of the IMO.

Main organs of the IMO are the Assembly, the Council and a Secretariat. IMO's policy-making body is the Assembly which meets every two years. The Council consisting of 40 members States, meets twice a year and is responsible for governing between Assembly sessions. Safety proposals are submitted to the Assembly by the 16 members Maritime Safety Committee, which meets annually. There are a number of sub-committees to deal with specific issues. A Secretariat is also maintained who is headed by the Secretary General. IMO has five main Committees : the Maritime Safety Committee, the Maritime Environment Protection Committee; the Legal Committee, the Technical Cooperation Committee and the Facilitating Committee with Headquarters in London.

(14) International Fund for Agricultural Development (IFAD) :

The proposal to set up the Fund was adopted by the World Food Conference held in Rome in 1974. Consequently, in 1976, a United Nations Conference was held in Rome, which adopted and initiated an agreement establishing an International Fund for Agricultural Development. IFAD was established in 1976 by the United Nations Conference. The International Fund became a specialized agency when the agreement was approved by the General

Assembly on December 15, 1977.

IFAD was established to solve one of the worst problems in the World food situation, i.e., the slow growth rate of food production in many developing countries. This was to be achieved by the Fund through the disbursement of the resources, partly through grants and mainly in the form of concessional loans to increase food production in developing countries. The Fund's proposed initial target of $ 1000 Million is more than the total concessional assistance available every year for agricultural or food production.

IFAD's members fall into three categories : Category I, 'Industrialized Countries'; Category II, 'Oil Petroleum exporting developing countries' and Category III, which includes more than 100 'recipient developing countries'. Countries in Category I and II are obliged to provide revenue for the Fund; countries in Category III may contribute but are not obliged to do so, though recipient countries must be members of IFAD.

The organizational structure of the Fund is innovative with the votes shared equally by three categories of countries.

The Fund operates through a Governing Council made up of the entire membership. The Chief Executive of the Fund is the President, assisted by the Vice-President and three Assistant Presidents. The President is responsible for the business of the Fund; he is also the Chairman of the 18 member Executive Board.

(15) World Intellectual Property Organisation (WIPO) :

WIPO was established in 1967 when it succeeded the United International Bureau for the Protection of Intellectual Property of 1893. The Convention establishing the WIPO was signed on 14th July, 1967. It entered into force on 26th July, 1970. WIPO Convention has 191 member States. The Headquarters of WIPO is at Geneva. WIPO became a specialized agency of the United Nations in 1974. The origin of the WIPO can be traced to the International Union for the Protection of Industrial Property of 1883, commonly called the Paris Convention or 'The Paris Union' and the International Union for the Protection of Literacy and Artistic Works of 1886 known as the Berne Convention or the 'Berne Union'. The two Unions were united in 1893 and functioned under various names, the last being the United International Bureaux for the Protection of Intellectual Property, known by the Franch acronyom 'BIRPI'. In practice, BIRPI has been replaced by WIPO but it still exists for those States who were the members of the Paris or Barne Union but have not become members of WIPO.

The main objectives of the WIPO are : (a) to promote the protection of intellectual property throughout the World through cooperation among States and where appropriate in collaboration with any international organisation; (b) to harmonise national intellectual property legislation and procedure; (c) to provide services for international applications for intellectual property rights; (d) exchange information on intellectual property; (e) provide legal and technical assistance to developing and other countries; and (f) facilitate the resolution of private intellectual property disputes.

WIPO performs its function through four organs : General Assembly, Conference, Coordinate Committee and the Secretariat. General Assembly consists of the States Parties to the Convention establishing WIPO which are the members of the Unions. Conference consists of the States Parties to the Convention. Coordinating Committee consists of the States Parties to the Convention which are the members of the Executive Committee of the Paris Union or the Berne Union or both. Secretariat or International Bureau is directed by the Director General. He is the Chief Executive of the WIPO.

Activities of the WIPO includes the administration of 11 treaties which set out internationally agreed rights and common standards for their protection. States Parties to the treaties agree to apply within their own territories.

In October 2004 WIPO agreed to adopt a proposal offered by Argentina and Brazil-Proposal for the Establishment of a Development Agenda for WIPO. The agreed "WIPO Development Agenda" consisting of 45 recommendations was the culmination of a long process of transformation for the Organisation from one that had historically been primarily aimed at protecting the interests of right holders to one that has increasingly incorporated the interests of other stakeholders in the international intellectual property system.

(16) United Nations Industrial Development Organisation (UNIDO) :

UNIDO was established on January 1, 1967 as an integral part of the United Nations system. Its purpose was 'to promote and accelerate the industrialization of the developing countries' with particular emphasis on manufacturing sector. In the Second General Conference of the UNIDO held in Lima (Peru), it was recommended that UNIDO be made a specialized agency of the United Nations. In September 1975, a Resolution 3362 (S-VII) was adopted at the Seventh Special Session of the General Assembly of the United Nations wherein the Lima recommendation was endorsed, and a committee was established to draw up a Constitution for the new agency. The Constitution of UNIDO as a specialized agency was adopted by consensus on April 8, 1979 by a Conference on Plenipotentiaries. Consequently, on June 21, 1985 UNIDO became a specialized agency of the United Nations. As of January 2017, 168 States are the members of the UNIDO.

The principal organ of the UNIDO is the Industrial Development Board consisting of members of the United Nations or of the intergovernmental agencies associated with the United Nations, elected by the General Assembly for a period of three years. A Permanent Committee, established in 1972 as a subsidiary organ, to oversee the implementation of UNIDO programmes when the Board is not in the session. Overall responsibility for UNIDO activities rests with the Executive Director, who is appointed by the Secretary General.

The primary objective of the UNIDO is the promotion of industrial development in the developing countries with a view to assisting the establishment of a New International Economic Order. It also promotes industrial development and co-operation on global, regional, national and secretariat levels. UNIDO also assists developing countries in establishing and operating industries; provides a forum and acts as an instrument to serve developing and industrialized countries in their contracts, consultations and negotiations; and develop special measures designed to promote co-operation among developing countries and between the developed and developing countries. While the Third General Conference of the UNIDO was held in New Delhi, UNIDO IV, the fourth General Conference was held in Vienna in 1984 wherein fifteen resolutions were adopted. Important amongst them were, firstly, it urged developed countries to increase their voluntary contributions for accelerating the development of developing countries' human resources for industrialization, as well as their contributions to the Industrial Development Fund; secondly, it urged co-operation in order to complete the international codes of conduct on the transfer of technology and on transnational corporations; thirdly, it invited developing countries to review their basic education system, in order to respond to changing industrial manpower needs, while placing more emphasis on science and technology; and fourthly, it recommended action to eliminate the negative effects of the "brain drain" from the developing countries and to promote the repatriation of skilled professionals from third world.

(17) World Tourism Organisation (WTO) :

Intergovernmental Conference on Tourism held in Sofia in 1969 recommended the creation of an intergovernmental organisation to promote tourism. The Statute of the World Tourism Organisation was adopted in Maxico City in 1970 and entered into force on January 2, 1975 after 51 ratifications. The General Council of the WTO and United Nations in the year 2003 agreed to establish the WTO as a specialized agency of the United Nations. By the end of July, 2017 the Organisation has 158 member States and seven territories as associate members. Its Headquarters are in Madrid.

WTO serves as a global forum for tourism policy issues and a practical source of tourism know-how. WTO plays a central and decisive role in promoting the development of responsible, sustainable and universaliy accessible tourism, paying particular attention to the interests of developing countries. The Organisation encourages the implementation of the Global Code of Ethics for Tourism, with a view to ensuring that member countries, tourist destinations and businesses maximise the positive economic, social and cultural effects of tourism and fully reap its benefits, while minimising its negative social and environmental impacts. Direct actions that strengthen the support and the efforts of National Tourism Administrations are carried out by the Organisation's regional representatives.

The structure of the WTO includes the General Assembly, Executive Council, Committees and Secretariat.

The General Assembly is the supreme organ of the Organisation. Its ordinary sessions are held in every two years which are attended by the delegates of the members and associate members. The Executive Council takes all necessary measures for the implementation of its own decisions and recommendations of the Assembly and reports thereon to the Assembly. In doing so the Council takes consultation of the Secretary-General of the Organisation. The Council consists of full members elected by the Assembly in the proportion of one member for every five members. The term of the office of members elected to the Council is four years. The Council meets at least twice a year. A number of committees with specific topics on tourism have been established which include World Committee on Tourism Ethics, Programme Committee, Committee on Budget and Finance and Committee on Market and Competitiveness. The Secretariat is led by the Secretary-General who supervises the staff at Madrid Headquarters. The Secretary-General is elected by the General Assembly.

Chapter 11

Related Organisations of the United Nations

In addition to the specialised agencies there are other inter-governmental organisations which are autonomous but are related to the United Nations. They are not specialised agencies as they have not been brought into relationship with the United Nations by concluding agreements. However, relationship of these organisations exists with the United Nations as they are required to make reports either to the General Assembly or to the Security-Council or to both. Such organisations include the following :—

(1) International Atomic Energy Agency (IAEA)

IAEA has its origin in a proposal made to the General Assembly of the United Nations in 1953 by the President of the United States, suggesting the establishment of a World organisation devoted exclusively to the peaceful uses of atomic energy. The General Assembly unanimously endorsed the proposal by adopting a resolution on December 4, 1954 wherein it expressed the hope that IAEA should be established to negotiate an appropriate form of agreement with the United Nations. Consequently, the United Nations International Conference on Peaceful uses of Atomic energy met in the year 1955 and a draft Statute for the establishment of the Agency was drawn up and circulated to members for their consideration. After a series of amendments the Statute was unanimously approved on October 26, 1956 and was signed by seventy States. The Agency legally came into being on July 29, 1957 with the deposit of the necessary ratifications of the Statute. Presently, IAEA has 172 members.

IAEA is an autonomous international organisation. It works through a Statute. Although IAEA was established independently of the United Nation a relationship agreement was concluded by the IAEA and the United Nations in the year 1957. IAEA reports to the General Assembly and the Security Council. Unlike other specialized agencies, IAEA does much of its work with the Security Council. The structure and the functions of the Agency are laid down in the Statute itself.

The functions of the IAEA are to seek to accelerate and enlarge the contribution of atomic energy to peace, health and prosperity throughout the World and to ensure, so far as it is able, that assistance provided by it or at its request or under its supervision or control, is not used in such a way as to further any military purposes.

The Agency in order to achieve the above aims assists in researches and also the practical application of atomic energy for peaceful purposes, including the production of electric power with special consideration to less developed areas. It acts as an intermediary between States members of the Agency, in providing services or supplying materials, equipment or facilities, fosters the exchange of scientific and technical information and encourages the exchange and training of scientists and experts. The IAEA also establishes and administers safeguards to ensure that fissionable and other materials are not used to further any military purposes and establishes safety standards and provides for the application of these standards.

IAEA has three main bodies—Board of Governors, General Conference and the Secretariat. The Board of Governors consists of 22 members designated by the outgoing Board and members elected by the General Conference. The outgoing Board designates ten members who are most advanced in atomic energy technology and the remaining three most advanced members from other areas that are not represented by the first ten. These members are designated for one year term. The General Conference elects 22 members from the remaining nations for a period of two year term. The Board is responsible for making most of the policies of the IAEA. The Board makes recommendations to the General Conference on IAEA activities and budget. It is responsible for publishing IAEA standards and appoints the Director General subject to the General Conference approval. The Board meets once in five year.

The General Conference consists of all members of the Statute. It meets once a year and takes its decisions by majority vote, except on financial matters, amendments to the Statute and suspension from membership which require a two-thirds majority. The Secretariat is organised in many departments. IAEA Headquarters are in Vienna.

The Agency has established a safeguard system based on material accountancy verified by IAEA inspectors in order to detect the dimension of nuclear materials for explosive or other military purposes. Non-nuclear weapon States parties to the Non-Proliferation Treaty undertake to conclude with the Agency safeguards arguments covering all their peaceful nuclear activities. The IAEA has expanded and adjusted its scientific programmes commensurate with the rapid development in the use of nuclear energy in recent years. The IAEA has formulated basic safety standards for radiation protection. It has also elaborated safety codes and guidelines on governmental organisations. To enhance the sharing of information and experience among IAEA Member States concerning the seismic safety of nuclear facilities, in 2008 the IAEA established the International Seismic Safety Centre.

IAEA and its former Director General were jointly awarded the Nobel Peace Prize in the year 2005.

(2) World Trade Organisation (WTO)

WTO come into existence on January 1, 1995 under the Marrakesh

Agreement replacing the General Agreement on Tariffs and Trade (GATT).[1] WTO deals with regulations of trade between participating countries and provides a framework for negotiating and formalising trade agreements. It provided a dispute resolution process aimed at enforcing participant's adherence to WTO agreements.

The structure of the WTO is dominated by its highest authority, the Ministerial Conference, consisted of representatives of all WTO members. It is required to meet at least once in every two years and it can take decisions on all matters under any of the multilateral trade agreements. The First Ministerial Conference took place in Singapore in 1996. The day-to-day work of the WTO is carried on by a number of subsidiary bodies mainly by the General Council consisting of all the WTO members. The Council has many bodies to perform specific tasks which are Council for Trade in Goods, Council for Trade Related Aspects of Intellectual Property Rights, Council for Trade in Services, Trade Negotiation Committee. In addition to the above, the General Council has several different committees, such as Trade and Environment, Trade and Development, working groups such as Trade, Debt and Finance and Trade and Technology Transfer. The Council is the highest level decision making body which meets regularly.

Secretariat of the WTO is headed by the Director-General who is appointed by the Ministerial Conference. Powers, duties, conditions of service and term of office are decided by the Ministerial Conference by adopting regulations.

The main functions of the WTO are firstly, it shall facilitate the implementation, administration and operation of the multilateral trade agreements, and secondly, it shall provide a forum for negotiations and for settling disputes. WTO has a procedure for resolving trade disputes between the members. States bring disputes to the WTO if they think that their rights under the agreements are being infringed. Decisions are given by specially appointed independent experts which are based on interpretations of the agreements and individual state's commitments. The dispute settlement system encourages states to settle their differences through consultations. Failing that, they can follow a carefully mapped out, stage by stage procedure that includes the possibility of a ruling by a panel of experts, and the chance to appeal the ruling or legal grounds. Additionally, it is the duty of the WTO to review and propagate the national trade policies and to ensure the coherence and transparency of trade policies through surveillance in global economic

---

1. GATT a temporary arrangement was the only international instrument since 1948 which laid down rules of conduct for trade and was accepted by the leading trading nations. It was a multilateral trade treaty embodying reciprocal rights and obligations. It laid four fundamental principles which are; Firstly, trade should be conducted on the basis of non-discrimination. In particular, all contracting parties are bound by the most-favoured nation clause in the application of import and export duties and charges and in their implementation. Secondly, protection shall be afforded to domestic industries exclusively through the customs tariff and not through other commercial measures. Thirdly, the concept of consultation aimed at avoiding damage to the trading interests of contracting parties and fourthly, it provided a framework within which negotiations can be held for the reduction of tariffs and other barriers to trade and a structure for embodying the results of such negotiations in a legal instrument.

policy-making. Another priority of the WTO is the assistance of developing, least-developed and low-income countries in transition to adjust the WTO rules and disciplines through technical cooperation and training. WTO is also a center of economic research and analysis. It cooperates closely with the IMF and the World Bank.

Fundamental principles of WTO are firstly non-discrimination which has two major components; the most favoured nation rule and the national treatment policy, secondly, reciprocity, thirdly, binding and enforceable commitments, fourthly, transparency and fifthly, safety valves.

WTO operates on the principle of one State, one vote but actual votes have never been taken. Decision is taken generally by consensus and relative market size is the primary source of bargaining power. The consensus decision making system is advantageous in the sense that it encourages efforts to find the most widely acceptable decision. However, the system suffers from disadvantage because it takes long time to take a decision and many rounds of negotiations are required to take place to develop a consensus.

The WTO has 164 members and a number of non-members are observers at WTO proceedings and are negotiating their membership. Some intergovernmental organisations have also been granted observer status to WTO.

(3) Comprehensive Test Ban Treaty Organisation (CTBTO) :

Article II of the Comprehensive Test Ban Treaty (CTBT)[1] provided for the establishment a CTBTO to achieve the objects and purposes of the Treaty and to ensure its implementation of the provisions including those for international verification of compliance with it and to provide a forum for consultation and cooperation among States parties (Para 1 Article II). All States Parties shall be members of the Organisation (Para 2 Article II). The seat of the Organisation shall be at Vienna. (Para 3 Article II).

The organs of the Organisation shall be the Conference of the States Parties, the Executive Council and the Technical Secretariat which shall include the International Data Centre (Para 4 Article II). While the Conference shall consist of all the States Parties, the Executive Council shall have 51 members. The Technical Secretariat shall assist the Conference and the Executive Council in the performance of their functions.

CTBT has not yet come into force, however the States signatories to the Treaty established an interim organisation known as Preparatory Commission for the Comprehensive Nuclear-Test-Ban Treaty on November 19, 1996 for the purpose of carrying out the necessary preparations for the effective implementation of the CTBT and for preparing the first session of the Conference of the States parties to the Treaty. The Commission is composed of all States which have signed the Treaty. Each State signatory shall have one representative in the Commission who may be accompanied by alternates and advisers. The Commission shall elect its Chairman and other officers and adopt

1. For detail *See* H.O. Agarwal, 'International Law And Human Rights', 23rd Edition (2021) Chapter 'Comprehensive Test Ban Treaty'.

its rules of procedure. It may meet as often as necessary and establish such committees as it deems useful. The seat of the Preparatory Commission is in Vienna (Austria).

The First meeting of the Commission was convened by the Secretary-General of the United Nations on November 20, 1996, *i.e.* within 60 days after the Treaty was signed by 50 States as stipulated by the Annex to the Resolution which established the Commission. The Preparatory Commission started operation with 58 signatories on March, 1997 and made steady progress in setting up the verification regime to monitor compliance with the CTBT.[1] In the Seventh Session held on November 16, 1998, the Commission adopted a number of recommendations for its subsidiary bodies relating to verification and budgetary issues.

The Commission on May 26, 2000 signed the agreement to regulate the Relationship between the United Nations and the Preparatory Commission commonly known as the relationship agreement[2] in New York. It was for the first time the United Nations concluded an agreement with an autonomous international organisation responsible for verification activities since the conclusion of relationship agreement between the United Nations and the International Atomic Energy Agency in 1957. Although the Preparatory Commission is not a part of the UN system, the agreement brings the Commission into formal working relationship with the United Nations and provides a framework of cooperation between the two organsiations. The Agreement entered into force following its approval by the CTBTO Preparatory Commission during its eleventh session held from May 2 to 5, 2001 and by the General Assembly on June, 2001.

Preparatory Commission will dissolve when the CTBT comes into force and the CTBTO will dissolve at the end of the first Conference of the States Parties of the CTBT after entry into force.

Organisation for the Prohibition of Chemical Weapons (OPCW) :

The Convention on the Prohibition of the Development, Production, Stockpiling and Use of Chemical Weapons and their Destruction commonly called the Convention on Chemical Weapons (CWC) of 1993 provided under Article VIII that the Organisation for the Prohibition of Chemical Weapons shall established as the implementating body of the CWC. The Organisation was given a mandate : firstly, to achieve the object and purpose of the Convention, secondly, to ensure the implementation of its provisions, including those for international verification of compliance with it, and thirdly, to provide a forum for consultation and cooperation among States parties, OPCW was established on April 29, 1997. All States parties to the CWC are automatically the members of OPCW. By the end of 2018 there were 193 States parties. Israel which is a signatory to the Chemical Weapons Convention has not ratified the Convention

---

1. On March, 18, 1997 a Host Country Agreement was entered into with the Republic of Austria which came into force on November 1, 1997. The purpose of the Agreement was to recognise the right of the Commission to establish its seat in Vienna and to carry out its activities.
2. Text of the Agreement was annexed to the General Assembly Resolution 54/280.

and is not a member of the Organisation. Non-members of the OPCW are Egypt, North Korea and South Sudan.

OPCW is an intergovernmental Organisation. It is not a specialised agency of the United Nations but cooperates both on policy and practical issues. OPCW and the United Nations on September 7, 2000 signed a Cooperation Agreement outlining how they were to coordinate activities. The Headquarters are in the Hague (the Neitherlands).

The Organisation promotes and verifies the adherence of the CWC which prohibits the use of chemical weapons and requires their destruction. The verification consists both of evaluation of declarations by member States and on-site inspections.

The main bodies of the OPCW are the Conference of States parties, the Executive Council and the Technical Secretariat. The Conference of States Parties is composed of all the States parties and they all have equal voting rights. It is convened once in a year. States are represented in the Conference by a permanent representative to the Organisation. The Conference decides on all main topics regarding the Organisation and the Convention. The Executive Council is the executive body of the Organisation consisting of 41 States parties. They are appointed by the Conference for a period of two years term. The Council oversees the budget and cooperates with the General Secretariat on all matters related to the Convention. The Technical Secretariat applies most of the activities mandated by the Council and is the body where most of the employees of the Organisation work. The main activities of the OPCW are performed by the verification and the inspection division.

By the end of 2017 OPCW has conducted more than 5,000 inspections in 86 countries and about 96% of the declared chemical weapons stock piles have been verifiably destroyed. In 2012, its inspections were called in to verify Syria's claims of destroying its chemical arsenal. About two dozen inspectors over see the destruction of an estimated 1000 tons of chemical weapons. OPCW was awarded Nobel Prize for Peace in the year 2013 for its extensive work to eliminate chemical weapons.

(5) International Organisation for Migration (IOM) :

IOM was initially established in 1951 by the name of Provisional Inter-governmental Committee for the Movement of Migrants from Europe (PIC MME) to help resettle people displaced by World War II. Its name was changed to the Inter-governmental Committee for European Migration (ICEM). Its Constitution was adopted in 1953 which came into force on November, 1954. Following amendments made to the Constitution, the International Organisation was renamed as Organisation for Migration (IOM) in 1989. IOM, an inter-governmental organisation became a related organisation of the United Nations in September 2016.

As of July, 2018 the Organisation had 165 member States and 8 observer States. India is a member of the IOM.

The main purpose of the IOM is to make arrangements for the organised transfer of migrants, for whom existing facilities are inadequate or who would not otherwise be able to move without special assistance to countries offering opportunities for orderly migration (Article 1(1)(a)). IOM also provide, at the request of and an agreement with the States concerned, migration services such as recruitment, selection, processing, language training, orientation activities and medical examination. In carrying out its functions, the Organisation shall cooperate closely with international organisations, governmental and non-governmental concerned with migration.

IOM performs its functions through its organs, the Council and the Administration. The Council determines the policies of the organisation. It also reviews the reports and approves the activities of the Organisation. The Council approves the programme, the budget, the expenditure and the accounts of the Organisation. The Council consists of the representatives of the Member States. It meets once in a year which is called regular session.

The Administration comprises a Director General, a Deputy Director General and such staff as the Council may determine. The Director General and Deputy Director General are elected by the Council. Director General shall be responsible to the Council. He shall discharge the administrative and executive functions of the Organisation in accordance with the Constitution and the policies and decisions of the Council and the rules and regulations established by it. He shall formulate proposals for appropriate action by the Council.

IOM has been publishing World Migration Report since 2000. World Migration Report 2018, the ninth in the series has been published during the 108th IOM Council. The report stated that the Indian diaspora is the largest in the World with over 15 million migrants from India living abroad. Mexico has the second largest diaspora after India followed by Russia, China, Bangladesh and Pakistan.

Chapter 12

Subsidiary Organs and Bodies of the United Nations

By the term subsidiary organs may mean auxiliary organs established by the principal organs competent to establish them under the Charter. The Charter has not defined the term 'subsidiary organs' but it has authorized the General Assembly under Article 22 and the Security Council under Article 29 to establish such subsidiary organs as they deem necessary for the performance of their functions. The use of the words 'may be established' 'as may be found necessary' under Part 2 of Article 7 implies that the establishment of such organs by them is optional.

They may be established by the General Assembly and the Security Council for the performance of all or some of the functions assigned to them. Establishment of such organs is beneficial to the Assembly and the Council as they allow them to do more important work; they have more time to go into details of the issue and they get the services of experts in various fields. They also assist the Assembly and the Council in new fields of concern.

The Charter has not provided as to the structure of the subsidiary organs established by the Assembly and the Council. Thus these two organs are free to compose the subsidiary organs for the performance of their functions. They may establish collegiate organ or appoint a single individual as a subsidiary organ. Collegiate organs may be composed of members of the Security Council or the General Assembly or in any other way. They may be called commission, committee or group. These subsidiary organs may set up their subsidiary units such as working groups, sub-committees and the like.

Subsidiary organs may be established on permanent basis or on adhoc basis. If they are required to perform more specific task they may be discontinued after the completion of the assigned task or definite mandate. They therefore fluctuate in number from year to year according to changing requirement.

Subsidiary organs may be referred to as subsidiary bodies of the United Nations, but all the subsidiary bodies of the United Nations are not subsidiary organs of the United Nations. A number of such bodies have been established by the principal organs of the United Nations for the performance of their functions in relation to economic, social and cultural fields. They have been created in different names such as funds, programmes, councils and offices. Their work within the United Nations system is of immense value in the sense that it would not have been possible for the Organisation to carry out the variety of functions without their assistance. Some of the organs and bodies of the United Nations are as follows :—

(1) International Law Commission (ILC)

Framers of the United Nations Charter were conscious of the need for the codification of International Law. Their desire was expressed in the Charter in clear terms under Article 13(1)(a) which lays down that the General Assembly shall initiate studies and make recommendations for the purpose of encouraging the progressive development of International Law and its codification. In order to implement the above obligations, the Assembly, in its meeting on December 11, 1946 adopted a resolution by which it established a Committee on the Progressive Development of International Law and its Codification. The Committee, known as Committee of Seventeen, met at Lake Success on May 12, 1947, and prepared a report along with a Draft Statute which was submitted to the General Assembly. The Assembly on November 21, 1947 adopted a resolution by which the International Law Commission was established as the subsidiary organ of the General Assembly. Its Statute, which governs the activities of the Commission, was also approved by the Assembly by the same resolution.

The Statute provided that the Commission shall consist of members who shall be persons of recognized competence in International Law [Article 2(1)]. The members are elected by the General Assembly for a period of five years in such a manner so as to ensure the representation of the main forms of civilization and of the principal legal systems of the world. The members acted in their individual capacity as experts in International Law. Initially, the number of members was fifteen. However, the strength was increased to twenty one in 1956, and to twenty five in 1961. At present, the Commission has thirty four members. The Commission meets normally in Geneva for a single session each year. Its records and documents and its annual reports to the General Assembly are published in the Year Book of the International Law Commission.

The topics for codification are chosen by the Commission itself. When the Commission considers that the codification of a particular topic is necessary or desirable, it submits its recommendations to the General Assembly. The Commission starts its work on a particular topic when the recommendation is approved by the General Assembly. The Assembly, on its own initiative, may also recommend to the Commission for codification of a particular topic. A greater part of the work of the Commission has been referred to it by the Assembly. When the Commission has chosen a particular topic for work and has reported it to the General Assembly for approval, or when the General Assembly has requested the Commission to work on a particular topic, its usual method of work is as follows. It approves one of its members as special rapporteur on that topic, and he prepares a draft usually in the form of draft articles with commentaries, for discussion and adoption by the Commission. After the Commission has provisionally submitted a set of draft articles, it decides to submit them to the governments of member States for their comments. Thereafter, the draft articles and commentaries are revised by the Commission in the light of the comments submitted in writing, or made orally in the debates of the General Assembly. When the revision of a set of draft articles has been completed, it is submitted to the General Assembly, which may decide to convoke an international Conference to conclude a Convention on the topic, or may decide upon some other disposition.

Functioning of the International Law Commission :

The Commission began its work in 1949. On the basis of the drafts prepared by the Commission, a number of multilateral Conventions have been adopted. Some important Conventions are the Geneva Conventions (four) on the Law of the Sea (1958); the Vienna Convention on Diplomatic Relations (1961); the Convention on Consular Relations (1963) Convention on Special Mission (1969); Convention on the Prevention and Punishment of Crimes Against Internationally Protected Persons, including Diplomatic Agents (1973); Vienna Convention on the Representation of States in Their Relations with Organisations of a Universal Character, Convention on the Law of Treaties (1969); the Vienna Convention on Succession of States in Respect of Treaties (1978); Vienna Convention on Succession of States in respect of State Property, Archives and Debts (1983); Convention on the Law of Treaties to which International Organisations are Parties (1986) and the Convention on the Law of the Non-Navigational Use of International Watercourses (1997). In 2004, the United Nations Convention on Jurisdictional Immunities of States and their property has been adopted by the General Assembly. The topics wherein Conventions have been formulated are of traditional International Law. Thus, a great deal of customary International Law has been transformed into treaty rules. One of the most outstanding contribution of the Commission has been the preparation of the draft Statute of the International Criminal Court.[1] On the basis of the draft, Rome Statute of the International Criminal Court was adopted on July 17, 1998.

The Commission has also prepared drafts on a few subjects where action has not been taken as yet. For instance, Draft Declaration on Rights and Duties of States (1949); Draft Code of Offences against the Peace and Security of Mankind (1951); Draft Convention on the Elimination of Future Statelessness (1954) and the Draft Articles on Responsibility of States for Wrongful Acts (2001). The Commission also worked on the subjects like, formulation of the Nuremberg Principles in 1950; Questions of Defining Aggression, Extended Participation in General Multilateral Treaties concluded under the auspices of the League of Nations and Ways to make the Evidence of Customary International Law more readily available (1950).

The Commission in its 71st Session held in 2019 discussed the topics which included Draft Model Clauses on Provisional application of treaties, Protection of the environment in relation to armed conflicts, protection of atmosphere, crime against humanity, general principles of International Law, Sea- level rise in relation to International Law, Prevention and repression of piracy and armed robbery at sea.

(2) United Nations Environment Programme (UNEP)

UNEP was set up as a result of the United Nations Conference on the Human Environment (commonly called Stockholm Conference) by the General

1. For detail *see* H.O. Agrawal, 'International Law and Human Rights', 21st Edition (2016), Chapter, 'International Criminal Court'.

Assembly through the adoption of a resolution on December 15, 1972.[1] The establishment of the UNEP was reaffirmed by the General Assembly in 1976.[2] It has its Headquarters in Nairobi (Kenya) and six regional offices and various country offices. UNEP comprises the United Nations Environment Assembly which is the governing body. It was created in 2012 to replace the Governing Council. The Assembly has 193 members and meets every two years in Nairobi. The Assembly is led by a Bureau and its President. The first session of the Assembly was held in 2014.

UNEP is the designated authority of the United Nations system on environmental issues at the global and regional level. Its mandate is to coordinate the development of environmental policy consensus by keeping the global environment under review and bringing emerging issues to the attention of governments and the international community for action. The mandate and objectives of the UNEP emanates from the Resolution 2997 (XXVII) of December 15, 1972 and subsequent amendments adopted at United Nations Conference on Environment and Development (UNCED) in 1992; the Nairobi Declaration on the Role and Mandate of UNEP and the Malmo Ministerial Declaration of May 31, 2000.

Main functions and responsibilities of the UNEP are as follows :

(a) To promote international co-operation in the environment field and to recommend, as appropriate, policies to this end;

(b) To provide general policy guidance for the direction and co-ordination of environmental programmes within the United Nations system;

(c) To receive and review the periodic reports of the Executive Director on the implementation of environmental programme within the United Nations system;

(d) To keep under review the world environmental situation in order to ensure that emerging environmental problems of wide international significance receive appropriate and adequate consideration by Governments;

(e) To promote the contribution of the relevant international scientific and other professional communities to the acquisition, assessment and exchange of environmental knowledge and information and, as appropriate, to the technical aspects of the formulation and implementation of environment programmes within the United Nations systems;

(f) To maintain under continuing review the impact of national and international environmental policies and measures on developing countries, as well as the problem of additional costs that may be incurred by developing countries in the implementation of environmental programmes and projects, and to ensure that such programmes and projects shall be compatible with the development plans and priorities of those countries;

1. General Assembly Resolution 2997 dated December 15, 1972.
2. General Assembly Resolution 32/12 dated December 16, 1976.

(g) To review and approve annually the programme of utilization of resources of the Environment Fund.

In addition to the above, Assenbly is required to report annually to the General Assembly of the United Nations through the Economic and Social Council, which will transmit to the Assembly such comments on the reports as may deem necessary.

The Governing Council (replaced by the Environment Assembly in 2012) held its first session in Geneva in 1973. Since then, it has met on many occasions and has discussed and reported different subjects relating to environment which includes : The Atmosphere, Marine Environment, Fresh-water Environment, Land Environment, Food and Agriculture Environment and Health, Energy, Environmental Pollution, Man and Environment, Environment management achievements. From the above list, it is evident that the Governing Council has given due emphasis to the people. The human impacts of diseases whose prevalence depends especially on environmental factors, the effects on people of chemicals in the environment and the ways in which human activities influence the environment, account for the bulk of activities.

The convening of the Habitat Conference in 1976 was the greatest contribution of the Governing Council of UNEP wherein it was declared that nations must avoid the pollution of the Biosphere of all environment resources, whether non-renewable or renewable in the long term. UNEP has contributed directly or indirectly to the development of several multilateral environmental treaties.[1]

(3) United Nations Commission for International Trade Law (UNCITRAL) :

When it became clear that the International Law Commission would not find time to take up questions of private law for codfication, the United Nations Commission for International Trade Law (UNCITRAL) was established by the General Assembly by adopting Resolution 2205(XXI) on December 17, 1966. In establishing the Commission, the General Assembly recognised that disparities in national laws governing international trade created obstacles to the flow of trade, and it regarded the Commission as the vehicle by which the United Nations could play a more active role in reducing or removing these obstacles. The Assembly gave the Commission the general mandate to further the progressive harmonization and unification of the law of international trade. The Commission has since come to be the 'core legal body' of the United Nations system in the field of International trade law.

The Commission was originally composed of twenty-nine governmental experts in the field of international trade law within the United Nations. Its membership was extended in 1973 to 36 and again in 2004 to 60 States.

The Commission has produced draft Conventions which were later adopted in diplomatic Conferences such as the Convention on the Limitation Period in the International Sale of Goods (1974); Convention on the Carriage of

1. For detail *see* H.O. Agrawal, 'International Law and Human Rights', 21st Edition (2016), Chapter, 'Environment'.

Goods by Sea (so-called Hamburg Rules) (1978) and the United Nations Convention on Contracts for the Sale of Goods (1980); United Nations Convention on the Liability of Operators or Transport Terminals in International Trade; United Nations Convention on International Bills of Exchange and International Promissory Notes (1988); United Nations Convention on Independent Guarantees and Stand-by Letters of Credit (1995) and the United Nations Convention on the Assignment of Receivables in International Trade (2001); the United Nations Convention on the use of Electronic Communications in International Contracts (2005) and the United Nations Convention on Contracts for the International Carriage of Goods Wholly or Partly by Sea (2008).

UNCITRAL has also adopted Model Law on different topics such as Model Law on International Commercial Arbitration (1985), Model Law on International Credit Transfers (1992), Model Law on Procurement of Goods and Construction (1994) Model Law on Procurement of Goods, Construction and Services (1994) and Model Law on International Commercial Conciliation (2002) and Model Legislative Provisions on Privately Financed Infrastructures Projects (2003).

(4) United Nations High Commissioner for Refugees (UNHCR) :

The General Assembly on December 3, 1949 adopted Resolution 319(iv) wherein it decided to establish UNHCR and on December 14, 1950 adopted the Statute of the Office of the United Nations High Commissioner for Refugees (UNHCR). It is a subsidiary organ of the General Assembly and acts under the authority of the General Assembly.

UNHCR came into existence on January 1, 1951 initially for a period of three years. Later, General Assembly decided to prolong the mandate for a further period of five years and made it renewable beginning from January 1, 1954. In the year 2000, the General Assembly resolved to continue UNHCR for a period of five years from January 1, 2004. Antonio Guterres of Portugal was appointed the High Commissioner on June 15, 2005 for a five years term. In April, 2010, the General Assembly re-elected Guterres to a second five years term.

The High Commissioner is required to report annually to the General Assembly, through the ECOSOC and its report is considered as a separate item. Its headquarters are in Geneva which coordinates the activities of 274 subordinate offices located in as many as sixty eight States. The Office also develops appropriate policy to curb the refugee problems.

The High Commissioner is elected by the General Assembly, on the nomination of the Secretary General and is responsible to the Assembly.

The Statute of the UNHCR provided that the High Commissioner shall seek the opinion of an Advisory Committee on Refugees, if it is established. In 1951, the ECOSOC established the Advisory Committee on Refugees to guide the High Commissioner, at his request in the exercise of his functions. The Committee consisted of 15 States of whom 12 were members of the United Nations and three were non-members. They were selected on the strength of their devotion to the solution of the refugee problems. Advisory Committee in

1955 was reconstituted by the General Assembly and ECOSOC as an Executive Committee known as UN Refugee Fund Executive Committee (UNRFE Committee) which retained the advisory functions of the Advisory Committee. The membership of the Committee had the original 15 member States of the Advisory Committee with an additional five members which became six in 1957. In 1958, the UNRFE Committee was replaced by the Executive Committee of the High Commissioner's Programme (EXCOM) which not only render advices to the High Commissioner, at his request, but it also reviews the use of the Emergency fund.

The High Commissioner's programme is administered by a thirty-member Executive Committee, which generally meets twice a year at Geneva. It consists of representatives of members of the United Nations and of the specialized agencies, who are elected by the Economic and Social Council on the widest geographical basis from among those States with a demonstrated interest in and devotion to the solution of the refugee problem.

Mandated refugees, as defined in the UNHCR Statute, are persons who, owing to well-founded fear of persecution for reason of race, religion, nationality or political opinion, are outside their country of origin and cannot or, owing to such fear, do not wish to avail themselves of the protection of that country. UNHCR is not, of course, concerned with all refugees throughout the World. For instance, refugees considered as nationals by the countries which have granted them asylum are not a UNHCR responsibility. Nor is UNHCR concerned with refugees for whom another United Nations body has assumed full responsibility, such as the Arab refugees from Palestine under the mandate of UNRWA.[1]

The work of UNHCR is humanitarian, social and non-political. Its basic tasks are to provide international protection to the refugees within the High Commissioner's mandate and to seek permanent solutions to their problems by facilitating their voluntary repatriation or their assimilation within new national communities. The above may mean that UNHCR tries to ensure that refugees are not refouled (deported) to their countries of origin or to a place where there lives are in danger and they are assured safety in the country of asylum. UNHCR also promotes standards of treatment of refugees that accrued with basic human rights standards.

The UNHCR initially focused its efforts on aiding refugees and displaced persons in Europe after World War II, but in later decades effort was shifted to resettling refugees who were the victims of war, political turmoil or natural disasters in Africa and parts of Asia and Latin America. It has facilitated the return of 2,50,00 Algerian refugees in 1962, repatriated 10 million Bangladeshis and 150000 Sudanese in 1972 and organized one of history's largest airlift population exchanges—a two way movement of large numbers of people

1. United Nations Relief and Works Agency for Palestine Refugees in the North East (UNRWA) was established by the General Assembly on December 8, 1949. Under the founding resolution, UNRWA's functions were primarily to carry out relief and works programmes in collaboration with local governments and also to consult with the interested Near Eastern governments concerning the measures they should takes against the time when international aid for such programmes would cease to be available.

between Bangladesh and Pakistan in 1973. The UNHCR was awarded the Nobel Peace Prize twice, in 1954 and 1981 for its excellent work. By 1997 UNHCR provided internal protection and assistance to more than 12 million people who fled from war or persecution. UNHCR has been an active office for the cause of refugees. Many States in many parts of the World are under considerable pressure from public and private groups to treat refugees in accordance with human rights norms.

UNHCR's mandate was to protect refugees but in recent years it has been involved in programmes for Internationally Displaced Persons (IDP) as well. The agency can act to help these people at the request of the Secretary General of the United Nations or a competent principal organ of the United Nations and with the consent of the government of the country involved. At various times and in operations of diverse magnitude, UNHCR has helped IDP in Afghanistan, Angola, Azerbaijan, Bosnia and Herzegovina, Croatia, El Slavador, Ethiopia, Georgia and Iraq. UNHCR—a humanitarian organization depends upon member States for funding and also on compliance of the minimum standards towards refugees.

(5) United Nations Development Programme (UNDP) :

The General Assembly on the recommendation of the Economic and Social Council decided to merge the Expanded Programme of Technical Assistance (EPTA)[1] and the Special Fund[2] into a programme to be known as United Nations Development Programme (UNDP). UNDP was founded on November 22, 1965. The Assembly while consolidating the two programmes expressed the conviction that it would simplify organisational arrangements and procedures and would facilitate over-all planning of the several types of technical cooperation programmes carried on within the United Nations System. UNDP is Headquartred in New York city. It has country offices in 177 countries where it works with local governments to meet development challenges and develop local capacity.

UNDP provides expert advice, training and grant support to developing countries with increasing emphasis on assistance to the least-developing countries. UNDP focuses on poverty reduction, HIV/AIDS, democratic governance, energy and environment, social development and crisis prevention and recovery. UNDP also encourages the protection of human rights and the empowerment of women in all of its programs. UNDP plays a significant coordination role for the activities of the United Nations in the field of development. This is mainly executed through the leadership of the UN Development Group (UNDG) and through the Resident Coordinator System.

Direct policy control is provided by the Governing Council of the UNDP who are elected from among the developing and developed countries. UNDP is managed by an Administrator who is the third highest ranking official of the United Nations after the Secretary-General and the Deputy Secretary-General. The Administrator along with Co-Administrator and their staff operates from the UN Headquarters. The Administrators are advised by an Inter-Agency

1. EPTA was established in 1950.
2. Special Fund was established in 1959.

Consultative Board composed of heads of the twelve executing agencies. UNDP is serviced in the field, in addition to the facilities provided by the executing agencies by field officers who work closely with governments and with the international organisations to identify needs for the assistance.

Resources of the UNDP are provided by the voluntary contributions of the U.N. Member States for carrying out UNDP projects.

(6) United Nations Children Fund (UNICEF) :

The United Nations International Children's Emergency Fund (UNICEF) also known as United Nations Children's Fund was created by the General Assembly in 1946 to provide relief to children suffering in the aftermath of the Second World War. In 1953 UNICEF became a permanent part of the United Nations System. When the Assembly in 1953 extended UNICEF's mandate indefinitely the words 'International' and 'Emergency' were dropped from its name but it is continued to be known by the popular acronym based on the old name. It is an intergovernmental organisation (IGO) and thus is accountable to these governments.

UNICEF provides long-term humanitarian and developmental assistance to children and mothers in developing countries. The Fund gives special attention on the widespread malnutrition, disease and illiteracy afflicting millions of children throughout the developing World.

The Fund has semi-autonomous status within the United Nations. It reports to Economic and Social Council and to the General Assembly. The Fund has its own Executive Board consisting of representatives of 36 States chosen by the Economic and Social Council usually for a period of three years. The Board establishes policies and approves programmes and overseas administrative and financial plans. The Board meets annually to review its programmes. UNICEF National Committees have been set up in 36 countries worldwide as an independent local non-governmental organisation.

Their main function is to raise funds. In addition to their fund-raising efforts, they help to inform the public about the needs of the children in the developing World and to explain how the Children's Fund works to meet these needs.

UNICEF is funded exclusively by voluntary contributions. Approximately, three quarters from Governments and the remainder from the general public, *i.e.*, contributions from corporations, civil society organisations and individual donors.

The Children's Fund provides a framework for advocacy on behalf of children and works to increase both decision-making and public awareness of the special needs of children. It undertakes analysis of national development plans, relates those plans to the well being of the children and the rates of death and disease among children. UNICEF was awarded Nobel Peace Prize in 1965 for its excellent work.

(7) Special Committee on the Question of Defining Aggression :

The task for defining aggression was entrusted to the International Law Commission by the General Assembly in 1950 on the proposal of the Soviet

Union. However, the Commission did not furnish the definition of the term by stating that the concept of aggression is a 'natural' one, which was not susceptible to definition. However, the General Assembly considered that a satisfactory definition of the term is 'possible and desirable' with a view to ensuring international peace and security. In 1952, the Assembly established a Special Committee for defining aggression as a subsidiary organ.[1] After a long exchange of views and deliberations, the Committee established in 1967[2] approved a definition by consensus and referred to the General Assembly. The Assembly thereupon adopted a resolution 'Definition of Aggression' on December 14, 1974.[3] The purpose of defining the term aggression is to recommend to the Security Council to take account of the definition as guidance in determining, in accordance with the Charter, the existence of an act of aggression so that it may recommend or decide as to what measures shall be taken by it in accordance with Articles 41 and 42, to maintain or restore international peace and security.

The resolution defines under Article 1 that 'aggression is the use of armed force by a State against the sovereignty, territorial integrity or political independence of another State, or in any other manner inconsistent with the Charter of the United Nations'.

The definition has asserted under Article 2 that 'the first use of armed force by a State in contravention of the Charter shall constitute *prima facie* evidence of an act of aggression'. It means that if a State, whatever grievance it may have, uses the armed force, shall be deemed aggressor. Thus, the concept of priority (first use of force), an objective criterion, has been regarded as a test for determining the act of aggression and the aggressor.

Acts Qualifying Aggression :

Article 3 of the definition has enumerated certain 'acts' which, if they are committed would be regarded as aggression 'regardless of a declaration of war'. These acts are as follows—

(a) Invasion or Attack :

The invasion or attack by the armed forces of a State on the territory of another State heads the list of clearly aggressive acts as provided under Para (1) of Article 3. Military occupation, however temporary, resulting from such invasion or attack, or any annexation are also added and are regarded as aggression.

(b) Bombardment and the Use of Weapons :

Para (b), Article 3 stipulates two different acts as aggressive acts : firstly, the bombardment by the armed forces of a State against the territory of another State, and secondly, the use of any weapons, by a State against the territory of another State. The expression 'any weapons' includes not only the use of nuclear, bacteriological and chemical weapons but also any other weapons of mass destruction.

1. General Assembly Resolution 688 (VII) December 20, 1952.
2. General Assembly Resolution 2330 (XXII) Dated December 18, 1967.
3. General Assembly Resolution 3314 (XXIX) December 14, 1974.

(c) Blockade :

Blockade of the 'ports or coasts' of a State by the forces of another State has been regarded as an aggressive act.

(d) Attack on Land, Sea or Air Forces or Marine or Air Fleets :

An attack by the armed forces of a State on the land, sea or air forces or marine or air-fleets of another State also constitute an act of aggression under Para (d) of Article 3. It implies that attack on vessels or aircraft would be aggression regardless of the fact as to whether they are military or civilian.

(e) The Use of Armed Forces in Contravention of Conditions provided in the Agreement :

Para (e) of Article 3 indicates that a State having its troops within the territory of another State where they have been lawfully stationed might be guilty of aggression if they use the forces in contravention of the conditions provided in the agreement between the sending State and the receiving State, or if they did not evacuate those troops beyond the termination of the agreement.

(f) Perpetration of an Act of Aggression :

The action of a State which has placed its territory at the disposal of another State shall be deemed aggression under Para (f) of the Article 3 if the latter uses this territory for perpetrating an act of aggression against a third State with the acquiescence or agreement of the former.

(g) Sending of Armed Bands, Groups, Irregulars or Mercenaries :

Para (g) of Article 3 provides that the sending by a State or on behalf of it, to another State armed bands, groups, irregulars or mercenaries which carry out grave acts or armed forces against another State would be deemed as aggression. The gravity and the substantial involvement of the armed bands, and whether their acts amount to aggression or not, would be considered by the Security Council after taking all the circumstances into account.

The above acts enumerated under Article 3 are not exhaustive. The Security Council may determine 'other acts' also as an act of aggression under the provisions of the Charter.[1] Thus, the definition does not curtail or fetter the discretionary power of the Security Council as provided under Article 39 of the Charter to determine the act of aggression. It was done so perhaps because of the fact that the Security Council has a primary responsibility for the maintenance of international peace and security as provided under Article 24 of the Charter.

(8) Committee on the Peaceful Uses of Outer Space (COPUOS)

The COPUOS was established by the General Assembly[2] in 1959 as a subsidiary organ to review the scope of international cooperation in peaceful uses of outer space. The Committee has two standing sub-committees : Legal and Scientific and Technological Sub-committees. The Legal Sub-committee was required to study and report on the legal problems which might arise from the

---

1. *See* Article 4.
2. General Assembly Resolution 1477 (XIV) dated December 12, 1959.

exploration and use of outer space. Question on the adoption of a Declaration of legal principles governing the activities of States in outer-space was first raised in 1962 before the legal sub-committee. In 1963 the General Assembly unanimously adopted a Declaration of Legal Principles Governing the Activities of States in the exploration and use of outer space. In the above Declaration nine principles were formulated which are as follows :

(1) The use of outer space for the benefit of mankind;
(2) Freedom of exploration and use of outer space and celestial bodies by all States in accordance with international law;
(3) prohibition of national appropriation of outer space and celestial bodies;
(4) the carrying out of activities of States in the exploration and use of outer space in accordance with the principles of international law;
(5) international responsibility of States for activities in outer space by their governmental agencies or by non-governmental entities;
(6) observance of corresponding interests of other States in outer space and conduct of appropriate international consultations;
(7) retention of ownership of objects launched into outer space and of jurisdiction and control by the State by registry over such objects, and personnel thereon while in outer space.
(8) international liability of States for damage caused by objects launched into outer space, and
(9) rendering of all posible assistance to, and return of astronauts in the event of accident, distress or emergency landing.

General Assembly on December 13, 1963 adopted a resolution wherein it recommended that consideration be given to incorporate these principles in an international agreement. The task was given to the Legal Sub-committee which began consideration in 1966 on the above questions. It has adopted five treaties and agreements which are : (1) Outer Space Treaty (1967); (2) Rescue Agreement (1968); (3) Liability Convention (1971); (4) Registration Convention (1974) and (5) Moon Treaty (1979).[1]

The Commitee on Peaceful Uses of Outer Space oversees the implementation of all the above treaties and agreements.

In addition to the above Conventions draft principles on Remote Sensing was adopted in 1986 by the Legal Sub-committee which was adopted by the General Assembly on December 3, 1987 wherein a set of fifteen principles relating to Remote Sensing of the Earth from Space was adopted.

(9) Military Staff Committee (MSC) :

MSC is the only subsidiary organ of the Security Council which is named in the Charter.[2] Its constitution and functions are laid down in the Charter under Article 46.[3] The MSC was required to plan UN military operation and assist in

1. For detail *see* H.O. Agrawal, International Law and Human Rights, 23rd Edition (2021), Chapter, 'Outer Space'.
2. *See* Chapter 'Security Council'.
3. *See Ibid*.

the regulation of armaments. But due to Cold War MSC could not be constituted and it became a 'dormant' part of the United Nations structure. Even after the end of Cold War MSC could not be constituted.

In the 2005 Summit of the World Leaders—Heads of State and Government was held which adopted the World Summit Outcome. The Outcome document laid down that the Security Council shall be requested to consider the composition, mandate and working methods of the MSC. However, MSC has not been constituted.

(10) Counter-Terrorism Committee :

The Security Council, in the wake of the 11 September, 2001 terrorist acts in the United States adopted Resolution 1373 on September 28, 2001 wherein it called on all States to work together urgently to bring the perpetrators to justice. The main thrust of the resolution was on the financing of terrorist operation and to stop providing safe haven to anyone who supports terrorists or their organisations. By the same resolution it established the 15 members Counter-Terrorism Committee to monitor implementation of the resolution with the assistance of the appropriate experts. The Council called upon all States to report to the Committee, not later than 90 days from the date of the adoption of the resolution on the steps they have taken to implement it.

The Committee has been effective in requiring member States to take steps to deny terrorists safe havens, prohibiting the raising or transferring of funds, freezing assets and sharing information about possible terrorist activities. The Council by adopting Resolution 1535 in the year 2004 created the Counter-Terrorism Committee Executive Directorate (CTED) to provide the Committee with experts advice on all areas covered by Resolution 1373. CTED was also required to facilitate technical assistance to countries and to provide cooperation and coordination both within the UN system of organisations and among regional and intergovernmental bodies. CTED was formerly declared operational in December 2005. Its mandate was extended to by the end of 2017.[1]

(11) Compensation Commission :

The United Nations Compensation Commission (UNCC) was established on May 20, 1991 by adopting Resolution 692 (1991) as a subsidiary organ of the Security Council. The UNCC was required to process claims and pay compensation for loses resulting from Iraq's invasion and occupation of Kuwait.[2] Compensation was required to be paid to successful claimants from a special fund that receives a percentage of the proceeds from sales of Iraqi oil.

The UNCC has three organs: Governing Council, Commissioners and the Secretariat. The Governing Council consists of all the fifteen members of the Security Council. The Council sets its policy within the framework of relevant resolutions of the Security Council. As such it establishes the criteria for the

1. Security Council Resolution 2129 (2013).
2. Security Council by adopting Resolution 687 on April 3, 1991 had established Iraq's legal responsibility under international law for any direct loss, damage including environmental damage and the depletion of natural resources, or injury to foreign Governments, nationals and corporations as a result of Iraq's unlawful invasion and occupation of Kuwait.

compensation of claims and set the rules and procedures for processing the claims, the guidelines for the administration and financing of the Compensation Fund and the procedures for the payment of compensation. It reports regularly to the Security Council on the work of the Commission. Commissioners verify and evaluate claims, and, in doing so they determine whether they are directly related to Iraq's invasion and occupation of Kuwait. They assess the value of the losses suffered by claimants and recommend compensation in reports to the Governing Council. Commissioners are appointed by the Executive Secretary who recommends the names of candidates to the Secretary-General. The Secretary General nominates them for the Governing Council's decision. The Council thereafter decides on their appointments. They are appointed for fixed terms. The Secretariat of the Commission provides service to the Governing Council and to the panels of Commissioners. They provide administrative, technical and legal support. The Secretariat also administers the Compensation Fund. The Secretariat is headed by the Executive Secretary.

UNCC on October 23, 2014 settled the damage claims of those who suffered loses in the 1990 Iraqi invasion of Kuwait by providing $ 1.06 billion dollers to the Government of Kuwait. With this payment, the total amount of compensation received by Kuwait amount to $ 47.8 billion doller.

(12) United Nations Conference on Trade and Development (UNCTAD) :

Rapid expansion in the World economy after the Second World War gave rise in the 1960's to the need for a multilateral organisation to assist developing countries in their efforts to industrialize and to participate in World trade. The General Assembly on December 30, 1964 by adopting a resolution decided to establish the United Nations Conference on Trade and Development (UNCTAD) as a principal organ of the Assembly. It is a permanent intergovernmental body. UNCTAD has 194 member States. Its Headquarter is located at Geneva (Switzerland).

The main functions of the UNCTAD are provided in the resolution of the General Assembly which are : (a) to promote international trade with a view to accelerate economic development; (b) to formulate principles and policies on international trade and related problems of economic development; (c) to review and facilitate the consideration of activities of other institutions within the United Nations System in the field of international trade and development; (d) to initiate actions, where appropriate, in cooperation with the competent organs of the United Nations, for the negotiations and adoption of multilateral agreements in the field of trade; and (e) to be available as a center for harmonising the trade and developmental policies of Governments and regional economic groupings.

The UNCTAD fulfils the above mandate by carrying out these important functions which are : firstly, it functions as a forum for intergovernmental deliberations, supported by discussions with experts and exchanges of experience, aimed at consensus building; secondly, it undertakes research, policy analysis and data collection for the debates of Government representatives and experts, and thirdly, it provides technical assistance tailored to the specific quirements of developing countries with special attention to the needs of the least developed countries.

The Conference comprises those States which are members of the United Nations, its Specialized Agencies or International Atomic Energy Agency. The first UNCTAD Conference took place in 1964 and since then Conference has been meeting regularly in the interval of four years. Thirteenth Conference met in Doha (Qatar) in 2012.

The Trade and Development Board, the permanent organ of the Conference is required to keep under review and take appropriate action for the implementation of the recommendations and other decisions of the Conference. The Board members are elected by the Conference from among its membership. The Board has set up main subsidiary organs for the effective discharge of its functions such as Committee on Commodities, the Committee on Manufacture; the Committee on Invisible and Financing related to Trade; the Committee on Shipping; the Committee on Preferences; the Committee on Transfer of Technology and the Committee on Economic Cooperation and Developing Countries.

The Secretariat of the UNCTAD is headed by a Secretary-General who is appointed by the Secretary-General of the United Nations and confirmed by the General Assembly. The headquarters of the Secretariat are in Geneva.

Chapter 13

Collective Security Under the United Nations

Collective security is an arrangement among States wherein it is agreed that collective action shall be taken by all the States against a State in response to threats to and breaches to peace. The above implies that the essential elements of the collective security system are : firstly, the prohibition of the use of force by all the States; secondly, collective guarantee of security by all for all States, and thirdly, the use of collective action in case aggression is committed by a State. Thus, the collective system is based on the idea that it would work with the cooperation of all and thereby on the principle 'one for all and all for one'. The system of collective security is formalized legally through a multilateral treaty. The main purpose of the collective security system is to establish a just and equitable universal and regional order whenever and wherever necessary.

Proper functioning of the collective security is dependent upon military, political and legal pre-requisites. They are required to be met for the effective collective security system. The first essential condition from the military point of view is that there should be sufficiently a strong peace-keeping force which should be stronger than the strongest single military force mobilized by an aggressor. The second pre-requisite for the proper functioning of collective security is the political solidarity or consensus among the member States. The third pre-requisite is that there should be general prohibition of the use of force except by the authorisation of the competent central organ of a collective system or in cases of self defence.

The first attempt to provide collective security system was introduced in modern time with the establishment of the League of Nations. Since the Covenant of the League neither completely outlawed war nor prohibited the use of force, the collective security system was imperfect. Complete lack of a coordinate central decision-making procedure for applying sanctions against the aggressor hampered the effective functioning of the collective security system. The idea of collective security was again adopted under the Charter of the United Nations. Drafters of the Charter were determined to avoid the weaknesses and errors of the Covenant.

The Charter like the Covenant of the League of Nations made elaborate provisions for the collective security system to fulfil one of its purpose *i.e.* to maintain international peace and security, *i.e.*, to preserve peace and prevent war. The United Nations was founded upon the assumption that the best way to promote lasting peace is through a system of collective security, which can both suppress aggression and give warning to potential aggressor so that aggression may not succeed. Article 1 of the Charter calls for the effective collective measures for the prevention and removal of threats to the peace and for the suppression of acts of aggression. It implies that the action shall be taken by the United Nations and, not by the members independently. The words 'effective collective measures' set the requirement of the application of tangible pressure and the words 'for the prevention and removal of threats to the peace and for the suppression of acts of aggression' directly set forth the limits of taking the collective measures particularly for serious categories of situations. Although the expression 'collective security' has not been used in the Charter of the United Nations, it has made elaborate provisions for taking the collective measures. Such measures may be taken by the two principal organs of the United Nations, *i.e.*, the Security Council and the General Assembly.

SECURITY COUNCIL

Maintenance of international peace and security is the primary responsibility of the Security Council. Members of the United Nations have conferred this responsibility to the Council under Article 24 Para 1 of the Charter. The members have also agreed that the Council shall act on their behalf in carrying out its duties under this responsibility and they agree to accept and carry out the decisions of the Security Council in accordance with the present Charter.[1] The Council performs functions relating to the maintenance of international peace and security in two ways, *i.e.*, by peaceful means which are laid down under Chapter VI of the Charter and by taking enforcement action.

The Security Council has been empowered to determine, under Article 39 of the Charter, that there exits threat to the peace, breach of the peace or act of aggression. If it decides so it may take enforcement action as provided under Chapter VII of the Charter which was recognised by the delegates to the San Francisco Conference as "the teeth of the United Nations". The enforcement action taken by the Security Council as provided under Chapter VII of the Charter comprising under Articles 39 to 51 is called the collective security measure.

The Security Council if it decides that there exists threat to the peace, breach of the peace or an act of aggression it may take action under Article 41 to apply measures like complete or partial economic blockade and interruptions of rail, sea, air, postal, telegraphic, radio and means of communication and the severance of diplomatic relations so as to give effect to its decisions. These measures are called short of military action. If the Security Council considers that measures provided for in Article 41 are not adequate or they have proved to be inadequate, it may take such action by air, sea or land forces as may be necessary to maintain or restore international peace and security. These may include demonstrations, blockade and other operations by air, sea or land forces of members of the United Nations to maintain international peace and security.[2]

In order to ensure prompt and effective action against the delict State, Article 43 of the Charter imposes an obligation on all the members of the United Nations to conclude special agreements[3] for the formation of a force

1. Article 25.
2. See Chapter 'Security Council'.
See *Ibid*.

permanently available at the disposal of the Security Council. The agreements mentioned under Article 43 have to be negotiated on the initiative of the Security Council and to be concluded between the members and the Security Council.

In order to enable the United Nations to take urgent military measures, members are required to provide their national air force contingent for combined international enforcement action. Provision for the creation of the Military Staff Committee[1] was also made in the Charter under Article 46 to advise and assist the Security Council on all military problems. In addition to the above the Council is also empowered to take provisional measures under Article 40 in order to prevent aggravation of the situation before making recommendations, or deciding the measures provided for in Article 39.

The United Nations was thus founded upon the assumption that the best way to promote peace and security is through a system of collective security, which can both suppress aggression and give warning to potential aggressor that aggression does not succeed. It was indeed a progressive development that the determination of delict and the guilty State, the decision on military and non-military sanction and the execution of the sanction were radically centralized in the Security Council. For the first time an organ of the international organisation, the Security Council, was created with real powers. Although the League of Nations had also made a provision for the collective security, it was stronger under the United Nations. It is so because all the members of the United Nations are legally bound to give every assistance in any action which the Security Council takes, and they are required to refrain from giving assistance to a State against which the United Nations is taking preventive or enforcement action. The theory is in reality the old Grotian concept of 'just war' which has presently revived and has become a leading principle of the United Nations. However, the collective security system under the Charter could not work effectively mainly because of the following reasons :

(1) Veto Power

It is difficult to determine the delict under Article 39 because the moment a permanent member is involved in the dispute either directly or indirectly by being in sympathy with the cause of the aggressor, the peace enforcement machinery breaks down. The permanent members may prevent the Council from taking any action against the aggressor by exercising their special power, 'veto' which if used has a potency to nullify the effect of all other affirmative votes cast by the other members of the Security Council. The practice of the Security Council reveals that on many occasions no action could be taken by the Council against a State only on account of its failure to determine the culprit State due to the veto power. The notorious and unjust veto power has therefore transformed the strength of the Security Council into a degree of impotency. Between 1946 to 1990 on 194 occassions veto power has been exercised. Thus, it had paralysed the whole sanctioning functions of the Security Council. The root cause of the failure of the Council in determining a situation under Article 39 has been the cold war because the 'big powers' exercised veto in each and every

1. See *Ibid*.

such efforts where a friend or ally of any of them was involved. With the end of the cold war, as a result of the political and economic transformation of the Soviet Union and the Eastern Europe, and later with the disintegration of the Soviet Union attitude of the Super Powers has changed towards the maintenance of the World Order. Perhaps, this reason led to the Council to declare in no time that the annexation of Kuwait by Iraq in 1990 is null and void. Further, acting under Article 39 of the U.N. Charter, it could also determine that there exists a breach of international peace and security as regards the Iraqi invasion on Kuwait.[1] During the cold war, on an action such as Iraq's, the Council would almost certainly not have been able to determine that international breach has occurred. One or the other Super Power would not have let it. The Council after the end of Cold War has also taken collective measures not involving use of force in many cases[2] including Cambodia (1991), Yugoslavia (1992), Somalia (1992), Libya (1992), Haiti (1993), Angola (1993), Rwanda (1994), Sudan (1996), Sierra Leone (1997) and Taliban (2000).

(2) Special Agreements

No substantial force can become available to the United Nations except through the member States. No standing United Nations forces were created in 1945, or after that, primarily because of the basic disagreement between the Soviet Union and the United States on the size of the United Nations armed forces, their location, bases, logistical support and other matters. These differences, which have made the conclusion of any agreements under Article 43 impossible, were political in origin and they continued till 1990. It is so despite the fact that Article 43 obliges members to make armed forces assistance and facilities available to the Security Council but only, 'in accordance with a special agreement or agreements'. Since no such agreement has yet entered into with any member of the Organisation, whether the forces shall be available to the United Nations, if the Security Council ever decides to take measures under Article 42 is again a question which is difficult to answer in affirmative.

The above limitations have placed the sanctioning functions of the Security Council in a difficult situation. It is to be noted that they have cropped up because of the basic disagreement between the East and West Blocs which emerged soon after the signing of the Charter. It resulted in the substantial failure of the collective security system. It became apparent that the great hopes entertained in 1944-45 would never become a reality. On many occasions it failed to perform its primary responsibility of the maintenance of international peace and security. However, it would be inappropriate to say that the Council has completely failed to contribute towards it. In the past, many disputes brought before it have been compromised, postponed or otherwise prevented from leading to serious international crisis. The Council has definitely played a useful role in defusing disputes that might otherwise lead to international explosions. In the case of Korea, Indo-Pakistan conflict, Congo, Cyprus, Palestine and Arab-Israeli conflict, the Council contributed to maintain international peace either by averting conflict or by suppressing it. Although in

1. Security Council Resolution 660 (1990) of August 2, 1990.
2. For detail *see* Chapter 'Security Council'.

these cases, the Council has avoided the worsening of the situation, it failed to find the political solution of the problem.

Efforts for Making Collective Security System Effective :

It is to be noted that the Council is fully aware of its limitations. It has admitted more than once that it had not always proved possible for it to eradicate the existence of various threats to the maintenance of peace and security. The Secretary-General of the United Nations in its report on the work of the Organisation submitted to the General Assembly in 1982 had stated that 'it may be useful for the Council to give renewed consideration to reviewing and streamlining its practices and procedures with a view to acting swiftly and decisively in crisis.' He had added, 'Adequate working relations between the permanent members of the Security Council are a *sine qua non* of the Council's effectiveness. Whatever, the relations may be outside the United Nations, within the Council the permanent members, which have special rights and special responsibilities under the Charter, share a sacred trust that should not go by default owing to their bilateral difficulties. When this happens, the Council, and therefore the United Nations are the losers, since the system of collective security envisaged by the Charter presupposes, at the minimum, a working relationship among the permanent members'. The Secretary-General made 'an appeal to the members of the Council, especially to its permanent members, to re-assess their obligations in that regard and to fulfil them at the high level of responsibility indicated in the Charter.'

The Security Council, consequent to the issuance of the above report stated the consideration of the role of the Council in the maintenance of international peace and security. President of the Council on September 28, 1984, issued a note on the above subject wherein on five main aspects a new round of discussions took place which are firstly, the role of the Council in the prevention of conflicts ; secondly, the role of the Council in promoting negotiations or other peaceful settlement procedures between the parties to a dispute ; thirdly, implementation of resolutions of the Council ; fourthly, measures for giving effect to Article 43 of the Charter including the role envisaged for Military Staff Committee in Articles 43 to 47 ; and fifthly, procedural improvements designed to facilitate the effective exercise by the Council of its functions under the Charter. The note stated that due emphasis was given to the special responsibility of the Council, acting on behalf of the international community, in collective maintenance of international peace and security. How far such deliberations would be effective is a question which is premature to answer.

Security Council Summit :

The first ever Security Council Summit held on January 31, 1992 was an encouraging step towards the effective collective security system. The topic before the Summit was the responsibility of the Security Council in the maintenance of international peace and security. The Declaration issued by the Summit reaffirmed their commitment to collective security to deal with threats to peace and reverse acts of aggression and to take concrete steps to enhance the effectiveness of the body—the World body. The realisation of the obligation for the maintenance of international peace and security which has been thrust upon the members of the Security Council in a world which is no longer threatened by cold war may be deemed as of immense importance.

The second meeting at the level of heads of States and Government of the members of the Security Council was held on September 7, 2000 wherein it was resolved to strengthen the central role of the United Nations in peace keeping and pledged to take concrete steps to achieve that goal. The Council voted unanimously to adopt a Declaration on ensuring an effective role of the Security Council in the maintenance of international peace and security, particularly in Africa. The Council identified pressing social and economic problems-poverty, the spread of infectious disease and the illicit trade in natural resources, particularly diamonds—as the root causes of many conflicts, which needed to be tackled as a fundamental part of efforts to establish peace and stability in many regions of the World. In a five-part text, the Council pledged to enhance the effectiveness of the United Nations in preventing conflict at all stages i.e., from prevention to settlement to post-conflict peace building. It also 'reaffirmed its commitment to give equal priority to the maintenance of peace in every region of the World.

Agenda for Peace :

In the area of peace-making and peace-keeping, the Council invited the Secretary-General to prepare by July 1, 1992 his analysis and recommendations on ways of strengthening and making more efficient the capacity of the United Nations for preventive diplomacy, for peace-making and for peace-keeping. Accordingly, the Secretary-General on June 23, 1992 issued a report entitled "An Agenda for Peace" containing an integrated programme of proposals aimed at enhancing the United Nations role in dealing with ongoing and future conflicts. Preventive diplomacy, peace-making and peace-keeping, peace-building was the subject of the report.

Peace-Keeping

With regard to peace-keeping operations, the Secretary-General in his report appealed to States for the information on the kind and number of personnel they were prepared to offer to the United Nations should the need for new operations arises. He urged action by the General Assembly to speed up the financing of new operations. He also supported financing of such missions out of Member States' defence budget rather than foreign affairs budget. The Secretary-General recommended in his report that Security Council should consider collective measures that would come into effect if there were attacks on United Nations military or civilian members. He also recommended that the United Nations should give serious thought to the idea of a 'rapid action' military force.

Peace-Building

With regard to post-conflict peace-building, the Secretary-General recommended a wide range of activities which included the joint efforts by the parties to repatriate refugees ; removal of land mines ; improvement of transformation ; monitoring of elections ; rebuilding of strengthening of governmental institutions and protection of human rights.

In 1995, the Secretary-General stated for the expanded role ir peace-building. He observed that in recent cases conflicts occurred within State wherein armies and irregular forces fought. The result was that State institution collapsed and humanitarian emergencies developed. In this context, he said tha peace-keeping efforts called for more complex interventions. The United Nation was being called upon to promote national reconciliation and re-establis effective government, in addition to carrying out its humanitarian and militar tasks. This kind of operation, the Secretary-General said, had been deploye with success in Namibia, Cambodia and Mozambique, where a negotiate settlement had already been reached. The United Nations was thus called t help the parties, implement the settlement and undertake an unprecedente variety of functions, *i.e.*, from the demobilization of forces to the organisation c elections.

Peace-building Commission

World Summit 2005 decided to establish a Peace-building Commission a an intergovernmental advisory body after recognising the need for a dedicate institutional mechanism to address the special needs of countries emerging fror conflict towards recovery, reintegration and reconstruction. In accordance wit the above proposal the Security Council and the General Assembly o December 20, 2005 established a Peace-building Commission. The Commissio shall be a subsidiary organ of the General Assembly and the Security Counci The Commission will include an Organisational Committee and Countr Specific Committee. The Organisational Committee shall consist of 31 membe (seven Security Council members including permanent members, selected by th Council, seven members of ECOSOC, elected from regional groups, five to contributors to U.N. budgets, funds, programmes and agencies and five to providers of military personnel and civilian police to United Nations mission The General Assembly would elect seven additional members). The Commissic will be an inter-governmental advisory body and will act only by consensus.

The main functions of the Commission will be, firstly, to propo integrated strategies for post-conflict peace-building and recovery; secondly, help to ensure predictable financing for early recovery activities and sustaine financial investment over the medium to long term period; thirdly, to extend th international community's period of attention to post-conflict recovery; and he best practices on issues that require extensive collaboration among politic military, humanitarian and development actions.

Requests for the Commission's advice can be made by the Gener Assembly, the Security Council, the Economic and Social Council and th Secretary-General, as well as by any member State. The Commission is likely deal only with countries emerging from conflict, following the establishment a peace accord and a cessation of violence.

Preventive Diplomacy :

The Security Council in order to maintain international peace and securi acts when the matter is brought before it after a conflict has arisen. In th process, disputes are often allowed to go inflamated before the Council takes an action or before it provides a solution. The Council or any other body do not keep an effective global watch over situations which are likely to lead to the conflict. Preventive diplomacy is one of the means by which situation is controlled from becoming bad to worst. The Agenda defined preventive diplomacy as an action to prevent disputes from arising between parties, to prevent existing disputes from escalating into conflicts and to limit the spread of the latter when they occur.[1] Preventive diplomacy therefore envisages as 'early warning' based on information gathering and informal or formal fact-finding. It is hoped that the 'early warning' system will prevent the existing dispute from escalating into a conflict.

The identification of potential dangers require constant monitoring of the global situation. It requires measures to create confidence and early warning based on information gathering and fact-finding and may also involve preventive deployment and, in some cases, demilitarized zones. Preventive diplomacy may be performed by the Secretary-General or through senior staff or specialized agencies and programmes. It may also be performed by the Security Council, the General Assembly or by the regional organisations in co-operation with the United Nations.

Preventive diplomacy may be carried on through the mechanism of satellite monitoring. The types of monitoring envisaged under this mechanism may include verification of compliance with cease-fire arrangements, surveillance of demilitarized zones, requirements of evidence of border violations or preparations for aggression etc. Preventing conflicts require the full support of all States for its efforts and those of relevant U.N. bodies.

Although members of the United Nations received the Agenda enthusiastically, later they became suspicious as it appeared to provide a legitimate base for intervention in their affairs and an infringement on one of the principles of the United Nations, *i.e.*, State sovereignty. The result was that many recommendations were not implemented.

As a follow up to the Agenda, the Secretary-General Boutros Ghali issued a 'Supplement to an Agenda for Peace' (hereinafter referred to as supplement) in January, 1995 on the occasion of the fiftieth anniversary of the United Nations. In a significant departure from the 'Agenda', supplement recognised the UN's limitations in imposing preventive and peace-keeping services on member States that did not want them and noted 'legally and politically their request for, or at least acquiescence in, U.N. action is a *sine qua non*. The supplement duly redefined peace-keeping highlighting the importance of the consent of the parties to the presence and mandate of a mission as a pre-requisite for its success.

Use of Force by the United Nations :

With regard to the use of military force by the United Nations the Secretary General stated that the Council has the power to take whatever action necessary—including the use of air, naval or ground forces to maintain

1. *See* Report of the Secretary-General.

international peace and security. But the Council has not so far made use of the most coercive of those measures—the action by military force foreseen in Article 42. That option, he stated, is essential to the credibility of the United Nations as a guarantor of international security. In that connection, under special agreements foreseen in Article 43, member States would make armed forces available to the Council not only on an *ad hoc* basis but also on a permanent basis. He noted that since such forces are not likely to be available for some time to come, and in view of the fact that the task of United Nations forces called upon to maintain a cease-fire on accession exceeds the mission of peace-keeping, he recommended that the Council should consider creating a new category of United Nations forces 'Peace Enforcement Units'. Such units would be deployed by the Security Council as a provisional measure under Article 40 of the Charter in defined circumstances and with their terms of reference specified in advance. Such units from member States would be available on call and would consist of troops that have volunteered for such service. The system of peace-enforcement units may prove to be advantageous in the sense that it can be despatched to a trouble-spot immediately.

Instances of Collective Action of Members

Non-conclusion of a special agreement or special agreements and the suspension of the working of the Military Staff Committee has made the Council impotent to take the collective action itself against the delict State. Neither it has any force available to it to maintain international peace and security nor any body which could advise and assist on the application of such force. Thus, if the Council ever decides to take an action it authorises members of the United Nations to take action against the delict State. If the members take action pursuant to a recommendation of the Council the action is quite within the scope of Article 42 of the Charter. Such an action has been referred to by Prof. Julius Stone as 'Voluntary action of members under the licence of the Security Council'.[1] The expression 'licence of the Council' may mean that members do not have liberty to resort to force unless they are authorized by the Council for doing so. Members are allowed to take action themselves as long as the purpose for which the action has been authorized is fulfilled or unless the Security Council has decided that the action henceforth shall be taken by itself. Latter decision may be taken by the Council, if the sufficient number of special agreements under Article 43 have been concluded by it with member States.

Voluntary action is taken by the members as the agents of United Nations. It is only with their cooperation and efforts that the purposes of the United Nations can be achieved. If they take any collective action to maintain international peace and security their act is regarded legal if they have been authorized to do so by the Council. Since the Security Council is unable to take collective action in the absence of special agreements with the members for the availability of the forces, assistance and facilities under Articles 43 and 45 and also because the Military Staff Committee which has suspended its activities since 1947 it is unlikely to decide any action by itself. It authorizes its members

1. 'Legal Control of International Conflict', Second Impression, Revised with Supplements, p. 234.

to take collective action against the delict State to maintain international peace and security. The collective action by the members in the past has been taken in the following cases :—

(1) Korean Crisis :

The Security Council, after an unprovoked attack by North Korea on South Korea on June 25, 1950, determined under Article 39 that armed attack by North Korea constituted a breach of the peace. The Security Council, in the absence of Soviet Union, called for an immediate cessation of hostilities and withdrawal of North Korean forces to the 38th parallel. Since the North Korea failed to comply with these directives the Security Council adopted a resolution[1] wherein it recommended to the members of the United Nations to furnish such assistance to the South Korea as may be necessary to repel the armed attack and to restore international peace and security.

It was given effect by the United States, on the same day, when it announced that it has ordered its air and sea forces to give cover and support to the troops of the South Korean Government in accordance with the resolution of June 25, 1950. Three days later, it informed the Council that it has ordered a naval blockade of the North Korean coast and authorized the use of ground forces as a further response to the resolution. The Council on July 7, 1950 adopted a Resolution S/1588 which recommended that all members providing military forces and other assistance make such forces and assistance available to the Unified Command under the United States. The resolution also requested the United States, to designate the Commander of such forces. It further authorized the Unified Command at its discretion to use the United Nations flag in the course of operations against North Korean forces concurrently with the flag of various nations participating in the operation.

The Unified Command was constituted according to the provisions of the resolution. General Douglos MacArthur was appointed by the President of the United States as the Commanding General of the military forces which the members of the United Nations placed under the Unified Command of the United Nations. Later, the Unified Command was designated the name United Nations Command and whose headquarters was Tokyo.

The operation control of the armed forces under the Unified Command was essentially American. The Commander took his orders and directives exclusively from the United States. Neither the forces were made available to the Council nor they were kept under the command of the Military Staff Committee. They were made available to the United Command in accordance with the agreements concluded by the United States with several countries concerning the logistical support of their forces in Korea. The Commander was neither the agent of the United Nations nor his headquarters was at the United Nations.

The action was taken by the members under the command of the unified forces voluntarily on the recommendation of the Security Council. Their action, under the licence of the Security Council may be deemed as an action of the Security Council. They took such an action only because the Security Council

1. See Security council Resolution S/1501 dated 25th June, 1950 and Resolution S/1511 dated 27th June, 1950.

did not have its own military forces in the absence of the conclusion of special agreements with the member States as laid down under Article 43 of the Charter.

It is to be noted that the use of UN flag at the time of operation and the blue helmet by the forces does not make any change in the form and character of the action. The use of UN flag was not binding on the Unified Command. Its discretionary power to use it was given by the Security Council itself. It was not desirable for the Council to authorize the Unified Command to use the UN flag which is meant for the use of UN forces only. The use of the flag by the United Command was therefore irregular but that does not make the operation illegal. Baxter has rightly concluded that no doubt the forces were endowed with the name and flag of the United Nations. They do however, logically entail that the acts of the United Command or the United Nations Command are not the acts of the United Nations itself.[1] Starke says that the 'United Nations' action in Korea was such in name only but not in substance.[2]

It may be concluded that in the Korean affair voluntary action was taken by the members under the leadership of the United Nations after obtaining the licence from the Security Council to repel the aggression committed. The action may be referred to as the collective action taken by the Security Council. It was a UN action as it was taken on the recommendation of the Security Council. While an action taken by the UN forces is a UN action, all UN actions need not necessarily be taken by the UN forces.

(2) Gulf Crisis :[3]

Iraq and Kuwait—the two neighbouring States of the Persian Gulf, were the members of the United Nations Organisation. While Iraq was an original member, Kuwait got membership in 1963, after it acquired independence in 1961. There is not even the slightest doubt as to the possession of sovereignty by Kuwait. On August 2, 1990 Iraqi tanks and troops invaded and occupied Kuwait and subjugated its sovereignty. The Emir of Kuwait fled to neighbouring Saudi Arabia. A week after occupation, Kuwait was annexed, and later it was made the 19th province of Iraq comprising of three districts—Kazimah, Al Jahra and Al Nidah (old name was Al Ahmadi).

Prohibition of Invasion, Occupation and Annexation :

At the outset it is to be noted that the act of invasion, occupation and annexation are unlawful and unjustified under Article 2, Para 4 of the U.N. Charter which lays down : All members shall refrain in their international relations from the threat or use of force against the territorial integrity or political independence of any State, or in any other manner inconsistent with

1. Constitutional Forms and Some Legal Problems of International Military Command, BYIL Vol. XXIX (1960) p. 283 at p. 284.
2. Starke's International Law, Eleventh Edition (1994) p. 585.
3. For detail see H.O. Agarwal, 'Legality of the Security Council Resolution' 678 (1990), IJIL, Vol. 29 (1989) p. 277.

the purposes of the United Nations.[1] Further, Declaration on Principles of International law concerning friendly relations and co-operation among States in accordance with the Charter of the United Nations also prohibits such acts by stating that "The territory of a State shall not be the object of military occupation resulting from the use of force in contravention of the provisions of the Charter. The territory of a State shall not be the object of acquisition by another State resulting from the threat or use of force.[2] Furthermore, the Iraqi acts against Kuwait amounted to aggression under Article 1 of the resolution entitled 'Definition of Aggression'.[3] which defines aggression as "the use of armed forces by a State against the sovereignty, territorial integrity or political independence of another State, or in any manner inconsistent with the Charter of the United Nations." The same resolution under Article 3 provides a list of clearly aggressive acts. Invasion, occupation and annexation heads the list of such acts since Article 3, Para (1), in particular provides : "invasion or attack by the armed forces of a State of the territory of another State, or any military occupation, however temporary, resulting from such invasion or attack, or any annexation by the use of force of the territory of another State or part thereof."

Iraqi invasion, occupation and annexation was condemned severely by the Security Council. On August 2, 1990, in an emergency meeting, in response to Kuwait's urgent request,[4] the Security Council promptly adopted a resolution, wherein it condemned the invasion and it demanded unconditional withdrawal of all Iraqi forces from Kuwait.[5] Later, on August 9, 1990 the Council adopted another resolution by which it decided that annexation of Kuwait by Iraq under any form and whatever pretext has no legal validity and is considered 'null and void.'[6] The resolution called upon all States, international organizations, and specialized agencies not to recognize that annexation, and to refrain from any action or dealing that might be interpreted as an indirect recognition of the

1. The same prohibition is contained in the draft Declaration on Rights and Duties of States, prepared by the International Law Commission which, in Article 9, provides that "Every State has the duty to refrain from the threat.......of force against the territorial integrity or political independence of another State, or in any other manner inconsistent with International Law and Order. Draft Declaration on the Enhancement of the Effectiveness of the Principles of Refraining from the Threat or Use of Force in International Relations, prepared by the Special Committee on Enhancing the Effectiveness of the Principle of Non-Use of Force in International Relations in 1987 also stated that the principle of refraining from the threat or use of force in international relations is universal in character and is binding regardless of each State's political economic, social or cultural system or relations of alliances.
2. *See* General Assembly Resolution 2625 (XXV), of October 24, 1970. Draft Code of Offences Against the Peace and Security of Mankind, adopted by the International Law Commission in 1951 also stated that acts of authorities of a State resulting in the annexation are contrary to International Law, or territory belonging to another State, or of territory under an international regime.
3. *See* General Assembly Resolution 3314 (XXIX), of December 14, 1974.
4. S/21423. A similar request was made by the United States as well (S/21424).
5. Security Council Resolution 660 (1990), of August 2, 1990. It was adopted by 14 votes in favour to none against. Yemen did not participate in the vote explaining that its representatives had not received instructions from his Government.
6. Security Council Resolution 662 (1990), dated August 9, 1990. The resolution was adopted unanimously. The resolution again demanded that Iraq withdraw immediately and unconditionally all its forces to the position in which they were located on August 1, 1990.

annexation. It again demanded that Iraq rescind its action purporting the annex Kuwait. Iraq's invasion and annexation was unacceptable to international community and therefore it demanded for immediate withdrawal of its forces from Kuwait.

Perhaps, no one would deny that Iraqi action was a flagrant violation of the United Nations Charter. It constituted an act of brazen aggression which is most serious and dangerous form of illegal use of force. It has been affirmed by the General Assembly as the greatest of all crimes against international peace and security of mankind. The plea of even 'military necessity' cannot be given for such acts because the law admits no necessity to initiate illegal aggression.[1]

Measures Involving Non-Use of Force :

After having determined the situation under Article 39 of the Charter, the Council took a number of measures involving non-use of force under Article 41. On August 6, 1990, the Council imposed mandatory economic sanctions against Iraq[2] which obliged States to prevent the import into their territories of all commodities and products exported from Iraq or Kuwait after August 6, and to keep their nationals and others operating in their territories from selling or supplying to Iraq or Kuwait any commodities or products, including weapons or any other military equipment. An exception was made for supplies intended strictly for medical purposes and, in humanitarian circumstances, foodstuffs. States were also required to prevent transfers of funds to Iraq or Kuwait. Later, on August 25, 1990, the Council adopted another resolution[3] wherein it called upon those States which are deploying maritime forces to the area to use such measures commensurate to the specific circumstances as may be necessary under the authority of the Security Council to halt all inward or outward maritime shipping in order to inspect and verify their cargoes and destinations and to ensure strict implementation of the provisions related to such shipping laid down in resolution 661 (1990) adopted on August 5. By the resolution, the Council invited member States to co-operate as may be necessary to ensure compliance with the mandatory sanction with maximum use of political and diplomatic measures. It is to be noted that it was the first occasion when the Council authorized member States to use the forces necessary to implement trade sanction against Iraq, aimed at its withdrawal from Kuwait.

---

1. *See* Quincy Wright, 'The Outlawry of War and the Law of War', AJIL Vol. 59 (1953) p. 365 at p. 371 ; Dunbar, 'Military Necessity in War Crimes Trial', 'BYIL Vol. XXIX (1952) p. 442.
2. Security Council Resolution 661 (1990), dated August 6, 1990. It was adopted by a vote of 13 in favour to none against with two abstentions (Cuba and Yemen). The Council by the above Resolution also appointed a Committee which is known formally as the Security Council Committee Established by Resolution 661 (1990) on 6 August concerning the Situation between Iraq and Kuwait. Informally it is called the Sanctions Committee. Sanctions imposed on Iraq were lifted by the Security Council on May 22, 2003 by the adoption of the Resolution 1483 (2003) with the exception of prohibitions related to the sale or supply to Iraq of arms and related material.
3. Security Council Resolution 665 (1990) dated August 25, 1990. It was adopted by a vote of 13 in favour and none against with two abstentions (Yeman and Cuba). Resolution 221 (1966) April 9, 1966).

On September 25, 1990, the Council imposed more sanctions against Iraq.[1] It decided that all States, notwithstanding the existence of any rights or obligations conferred or imposed by any international agreement or any contract entered into or any licence or permit granted before the present resolution, shall deny permission to take any aircraft to take off from their territory if the aircraft would carry any cargo to or from Iraq or Kuwait other than food in humanitarian circumstances, subject to authorization by the Council or the Sanctions Committee, or supplies intended strictly for medical purposes or solely for UNIIMOG. The Council further decided that all States shall deny permission to any aircraft destined to land in Iraq and Kuwait, whatever its State of registration to overfly its territory.

The striking feature of the resolutions imposing sanctions under Article 41 of the Charter was the voting pattern of the permanent members. Unanimity of all the permanent members in adoption of these resolutions was indeed historic. Their unanimity exhibited that their commitment to act effectively in order to maintain or restore international peace and security, which they have made at the time of the framing of the Charter, is still firm and strong. They condemned the blatant aggression by Iraq against Kuwait and were determined to see the Iraqi withdrawal from Kuwait.

There is no doubt that unanimity of the permanent members of the Council in dealing with *Gulf Crisis* was tremendous. Had they not remained unanimous, or to say, even if one of them had shown its dissent, the situation would have been entirely different. The truth is that the principle of unanimity is the cornerstone of the structure of the United Nations.

Authorisation to Members for Their Voluntary Action :

When the measures taken under Article 41 were found inadequate to restore the political independence and sovereignty of Kuwait, the Council moved to take action involving use of force under Article 42 of the Charter. The Council on November 29, 1990 adopted a Resolution 678 which authorized member States co-operating with the Government of Kuwait to uphold and implement the Security Council resolution unless Iraq withdraws from Kuwait on or before January 15, 1991 on its own. The resolution demanded States 'to keep the Security Council regularly informed on the progress of actions'. Members States were recommended to provide appropriate support.

Resolution 678 has been branded as illegal as being in violation of the Charter. It has been asserted that the Council has not been empowered under the Charter to authorize the member States to use all necessary means against the delict State. No doubt, the Council was acting under Article 39 of the Charter, it is being criticized because no specific Article was mentioned in Resolution 678. It is to be noted that Article 42 of the U.N. Charter provides for the collective enforcement action involving use of force by stating :

Should the Security Council consider that measures provided for in Article 41 would be inadequate or have proved to be inadequate, it may take such action by air, sea or land forces as may be necessary to maintain or restore

1. Security Council Resolution 670 (1990) dated September 25, 1990. It was adopted by a vote of 14 in favour to 1 against (Cuba).

international peace and security. Such action may include demonstrations, blockade, and other operations by air, sea or land forces of Members of the United Nations.

The word 'it' in the first sentence of Article 42 has been used for the Security Council. In other words, collective enforcement action involving use of force may be taken by the Security Council itself against the delict State if the measures taken under Article 41 to maintain international peace and security are found inadequate. It may take such action by air, sea or land forces as may be necessary to maintain or restore international peace and security. Armed forces, assistance and facilities including right of passage shall be made available to the Council by members on its call and in accordance with a special agreement or agreements.[1] The agreement or agreements shall be negotiated as soon as possible on the initiative of the Security Council and groups of members.[2] These agreements shall govern the members and types of forces, their degree of readiness and general location, and the nature of the facilities and assistance to be provided.[3] When the Council decides to take any action itself, it also determines the part to be played by all the members of the United Nations.[4] Whether the action shall be taken by all the members or by some of them is determined by the Council itself. Even if only some of the members are required to carry out the action, all of them shall join in affording mutual assistance in carrying out the measures decided upon by the Security Council.[5] The tragedy of the United Nations is that not even a single agreement has been concluded as yet by the Council with the members, and therefore, the question of the availability of armed forces, the assistance and facilities provided by each member in an action taken by it does not arise.

Voluntary Action of Members was U.N. Action :

Non-conclusion of a special agreement or special agreements and the suspension of the working of the Military Staff Committee had virtually made the Council impotent to take the collective action itself against a delict State. Neither it has any force available to it to maintain international peace and security nor any body which could advise and assist on the application of such force.

It is true that in the Gulf crisis the action was taken not by the Council itself, instead it authorized under resolution 678 (1990) to member States to take necessary action to liberate Kuwait. By authorizing members to take action, it has not violated the provisions of the U.N. Charter. The Charter has made an explicit provision for such an authorization. While under the first sentence of Article 42, the Council itself is empowered to take collective enforcement action against the delict State, the second sentence of Article 42 lays down that such

1. Para 1 of Article 43.
2. Para 3 of Article 43. This para also lays down that if such an agreement or agreements are concluded, they shall be subject to ratification by the signatory States in accordance with their respective constitutional processes.
3. Para 2 of Article 43. During the negotiation of such agreement, a member State is entitled to insist that some part of the expenses would be borne by the Organisation. (See Certain Expenses of the United Nations Case, op. cit., at p. 81.)
4. *See* Para 2 of Article 48.
5. *See* Article 49.

action may include demonstrations, blockade, and other operation by air, sea or land forces of members of the United Nations. The above implies that the action taken by the Council includes the action taken by the members. It also follows that if the action is taken by the members, that would be regarded as an action of the Security Council. However taking of an action by the members is lawful only if that has been authorised by the Council.

Voluntary action of the Members under the licence of the Security Council may be referred to as U.N. action if the term is taken to be used for those actions which are 'recommended and directed by the United Nations'.[1] It follows that the action taken by the Security Council under Article 42 with the assistance of the Military Staff Committee, or by the General Assembly under the Uniting for Peace Resolution[2] would be termed as U.N. action in the sense that they satisfy both the elements- recommendation and direction by the United Nations. In addition to the above, an action taken by the Members themselves would also be called a U.N. action, if recommended by the Council under Article 39, but not directed by the United Nations. It is so because the action taken by the Security Council includes the action of the members, if recommended by the Council under Article 39 of the Charter. In such cases power of direction and operation of the action is controlled and supervised by the members themselves.

It is true that in the Gulf Crisis it was not possible for the Council to take action by itself because it had not concluded special agreements with members for the availability of the forces, assistance and facilities under Articles 43 and 45 and also because the Military Staff Committee which had suspended its activities in 1947, could never be activitiated. It appears that as long as mechanism laid down under Chapter VII for the enforcement action does not function, the Council is likely to decide not to take any action by itself. In such a State of affairs, it has to depend upon its members for the maintenance of international peace and security. Perhaps, there is no way out to fulfil this very purpose of the United Nations. In the instant case, had it not authorized its members to take necessary action even in the case of flagrant armed attack on one of its members, the purpose for which the United Nations was created would have been defeated. Perhaps, that would have been the beginning of the end of the United Nations, just as to having done nothing in the case of Japan's invasion of Manchuria in 1931 was the beginning of the end of the League of Nations.

It is significant to note that the voluntary action of the members of the United Nations is distinct from the action taken by the Council itself. In the former case contingents are kept under the individual command[3] whereas in the latter case, contingents are placed under the U.N. command and their operations are controlled by the Military Staff Committee. Further, when an action is taken by the Security Council, it uses U.N. Flag and contingents are required to use blue helmet. However, in the voluntary action taken by the members they are not required to fulfil these formalities. Although voluntary action and the action

1. Baxter, 'Constitutional forms and Some Legal Problems of International Military Command,' BYIL, Vol. XXIX (1960) p. 283 at p. 334.
2. *See* General Assembly Resolution 377 (v), November 3, 1950.
3. Stone, op cit., p. 197, f.n. 67.

taken by the Council differ, both are the collective actions of the United Nations. While in the former, members take action themselves after obtaining the permission of the Security Council, as organs of the United Nations, in the latter case, they take action after concluding the special agreements with the Security Council. The former course is adopted by the members in view of the incapability of the Council in concluding the special agreements. The purpose of both the courses is to maintain international peace and security.

In the Gulf crisis, members of the United Nations themselves constituted a force to liberate Kuwait, when Iraq did not withdraw its force on the expiry of the dead-line set in the Resolution 678 (1990). The force generally known as multinational forces consisted of the contingents of 28 States. In addition to them, a number of States, who had not sent combat units contributed to the war fund or sent medical units to the action. The contribution of all the members taken together suggests that the multinational forces have the forces of three permanent members of the Security Council, i.e., U.K., U.S.A. and France, and consisting of States spread over all the continents of the world. The troops of these States operated under their national flags, but their operation was led by the United States.

The action of the multinational forces was led by the United States, and therefore, the action is referred to as the U.S. led multinational forces. The United States became the leader because it happened to be the largest country in size and fully equipped with the latest war technology. It alone supplied nearly 63 per cent of the ground forces, 65 per cent of the naval deployment and 45 per cent of the air craft. No doubt, the United States took the initiative for taking action in the instant case, it was not undesirable, as no international enforcement action is likely to take place effectively unless one of the Great Powers shows its willingness to take initiative in it either directly or indirectly, and unless one of them becomes interested, for whatsoever reason may be. On this proposition, it may be stated that had the U.S.A. not taken initiative to liberate Kuwait, some other Big Power would have to show its willingness to take the initiative in this regard, failing which, no action would have been taken at all in view of the existing situation, as no State from Third World would have taken the initiative in this regard, failing which, no action would have taken against Iraq which had become stronger not just in the Arab and Islamic States but throughout the non-Western World. Had one of the Big Powers, who are regarded as custodian for maintaining international peace and security, not taken initiative to take necessary measures to restore the independence and sovereignty of Kuwait pursuant to resolution 678 of the Security Council, they would have been condemned and criticised more ruthlessly. That situation would have made clear that members have complete freedom to ignore even those recommendations of the Council which are directed for achieving one of the purposes of the United Nations, i.e., to maintain international peace and security.

Action taken by the multinational forces in Gulf Crisis pursuant to the Resolution 678 of the Security Council was justified. Members' voluntary action would have been unlawful only if it could be said to have been directed against the territorial integrity or political independence of Iraq. In the instant case, it was not so. The action was taken to restore the political independence and sovereignty of Kuwait, *vis-a-vis,* to maintain international peace and security. The action was permitted by the Security Council and was taken by a large number of States. Those who did not participate in the action nevertheless approved it. Moreover, members' action was not the first case in the history of the United Nations. In Korean affair too, the similar action was taken by the members to repel the North Korean aggression. The Council by authorizing members to take action has demonstrated that even though it has no armed forces at it's disposal, as provided in Article 43 of the Charter, it was not impotent in the face of open and naked aggression.

(3) Military Operation in Somalia :

In Mogadishu—the Capital of Somalia, heavy fighting broke out between rebels of the United Somali Congress and troops of the Interim President Mohamed Siad Barre in January 1991 because the former did not recognise the latter. The President was driven out of the capital. All the embassies were evacuated except for the Egyptian and with them most aid providing agencies left the capital. United Nations staff was forced to withdraw in November 1991. The mass exit placed civilians beyond the protective reach of international observance and facilitated human rights abuses. In the Capital, conditions quickly deteriorated from mere banditry and hunger into outright war.

Somalia on January 20, 1992 requested the Council to consider the 'deteriorating human dilemma prevailing in Somalia' following the civil war situation which was 'worsening day by day'.[1] The Council on January 23, 1992 unanimously adopted a resolution[2] by which it decided that States should for establishing peace and stability in Somalia, immediately implement a general and complete embargo on all deliveries of weapons and military equipment to that country until it decided otherwise.

Authorisation to Members for Military Operation :

When the situation in Somalia did not improve, the Secretary-General on November 30, 1992 stated that the existing course of the U.N. Operation in Somalia (UNOSOM) would not 'be an adequate response' to the tragedy, where unique character was of a deteriorating complex and extraordinary nature, requiring an immediate and exceptional response recommended to the Security Council for the authorisation of military operation for providing humanitarian relief and promote national reconciliation and reconstruction of Somalia. Later, a draft resolution was proposed in the Security Council for providing military backed humanitarian relief operation in Somalia and to authorise the member States contributing troops to "use all necessary means" to establish a secure environment. The draft resolution invokes Chapter VII of the Charter after determining the situation in Somalia in particular obstacles made to the distribution of humanitarian assistance, constitutes a threat to international peace and security of the area.

The Security Council on December 3, 1992 adopted unanimously a

1. S-23445.
2. Security Council Resolution 733 (1992), dated January 23, 1992.

Resolution 794 (1992) wherein it called on all member States, which are in a position to do so, to provide military forces and to make additional contributions to such an operation. The resolution authorized the Secretary-General and member States co-operating to use "all necessary means" to establish as soon as possible, a secure environment for humanitarian relief operations in Somalia. The Secretary-General and member States contributing to the international forces were authorized to make arrangements for the Unified Command and control of forces. This is the first time that the World body has decided to send troops for humanitarian relief without the consent of the parties concerned. The Council in the resolution has taken some safeguards to keep tabs on the operation so that it does not lose all control as had happened during the Gulf Crisis. But still the timing for the beginning and ending of the operation will in effect be decided by the United States.

The United States led Unified Task Force (UNITAF) began its operation—'Restore Hope' on December 9, 1992 in order to disarm the warring factions in its area of operation. Twenty other States contributed in the operation which is generally called 'operation' 'Restore Hope'. The aim of the operation was not to maintain international peace and security which is within the jurisdiction of the Security Council, but restoring law and order to distribute food to starving people without an effective government. It is to be noted that like the Gulf Crisis, the military operation was not carried on by the U.N. forces mainly because it still did not have any force. However, it may be called an U.N. operation because it was authorized by the Security Council.

(4) Military Operation in Rwanda :

Rwanda is inhabitated by two tribes Tutis and Hutus. While Tutis have domination there, Hutus are in a larger number. When the President of Rwanda, a Hutus, was travelling in the aircraft, the plane was brought down and, the President was killed in mysterious circumstances by the air-missile launched by the Partriotic Front, an insurgent group of Tutis. This led to the killing of one tribe to another. Civil strife worsened in October 1990 when a number of clashes occurred on its border with Uganda. After a lull, armed fighting in the North of Rwanda resumed in February 1993.

Multinational Operation in Rwanda : Security Council after having determined that the magnitude of the humanitarian crisis in Rwanda was a threat to peace and security, it authorised the member States co-operating with the Secretary-General to conduct the operation until the UNAMIR was brought upto necessary strength.[1] The operation will contribute to the security and protection of displaced persons, refugees and civilians in the country. The Council limited the operation to two months, unless the Secretary-General determined at an earlier date that the expended UNAMIR was able to carry out its mandate. The Council also called on member States to respond urgently to the Secretary General's request for resources, including logistical support, so that UNAMIR could carry out its mandate as soon as possible.

1. Security Council Resolution 929 (1994) dated June 22, 1994. The resolution was adopted by 10 votes in favour and 5 abstentions (China, Nigeria, New Zealand, Brazil and Pakistan).

In accordance with the Council's resolution, the French military, whose code name was 'Operation Turquoise' stepped up its operation in South-Western Rwanda. France sought support from the European and African countries but many countries were of the view that the Operation under the leadership of France will not be neutral and therefore they decided to remain aloof from the Operation. However, Senegal and Ivory Coast sent its forces and Egypt and Italy have also shown their willingness in the Operation.

(5) Military Operation in Haiti :

When the oil and arms embargo imposed against Haiti did not succeed in reinstating the democratically elected government headed by the exiled President of Jean Bertrand Aristide, and the Commander-in-Chief of the Armed Forces did not implement the Agreement concluded with the ousted President, the United States of America proposed a draft resolution before the Security Council for taking collective military action under Article 42 of the Charter to oust Haiti's military rulers by force. The proposed U.S. resolution authorising force to restore the elected government in Haiti was similar to the resolution authorising force against Iraq after the August 1990 invasion of Kuwait.

Authorisation to Members for their Voluntary Action : The Security Council on July 31, 1994 adopted a resolution[1] wherein it authorized the member States to form multilateral force known as 'Operation Uphold Democracy' under a Unified Command and use all necessary means to remove the military leadership. The resolution also provided for the U.N. observers to monitor any invasion and envisages a 6,000 strong U.N. peace-keeping force to take over when invaders leave after a secure and stable government has been created. The resolution did not fix any deadline for the use of force. However, it stipulated that the multilateral force will terminate its mission when a secure and stable environment will be established.

The resolution was adopted by 12 votes with 2 absentions (Brazil and China). Rwanda a member of the Council has vacated the seat.

Implementation of the Resolution : Unlike the Gulf Crisis, the resolution did not fix any dead-line for the use of force, and therefore it depended upon the members of the United Nations to take military action whenever they consider it appropriate. Like the Gulf-Crisis, the action was to be led by the United States of America. Although, the United States and its allies were granted permission to invade Haiti, it has been waiting to take action in the hope that the threat for the military action may drive out military leaders without a fight.

In the meantime an agreement was concluded between Jimmy Carter, the former President of the United States and the Lt. Gen. Cedras on September 19, 1994 wherein the latter agreed to leave power by October 15, 1994. Accordingly, Jean Bertrand Aristide, the democratically elected President took over the power in Haiti.[2] This averted the military action of the U.S. led multinational forces earlier authorized by the Security Council.

Authorisation to the member States to take military action by the Security

1. Security Council Resolution 940 (1994) dated July 31, 1994.
2. Security Council Resolution 944 dated September 29, 1994.

Council to replace an usurper regime with an earlier democratically elected one in Haiti is unprecedented. The sanctioned military operation neither fall into the category of those dealing with aggression as in case of North Korea and Iraq, nor it is a peace-keeping operation as in Somalia and Rwanda.

(6) Military Operation in Libya :

In the Libyan civil war hundreds of people died because of the large scale violence committed by Gaddafi regime. Thousands of people were tortured and displaced. The systematic violation of human rights including arbitrary detentions, enforced disappearances, torture and summary execution constituted crimes against humanity. These crimes were committed on Libyan civilians specially in those areas which were dominated in the east of Libya.

In order to protect the civilians and civilian populated areas and to provide humanitarian assistance and safety of humanitarian personnel, the Security Council, acting under Chapter VII of the Charter, adopted Resolution 1973 (2011) on March 18, 2011 wherein member States were authorized under Para 4 to take all necessary measures to protect civilians and civilian populated areas under threat of attack in Libya including Benghazi and requested member States concerned to inform the Secretary-General immediately of the measures they take pursuant to the authorization conferred to them. Resolution also imposed a ban on all flights in the air-space of the Libyan Arab Jamahiriya in order to help protect civilians.[1] Travel restrictions on certain individuals[2] and freezing of assets including funds and other financial assets and economic resources owned by Libyan authorities directly or indirectly were also imposed by the Resolution.[3]

In accordance with Para 4 of the Resolution which authorized member States to take all necessary measures to protect civilians, international military action through air strikes and cruise missiles led by France, U.K. and USA was taken. The operation taken by them was known as Operation 'Odysey Dawn'. Its main aim was to protect the civilians from Gaddafi regime who was using his own military to suppress a pro-democracy movement.

GENERAL ASSEMBLY

Maintenance of international peace and security is the primary responsibility of the Security Council and therefore provisions for the collective measures by the Assembly were not laid down in the Charter. Thus the Assembly was not authorized to take collective measures for the maintenance of international peace and security. However, due to veto power exercised by the big powers, especially by the Soviet Union in the Security Council, it failed to perform its primary responsibility of maintaining international peace and security. It therefore became necessary to find out a solution to achive the main

1. The ban imposed shall not apply to flights whose sole purpose is humanitarian, such as delivering or facilitating the delivery of assistance, including medical supplies, food, humanitarian workers and related assistance, or evacuating foreign nationals from Libya. Ban shall also not apply to flights which are deemed necessary by States for the benefit of Libyan people.
2. Listed in Annex I of the Resolution.
3. Listed in Annex II of the Resolution.

purpose of the maintenance of international peace and security. The United States, with the support of France and Great Britain brought before the General Assembly an item 'Uniting for Peace' on November 3, 1950 which was adopted on the same date. The Assembly adopted three resolutions under the item 'Uniting for Peace Resolution.[1] The main objective of the resolution was therefore to improve the machinery of the United Nations to preserve peace.

The above resolution provided that if the Security Council fails to discharge its primary responsibility in the maintenance of international peace and security because of the lack of unanimity of the permanent members the Assembly may meet for making recommendations to members for taking collective measures including in the case of a breach of the peace or an act of aggression, the use of armed force when necessary to maintain international peace and security. The Assembly may meet in emergency special session within twentyfour hours, if it is not in session, on a request by the Security Council on a vote of seven members (nine members after the amendment made in the year 1965) or by a majority of the members of the United Nations.

A Peace Observation Commission of fourteen members including the five permanent members of the Security Council was established to observe and report the situation to the General Assembly in areas where peace was threatened. Members of the United Nations were invited to survey their resources in order to determine the nature and scope of the assistance they might be in a position to render in support of any recommendation of the Security Council or the General Assembly for the maintenance of international peace and security. The resolution also recommended to the members to maintain within their national armed forces elements that could promptly be made available for service as a United Nations unit or units, upon recommendation of the Council or the Assembly.

A Collective Measures Committee consisting of fourteen members was also established to make a report to the Security Council and the General Assembly on methods which might be used collectively to maintain peace.

The Uniting for Peace Resolution has thus empowered the General Assembly to take collective measures including the use of force for the maintenance of international peace and security. However, the resolution has many limitations[2] which have made it difficult to take the collective action.

The system of collective action by the General Assembly is indeed a remarkable development in the history of the United Nations. The Assembly acquired this power by adopting a resolution itself despite the fact that the Charter did not lay down for the enforcement action to be taken by the Assembly. Although the collective measures of the Uniting for Peace Resolution has been criticised on the ground that it is an attempt to break down the original plan not permissible under the Charter, it may be stated that the resolution was adopted to fulfil one of the purposes of the United Nations *i.e.*, to maintain international peace and security and to that end it may take effective collective measures for the removal of threats to the peace and for the suppression of acts

1. For detail see Chapter 'General Assembly'.
2. For detail see Chapter 'General Assembly'.

of aggression or other breaches of the peace. The above implies that the maintenance of international peace and security is the responsibility of the United Nations as a whole.

Chapter 14

Peace Keeping Operations

United Nations has been engaged in various types of peace-keeping activities for maintaining international peace and security. The term 'peace-keeping operations' has not been used in the Charter of the United Nations. It is one of the creations of the United Nations and it has proved to be a valuable instrument in controlling conflicts and maintaining international peace and security. The expression 'peace keeping operations cannot be precisely defined to the satisfaction of all the concerned. In a generic sense it can be said that any operation which is taken to insulate the areas of conflict and to neutralize them by providing presence in various forms to avoid dangerous situations may be called peace keeping operations.[1] Their necessity arose in view of the absence of the conclusion of the special arguments for the availability of the armed forces and facilities by the members in accordance with Article 43 of the Charter. Accordingly, a number of operations have evolved since the inception of the United Nations for the maintenance of international peace and security.

The basis for such operations and activities, in the absence of any provision for peace-keeping operations in the Charter, lies in the general provisions of the Charter. For instance, the Security Council may establish such subsidiary organs as it deems necessary for the performance of its functions (Article 29) such as power of investigation (Article 34), power to recommend appropriate procedures or methods of disputes settlement (Articles 36-37 and 38); power of recommendation or decision in order to maintain international peace and security (Article 39) and power to take such action by land, sea or air forces as may be necessary to maintain international peace and security (Article 42). The Security Council may entrust functions to the Secretary-General under Article 98 and this mechanism has proved significant in the practice of peace keeping operations. Peace keeping operations have the following distinguishing features :—

(1) Scope of the Peace-keeping Operations.—Peace-keeping operations include observer operations as well as operations involving the deployment of armed forces. In those cases where armed forces are deployed, the operation is essentially of defensive or protective nature. A notable exception to this feature took place during the Congo conflict wherein the Security Council adopted a

1. The former UN Legal Counsel has defined the peace keeping operations as "actions involving the use of military personnel in international conflict situations on the basis of the consent of all parties concerned without resorting to armed force except in cases of self-defence. (E. Suy, 'Peace-keeping Operations in a Hand book on International Organisations) edited by R.J. Dupuy, 1988, p. 379.

resolution by which the use of force beyond self-defence was authorized if necessary, in order to prevent the occurrence of civil war in Congo.[1] The former Security-General of the United Nations Dag Hamarskjold therefore called the peace-keeping operations as 'preventive diplomacy'. It is to be noted that the armed forces are not composed of contingents provided by any of the five permanent members of the Security Council so as to avoid the involvement of any of them. Cyprus was an exception wherein the troops of the United Kingdom contributed to the United Nations forces on the ground that they were already stationed in the area under the bilateral agreement.

(2) Deployment the Peace-keeping Operations.—Questions relating to the involvement of the peace-keeping operations are normally examined in the first place by the Security Council. However, if it is paralysed by the 'veto' power exercised by the permanent members of the United Nations, and it therefore is unable to take decisions, there is nothing to prevent the General Assembly from considering the matter immediately and making appropriate recommendations. In the Suez Crisis and Gaza the United Nations Emergency Force (UNEF) was sent on the initiative of the General Assembly. Similarly, in the case of West Irian (West New Guinea) the initiative for setting United Nations Security Force (UNSF) came from the General Assembly. However, if the operation takes on the initiative of the Security Council, it has an advantage in the sense that the operation is likely to have the support of the big powers. Direction of the operation, whether it is by the Security Council or by the General Assembly, is entrusted to the Secretary General. He is given power of control although he always acts under the supervision of the Council or the Assembly.

(3) Cooperation of the Parties.—Peace keeping operations are sent on a detailed agreement between the parties in conflict, and therefore it is consensual. U. Thant, the former Secretary-General of the United Nations has once remarked that 'the consent of the host country is a basic principle which had applied to all the United Nations peace-keeping operations'. In 1983, the General Assembly adopted a resolution that the peace-keeping operations are conducted with the consent of the host countries, with due respect for their sovereignty and territorial integrity. In November 1987, Pakistan and Turkey pressed for deletion of the reference to the consent of the host countries. Accordingly, a resolution was adopted by the Special Committee wherein reference to the consent of the host countries has been deleted. It is to be noted that if one of the parties in conflict opposes or has strong reservations, the operation becomes an additional source of controversy and friction. Thus, the fundamental pre-requisite of the successful peace-keeping operations is the co-operation of the parties concerned.

(4) Expenses of the Peace-keeping Operations.—The financial support for the forces is provided by the voluntary contributions of the member States. In 1962, the International Court of Justice in the Advisory Opinion on Certain Expenses of the United Nations observed that the expenses of the operations are the expenses of the Organization.[2]

The origin of the peace-keeping operations may be traced to the truce

1. See Resolution S/4741-A of February 21, 1961).
2. ICJ Reports 1962, p. 151.

supervision activities. The first such activity took place in Greece when an eleven member United Nations Special Committee on the Balkans (UNSCOB) was set up by the General Assembly in 1947.[1] The UN Truce Supervision Organsiation (UNTSO) was established in 1948 to supervise the truce in the Middle East armed conflict.[2] Later, the UN Military Observer Group in India and Pakistan (UNMOGIP) was established by the Secretary-General in 1948 to supervise the ceasefire in Jammu and Kashmir.[3] The truce supervision activities were later transformed into peace keeping operations when the Security Council faced the problem of the maintenance of international peace and security during the cold war.

The first peace-keeping operation took place in 1956 when the United Nations Emergency Force (UNEF) was created by the General Assembly for observing and patrolling the demarcation line in the Gaza strip and the frontier between the United Arab Republic and Israel. General Assembly was involved as the Security Council was unable to act as two permanent members (U.K. and France) were directly involved in the crisis and vetoed the resolution.

Since then peace-keeping operations have been organised in different names such as groups, missions, observers and interim forces. They have performed different functions including observations, patrolling cease-fire and truce supervisions and internal patrolling. Thus, presently the scope of these missions has become much wider than the traditional peace-keeping operations of monitoring cease fire. However, peace-keeping mission is withdrawn when it is considered that they have completed their assigned functions. Names of some of the withdrawn missions are : United Nations Emergency Force (UNEF–I); U.N. Observation Group in Lebanon (UNOGIL); UN Operation on Congo (ONUC); UN Security Forces in West New Guinea (West Irian); UN Yeman Observation Mission (UNYOM); UN Emergency Force (UNEF-II); UN Good Office Mission in Afghanistan and Pakistan (UNGOMAP) and UN Observer Group in Central America (ONUCA).[4]

The United Nations Military Observers Group in India and Pakistan (UNMOGIP) is the longest peace keeping operation. It was set up in January 1949 by the Secretary General Trygve Lie, under the Command of Lt. General Maurice Delvoi. The Observers Group initially consisting of 36 personnels was sent to help India and Pakistan in arriving at an armistice and supervise the cease-fire along a line of more than five hundred miles in primitive mountaneous country. The number of observers was later on increased. It has been observing the cease-fire even today with 44 uniformed personnel.

It is significant to note that peace-keeping operations have proved useful for the purpose of making the contesting parties stop fighting thereby avoiding more bloodshed. These operations do not find solutions to the dispute. They

1. General Assembly Resolution 109. The Operation continued upto 1954.
2. Security Council Resolution 50 (1948). UNTSO was composed of international observers and headed by a Chief of the Staff.
3. Security Council Resolution 47 (1948).
4. The U.N. Flag was used for instance, by the U.N. Security Forces in West New Guinea (West Irian); The U.N. Forces in the Corgo and the U.N. Force in Cypres. The forces operating in Korea were given the name and the flag of the United Nations by a Resolution of the Security Council adopted in 1950.

simply create conditions in which peace making can take place. However, many peace keeping operations have not been able to fulfil the task for which they were employed. Some of them got limited success in temporarily preventing major disturbances but they failed to prevent the 1967 Arab-Israeli war and the 1974 Turkish invasion of Cyprus. Success of the peace keeping operations depend upon the consent of the host State and the support of the Security Council.

It is to be noted that since 1948 to 2010 sixty four peace keeping operations have been established. In recent years they have been playing greater role than the earlier years. By 1998, 35 such operations have been created since 1988 as compared to 14 in the previous 40 years of existence of the United Nations. By the end of January 2019 there were 16 peace-keeping operations consisting of military, police and civilian personnels, who work to deliver security, political and early peace-keeping support. Their persistent and dedicated work resulted to the award of the Noble Peace Prize in 1988.

In a number of operations, especially in Somalia and Bosnia, the United Nations personnel involved in a humanitarian assistance or peace-keeping missions have been attacked knowingly and intentionally and acts of violence have been committed against them. In order to protect the personnel, General Assembly on December 9, 1994 adopted the Convention on the Safety of United Nations and Associated Personnel[1] which stated that it is an obligation of States to provide safety and security of such personnel and to release or return those who have been captured or detained. The Convention further provided that States shall ensure that the crimes committed against such personnel do not go unpunished, offenders shall be either prosecuted or extradited.

It is submitted that in order to make peace-keeping operations more effective, a permanent U.N. force for peace-keeping be created with a peace-keeping fund, and a staff college for peace keeping officers.

Standby Arrangement System (SAS) :

Although the role of the peace-keeping operations have enhanced recently in number and complexity, there is no such force available to the United Nations which may be used at short notice. In order to overcome this eventuality, the Secretary-General in his report 'Agenda for Peace'[2] submitted to the Security Council in 1992, made a provision under Para 51 for the Standby Forces. Standby Forces may mean the troops and resources which are made available to the United Nations by the member States at short notice, when necessary. The standby system is based upon commitment of member States to contribute

---

1. General Assembly Resolution 49/59, dated December 9, 1994.
2. For detail *see* Chapter 'Security Council'.

specified resources within agreed response time[1] for peace-keeping operations. It is to be noted that the purpose of the Standby forces is the availability of the forces for peace-keeping missions. The resources agreed upon remain on standby in their home country. It is different from peace-enforcement units[2] which are meant in response to "outright aggression, imminent or actual."

In accordance with the report of the Secretary-General, the Security Council on October 29, 1992, encouraged Member States to inform the Secretary General of the willingness to provide forces or capabilities to the U.N. for peace-keeping operations and the type of units or capabilities that might be available at short notice, "subject to overriding national defence requirements and the approval of the Governments providing them."

The appeal of the Security Council yielded fruitful results. The Netherland became the first Member State to commit to contribute military units for the peace enforcement units. The Netherland on June 20, 1994 notified to the Secretary General that by putting its military units at the disposal of the Standby system, the United Nations should be able to respond rapidly and effectively to calls by the Security Council for deployment of peace keeping forces. The letter announced the specific units—Royal Netherlands Navy, Army, Air Force and Military Constabulary—which was prepared to the United Nations Standby Arrangement System.

As of January 2001, eighty-nine member States have confirmed commitments to provide Standby resources consisting mainly of infantry but some with equipment and logistic support. Forty per-cent of the above forces can be ready for use in the mission area within 30 days or less. The Secretariat's initiative and efforts in this regard is commendable.

---

1. Response time is defined as the time that elapses between the moment a formal request from the Secretary-General is received by the Permanent Representative of the Member State concerned and the time when the resources are ready to be picked up for deployment at specified points of embarkation. To ensure that forces will be expeditiously organized and rapidly deployed, the preferred response time given as guidance to contributing member States is seven days for individual personnel; fifteen days for units/sub-units/elements involved in the reception phase and thirty days for other units/sub-units/elements.
2. For detail *see* Chapter Security Council.

Chapter 15

Regional Organisations

In International law the term 'region' may mean an area embracing the territories of a group of States. It is not necessary that the States constituting a region should belong to same Continent or they should be contiguous. What is essential is that the States should be bound together by the ties of common interest, *i.e.,* there should atleast be an identity of certain minimum values and standards. Some common interest may bring a set of States together. Regional arrangements and treaties are concluded by States. Such treaties have regional character. Thus, a regional arrangement may be created by grouping the States on the basis of economic, social, cultural or political factors. It may also be constituted by States having affinities of race, institutions or political interests. It is not essential that all the States of a region should be members of regional organisation. A State may, if it wishes, remain outside the organisation. For instance, in the organisation of American States, Canada is not a member. Further, some of the regional organisations may even have members from outside the region. For instance, Italy, Greece and Turkey are members of North Atlantic Treaty Organisation despite of their not being the States of North Atlantic. The above implies that geographical proximity is not the only criterion for the creation of the regional organisations. Regional agreements may be created for a wide range of purposes, such as, security, defence, political or socio-economic functions and responsibilities. States constituting a regional arrangement are required to conclude a standing agreement. Regional arrangements are therefore a more limited community than those of international institutions. Such organisations are established as it is easier to develop a sense of community in a compact geographical area.

The trend towards regionalism and regional arrangements is one of the interesting developments in recent international relations. The Covenant of the League of Nations under Article 21 had made a provision for the regional arrangements by stating that "Nothing in the Covenant shall be deemed to affect the validity of international engagements such as the treaties of arbitration or regional understanding like the Monroe Doctrine for securing the maintenance of peace." The above provision no doubt expressly provided for the creation of regional arrangements but the concept of regionalism was still unknown to many social and economic fields. Even in security matters it was not effective because the task set was World-wide and not limited to regions.

Regional Arrangements and the United Nations

The United Nations under the Charter gave due importance to regional arrangements for the maintenance of international peace and security. Chapter

VIII of the Charter consisting of Articles 52 to 54 is devoted exclusively to regional arrangements. Article 52 Para 1 provides that regional arrangements or agencies may be made 'for dealing with matters relating to maintenance of international peace and security as are appropriate for regional action provided that the activities of such arrangements or agencies and their activities are consistent with the purposes and principles of the United Nations.

Functions of Regional Arrangements

Regional arrangement may be made by the States for the performance of certain functions which are laid down in the Charter :—

(1) Settlement of Disputes.—Article 52 Para 2 provides that members of the United Nations making regional arrangements shall make every effort to achieve pacific settlement of local disputes through such arrangements before referring to the Security Council. Security Council shall encourage the development of pacific settlement of local disputes through regional arrangements either on the initiative of the States concerned or by reference from the Security Council (Article 52 Para 3).

(2) Enforcement Action.—The Security Council may authorize such regional agencies, if it considers appropriate, for enforcement action which it takes. Further, no enforcement action shall be taken by any regional agencies without the authorization of the Security Council. (Article 53). The Security Council, as provided under Article 54, shall at all times be kept fully informed of activities undertaken under regional arrangements for the maintenance of international peace and security.

Regional arrangements may take enforcement action even without the authorisation of the Security Council in three cases : (a) enforcement action may be taken as a measure against any enemy State as provided under Article 107; (b) enforcement action provided for in regional arrangements directed against removal of aggressive policy on the part of any enemy State; and (c) enforcement action in the exercise of collective self-defence under Article 51 of the Charter.[1] Although this is not mentioned repressly under Article 51, the right of collective self-defence implies the right of using force organised by the regional arrangements.

Article 103 of the Charter provides that in the event of a conflict between the obligations of the members of United Nations under the Charter and their obligations under regional arrangements, obligations of the members under the Charter shall prevail. Thus the obligations undertaken by the members under the Charter are supreme and they cannot be contradicted by the members before or after the establishment of the organisation. It is so perhaps because the principles contained in the Charter have acquired the status of *jus cogens*.

Regional arrangements or agencies being treaties are required to be registered with the Secretariat of the United Nations in accordance with Article 102 of the U.N. Charter.

---

1. Regional agencies may take collective action in self defence if an armed attack occurrs against a member of the United Nations until the Security Council has taken measures necessary to maintain international peace and security (Article 51).

Important Regional Agencies

The Charter has made provisions for the creation of the regional agencies for the maintenance of international peace and security. It did not lay down under Chapter VIII that such an arrangement can be made in relation to other fields as well. It may be stated that what applies to maintenance of international peace and security applies to other spheres as well such as economic, social and cultural. In the last sixty years regional arrangements have been made for a wide range of security, political and socio-economic functions and responsibilities. Some of the important regional organisations are as follows :—

(1) Organisation of American States (OAS) :

The pursuit of regional solidarity and cooperation in the American Hemisphere came in 1890 at the First International Conference of American States. In the Ninth International Conference of American States held in Bogota the Charter of the OAS was adopted on April 30, 1948. Article 1 of the Charter provided the goal for the creation of the OAS which was to achieve peace and justice, to promote their solidarity, to strengthen their collaboration, and to defend their sovereignty, their national integrity and their independence.

The purposes of the OAS were laid down under Article 2 of the Charter which were : (1) to strengthen the peace and security of the Continent; (2) to promote and consolidate democracy; (3) to ensure the pacific settlement of disputes among the member States; (4) to provide for common action on the part of these States in the event of aggression; (5) to seek the solution of political, judicial and economic problems; (6) to promote economic, social and cultural development; (7) to eradicate extreme poverty and (8) to achieve effective limitation of conventional weapons.

Membership of the OAS is open to all the American States including Canada. Presently, all 35 independent States of the Americas are members of OAS. In addition to members there are 69 permanent observer countries as well as the European Union. A member can withdraw from the Organisation by serving two years notice.

Organisational structure of the OAS includes the : (a) General Assembly; (b) Meetings of the Consultation of Ministers of Foreign Affairs; and (c) Permanent Council. The supreme body of the OAS is the General Assembly which holds annual session to discuss urgent issues. It consists of all members having equal vote. The Permanent Council convenes meetings of Consultation of Ministers of Foreign Affairs. Several Councils are empowered with executive functions. The Permanent Council, the Inter-American Economic and Social Council and the Inter-American Council for Education, Science and Culture. These three Councils are directly subordinated to the General Assembly. Central permanent administrative body is the General Secretariat (before 1970, the Pan American Union). It has a number of Committees such as the Committee on Judicial and Political Affairs, the Committee on Administrative and Budgetary Affairs, the Committee on Hemispheric Security and the Committee on Inter-American Summits Management and Civil Society Participation in OAS Activities.

OAS contribution towards the promotion of human rights is noteworthy.

In 1959 it adopted the Inter-American Commission on Human Rights which has since then undertaken important investigative activities concerning human rights activties in the American States.[1] Later, American Convention on Human Rights was adopted in November, 1969 in the Inter-American Specialized Conference on Human Rights. The Convention so-called 'Pact of San Jose de Costa Rica' came into force on July 11, 1978.[2] American Convention to Prevent and Punish Torture was adopted in 1985.[3] In order to abolish death sentence, States parties concluded a Protocol in 1990 to abolish death penalty. OAS also constituted the Inter-American Court of Human Rights in the Ninth Regular Session of the General Assembly held at Bolivia in October, 1979. Under Article 60 of the Convention it was empowered to draw up its Statute and submit it to the General Assembly for approval. Accordingly, the Statute of the Inter-American Court on Human Rights was adopted which came into force on January 1, 1980.

(2) Arab League (League of Arab States) :

Arab League officially called the League of Arab States is a regional organisation of Arab States in the Middle East. It was formed on March 22, 1945 in Cairo with six members. Founding members of the League were Egypt, Iraq, Transjordon (presently Jordon), Lebanon, Saudi Arabia and Syria. Presently, the League has 22 members[4] and five observers.[5]

The main aims of the League were : (a) to strengthen relations between the member States; (b) to coordinate the political activities of its member States in order to attain the goal of independence and sovereignty of member States; (c) to promote cooperation among members in economic and financial affairs, communication, cultural affairs, nationality problems, and social and health problems.

The League Council is the supreme body of the League. Each member State has one vote in the Council. Decisions of the Council are binding only for those States which have voted for them. The Secretariat of the League is situated at Cairo. The Secretary-General is the Head of the Secretariat. The League established the Arab League Educational, Cultural and Scientific Organisation (ALECSO) and the Economic and Social Council of Arab League's Council of Arab Economic Unity (CAEU) to facilitate political, economic, cultural, scientific and social programmes in the interest of the member States. In March 2015, the Secretary-General of the Arab League announced the establishment of the Joint

1. For detail *see* H.O. Agarwal, 'Human Rights', 17th Edition, (2020), Chapter 'Regional Conventions on Human Rights'.
2. For detail *see ibid*. The Convention under Article 4 recognised the right to life and restricted the application of death penalty.
3. Although Article 5 Para 2 of the American Convention on Human Rights clearly stipulated that no one shall be subjected to torture or to cruel, inhuman, or degrading punishment or treatment, the American States in order to elaborate the above right considered themselves necessary to conclude a Convention that prevents and punishes torture. Accordingly, in 1985 a Convention known as American Convention to Prevent and Punish Torture was adopted. For detail see H.O. Agarwal, Op. cit.
4. Syria's participation has been suspended since November, 2011.
5. Observer status is a status that entitles a State to express its opinion and give advice without vote. Five States having observer status are : Eritrea, Brazil, Venezuela, India and Armenia.

Arab Force with the aim of counter-acting extremists and other threats to the Arab States.

The League has played an important role in the social, economic and cultural fields by advancing the role of women in the Arab societies, promoting child welfare, preserving Arab cultural heritage and fostering cultural exchanges between the member States. However, the League is weakened by internal dissension on political issues especially those concerning Israel and the Palestine.

(3) African Union (AU) :

AU was established on July 9, 2002 in Sirte (Libya) as a successor of the Organisation of African Unity (OAU).[1] It is a Union Consisting of 55 African States. AU was formed with the object : (a) to achieve greater unity, cohesion and solidarity between the African countries; (b) to defend the sovereignty, territorial integrity and independence of member States; (c) to accelerate the political and socio-economic integration of the Continent; (d) to promote and defend the African common position on issues of interest to the Continent and its peoples; (e) to achieve peace and security in Africa; and (f) to promote democratic institutions, good governance and human rights.

The African Union has a number of official bodies. The Assembly consisting of all the Heads of State of the member States takes the most important decisions. It meets once a year and takes its decisions by consensus or by a two-thirds majority. Executive Council is composed of ministers designated by the Governments of member States. It decides on matters such as foreign trade, social security, food, agriculture and communications. The Council is accountable to the Assembly and prepares material for the Assembly to discuss and approve. Permanent-Representative's Committee is made up of the nominated permanent representatives of the member States. The Committee prepares the work for the Executive Council. Peace and Security Council (PSC) was established in 2004 by a Protocol to the Constitutive Act adopted by the Assembly in 2002. The Protocol on the PSC was a collective security for early warning arrangement to facilitate timely and effective response to conflict and crisis situations in Africa. The Secretariat of the African Union is composed of the commissions and supporting staff. Its Headquarters is in Addis Ababa (Ethiopia). It is responsible for the administration and coordination of the activities and meetings of the African Union.

---

1. OAU was established by the Conference of Independent African States on May 25, 1963 to resolve mainly their political problems. The main objectives of the OAU were : (a) to promote the unity and solidarity of the African States and to act as collective voice for the African Continent; (b) to eradicate all forms of colonialism on the Continent and to protect African State's sovereignty, territorial integrity and independence. The OAU proposed two ways to get rid of the Continent from colonialism, *i.e.*, firstly, it shall defend the interests of independent countries and help to pursue those which are still colonies, and secondly, it would remain neutral in terms of world affairs, preventing its members from being controlled once more by outside Powers especially during the cold war. OAU has originally 32 members.
The principal organs of the OAU were the Assembly of Heads of States and Governments, Council of Ministers and the General Secretariat. The OAU was replaced by the African Union on July 9, 2002.

The Constitutive Act of the African Union had made a provision for a Court of Justice to settle disputes relating to the interpretation of treaties. Consequently, a Protocol to set up the Court of Justice was adopted in the year 2003 which entered into force in 2009. However, the Protocol was the creation of the African Court of Justice superseded by a Protocol creating an African Court of Justice and Human Rights which will incorporate the already established African Court of Justice and the African Court on Human and People's Rights.[1] The Court of Justice and Human Rights will have two Chambers—one for general legal matters and other for rulings on the human rights treaties.

AU for the first time intervened in Burundi when it deployed a peace-keeping force of soldiers of some of the member States to oversee the implementation of the various agreements. It also deployed troops in Sudan for peace-keeping in the Darfur conflict and a peace-keeping mission to Somalia.

(4) Association of South-east Asian Nations (ASEAN) :

ASEAN[2] was formed on August 8, 1967 in Bangkok by Indonesia, Malaysia, the Philippines, Singapore and Thailand—the countries of South-east Asia. Since then, the membership of the Organisation has expanded to include Brunei, Myanmar, Cambodia, Laos and Vietnam. In addition to the above Timor Leste and Papua New Guinea are the permanent observers.

ASEAN is a political and economic organisation of South-east Asian Countries. Its main objective is to accelerate the economic growth, social progress, cultural development amongst the members. ASEAN also protects peace and stability in the region and provides opportunities for member countries to discuss differences amongst them peacefully.

ASEAN's organisational structure consists of Summit Meetings; Ministerial Conferences of the foreign ministers of the member States held annually in each country by rotation; the Standing Committee consisting of the foreign minister of the country that is host to the Ministerial Conference and the ambassadors of the other member States which conducts business between Ministerial Conferences and a Permanent Secretariat in Jakarta (Indonesia) headed by Secretary General and a number of other committees, sub-committees and *ad hoc* groups.

In 1990 Malaysia proposed for the creation of an East Asia Economic Caucus comprising of the members of ASEAN as well as China, Japan and South Korea (Plus Three Countries) with the intention of counter-balancing the growing influence of the United States in the Asia-Pacific Economic Cooperation (APEC) as well as in the Asian region as a whole. Although the proposal failed at that time the member States continued to work for further integration and ASEAN Plus Three countries was created in 1997. This was followed by a larger East Asia Summit (EAS) which included ASEAN plus three as well as India, Australia and New Zealand. ASEAN plus six is the main body for the economic,

1. For detail *see* H.O. Agarwal, 'Human Rights', 17th Edition (2020), Chapter 'Regional Conventions on Human Rights'.
2. ASEAN was preceded by an Organisation called the Association of South-east Asia (ASA) formed in the year 1961 by Philippines, Malaysia and Thailand.

political security and the socio-cultural development of the Asia Pacific region.

ASEAN on December 15, 1995 concluded the South East Asian Nuclear-Free Zone Treaty in order to make South East Asia into a Nuclear-Weapon Free Zone. It came into force on June 21, 2001. Member States of the ASEAN also concluded a few treaties on environmental issues. ASEAN Agreement on Transboundry Haze Pollution was signed in 2002 but the Agreement failed due to outbreak of the Malaysian Haze in 2005 and the South East Asian Haze in 2006. They also concluded Cebu Declaration on East Asian Energy Security and the ASEAN Wild Life Enforcement Network (ASEAN-WEN) in 2005. In November, 2007 the ASEAN members signed the ASEAN Charter—a Constitution governing relations among the ASEAN members. ASEAN concluded Human Rights Declaration on November 19, 2012 in Phnom Penh (Cambodia) which recognised that all persons are born free and equal in dignity and right and all human rights are universal, indivisible, interdependent and interrelated. ASEAN was given observer status in the General Assembly of the United Nations in the year 2006.

(5) North Antlantic Treaty Organisation (NATO) :

NATO—an intergovernmental military alliance was signed on April 4, 1949. It came into force on August 24, 1949. NATO was established to counter weight the Soviet military presence in post-war Eastern Europe. It therefore constitutes a system of collective defence arrangements under Article 51 of the U.N. Charter whereby its member States agree to mutual defence in response to an attack by an external party.

NATO originally had 14 members. Later, new members were added on many occasions. Presently, it has 30 members. New membership in the alliance has been largely from Eastern Europe and the Balkans, including former members of the Warsaw Pact. North Macedonia was the most recent member of NATO which became member on March 27, 2020. Its main Headquarters is located in Brussels.

Main purpose for the creation of NATO was the collective defence of the member States. Parties of the NATO agreed that an armed attack against one or more of them in Europe or North America shall be considered an attack against all of them. Consequently, they agreed that, if such an armed attack occurs, each of them, in exercise of the right of individual or collective self-defence will assist the Party or Parties being attacked, individually and in consultation with the other Parties, such action as it deems necessary, including the use of armed force, to restore and maintain the security of the North Atlantic Area.

NATO is governed by North Atlanic Council (NAC) composed of ministerial representatives of the member States. The Council meets twice a year. Its Chairman is chosen by rotation among the member States. The Parliamentary Assembly of the NATO sets broad strategic goals and meets at the annual session and one other during the year. The Assembly directly interacts with the parliamentary structures of the national governments of the member States which appoints permanent members as ambassador to NATO.

NATO has a strong military organisation for possible war time use. The Military Committee consists of the Chiefs of Staff of the member States. The

Committee recommends to NATO's political authorities to take those measures which it considered necessary for the common defence of the NATO area. Its principal role is to provide direction and advice on military policy and strategy. It also provides guidance on military matters to the NATO strategic commanders.

Soviet Union's formation of the Warsaw pact signed on May 14, 1955 by the Soviet Union and the countries of the Eastern Europe forced the NATO to develop concrete military plans. Its forces were systematically improved. Although number of its forces were less than the Warsaw Pact huge ground forces, the NATO's superior weaponry and training rendered them roughly equal in strength to their potential adversaries. The situation continued in 1980's by which time the NATO forces had at their disposal nuclear armed intermediate-range (under U.S. Control) as well as large conventional forces. The end of the cold war and the dissolution of the Warsaw Pact in 1991 removed the main adversary of the NATO. This caused a strategic re-evaluation of NATO's purpose, nature and task.

NATO intervened in Balkans by causing first military operation in the conflict in the former Yugoslavia. Its 'Operation Sharp Guard' continued from June 1993 to October 1996. It provided maritime enforcement of the arms embargo and economic sanctions against Federal Republic of Yugoslavia. In 1994 NATO took its first military action by shooting down four Bosnian Serb crusing aircraft. NATO bombing campaign 'Operations Deliberate Force' began in August, 1995 against the army of the Republic Srpska after the Srebrenica massacre. NATO air strikes helped to bring the end of war in Bosnia resulting in the Dayton Agreement. NATO deployed a peace-keeping force there from 1996 to 2004. NATO in 1999 made the first broad scale military engagement in the Kosovo War.

NATO for the first time invoked Article 5 of the Charter after attack in the United States on September 11, 2001. The Article lays down that an attack on any member shall be considered as an attack on all members of the NATO. Eight officials were taken by NATO on October 4, 2001 which included naval operation in the Mediterarean Sea to prevent the movement of terrorists or weapons of mass destruction as well as to enhance the security of shipping in general. NATO showed greater unity on the issue of Afghanistan when in 2003 it agreed to take command of the International Security Assistance Force (ISAF). The NATO has operated a range of additional roles since then including sending trainers to Iraq, assisting in counter in piracy operations and in 2011 enforcing a no-fly zone over Libya in accordance with U.N. Security Council Resolution 1973.

(6) South Asian Association for Regional Cooperation (SAARC) :

The concept of SAARC was adopted by Bangladesh when it made a proposal for its creation on May 2, 1980. The proposal was responded positively by other South Asian nations. After the preparatory activities a Declaration was adopted by the Foreign Ministers of the seven South Asian States, *viz.*, Bangladesh, Bhutan, India, Maldives, Nepal, Pakistan and Sri Lanka in New Delhi in August, 1983 for achieving cooperation in certain selected areas. Later, on December 8, 1985 SAARC was created by all the above States with the adoption of the Charter. Charter therefore is a constituent instrument of the SAARC. The above seven States were the founding members of the SAARC. Iran and Afghanistan joined the Organisation in 2007. Australia, China, Myanmar, European Union, Japan, Mauritius, South Korea, Iran and the United States have been given observer status. SAARC Secretariat was established in Kathmandu (Nepal) on January 16, 1987.

Objectives for the creation of the SAARC are laid down under Article 1 of the Charter which are : (a) to promote the welfare of the peoples of the South Asia and to improve their quality of life; (b) to accelerate economic growth, social progress and cultural development in the region and to provide all individuals the opportunity to line in dignity and to realise their full potentials; (c) to promote and strengthen collective self-reliance among the countries of South Asia; (d) to contribute to mutual trust, understanding and appreciation of one another's problems; (e) to promote active collaboration and mutual assistance in the economic, social, cultural, technical and scientific fields; (f) to strengthen cooperation with other developing countries; (g) to strengthen cooperation among themselves in international forums on matters of common interest; and to cooperate with international and regional organisations with similar aims and purposes. The above implies that objectives of the SAARC were mainly to achieve economic cooperation.

The Charter has provided for a five-tier institutional framework which are Meetings of the Heads of State or Government, Council of Ministers, Standing Committee, Technical Committees and Secretariat.

Article III of the Charter merely States that the 'Heads of State or Government shall meet annually'. Article IV provides that the Council of Ministers consisting of the Foreign Ministers of the member States shall meet in regular session as often as possible to : (a) formulate policies of the Association; (b) review the progress of cooperation under the Association; (c) decide on new areas of cooperation; (d) establish additional mechanism under the Association as deemed necessary; and (e) to decide on other matters of general interest to the Association. Extra Ordinary sessions of the Council of Ministers may be held by agreement among member States.

Article V of the Charter lays down that the Standing Committee comprising of foreign secretaries shall meet as often as deemed necessary but at least once a year. The Standing Committee shall perform following functions; (a) overall monitoring and coordination of programmes of cooperation; (b) approval of projects and programmes, and the modalities of their financing; (c) mobilisation of regional and external resources; and (d) identification of new areas of cooperation based on appropriate studies. The Standing Committee is required to submit periodic reports to the Council of Ministers.

Provisions relating to Technical Committees are provided under Article VI of the Charter. Technical Committees shall comprise representatives of all member States and shall be responsible for the implementation, coordination and monitoring of the programmes in their respective areas of cooperation. The Technical Committees shall submit periodic reports to the Standing Committee.

Article VII of the Charter provides that the Standing Committee may set up Action Committees comprising member States concerned for implementation of projects involving more than two but not all member States.

The Council of Ministers shall consider at an appropriate time, the establishment of a Secretariat for the Association and its organisation, function and funding modalities. (Article VIII). Accordingly, the Secretariat of the SAARC was established in Kathmandu on January 16, 1986. It is headed by the Secretary-General who is appointed by the Council of Ministers from Member countries in alphabetical order for a period of three years. He is assisted by the professionals and the General Services Staff. The Secretariat has a number of functional units which are called Divisions assigned to Directors on deputation from Member States. The Secretariat coordinates and monitors implementation of activities, prepares for and services meetings and serves as a channel of communication between the Association and its member States as well as other regional organisations.

Article X (1) of the Charter States that decisions at all levels shall be taken on the basis of unanimity. Although unanimity in decision-making is a fundamental principle of the SAARC this rule has a tendency to create problems for smooth running of any organisation including SAARC and may lead to frustration among the members. The Charter has provided under Article X(2) that bilateral and contentious issues shall be excluded from the deliberations.' It may be stated that it is difficult to exclude bilateral issues from the discussion in the SAARC as some of the bilateral issues have multilateral and regional dimensions. However, the exclusion of these matters in the deliberations reflects the South Asian political reality.

(7) European Communities (EC) :

A variety of Western European Organisations developed after the Second World War to avoid rivalry especially between France and Europe. The Treaty of Paris in 1952 established the European Coal and Steel Community (ECSC) wherein Belgium, France, Italy, Luxemburg, the Neitherland and West Germany agreed to combine coal and steel industries of its members and to create a single market and remove distributive restrictions for coal and steel among the six participating countries. In 1957, European Economic Community (EEC) was formed by the above six countries wherein the Common Market was established for eliminating all trade barriers. European Atomic Energy Community (Euratom or EAEC) was established in 1957 whose primary purpose was to stimulate and safeguard the development of atomic energy for peaceful purposes. Each separate organisation had its own Council. EEC and EAEC were created by the Treaty of Rome. ECSE, EAEC and Euratom were consolidated in 1967 by the above six countries into a single massive organisation—the European Communities. The six were joined in January, 1973 by Britain, Denmark and Ireland, in 1981 by Greece and in 1986 by Portugal and Spain.

The institutional structure of the EC included the two executive bodies—the Council of Ministers and the Commission. The Council is headed by the foreign ministers of the participating States. Decisions in the Council are taken by unanimity and are binding on members. The Commission is the key administrative organ of the Community consisting of nine members and is supported by a large professional staff. The Headquarters of the Commission is situated in Brussels and is referred to as the 'Eurocracy'. The Commission is a powerful body which makes recommendations to the Council of Ministers. The Council of Ministers generally accepted the recommendations without much difficulty. The judicial core of the European Community is the European Court of Justice. The main task of the Court of Justice is to interpret the founding treaties and settle disputes among the members. The Court has compulsory jurisdiction over member States. It was also empowered to hear cases initiated by individuals, corporations, and other legal entities.

The purposes of the EC were outlined in the Treaty of Rome (1958). The main task of the EC was to prepare the groundwork for the establishment of a *bona fide* European Federation. The EC was to coordinate and standardize European policies for dealing with monopolies, fixing prices, regulating internal trade flows, rationalizing production, arriving at common standards for working conditions and developing social security and effective bargaining methods between management and labour groups.

EC has been able to achieve the purposes in many areas despite the occasional friction among the members. For instance, in 1968, it abolished customs duties and quota restrictions for trade among member States; common external tariffs was agreed upon as a means of regulating trade with all other States. In 1962, the Community began to put into operation structures designed to implement a common agricultural regime. The most important of them is the European Agricultural Guidance and Guarantee Fund (EAGGF). In order to reduce regional disparities in economic growth, the European Regional Development Fund (ERDF) was created.

Economic Communities came to be known as European Community in 1980's. In 1993, the European Community became the basis for the European Union. ECSC and EAEC continued to function in a subordinate position and existed separately in a legal sense but were governed by the institutions of the European Union as if they were its own. The treaty of ECSC was made for fifty years and therefore it expired after the completion of the stipulated period in the year 2002. All its activities were absorbed into the European Community. The European Community was dissolved into the European Union (EU) by the Lisbon Treaty of 2009. The EU became the successor of the Community. Euratom remained an entity distinct from the EU.

(8) European Union (EU) :

European Union is the most important regional institution of the European Countries. It is an economic and political Union which came into existence with the conclusion of the Treaty on European Union (Maastricht Treaty) signed on February 7, 1992. The Treaty came into force on November 1, 1993. EU superseded and absorbed the European Communities. Lisbon Treaty which entered into force on December 1, 2009 made many reforms particularly in the legal structure of the EU. EU has been granted the observer status in the United Nations and is a signatory to a number of treaties. It maintains diplomatic mission in many countries. EU was given Nobel Peace Prize in the year 2012 for its contribution to the advancement of peace and reconciliation, democracy and human rights.

A State in order to become a member of the EU is required to meet certain criteria laid down in the Copenhegen European Council of 1993. They are : stable democracy that respects human rights and the rule of law; a functioning market economy capable of competition within the EU and the acceptance of the obligations of membership including the EU law. The fulfilment of these criteria is evaluated by the European Council. Article 50 of the Lisbon Treaty provided for the withdrawal of a member from the EU. Two members withdraw from the EU. They are Greenland in 1985 and the United Kingdom in 2020. EU has 27 members.

One of the main objectives of the EU is the integration of its member's economies into a single unified market without any barrier of the border through a standardized system of law which applies in all member States including the abolition of passport control. The EU also aimed at the establishment of common currency and the common Central Bank. The object implies that there shall be free movement of people, goods, services and capital. The EU maintains common policies on trade, agriculture, fisheries and regional development.

The institutions of EU comprises primarily the European Parliament, the Council of the European Union, the Commission and the Court of Justice.

The European Parliament is the legislative branch of the EU. It consists of 705 members at present who are directly elected by EU citizens every five years on the basis of proportional representation to the share of votes collected by each political party. The Parliament and the Council pass legislation jointly in all areas under the ordinary legislative procedure. Parliament's approval is required for international agreements such as the accession of new member States and the association agreements with third States. The budget of the EU is approved by the Parliament. It may propose modifications and amendments to the proposal initiated earlier by the Commission.

The Council of the European Union also called the Council consists of one representative from each of the member States. It is the ultimate political authority in the Union by having real power of decision in the Union. It determines how the intents of the treaties are to be carried out and how the separate economic powers of the member States are to be coordinated towards that end. Subordinate to the Council and subject to parliamentary control is the European Commission. Presently, the Commission has 27 members. They are selected on the basis of their individual competence and act independently of governmental control. The President of the Commission is chosen by the European Council subject to the approval of the Parliament, while the other members of the Commission are nominated by the member States in consultation with the President. The Commission acts as the executive arm of the Union. It is responsible for initiating legislation and implementation of various treaties of the Union and various rules issued by the Council.

The Court of Justice formally called the Court of Justice of the European Union consists of fifteen judges. The Court of Justice consists of two Courts : the

Court of Justice and the General Court. Together, they interpret and apply the treaties and the law of the EU. The Court of Justice primarily deals with cases taken by member States, the institutions, and cases referred to it by the Courts of member States. The General Court mainly deals with cases taken by individuals and companies directly before the EU's Court. Appeals may be made from the decisions of the General Court to the Court of Justice but only on a point of law.

(9) The Council of Europe :

The Council of Europe was created on May 5, 1949 with the conclusion of the Treaty of London (or the Statute of the Council of Europe) by 10 States. Article 4 of the Statute provides that membership is open to any 'European' State. Thus, all the European States except Belarus, Kazakhistan, and Vatican City are the members of the Council. Presently, the Council has 47 member States. Its Headquarters is in Strasbourg (France).

The Statute under Article 1(a) States that the aim of the Council of Europe is to achieve a greater unity between its members for the purpose of safeguarding and realising the ideals and principles which are their common heritage and facilitating their economic and social progress. Thus, the Council could discuss questions of common concern to European States in order to reach agreements and take joint action in economic, social, cultural, scientific, legal and administrative matters. The Council would promote an environment protecting human rights and fundamental freedoms. Thus the Council was created with wide-ranging cooperative aims. The Council was therefore the first regional organisation towards European integration and a timid step in the direction of creating a 'United States of Europe.'

The structure of the Council comprises the Committee of Ministers, Parliamentary Assembly and a Secretariat.

The Committee of Ministers comprises the Ministers of Foreign Affairs of all the members who are represented by their Permanent Representatives and Ambassadors accredited to the Council. The Committee can conclude conventions and agreements, and may make recommendations to member States and issue declarations. However, its recommendations are not binding on the governments of members. The committee may invite States to become full or associate members of the Council and it can suspend States from membership.

The Parliamentary Assembly, earlier the Consultative Assembly, consists of the representatives from all member States. Representation in the Assembly is determined in proportion to population of the members. The representatives are elected by national parliament. Members of the Assembly elect its President for a period of one year with the possibility of being re-elected for another year. The Parliamentary Assembly is only the deliberative organ of the Council. It may recommend action upon matters referred to it by the Committee of Ministers and may adopt resolutions. Recommendations require a two-thirds majority and resolutions require a simple majority.

The Secretary-General is the head of the Secretariat. He is elected for a term of five years by the Parliamentary Assembly.

The most important work of the Council of Europe is the preparation and conclusion of conventions and protocols. A number of conventions have been concluded dealing with the protection of human rights and fundamental rights, cultural and educational questions and conventions covering patents, extradition, migration, State immunity, terrorism and others. The most important amongst them is the European Convention for the Protection of Human Rights and Fundamental Freedoms[1] of November 4, 1950 which came into force on September 3, 1953 and the European Social Charter of October 18, 1961 which came into force on February 26, 1965.[2]

(10) Shanghai Cooperation Organisation (Shanghai Pact) (SCO) :

SCO was signed in June, 2002 in Shanghai and entered into force on September 19, 2003. Originally, it had six members, *i.e.,* China, Kazakistan, Kyrgystan, Russia, Tajakistan and Ujbekistan. Later, India and Pakistan joined the Organisation on June 9, 2017. In addition to full members SCO also grants observer status. Afghanistan, Belarus, Iran and Mongolia have been granted observer status.

The Council of Heads of State is the highest decision-making body in the SCO. The Council meets at the SCO summit held each year. The Council of Heads of Government, second important body also meets annually to discuss issues of multilateral cooperation. The Council of foreign ministers also hold regular meetings to discuss the current international situations. Secretariat of the SCO is the primary executive body of the Organisation which is located in Beijing.

SCO was established to secure cooperation amongst the member States on security related matters, military cooperation, economic and cultural cooperation. As to security cooperation the SCO established the Regional Anti-Terrorist Structure (RATS) in June 2004. As to military cooperation SCO regularly conducted military exercises among members to maintain regional peace and stability. The first joint military exercises were conducted in Kazakistan and China in 2003. In economic field a framework agreement to enhance economic cooperation was signed by the member States on September 23, 2003.

---

1. For detail *see* H.O. Agarwal, 'Human Rights', Chapter 'Regional Conventions on Human Rights', 17th Edition (2020).
2. For detail *see ibid.*

Chapter 16

Non-Governmental Organisations

Non-Governmental Organisations (NGOs) are non-profit private organisations consisting of private groups of religious, scientific, cultural, philanthropic, technical or economic orientation. They are neither inter-governmental agreements nor involve direct government participation. The Economic and Social Council of the United Nations by adopting a resolution [288(x)] on February 27, 1950 defined the non-governmental organisations as 'any international organisation which is not established by inter-governmental agreements'. In wider sense, the term can be applied to any non-profit organisation that is independent of government. The World Bank has defined NGOs as 'private organisations that pursue activities to relieve the suffering and promote the interests of the poor, protect the environment, provide basic social services or undertake community development. Examples of such organisations are International Chamber of Commerce, Inter-Parliamentary Union, World Veterans Federation, Federation of Trade Union and Women's International Democratic Federation. In recent past terrorist movements and terrorist groups have begun to be referred as NGOs but it is not proper to call them NGOs. NGOs do not promote violence and do not create hatred and terror in the minds of people. It will go against the spirit of NGOs if they are included in this category. These groups might have been referred as NGOs in order to discredit them.

NGOs may be either national (or domestic) or international (global). Private organisations formed at national level have national membership and they define therein goals in their Constitutions. International NGOs having international membership perform their activities at international level. They may be considered analogous to the public interest groups in the sense that their activities are meant not for particular and expediential interests of their members but for the public good. The activities of these groups, therefore, produce no direct and immediate benefit to the members of the group or organisation (except for physical satisfaction).

Non-governmental organisations are not a homogenous group. The long list of acronyms has developed around the term NGO. These include INGOs (International NGOs), BINGOs (business oriented international NGOs), RINGOs (religious international NGOs), ENGOs (environmental NGOs), GONGOs (government-operated NGOs) and QUANGOs (quasi-non-governmental organisations).

NGOs and the United Nations

NGOs pursue a number of activities to remove sufferings, promote the interests of the poor, protect the environment, provide basic social services, undertake community development and promote human rights. They vary in their methods. While some act primarily as lobbyists others conduct primarily programmes and activities. Literally speaking, NGOs are not inter-State or international organisations. Dumbarton Oaks Proposals of October 7, 1944 put forth by the four major Powers (U.S., U.K., U.S.S.R. and China) did not make any reference to the role of NGOs. It was only in the San Francisco Conference (1945) the U.S. delegates included representatives of 42 national NGOs as consultants. This led to the recognition of NGOs by the U.N. Charter[1] under Article 71 which provides as under—

> The Economic and Social Council may make suitable arrangements for consultation with non-governmental organisations which are concerned with matters within their competence. Such arrangements may be made with international organisations and where appropriate, with national organisations after consultation with the Members concerned of the United Nations.

The above provision of the Charter implies that these organisations by possessing special experience or technical knowledge in the field of their competence could have suitable arrangements for consultation. They may be proved to be true partners of the United Nations, not only in mobilizing public opinion, but also in the process of deliberation and policy formulation, and, even more important, in the execution of policies, in work on the ground. They may be of great value to the Council in its work and therefore they may be given an opportunity to express their views. The Council, therefore, may consult such organisations on matters of concern to them that fall within their competence.

The Committee on Non-Governmental Organisations

A Standing Committee of the Economic and Social Council was established by the Council Resolution 3(ii) on June 21, 1946. The Committee reports directly to the ECOSOC. The Committee consists of nineteen members who are elected on the basis of equitable geographical representation.[2] In accordance with ECOSOC decision taken on January 28, 1975, the term of office of its members is four years. The current terms of reference of the Committee are set out in Resolution 1996/31 of July 25, 1996. The main tasks of the Committee are : (1) the consideration of applications of consultative status and requests for re-classification submitted by NGO's; (2) consideration of reports submitted by NGO's; (3) monitoring of consultative relationship; and (4) consideration of any other issues which the ECOSOC may request the Committee. Consultative relationship may be established with international, regional, sub-regional and national non-governmental, non-profit, public or voluntary organisations. NGO's affiliated to an international organisation already in status may be admitted provided that they can demonstrate that their programme of work is of direct relevance to the aims and purposes of the United Nations. In the case

1. Although the phrase non-governmental organisations became popular only after the establishment of the United Nations, it has a history dating back to at least 1839. It has been estimated that by 1914 there were 1083 NGOs.
2. See ECOSOC Resolution 1981/50 dated July 7, 1980.

of national organisations consultation with the Member State concerned is required.

To be eligible for consultative status, an NGO must have in existence for at least two years, must have an established Headquarters, a democratically adopted constitution, authority to speak for its members, a representative structure, appropriate mechanisms of accountability and democratic and transparent decision-making processes. The basic resources of the organisation must be derived in the main part from contributions of the national affiliates or other components or from individual members.

There are three categories of consultative status. They are : General consultative status, Special consultative status and Roster status. General consultative status is granted to those large international NGOs whose area of work covers most of the issues on the agenda of ECOSOC and its subsidiary bodies. These tend to be fairly large, established international NGOs with a broad geographical reach. Special consultative status is granted to those NGOs which have a special competence in, and are concerned specifically with, only a few of the fields of activity covered by ECOSOC. Such NGOs tend to be smaller than those belonging to the category of general consultative status. NGO's that apply for consultative status but do not fit in any of above two catagories are usually included in Roaster. They can make occasional useful contribution to the work of the Council and listed on the Roaster. They tend to have a rather narrow and/or technical focus. NGOs that have formal status with other UN bodies or specialized agencies such as FAO, ILO, UNCTAD, UNESCO and others can be included in this category. NGOs role has been increasing as Consultative status in the ECOSOC functioning. The number of NGOs which were granted consultative status was 41 in 1946 and by the year 1993 the number increased to 978. In the year 2007 the number has increased to 3050. As of September 2018 there are a total of 5161 organisations in general consultative status, 4052 are in special consultative status. Roaster as has 971 NGO's.

The NGOs may designate authorized representatives to sit as observers at public meetings of the Council and its bodies and they may submit written statements relevant to the work of the Council and its bodies for circulation as United Nations documents. All the three categories of NGOs may consult with the United Nations Secretariat on matters of mutual concern. NGOs as Consultative status have contributed immensely to the United Nations in different ways. They have influenced the General Assembly and other U.N. organs to pass resolutions on disarmament, on development, on human rights and on other subjects related to the underlying sources of conflicts. They have helped to develop new U.N. institutions and treaties. They have been instigators of putting new issues on the U.N. agenda such as environment, women's rights and child's soldiers. They have delivered humanitarian assistance and aided refugees and have worked on development of societies that have experienced violent conflict.

NGOs have been established in almost every country. It has been estimated that the number of Internationally operating NGOs is about 40000. Number of national NGOs is even higher. It was estimated in 1994 that the number of NGOs in the United Kingdom was 275000 and roughly 20000 in the poor countries.[1] Since then, their growth has been considerably accelerated. It was estimated that in the year 1999 their number Worldwide was two million. The number has gone up considerably since then. It has been estimated that in the year 2010 Russia has 277000 NGOs. India is estimated to have around 2 million NGOs in 2009. In the United States estimated number of NGO is 1.5 million.

Activities of NGOs

NGOs, whether their activities are spread Worldwide or confined to one country, contribute substantially in different ways especially in developing and undeveloped countries. They are concerned with varieties of issues such as religion, emergency aid, poverty alleviation, humanitarian affairs and protection of human rights. They perform different functions depending upon the purposes for which they are established. Their performance of functions also depend upon their resources, the geographical regions where they operate and the nature and number of the membership. Some of the functions which they may perform are as follows :—

(1) Mobilization of Public Opinion.—NGOs can play an important role in mobilising the public opinion by arranging seminars, Conferences and meetings on different aspects. Administrative officers, jailors, police officers, judges, advocates and journalists may be invited to participate therein. This would make them more knowledgable about international treaties concluded on different areas and their implications. Increased political influence from the NGO's sector is essential to the development and use of more effective formal means of protection.

(2) Collection of Information.—NGOs may contribute to the society by providing information and data preparing reports on survey conducted as to the conditions of jails, treatment meted to prisoners, especially to undertrials in jails and the number of undertrials and their duration in prison. They supply information to Government and urge them to take action they recommend on these issues. Their reports may be circulated as widely as possible to make the people and the Government conscious of the facts. Thus, fact-finding and publicity task can be performed by the NGOs.

(3) By Providing Direct Service.—NGOs may work directly with victims and assist in solving their problems. Thus, they may perform the task of service providers. Since NGOs concentrate more on service provision they often collaborate with advocacy groups to provide legal assistance before the Government authorities and the Court to ensure full protection to victim's rights. Thus, NGOs may perform the task of trial observations in the Court. They may provide care to help trafficking victims recover from physical and phychological abuse.[2] They may defend the human rights particularly to the vulnerable sections of the society such as to women, children, refugees, older people and disabled persons by contacting them directly and providing the required services.

(4) Dialogue with Governments and International Bodies.— NGOs can

1. Figures cited in Jagdish Bhagwati, 'In Defense of Globalization,' p. 36.
2. Vital Voices Global Partnership (VVGP)—an International NGO works with an extensive network of NGOs and is engaged in the fight against human trafficking.

have a dialogue with the Government to respect international standards on a particular aspect. For instance they can pressurise the Government to keep a check on the growing problem of torture and inhuman treatment of police and jail authorities and to submit their reports in time to the various international committees set up under different international Conventions.

NGOs can also extend pressure on international bodies. The persistent pressure of Amnesty International on the UN General Assembly to adopt a Convention Against Torture and Other Cruel, Inhuman, or Degrading Treatment or Punishment, or of the American Jewish Committee to win the General Assembly's acceptance of a Declaration on the Elimination of All Forms of Intolerance and Discrimination Based on Religion or Belief, for another, lends credence to the conclusion that international human rights law has been greatly advanced by global popular support.[1]

(5) Legal Assistance.—They may take initiative in bringing those cases before the Courts of law where a right has been violated but no action has been taken by the victim to secure the redress either because of the lack of resources or because of the ignorance.

In *Center of Legal Research* v. *State of Kerala,*[2] the Supreme Court of India observed that the voluntary organisations and social action groups must be encouraged and supported by the State in operating the legal aid programmes.[3] The Court further observed that such voluntary organisations or social action groups must not be under the control or direction or supervision of the State Government or the State Legal Aid and Advisory Board because voluntary organisations and social action groups operating these programmes should be totally free from Governmental Control.[4]

(6) Filing of Writ Petitions.—NGOs may file writ petitions before the Courts by way of public interest litigation (PIL) for the purpose of providing access to justice to a large masses of people who are denied their basic human rights and to whom freedom and liberty have no meaning.

(7) Processing of Information.—NGOs may perform the task of processing of information, *i.e.*, educating people about the extent of their rights and disseminating information about rights violation. This dissemination of information about rights includes publishing reports about rights violations, an activity that involves, as well, gathering and evaluating information. Thus, NGOs may spread the movement of human rights by educating people who have right to know their rights in order to assist and defend them. In order to realise this right they are free to seek assistance from other non-governmental organisations and institutions.

(8) Human Rights Education.—Human Rights NGOs are required to create awareness as to human rights among the people. Formal education system alone cannot succeed in this endeavour. The non-formal sector has to play an active and ever increasing role in conscientising the masses. Role of

1. Richard Pierra Claude and Burn H. Weston, 'Human Rights in the World Community', p. 10.
2. AIR 1986 Supreme Court p. 1322.
3. *Ibid.*
4. *Ibid.*

NGOs to make people aware as to human rights is essential at least in those States where people are deprived of the formal education. It is to be noted that the most important function of the NGOs is to provide checks and balances to government power. Thus, they serve as the watchdog of democratic institutions. NGOs in this context are not an adversary of the government but they encourage the government to promote human rights and to eliminate corruption, inefficiency, and unaccountable practices.

Leading International NGOs

Some of the leading NGOs having international activities and membership are as follows :

(1) Amnesty International (AI)—AI was founded in 1961 by British lawyer Peter Beneson and is independent of any government, political ideology, economic interest or religion. It does not support or oppose any government or political system, nor does it support or oppose the views of the victims whose rights it seeks to protect. It is concerned with the impartial protection of human rights by drawing attention to its abuses and complain for the compliances with International Law standards. It works to mobilize public opinion to put pressure on governments that let abuse take place. It is a worldwide movement of people who campaign for internationally recognised human rights. AI has a varied network of members and supporters around the World. Presently, there are more than 1.8 million members, supporters and subscribers in over 150 countries. Although they come from many different backgrounds and have widely different political and religious beliefs, they are united by a determination to work for a World where everyone enjoys human rights.

AI's vision is of a World in which every person enjoys all the human rights enshrined in the Universal Declaration of Human Rights and other human rights standards. In pursuit of this vision, Amnesty International's mission is to undertake research and action focused on preventing and ending grave abuses of the rights to physical and mental integrity and freedom of conscience and expression, and freedom from discrimination, within the context of the work to promote all human rights.

Amnesty International has its own methods to protect the rights of the human beings. It addresses governments, inter-governmental organisations, armed political groups, companies and other non-State actors. It seeks to disclose human rights issues accurately, quickly and persistently. It systematically and impartially researches the facts of individual cases and patterns of human rights abuses. These findings are publicized, and members, supporters and staff mobilize public pressure on governments and others to stop the abuses. In addition to its work on specific abuses of human rights, Amnesty International urges all governments to observe the rule of law, and to ratify and implement human rights standards. It also carries out a wide range of human rights educational activities. It encourages inter-governmental organisations, individuals and all organs of society to support and respect human rights.

Amnesty International operates through an International Council, International Board formerly known as International Executive Committee, Sections, Structures, International Networks and International Secretariat.

International Council is the final authority for the conduct of the affairs of Amnesty International. It consists of the members of the International Board and of the representatives of Sections. It meets at intervals of not more than two years on a date fixed by the International Board. Only representatives of Sections shall have the right to vote at the International Council. The primary functions of the International Council are (1) to focus on strategy; (2) to set Amnesty International's vision, mission and core values; (3) to determine Amnesty International's integrated strategic plan including its financial strategy; (4) to establish systems and bodies of governance and delegation for the movement, to elect members to those bodies, and to hold those bodies and their members accountable; (5) to evaluate the movement's performance against its agreed strategies and plans, and (6) to hold sections, structures and other bodies accountable.

International Board consists of the treasurer and eight regular members who shall be individual or international members of Amnesty International. The regular members and treasurer shall be elected by the International Council. It meets not less than twice a year. Members of the International Board shall hold office for a period of two years and shall be eligible for re-election for a maximum tenure of three consecutive terms. The primary role of the International Board is to provide leadership and stewardship for the whole of Amnesty International worldwide. Its other functions are (1) to take international decisions on behalf of Amnesty International; (2) to ensure that there is sound financial policy for Amnesty International and that the financial policy is consistently implemented across the international organisation; (3) to ensure implementation of the Integrated Strategy plan; (4) to ensure compliance with the Statute; (5) to ensure human resources development; (6) to hold Sections, Structures and other bodies of Amnesty International accountable for their functioning by presenting reports to the International Council.

A Section of Amnesty International may be established in any country, State, territory or region with the consent of the International Board. All sections shall have the right to appoint a representative to the International Council. A Section, in order to be recognised as such shall (a) demonstrate its ability to organise and maintain basic Amnesty International activities; (b) submit its Statute to the International Board for approval; (c) pay such annual fee as may be determined by the International Council, and (d) be registered as such with the Secretariat on the decision of the International Board. Sections shall take no action on matters that do not fall within the stated vision and mission of Amnesty International.

Structure is a national or regional body established by the International Board, to promote and implement the movement's vision and mission. The purpose of a Structure is to coordinate a sustained programme of human rights activities and consolidate its national or regional organisations.

International Network exists to promote and implement the movement's vision and mission, primarily on the basis of a specific theme or identity. The Secretariat includes the Secretary General and the staff. The head of the Secretariat *i.e.,* the Secretary General is appointed by the International Board. He is responsible for the conduct of the affairs of Amnesty International and for the implementation of the decisions of the International Councils.

(2) Human Rights Watch (HRW).—Human Rights Watch based in New York city, USA started in 1978 in the name of Helsinki Watch to monitor the Soviet Union's compliance with the Helsinki Accords. Other Watch organisations were started to cover other parts of the World. They all were united in 1988 and formed Human Rights Watch. HRW researchers conduct fact-finding investigations in human rights abuses in all regions of the World. The main purpose of the investigation is to draw international attention to abuses and to put pressure on governments and international organisations. The Organisation then publishes those findings in books and reports every year. For instance, HRW reported in 2004 that Iraqi security forces are systematically torturing detainees by beating them with hosepipes and cables and passing electric shock to their genitals. The HRW group interviewed ninety detainees, 72 of whom alleged torture or ill-treatment, particularly under interrogation. In several cases, the detainees suffered what may be permanent physical disability. Detainees were also reported of being deprived, by Iraqi security forces, of food and water and being crammed into small cells with standing room only.

HRW has been criticized by various human rights activists and non-governmental organisations as having an anti-semitic or anti-Israel bias.

The HRW while commenting on the situation in Nepal following the take-over of power by King Gyanendra stated that international community should help end arbitrary detention of political workers and journalists in the Himalayan Kingdom. It also stated that with ongoing arrests reported around the country, there is a risk that some of those being arrested will be disappeared by the security forces. The HRW further stated that in handling the Army's unbridled power, the King will also be responsible for the predictable human rights abuses the Army commits under the State of emergency.

(3) International Chamber of Commerce (ICC).—ICC was established in 1919 with the main object of serving World business by promoting trade and investment. Its other aims were to open markets for goods and services and the free flow of capital. ICC has acted on behalf of business, in making representations to governments and inter-governmental organisations. ICC was granted the highest level Consultative status with the United Nations.

Structure of the ICC includes the World Council which is an assembly of a major intergovernmental organisations. Their delegates are business executives and not government officials. National committees appoint delegates to the Council which normally meets twice a year.

The Council elects the Chairman and Vice-chairman for a two year term. The Council also elects the Executive Board which is responsible for implementing ICC policy, on the recommendations of the Chairman. The Executive Board has members whose number varies between 15 to 30. Members are appointed for a period of three years with one third retiring at the end of each year. The ICC has a Paris based International Secretariat which is headed by the Secretary-General.

ICC has activity participated in global UN Conferences such as the

Conference on Financing and Development, and the World Summit on Sustainable Development. It has been playing active role in the work of the Economic and Social Council.

(4) International Commission of Jurists (ICJ).—ICJ is an international human rights NGO. It was established in 1952 by a group of lawyers dedicated to the defence of human rights through the rule of law. Presently, ICJ has national sections and affiliates in over 70 countries.

ICJ has been actively devoted to fulfil the purpose for which it was created. In 1959 the Declaration of Delhi was adopted on the rule of law. In 1978, ICJ established the Center for the Independence of Judges and Lawyers. It was instrumental in the formulation and adoption of the UN Basic Principles on the Independence of the Judiciary and the UN Basic Principles on the Role of Lawyers. In 1990s a number of international developments took place as a result of initiatives by the ICJ which included the UN Declaration on the Protection of All Persons from Enforced Disappearance and the recommendations by the Programme of Action of the World Conference on Human Rights in Vienna to work on the setting up of an International Criminal Court.

(5) Inter-Parliamentary Union (IPU).—IPU was established in 1889 as the first international forum for political multilateral negotiations. Initially, the individual parliamentarians participated in the IPU but later the Union was transformed into an international organisation of the parliaments of sovereign States. The national parliaments of 143 countries are members of the IPU. It is the duty of the members of the Union to submit the resolutions of the Union within their respective Parliament in the most appropriate forum; to communicate them to the government; to stimulate their implementation and to inform the Secretariat of the Union as to the steps taken and the results obtained. The Headquarters of the IPU are in Geneva.

The organs of the IPU are the Assembly, Governing Council and the Executive Committee. The Executives Committee is the administrative organ of the IPU.

APPENDIX I
CHARTER OF THE UNITED NATIONS

Preamble

WE THE PEOPLES OF THE UNITED NATIONS DETERMINED

to save succeeding generations from the scourge of war, which twice in out lifetime has brought untold sorrow to mankind, and

to reaffirm faith in fundamental human rights, in the dignity and worth of the human person, in the equal rights of men and women and of nations large and small, and

to establish conditions under which justice and respect for the obligations arising from treaties and other sources of international law can be maintained, and

to promote social progress and better standards of life in large freedom,

AND FOR THESE ENDS

to practise tolerance and live together in peace with one another as good neighbours, and

to unite our strength to maintain international peace and security, and

to ensure, by the acceptance of principles and the institution of methods, that armed force shall not be used, save in the common interest, and

to employ international machinery for the promotion of the economic and social advancement of all peoples,

HAVE RESOLVED TO COMBINE OUR EFFORTS TO ACCOMPLISH THESE AIMS

Accordingly, our respective Governments, through representatives assembled in the city of San Francisco, who have exhibited their full powers found to be in good and due form, have agreed to the present Charter of the United Nations and do hereby establish an international organization to be known as the United Nations.

CHAPTER I
PURPOSES AND PRINCIPLES

Article 1

The Purposes of the United Nations are :

1. To maintain international peace and security, and to that end: to take effective collective measures for the prevention and removal of threats to the peace, and for the suppression of acts of aggression or other breaches of the peace, and to bring about by peaceful means, and in conformity with the principles of justice and international law, adjustment or settlement of international disputes or situations which might lead to a breach of the peace;

2. To develop friendly relations among nations based on respect for the principles of equal rights and self-determination of peoples, and to take other appropriate measures to strengthen universal peace;

3. To achieve international cooperation in solving international problems of an economic, social, cultural, or humanitarian character, and in promoting and encouraging respect for human rights and for fundamental freedoms for all without distinction as to race, sex, language, or religion; and

4. To be a center for harmonizing the actions of nations in the attainment of these common ends.

Article 2

The organization and its Members, in pursuit of the Purposes stated in Article 1, shall act in accordance with the following Principles:

1. The Organization is based on the principle of the sovereign equality of all its Members.

2. All Members, in order to ensure to all of them the rights and benefits resulting from membership, shall fulfill in good faith the obligations assumed by them in accordance with the present Charter.

3. All Members shall settle their international disputes by peaceful means in such a manner that international peace and security, and justice, are not endangered.

4. All Members shall refrain in their international relations from the threat or use of force against the territorial integrity or political independence of any State, or in any other manner inconsistent with the Purposes of the United Nations.

5. All Members shall give the United Nations every assistance in any action it takes in accordance with the present Charter, and shall refrain from giving assistance of any State against which the United Nations is taking preventive or enforcement action.

6. The Organization shall ensure that States which are not Members of the United Nations act in accordance with these Principles so far as may be necessary for the maintenance of international peace and security.

7. Nothing contained in the present Charter shall authorize the United Nations to intervene in matters which are essentially within the domestic jurisdiction of any State or shall require the Members to submit such matters of settlement under the present Charter, but this principle shall not prejudice the application of enforcement measures under Chapter VII.

CHAPTER II
MEMBERSHIP

Article 3

The original Members of the United Nations shall be the States which, having participated in the United Nations Conference on International Organization at San Francisco, or having previously signed the Declaration of United Nations January 1, 1942, sign the Charter and ratify it in accordance with Article 110.

Article 4

1. Membership in the United Nations is open to all other peace-loving States which accept the obligations contained in the present Charter and, in the judgment of the Organization, are able and willing to carry out these obligations.

2. The admission of any such state to membership in the United Nations will be effected by a decision of the General Assembly upon the recommendation of the Security Council.

Article 5

A Member of the United Nations against which preventive or enforcement action has been taken by the Security Council may be suspended from the exercise of the rights and privileges of membership by the General Assembly upon the recommendation of the Security Council. The exercise of these rights and privileges may be restored by the Security Council.

Article 6

A Member of the United Nations which has persistently violated the Principles contained in the present Charter may be expelled from the Organization by the General Assembly upon the recommendation of the Security Council.

CHAPTER III
ORGANS

Article 7

1. There are established as the principal organs of the United Nations : a General Assembly, a Security Council, an Economic and Social Council, a Trusteeship Council, an International Court of justice, and a Secretariat.

2. Such subsidiary organs as may be found necessary may be established in accordance with the present Charter.

Article 8

The United Nations shall place no restrictions on the eligibility of men and women to participate in any capacity and under conditions of equality in its principal and subsidiary organs.

CHAPTER IV
THE GENERAL ASSEMBLY

COMPOSITION
Article 9

1. The General Assembly shall consist of all the Members of the United Nations.

2. Each member shall have not more than five representatives in the General Assembly.

FUNCTIONS AND POWERS
Article 10

The General Assembly may discuss any questions or any matters within the scope of the present Charter or relating to the powers and functions of any organs provided for in the present Charter, and, except as provided in Article 12, may make recommendations to the Members of the United Nations or to the Security Council or to both on any such questions or matters.

Article 11

1. The General Assembly may consider the general principles of cooperation in the maintenance of international peace and security, including the principles governing disarmament and the regulation of armaments, and may make recommendations with regard to such principles to the Members or to the Security Council or to both.

2. The General Assembly may discuss any questions relating to the maintenance of international peace and security brought before it by any Member of the United Nations, or by the Security Council, or by a State which is not a Member of the United Nations in accordance with Article 35, paragraph 2, and, except as provided in Article 12, may make recommendations with regard to any such questions to the State or States concerned or to the Security Council or to both. Any such question on which action is necessary shall be referred to the Security Council by the General Assembly either before or after discussion.

3. The General Assembly may call the attention of the Security Council to situations which are likely to endanger international peace and security.

4. The powers of the General Assembly set forth in this Article shall not limit the general scope of Article 10.

Article 12

1. While the Security Council is exercising in respect of any dispute or situation the functions assigned to it in the present Charter, the General Assembly shall not make any recommendation with regard to that dispute or situation unless the Security Council so requests.

2. The Secretary-General, with the consent of the Security Council, shall notify the General Assembly at each session of any matters relative to the maintenance of international peace and security which are being dealt with by the Security Council and shall similarly notify the General Assembly, or the Members of the United Nations if the General Assembly is not in session, immediately the Security Council ceases to deal with such matters.

Article 13

1. The General Assembly shall initiate studies and make recommendations for the purpose of:

(a) promoting international cooperation in the political field and encouraging the progressive development of International Law and its codification;

(b) promoting international cooperation in the economic, social, cultural, educational, and health fields, and assisting in the realization of human rights and fundamental freedoms for all without distinction as to race, sex, language, or religion.

2. The further responsibilities, functions and powers of the General Assembly with respect to matters mentioned in paragraph 1 (b) above are set forth in Chapters IX and X.

Article 14

Subject to the provisions of Article 12, the General Assembly may recommended measures for the peaceful adjustment of any situation, regardless of origin, which it deems likely to impair the general welfare or friendly relations among nations, including situations resulting from a violation of the provisions of the present Charter setting forth the Purposes and Principles of the United Nations.

Article 15

1. The General Assembly shall receive and consider annual and special reports from the Security Council; these reports shall include an account of the measures that the Security Council has decided upon or taken to maintain international peace and security.
2. The General Assembly shall receive and consider reports from the other organs of the United Nations.

Article 16

The General Assembly shall perform such functions with respect to the international trusteeship system as are assigned to it under Chapters XII and XIII, including the approval of the trusteeship agreements for areas not designated as a strategic.

Article 17

1. The General Assembly shall consider and approve the budget of the Organisation.
2. The expenses of the Organization shall be borne by the Members as appointed by the General Assembly.
3. The General Assembly shall consider and approve any financial and budgetary arrangements with specified agencies referred to in Article 57 and shall examine the administrative budgets of such specialized agencies with a view to making recommendations to the agencies concerned.

VOTING

Article 18

1. Each member of the General Assembly shall have one vote.
2. Decisions of the General Assembly on important questions shall be made by a two-thirds majority of the members present and voting. These questions shall include recommendations with respect to the maintenance of international peace and security, the election of the non-permanent members of the Security Council, the election of the members of the Economic and Social Council, the election of the members of the Trusteeship Council in accordance with paragraph 1 (c) of Article 86, the admission of new Members to the United Nations, the suspension of the rights and privileges of membership, the expulsion of Members, questions relating to the operation of the trusteeship system, and budgetary questions.
3. Decision on other questions, including the determination of additional categories of questions to be decided by a two-thirds majority, shall be made by a majority of the members present and voting.

Article 19

A member of the United Nations which is in arrears in the payment of its financial contributions to the Organization shall have no vote in the General Assembly if the amount of its arrears equals or exceeds the amount of the contributions due from it for the preceding two full years. The General Assembly may, nevertheless, permit such a Member to vote if it is satisfied that the failure to pay is due to conditions beyond the control of the Member.

PROCEDURE

Article 20

The General Assembly shall meet in regular annual sessions and in such special sessions as occasion may require, Special sessions shall be convoked by the Secretary-General at the request of the Security Council or of a majority of the Members of the United Nations.

Article 21

The General Assembly shall adopt its own rules of procedure. It shall elect its President for each session.

Article 22

The General Assembly may establish such subsidiary organs as it deems necessary for the performance of its functions.

CHAPTER V
THE SECURITY COUNCIL

COMPOSITION

Article 23

1. The Security Council shall consist of fifteen Members of the United Nations. The Republic of China, France, the Union of Soviet Socialist Republics, the United Kingdom of Great Britain and Northern Ireland, and the United States of America shall be permanent members of the Security Council. The General Assembly shall elect ten other Members of the United Nations to be Non- permanent members of the Security Council, due regard being specially paid, in the first instance to the contribution of Members of the United Nations to the maintenance of international peace and security and to the other purposes of the Organization, and also to equitable geographical distribution.

2. The non-permanent members of the Security Council shall be elected for a term of two years. In the first election of the non-permanent members after the increase of the membership of the Security Council from eleven to fifteen, two of the four additional members shall be chosen for a term of one year. A retiring members shall not be eligible for immediate re- election.

3. Each member of the Security Council shall have one representative.

FUNCTIONS AND POWERS

Article 24

1. In order to ensure prompt and effective action by the United Nations, its Members confer on the Security Council primary responsibility for the maintenance of international peace and security, and agree that in carrying out its duties under this responsibility the Security Council acts on their behalf.

2. In discharging these duties the Security Council shall act in accordance with the Purposes and Principles of the United Nations. The specific powers granted to the Security Council for the discharge of these duties are laid down in Chapters VI, VII, VIII and XII.

3. The Security Council shall submit annual and, when necessary, special reports to the General Assembly for its consideration.

Article 25

The Members of the United Nations agree to accept and carry out the decisions of the Security Council in accordance with the present Charter.

Article 26

In order to promote the establishment and maintenance of international peace and security with the least diversion for armaments of the world's human and economic resources, the Security Council shall be responsible for formulating, with the assistance of the Military Staff Committee referred to in Article 47, plans to be submitted to the Members of the United Nations for the establishment of a system for the regulation of armaments.

VOTING

Article 27

1. Each member of the Security Council shall have one vote.
2. Decisions of the Security Council on procedural matters shall be made by an

affirmative vote of nine members.

3. Decisions of the Security Council on all other matters shall be made by an affirmative vote of nine members including the concurring votes of the permanent members; provided that, in decisions under Chapter VI, and under paragraph 3 of Article 52, a party to a dispute shall abstain from voting.

PROCEDURE

Article 28

1. The Security Council shall be so organized as to be able to function continuously. Each member of the Security Council shall for this purpose be represented at all times at the seat of the Organisation.

2. The Security Council shall hold periodic meetings at which each of its members may, if it so desires, be represented by a member of the Government or by some other specially designated representative.

3. The Security Council may hold meetings at such places other than the seat of the Organization as in its judgment will best facilitate its work.

Article 29

The Security Council may establish such subsidiary organs as it deems necessary for the performance of its functions.

Article 30

The Security Council shall adopt its own rules of procedure, including the method of selecting its.

Article 31

Any Member of the United Nations which is not a member of the Security Council may participate, without vote, in the discussion of any question brought before the Security Council, whenever the latter considers that the interests of that Member are specially affected.

Article 32

Any Member of the United Nations which is not a member of the Security Council or any State which is not a Member of the United Nations, if it is a party to a dispute under consideration by the Security Council, shall be invited to participates, without vote, in the discussion relating to the dispute. The Security Council shall lay down such conditions as it deems just for the participation of a State which is not a Member of the United Nations.

CHAPTER VI

PACIFIC SETTLEMENT OF DISPUTES

Article 33

1. The parties to any dispute, the continuance of which is likely to endanger the maintenance of international peace and security, shall, first of all, seek a solution by negotiation, enquiry, mediation, conciliation, arbitration, judicial settlement, resort to regional agencies or arrangements, or other peaceful means of their own choice.

2. The Security Council shall, when it deems necessary, call upon the parties to settle their dispute by such means.

Article 34

The Security Council may investigate any dispute, or any situation which might lead to international friction or give rise to a dispute, in order to determine whether the continuance of the dispute or situation is likely to endanger the maintenance of international peace and security.

Article 35

1. Any member of the United Nations may bring any dispute, or any situation of the nature referred to in Article 34, to the attention of the Security Council or of the General Assembly.

2. A State which is not a Member of the United Nations may bring to the attention of the Security Council or of the General Assembly any dispute to which it is a party if it accepts in advance, for the purposes of the dispute, the obligations of pacific settlement provided in the present Charter.

3. The proceedings of the General Assembly in respect of matters brought to its attention under this Article will be subject to the provisions of Articles 11 and 12.

Article 36

1. The Security Council may, at any stage of a dispute of the nature referred to in Article 33 or of a situation of like nature, recommend appropriate procedure or methods of adjustment.

2. The Security Council should take into consideration any procedures for the settlement of the dispute which have already been adopted by the parties.

3. In making recommendations under this Article, the Security Council should also take into consideration that legal disputes should as a general rule be referred by the parties to the International Court of Justice in accordance with the provisions of the Statute of the Court.

Article 37

1. Should the parties to a dispute of the nature referred to in Article 33 fail to settle it by the means indicated in that Article, they shall refer it to the Security Council.

2. If the Security Council deems that the continuance of the dispute is in fact likely to endanger the maintenance of international peace and security, it shall decide whether to take action under Article 36 or to recommend such terms of settlement as it may consider appropriate.

Article 38

Without prejudice to the provisions of Articles 33 to 37, the Security Council may, if all the parties to any dispute so request, make recommendations to the parties with a view to a pacific settlement of the dispute.

CHAPTER VII
ACTION WITH RESPECT TO THREATS TO THE PLACE, BREACHES OF THE PEACE, AND ACTS OF AGGRESSION

Article 39

The Security Council shall determine the existence of any threat to the peace, breach of the peach, or act of aggression and shall make recommendations, or decide what measures shall be taken in accordance with Articles 41 and 42, to maintain or restore international peace and security.

Article 40

In order to prevent an aggravation of the situation, the Security Council may, before making the recommendations or deciding upon the measures provided for in Article 39, call upon the parties concerned to comply with such provisional measures as it deems necessary or desirable. Such provisional measures shall be without prejudice to the rights, claims, or position of the parties concerned. The Security Council shall duly take account of failure to comply with such provisional measures.

Article 41

The Security Council may decide what measures not involving the use of armed forces are to be employed to give effect to its decisions, and it may call upon the Members of the United Nations to apply such measures. These may include complete or partial interruption of economic relations and of rail, sea, air, postal, telegraphic, radio, and other means of communication, and the severance of diplomatic relations.

Article 42

Should the Security Council consider that measures provided for in Article 41 would be inadequate or have proved to be inadequate, it may take such action by air, sea, or land forces as may be necessary to maintain or restore international peace and security. Such action may include demonstrations, blockade, and other operations by air, sea, or land forces of Members of the United Nations.

Article 43

1. All members of the United Nations, in order to contribute to the maintenance of international peace and security, undertake to make available to the Security Council, on its call and in accordance with a special agreement or agreements, armed forces,

assistance, and facilities, including rights of passage, necessary for the purpose of maintaining international peace and security.

2. Such agreement or agreements shall govern the numbers and types of forces, their degree of readiness and general location, and the nature of the facilities and assistance to be provided.

3. The agreement or agreements shall be negotiated as soon as possible on the initiative of the Security Council. They shall be concluded between the Security Council and Members or between the Security Council and groups of Members and shall be subject to ratification by the signatory States in accordance with their respective constitutional processes.

Article 44

When the Security Council has decided to use force it shall, before calling upon a Member not represented on it to provide armed forces in fulfilment of the obligators assumed under Article 43, invite that Member, if the Member so desires, to participate in the decisions of the Security Council concerning the employment of contingents of that Member's armed forces.

Article 45

In order to enable the United Nations to take urgent military measures, Members shall hold immediately available national air-force contingents for combined international enforcement action. The strength and degree of readiness of these contingents and plans for their combined action shall be determined, within the limits laid down in the special agreement or agreements referred to in Article 43, by the Security Council with the assistance of the Military Staff Committee.

Article 46

Plans for the application of armed forces shall be made by the Security Council with the assistance of the Military Staff Committee.

Article 47

1. There shall be established a Military Staff Committee to advice and assist the Security Council on all questions relating to the Security Council's military requirements for the maintenance of international peace and security, the employment and command of force placed at its disposal, the regulation of armaments, and possible disarmament.

2. The Military Staff Committee shall consist of the Chiefs of Staff of the permanent members of the Security Council or their representatives. Any members of the United Nations not permanently represented on the Committee shall be invited by the Committee to be associated with it when the efficient discharge of the Committee's responsibilities requires the participation of that Member in its work.

3. The Military Staff Committee shall be responsible under the Security Council for the strategic direction of any armed forces placed at the disposal of the Security Council. questions relating to the command of such forces shall be worked out subsequently.

4. The Military Staff Committee, with the authorization of the Security Council and after consultation with appropriate regional agencies, may establish regional sub-committees.

Article 48

1. The action required to carry out the decisions of the Security Council for the maintenance of international peace and security shall be taken by all the Members of the United Nations or by some of them, as the Security Council may determine.

2. Such decisions shall be carried out by the Members of the United Nations directly and through their action in the appropriate international agencies of which they are members.

Article 49

The Members of the United Nations shall join in affording mutual assistance in carrying out the measures decided upon by the Security Council.

Article 50

If preventive or enforcement measures against any State are taken by the Security Council, any other State, whether a Member of the United Nations or not, which finds itself confronted with special economic problems arising from the carrying out of those measures shall have the right to consult the Security Council with regard to a solution of those problems.

Article 51

Nothing in the present Charter shall impair the inherent right of individual or collective self-defence if an armed attack occurs against a member of the United Nations, until the Security Council has taken measures necessary to maintain international peace and security. Measures taken by Members in the exercise of this right of self-defence shall be immediately reported to the Security Council and shall not in any way affect the authority and responsibility of the Security Council under the present Charter to take at any time such action as it deems necessary in order to maintain or restore international peace and security.

CHAPTER VIII
REGIONAL ARRANGEMENTS

Article 52

1. Nothing in the present Charter precludes the existence of regional arrangements or agencies for dealing with such matters relating to the maintenance of international peace and security as are appropriate for regional action, provided that such arrangements or agencies and their activities are consistent with the purposes and principles of the United Nations.

2. The members of the United Nations entering into such arrangements or constituting such agencies shall make every effort to achieve pacific settlement of local disputes through such regional arrangements or by such regional agencies before referring them to the Security Council.

3. The Security Council shall encourage the development of pacific settlement of local disputes through such regional arrangements or by such regional agencies either on the initiative of the States concerned or by reference from the Security Council.

4. This Article in no way impairs the application of Articles 34 and 35.

Article 53

1. The Security Council shall, where appropriate, utilize such regional arrangements or agencies for enforcement action under its authority. But no enforcement action shall be taken under regional arrangements or by regional agencies, without the authorization of the Security Council, with the exception of measures against any enemy State, as defined in paragraph 2 of this Article, provided for pursuant to Article 107 or in regional arrangements directed against renewal of aggressive policy on the part of any such State, until such time as the Organization may, on request of the Governments concerned, be charged with the responsibility for preventing further aggression by such a State.

2. The term enemy state as used in paragraph 1 of this Article applies to any State which during the Second World War has been an enemy of any signatory of the present Charter.

Article 54

The Security Council shall at all times be kept fully informed of activities undertaken or in contemplation under regional arrangements or by regional agencies for the maintenance of international peace and security.

CHAPTER IX
INTERNATIONAL ECONOMIC AND SOCIAL CO-OPERATION

Article 55

With a view to the creation of conditions of stability and well-being which are necessary for peaceful and friendly relations among nations based on respect for the principle of equal rights and self-determination of peoples, the United Nations shall promote:

(a) higher standards of living, full employment, and conditions of economic and social progress and development;

(b) solutions of international economic, social, health, and related problems;

and international cultural and educational co-operation; and

(c) universal respect for, and observance of, human rights and fundamental freedoms for all without distinction as to race, sex, language, or religion.

Article 56

All Members pledge themselves to take joint and separate action in co-operation with the Organization for the achievement of the purposes set forth in Article 55.

Article 57

1. The various specialized agencies, established by inter-governmental agreement and having wide international responsibilities, as defined in their basic instruments, in economic, social, cultural, educational, health, and related fields, shall be brought into relationship with the United Nations in accordance with the provisions of Article 63.

2. Such agencies thus brought into relationship with the United Nations are hereinafter referred to as specialized agencies.

Article 58

The Organisation shall make recommendations for the coordination of the policies and activities of the specialized agencies.

Article 59

The Organization shall, where appropriate, initiate negotiations among the States concerned for the creation of any new specialized agencies required for the accomplishment of the purposes set forth in Article 55.

Article 60

Responsibility for the discharge of the functions of the Organization set forth in this Chapter shall be vested in the General Assembly and, under the authority of the General Assembly, in the Economic and Social Council, which shall have for this purpose the powers set forth in Chapter X.

CHAPTER X
THE ECONOMIC AND SOCIAL COUNCIL

COMPOSITION

Article 61

1. The Economic and Social Council shall consist of fifty-four Members of the United Nations elected by the General Assembly.

2. Subject to the provisions of paragraph 3, eighteen members of the Economic and Social Council shall be elected each year for a term of three years. A retiring member shall be eligible for immediate re-election.

3. At the first election after the increase in the membership of the Economic and Social Council from twenty-seven to fifty-four members, in addition to the members elected in place of the nine members whose term of office expires at the end of that year, twenty-seven additional members shall be elected. Of these twenty-seven additional members, the term of the office of nine members so elected shall expire at the end of one year, and of nine other members at the end of two years, in accordance with arrangements made by the General Assembly.

4. Each member of the Economic and Social Council shall have one representative.

FUNCTIONS AND POWERS

Article 62

1. The Economic and Social Council may make or initiate studies and reports with respect to international economic, social, cultural, educational, health, and related matters and may make recommendation with respect to any such matters to the General Assembly, to the Members of the United Nations, and to the specialized agencies concerned.

2. It may make recommendations for the purpose of promoting respect for, and observance of, human rights and fundamental freedoms for all.

3. It may prepare draft conventions for submission to the General Assembly, with respect to matters falling within its competence.

4. It may call, in accordance with the rules prescribed by the United Nations,

international conference on matters falling within its competence.

Article 63

1. The Economic and Social Council may enter into agreements with any of the agencies referred to in Article 57, defining the terms on which the agency concerned shall be brought into relationship with the United Nations. Such agreements shall be subject to approval by the General Assembly.

2. It may coordinate the activities of the specialized agencies through consultation with the recommendations to such agencies and through recommendations to the General Assembly and to the Members of the United Nations.

Article 64

1. The Economic and Social Council may take appropriate steps to obtain regular reports from the specialized agencies. It may make arrangements with the Members of the United Nations and with the specialized agencies to obtain reports on the steps taken to give effect to its own recommendations and to recommendations on matters falling within its competence made by the General Assembly.

2. It may communicate its observations on these reports to the General Assembly.

Article 65

The Economic and Social Council may furnish information to the Security Council and shall assist the Security Council upon its request.

Article 66

1. The Economic and Social Council shall perform such functions as fall within its competence in connection with the carrying out of the recommendations of the General Assembly.

2. It may, with the approval of the General Assembly, perform services at the request of Members of the United Nations and at the request of specialized agencies.

3. It shall perform such other functions as are specified elsewhere in the present Charter or as may be assigned to it by the General Assembly.

Article 67

1. Each member of the Economic and Social Council, shall have one vote.

2. Decisions of the Economic and Social Council shall be made by a majority of the members present and voting.

PROCEDURE

Article 68

The Economic and Social Council shall set up commissions in economic and social fields and for the promotion of human rights, and such other commissions as may be required for the performance of its functions.

Article 69

The Economic and Social Council shall invite any Member of the United Nations of participate, without vote, in its deliberations on any matter of particular concern to that Member.

Article 70

The Economic and Social Council may make arrangements for representatives of the specialized agencies to participate, without vote, in its deliberations and in those of the commissions established by it, and for its representatives to participate in the deliberations of the specialized agencies.

Article 71

The Economic and Social Council may make suitable arrangements for consultation with non-governmental organizations which are concerned with matters within its competence. Such arrangements may be made with international organizations and, where appropriate, with national organizations after consultation with the Member of the United Nations concerned.

Article 72

1. The Economic and Social Council shall adopt its own rules of procedure, including the method of selecting its President.

2. The Economic and Social Council shall meet as required in accordance4 with its

rules, which shall include provision for the convening of meetings on the request of a majority of its members.

CHAPTER XI
DECLARATION REGARDING NON-SELF-GOVERNING TERRITORIES

Article 73

Members of the United Nations which have or assume responsibilities for the administration of territories whose people have not yet attained a full measure of self-government recognize the principle that the interests of the inhabitants of these territories are paramount, and accept as a sacred trust the obligation to promote to the utmost, within the system of international peace and security established by the present Charter, the well-being of the inhabitants of these territories, and, to this end:

(a) to ensure, with due respect for the culture of the peoples concerned, their political, economic, social, and educational advancement, their just treatment, and their protection against abuses;

(b) to develop self-government, to take due account of the political aspirations of the peoples, and to assist them in the progressive development of their free political institutions according to the particular circumstances of each territory and its peoples and their varying stages of advancement;

(c) to further international peace and security;

(d) to promote constructive measures of development, to encourage research and to cooperate with one another and, when and where appropriate, with specialized international bodies with a view to the practical achievement of the social, economic, and scientific purposes set forth in this Article, and

(e) to transmit regularly to the Secretary-General for information purposes, subject to such limitation as security and constitutional considerations may require, statistical and other information of a technical nature relating to economic social, and education conditions in the territories for which they are respectively responsible other than those territories to which Chapters XII and XIII apply.

Article 74

Members of the United Nations also agree that their policy in respect of the territories to which this Chapter applies, no less than in respect of their metropolitan areas, must be based on the general principle of good neighbourliness, due account being taken of the interests and well-being of the rest of the world, in social, economic, and commercial matters.

CHAPTER XII
INTERNATIONAL TRUSTEESHIP SYSTEM

Article 75

The United Nations shall establish under its authority an international trusteeship system for the administration and supervision of such territories as may be placed thereunder by subsequent individual agreements. These territories hereinafter referred to as trust territories.

Article 76

The basic objectives of the trusteeship system, in accordance with the purposes of the United Nations laid down in Article 1 of the present Charter, shall be :

(a) to further international peace and security;

(b) to promote the political, economic, social, and educational advancement of the inhabitants of the trust territories, and their progressive development towards self-government or independence as may be appropriate to the particular circumstances of each territory and its peoples and the freely expressed wishes of the peoples concerned, and as may be provided by the terms of each trusteeship agreement;

(c) to encourage respect for human rights and for fundamental freedoms for all without distinction as to race, sex, language, or religion, and to encourage recognition of the interdependence of the peoples of the world; and

(d) to ensure equal treatment in social, economic, and commercial matters for all Members of the United Nations and their nationals, and also equal treatment for the latter in the administration of justice, without prejudice to the attainment of the foregoing objectives and subject to the provisions of Article 80.

Article 77

1. The trusteeship system shall apply to such territories in the following categories as may be placed thereunder by means of trusteeship agreements;

(a) territories now held under mandate;

(b) territories which may be detached from enemy States as a result of the Second World War; and

(c) territories voluntarily placed under the system by States responsible for their administration.

2. It will be a matter for subsequent agreement as to which territories in the foregoing categories will be brought under the trusteeship system and upon what terms.

Article 78

The trusteeship system shall not apply to territories which have become Members of the United Nations, relationship among which shall be based on respect for the principle of sovereign equality.

Article 79

The terms of trusteeship for each territory to be placed under the trusteeship system, including any alteration or amendment, shall be agreed upon by the states directly concerned, including the mandatory power in the case of territories held under mandate by a Member of the United Nations, and shall be approved as provided for in Articles 83 and 85.

Article 80

1. Except as may be agreed upon in individual trusteeship agreements, made under Articles 77, 79 and 81, placing each territory under the trusteeship system, and until such agreements have been concluded nothing in this Chapter shall be construed in or of itself to alter in any manner the rights whatsoever of any States or any peoples or the terms of existing international instruments to which Members of the United Nations may respectively be parties.

2. Paragraph 1 of this Article shall not be interpreted as giving grounds for delay or postponement of the negotiation and conclusion of agreements for placing mandated and other territories under the trusteeship system as provided for in Article 77.

Article 81

The trusteeship agreement shall in each case include the terms under which the trust territory will be administered and designate the authority which will exercise the administration of the trust territory. Such authority hereinafter called the administering authority, may be one or more State or the Organization itself.

Article 82

There may be designated, in any trusteeship agreement, a strategic area or areas which may include part or all of the trust territory to which the agreement applies, without prejudice to any special agreement or agreements made under Article 43.

Article 83

1. All functions of the United Nations relating to strategic areas, including the approval of the terms of the trusteeship agreements and of their alteration or amendment, shall be exercised by the Security Council.

2. The basic objectives set forth in Article 76 shall be applicable to the people of each strategic area.

3. The Security Council shall, subject to the provisions of the trusteeship agreements and without prejudice to security considerations, avail itself to the assistance of the Trusteeship Council to perform those functions of the United Nations under the trusteeship system relating to political, economic social, and educational matters in the strategic areas.

Article 84

It shall be the duty of the administering authority to ensure that the trust territory shall play its part in the maintenance of international peace and security. To this end the administering authority may make use of volunteer forces, facilities, and assistance from the trust territory in carrying out the obligations towards the Security Council undertaken in this regard by the administering authority, as well as for local defence and the maintenance of law and order within the trust territory.

Article 85

1. The functions of the United Nations with regard to trusteeship agreements for all areas not designated as strategic, including the approval of the terms of the trusteeship agreements and of their alternation or amendment, shall be exercised by the General Assembly.

2. The Trusteeship Council, operating under the authority of the General Assembly, shall assist the General Assembly in carrying out these functions.

CHAPTER XIII
THE TRUSTEESHIP COUNCIL
COMPOSITION
Article 86

1. The Trusteeship Council shall consist of the following Members of the United Nations:

(a) those Members administering trust territories;

(b) such of those Members mentioned by name in Article 23 as are not administering trust territories; and

(c) as many other Members elected for three-year terms by the General Assembly as may be necessary to ensure that the total number of members of the Trusteeship Council is equally divided between those Members of the United Nations which administer trust territories and those which do not.

2. Each member of the Trusteeship Council shall designate one specially qualified person to represent therein.

FUNCTIONS AND POWERS
Article 87

The General Assembly and, under its authority, the Trusteeship Council, in carrying out their functions, may :

(a) consider reports submitted by the administering authority;

(b) accept petitions and examine them in consultation with the administering authority;

(c) provide for periodic visits to the respective trust territories at times agreed upon with the administering authority; and

(d) take these and other actions in conformity with the terms of the trusteeship agreements.

Article 88

The Trusteeship Council shall formulate a questionnaire on the political, economic, social, and educational advancement of the inhabitants of each trust territory, and the administering authority for each trust territory within the competence of the General Assembly shall make an annual reports to the General Assembly upon the basis of such questionnaire.

VOTING
Article 89

1. Each member of the Trusteeship Council shall have one vote.

2. Decisions of the Trusteeship Council shall be made by a majority of the members present and voting.

PROCEDURE
Article 90

1. The Trusteeship Council shall adopt its own rules of procedure, including the method of selecting its President.

2. The Trusteeship Council shall meet as required in accordance with its rules, which shall include provision for the convening of meetings on the request of a majority of its members.

Article 91

The Trusteeship Council shall, when appropriate avail itself of the assistance of the Economic and Social Council and of the specialized agencies in regard to matters with which they are respectively concerned.

CHAPTER XIV
THE INTERNATIONAL COURT OF JUSTICE

Article 92

The International Court of Justice shall be the principal judicial organ of the United Nations. It shall function in accordance with the annexed Statute, which is based upon the Statute of the Permanent Court of International Justice and forms and integral part of the present Charter.

Article 93

1. All members of the United Nations are *ipso facto* parties to the Statute of the International Court of Justice.

2. A State which is not a Member of the United Nations may become a party to the Statute of the International Court of justice on conditions to be determined in each case by the General Assembly upon the recommendation of the Security Council.

Article 94

1. Each Member of the United Nations undertakes to comply with the decision of the International Court of Justice in any case to which it is a party.

2. If any party to a case falls to perform the obligations incumbent upon it under a judgment rendered by the Court, the other party may have recourse to the Security Council, which may, if it deems necessary, make recommendations or decide upon measures to be taken to give effect to the judgment.

Article 95

Nothing in the present Charter shall prevent Members of the United Nations from entrusting the solution of their differences to other tribunals by virtue of agreements already in existence or which may be concluded in the future.

Article 96

1. The General Assembly or the Security Council may request the International Court of Justice to give an advisory opinion on any legal question.

2. Other organs of the United Nations and specialized agencies, which may at any time be so authorized by the General Assembly, may also request advisory opinions of the Court on legal questions arising within the scope of their activities.

CHAPTER XV
THE SECRETARIAT

Article 97

The Secretariat shall comprise a Secretary-General and such staff as the Organization may require. The Secretary-General shall be appointed by the General Assembly upon the recommendation of the Security Council. He shall be the Chief administrative officer of the Organization.

Article 98

The Secretary General shall act in that capacity in all meetings of the General Assembly, of the Security Council, of the Economic and Social Council, and of the Trusteeship Council, and shall perform such other functions as are entrusted to him by these organs. The Secretary-General shall make an annual report to the General Assembly on the word of the Organization.

Article 99

The Secretary-General may bring to the attention of the Security Council any matter which in his opinion may threaten the maintenance of international peace and security.

Article 100

1. In the performance of their duties the Secretary-General and the staff not seek

or receive instructions from any Government or from any other authority external to the Organization. They shall refrain from any action which might reflect on their position as international officials responsible only to the Organization.

2. Each member of the United Nations undertakes to respect the exclusively international character of the responsibilities of the Secretary-General and the staff and not to seek to influence them in the discharge of their responsibilities.

Article 101

1. The staff shall be appointed by the Secretary-General under regulations established by the General Assembly.

2. Appropriate staffs shall be permanently assigned to the Economic and Social Council, the Trusteeship Council, and, as required, to other organs of the United Nations. These staffs shall form a part of the Secretariat.

3. The paramount consideration in the employment of the staff and in the determination of the conditions of service shall be the necessity of securing the highest standards of efficiency, competence, and integrity. Due regard shall be paid to the importance of recruiting the staff on as wide a geographical basis as possible.

CHAPTER XVI
MISCELLANEOUS PROVISIONS

Article 102

1. Every treaty and every international agreement entered into by any Member of the United Nations after the present Charter comes into force shall as soon as possible be registered with the Secretariat and published by it.

2. No party to any such treaty or international agreement which has not been registered in accordance with the provisions of paragraph 1 of this Article may invoke that treaty or agreement before any organ of the United Nations.

Article 103

In the event of a conflict between the obligations of the Members of the United Nations under the present Charter and their obligations under any other international agreement, their obligations under the present Charter shall prevail.

Article 104

The Organization shall enjoy in the territory of each of its Members such legal capacity as may be necessary for the exercise of its functions and the fulfilment of its purposes.

Article 105

1. The Organization shall enjoy in the territory of each of its Members such privileges and immunities as are necessary for the fulfilment of its purposes.

2. Representatives of the Members of the United Nations and officials of the Organization shall similarly enjoy such privileges and immunities as are necessary for the independent exercise of their functions in connection with the Organization.

3. The General Assembly may make recommendations with a view to determining the details the application of paragraphs 1 and 2 of this Article or may proposes conventions to the Members of the United Nations for this purpose.

CHAPTER XVII
TRANSITIONAL SECURITY ARRANGEMENTS

Article 106

Pending the coming into force of such special agreements referred to in Article 43 as in the opinion of the Security Council enable it to begin the exercise of its responsibilities under Article 42, the parties to the Four-Nation Declaration, signed at Moscow, October 30, 1943, and France, shall, in accordance with the provisions of paragraph 5 of that Declaration, cousult with one another and as occasion requires with other Members of the United Nations with a view to such joint action on behalf of the Organization as may be necessary for the purpose of maintaining international peace and security.

Article 107

Nothing in the present Charter shall invalidate or preclude action, in relation to any

State which during the Second World War has been an enemy of any signatory to the present Charter, taken or authorized as a result of that war by the Governments having responsibility for such action.

CHAPTER XVIII
AMENDMENTS
Article 108

Amendments to the present Charter shall come into force for all Members of the United Nations when they have been adopted by a vote of two-thirds of the members of the General Assembly and ratified in accordance with their respective constitutional processes by two-thirds of the Members of the United Nations, including all the permanent members of the Security Council.

Article 109

1. A General Conference of the Members of the United Nations for the purpose of reviewing the present Charter may be held at a date and place to be fixed by a two-thirds vote of the members of the General Assembly and by a vote of any nine members of the Security Council. Each Member of the United Nations shall have one vote in the conference.

2. Any alteration of the present Charter recommended by a two- thirds vote of the conference shall take effect when ratified in accordance with their respective constitutional processes by two- thirds of the Members of the United Nations including all the permanent members of the Security Council.

3. If such a conference has not been held before the tenth annual session of the General Assembly following the coming into force of the present Charter, the proposal to call such a conference shall be placed on the agenda of that session of the General Assembly, and the conference shall be held if so decided by a majority vote of the members of the General Assembly and by a vote of any seven members of the Security Council.

CHAPTER XIX
RATIFICATION AND SIGNATURE
Article 110

1. The present Charter shall be ratified by the signatory States in accordance with their respective constitutional processes.

2. The ratifications shall be deposited with the Government of the United States of America, which shall notify all the signatory States of each deposit as well as the Secretary-General of the Organization when he has been appointed.

3. The present Charter shall come into force upon the deposit of ratifications by the Republic of China, France, the Union of Soviet Socialist Republics, the United kingdom of Great Britain and Northern Ireland, and the United States of America, and by a majority of the other signatory States. A protocol of the ratifications deposited shall thereupon be drawn up by the Government of the United States of America which shall communicate copies thereof to all the signatory States.

4. The States signatory to the present Charter which ratify it after it has come into force will become original Members of the United Nations on the date of the deposit of their respective ratifications.

Article 111

The present Charter, of which the Chinese, French, Russian, English, and Spanish texts are equally authentic, shall remain deposited in the archives of the Government of the United States of America. Duly certified copies thereof shall be transmitted by that Government to the Governments of the other signatory States.

IN FAITH WHEREOF the representatives of the Governments of the United Nations have signed the present Charter.

DONE at the city of San Francisco the twenty-sixth day of June, one thousand nine hundred and forty-five.

APPENDIX II

STATUTE OF THE INTERNATIONAL COURT OF JUSTICE

Article 1

THE INTERNATIONAL COURT OF JUSTICE established by the Charter of the United Nations as the principal judicial organ of the United Nations shall be constituted and shall function in accordance with the provisions of the present Statute.

CHAPTER 1

ORGANIZATION OF THE COURT

Article 2

The Court shall be composed of a body of independent judges, elected regardless of their nationality from among persons of high moral character, who possess the qualifications required in their respective countries for appointment to the highest judicial offices, or are jurisconsults of recognized competence in International Law.

Article 3

1. The Court shall consist of fifteen members, no two of whom may be nationals of the same state.

2. A person who for the purposes of membership in the Court could be regarded as a national of more than one state shall be deemed to be a national of the one in which he ordinarily exercises civil and political rights.

Article 4

1. The members of the Court shall be elected by the General Assembly and by the Security Council from a list of persons nominated by the national groups in the Permanent Court of Arbitration, in accordance with the following provisions.

2. In the case of Members of the United Nations not represented in the Permanent Court of Arbitration, candidates shall be nominated by national groups appointed for this purpose by their Governments under the same conditions as those prescribed for members of the Permanent Court of Arbitration by Article 44 of the Convention of the Hague of 1907 for the pacific settlement of international disputes.

3. The conditions under which a state which is a party to the present Statute but is not a Member of the United Nations may participate in electing the members of the Court shall, in the absence of a special agreement, be laid down by the General Assembly upon recommendation of the Security Council.

Article 5

1. At least three months before the date of the election, the Secretary-General of the United Nations shall address a written request to the members of the Permanent Court of Arbitration belonging to the states which are parties to the present Statute, and to the members of the national groups appointed under Article 4, paragraph 2, inviting them to undertake, within a given time, by national groups, the nomination of persons in a position to accept the duties of a member of the Court.

2. No group may nominate more than four persons, not more than two of whom shall be of their own nationality. In no case may the number of candidates nominated by a group be more than double the number of seats to be filled.

Article 6

Before making these nominations, each national group is recommended to consult its highest court of justice, its legal faculties and schools of law, and it national academies and national actions of international academies devoted to the study of law.

Article 7

1. The Secretary-General shall prepare a list in alphabetical order of all the persons thus nominated. Save as provided in Article 12, paragraph 2 these shall be the only

persons eligible.

2. The Secretary-General shall submit this list to the General Assembly and to the Security Council.

Article 8

The General Assembly and the Security Council shall proceed independently of one another to elect the members of the Court.

Article 9

At every election, the electors shall bear in mind not only that the persons to be elected should individually posses the qualifications required, but also that in the body as a whole the representation of the main forms of civilization and of the principle legal systems of the world should be assured.

Article 10

1. Those candidates who obtain an absolute majority of votes in the General Assembly and in the Security Council shall be considered as elected.

2. Any vote of the Security Council, whether for the election of judges or for the appointment of members of the conference envisaged in Article 12, shall be taken without any distinction between permanent and the non-permanent members of the Security Council.

3. In the event of more than one national of the same state obtaining an absolute majority of the votes both of the General Assembly and of the Security Council, the eldest of these only shall be considered as elected.

Article 11

If after the first meeting held for the purpose of the election, one or more seats remain to be filled, a second and, if necessary, a third meeting shall take place.

Article 12

1. If, after the third meeting, one or more seats still remain unfilled, a joint conference consisting of six members, three appointed by the General Assembly and three by the Security Council, may be formed, at any time at the request of either the General Assembly or the Security Council, for the purpose of choosing by the vote of an absolute majority one name for each seat still vacant, to submit to the General Assembly and the Security Council for their respective acceptance.

2. If the joint conference is unanimously agreed upon any person who fulfills the required conditions, he may be included in its list, even though he was not included in the list of nominations referred to in Article 7.

3. If the joint conference is satisfied that it will not be successful in procuring an election, those members of the Court who have already been elected shall, within a period to be fixed by the Security Council, proceed to fill the vacant seats by selection from among those candidates who have obtained votes either in the General Assembly or in the Security Council.

4. In the event of an equally of votes among the judges, the eldest judge shall have a casting vote.

Article 13

1. The members of the Court shall be elected for nine years and may be re-elected; provided, however, that of the judges elected at the first election, the terms of five judges shall expire at the end of three years and the terms of five more judges shall expire at the end of the six years.

2. The judges whose terms are to expire at the end of the above-mentioned initial periods of three and six years shall be chosen by lot to be drawn by the Security-General immediately after the first election has been completed.

3. The members of the Court shall continue to discharge their duties until their places have been filled. Though replaced, they shall finish any cases which they may have begun.

4. In the case of the resignation of a member of the Court, the resignation shall be addressed to the President of the Court for transmission to the Secretary-General. The last notification makes the place vacant.

Article 14

Vacancies shall be filled by the same method as that laid down for the first election, subject to the following provision; the Secretary-General shall, within one month of the occurrence of the vacancy, proceed to issue the invitations provided for in Article 5, and the date of the election shall be fixed by the Security Council.

Article 15

A member of the Court elected to replace a member whose term of office has not expired shall hold office for the remainder of his predecessor's term.

Article 16

1. No member of the Court may exercise any political or administrative function, or engage in any other occupation of a professional nature.
2. Any doubt on this point shall be settled by the decision of the Court.

Article 17

1. No member of the Court may act as agent, counsel, or advocate in any case.
2. No member may participate in the decision of any case in which he has previously taken part as agent, counsel, or advocate for one of the parties, or as a member of a national or international court, or of a commission of enquiry, or in any other capacity.
3. Any doubt on this point shall be settled by the decision of the Court.

Article 18

1. No member of the Court can be dismissed unless, in the unanimous opinion of the other members, he has ceased to fulfill the required conditions.
2. Formal notification thereof shall be made to the Secretary-General by the Registrar.
3. This notification makes the place vacant.

Article 19

The members of the Court, when engaged on the business of the Court, shall enjoy diplomatic privileges and immunities.

Article 20

Every member of the Court shall, before taking up his duties, make a solemn declaration in open court that he will exercise his powers impartially and conscientiously.

Article 21

1. The Court shall elect its President and Vice-President for three years; they may be re-elected.
2. The Court shall appoint its Registrar and may provide for the appointment of such other officers as may be necessary.

Article 22

1. The seat of the Court shall be established at The Hague. This, however, shall not prevent the Court from sitting and exercising its functions elsewhere whenever the Court considers it desirable.
2. The President and the Registrar shall reside at the seat of the Court.

Article 23

1. The Court shall remain permanently in session, except during the judicial vacations, the dates and duration of which shall be fixed by the Court.
2. Members of the Court are entitled to periodic leave, the dates and duration of which shall be fixed by the Court, having in mind the distance between The Hague and the home of each judge.
3. Members of the Court shall be bound, unless they are no leave or prevented from attending by illness or other serious reasons duly explained to the President, to hold themselves permanently at the disposal of the court.

Article 24

1. If, for some special reason, a member of the Court considers that he should not take part in the decision of a particular case, he shall so inform the President.
2. If the President considers that for some special reason one of the members of

the Court should not sit in a particular case, he shall give him notice accordingly.

3. If in any such case the member of the Court and the President disagree, the matter shall be settled by the decision of the Court.

Article 25

1. The full Court shall sit except when it is expressly provided otherwise in the present Statute.

2. Subject to the condition that the number of judges available to constitute the Court is not thereby reduced below eleven, the Rules of the Court may provide for allowing one or more judges, according to circumstances and in rotation, to be dispensed from sitting.

3. A quorum of nine judges shall suffice to constitute the Court.

Article 26

1. The Court may from time to time form one or more chambers, composed of three or more judges as the Court may determine, for dealing with particular categories of cases; for example, labour cases and cases relating to transit and communications.

2. The Court may at any time form a chamber for dealing with a particular case. The number of judges to constitute such a chamber shall be determined by the Court with the approval of the parties.

3. Cases shall be heard and determined by the Chambers provided for in this Article if the parties so request.

Article 27

A judgment given by any of the chambers provided for in Articles 26 and 29 shall be considered as rendered by the Court.

Article 28

The chambers provided for in Articles 26 and 29 may, with the consent of the parties, sit and exercise their functions elsewhere than at The Hague.

Article 29

With a view to the speedy dispatch of business, the Court shall form annually a chamber composed of five judges which, at the request of the parties, may hear and determine cases by summary procedure. In addition, two judges shall be selected for the purpose of replacing judges who find it impossible to sit.

Article 30

1. The Court shall frame rules for carrying out its functions. In particular, it shall lay down rules of procedure.

2. The Rules of the Court may provide for assessors to sit with the Court or with any of its chambers, without the right to vote.

Article 31

1. Judges of the nationality of each of the parties shall retain their right to sit in the case before the Court.

2. If the Court includes upon the Bench a judge of the nationality of one parties, any other party may choose a person to sit as judge. Such person shall be chosen preferably from among those persons who have been nominated as candidates as provided in Articles 4 and 5.

3. If the Court includes upon the Bench no judge of the nationality of the parties, each of these parties may proceed to choose a judge as provided in paragraph 2 of this Article.

4. The provisions of this Article shall apply to the case of Articles 26 and 29. In such cases, the President shall request one or, if necessary, two of the members of the Court forming the chamber to give place to the members of the Court ot the nationality of the parties concerned, and, failing such, or if they are unable to be present, to the judges specially chosen by the parties.

5. Should there be several parties in the same interest, they shall, for the purpose of the preceding provisions, be reckoned as one party only. Any doubt upon this point shall be settled by the decision of the Court.

6. Judges chosen as laid down in paragraphs 2, 3 and 4 of this Article shall fulfil

the conditions required by Articles 2, 17 (paragraph 2), 20 and 24 of the present Statute. They shall take part in the decision on terms of complete equally with their colleagues.

Article 32

1. Each member of the Court shall receive an annual salary.
2. The President shall receive a special annual allowance.
3. The Vice-President shall receive a special allowance for every day on which he acts as President.
4. The judges chosen under Article 31, other than members of the Court, shall receive compensation for each day on which they exercise their functions.
5. These salaries, allowances, and compensation shall be fixed by the General Assembly. They may not be decreased during the term of office.
6. The salary of the Registrar shall be fixed by the General Assembly on the proposal of the Court.
7. Regulations made by the General Assembly shall fix the conditions under which retirement pensions may be given to members of the Court and to the Registrar, and the conditions under which members of the Court and the Registrar shall have their travelling expenses refunded.
8. The above salaries, allowances, and compensation shall be free of all taxation.

Article 33

The expenses of the Court shall be borne by the United Nations in such a manner as shall be decided by the General Assembly.

CHAPTER II
COMPETENCE OF THE COURT

Article 34

1. Only states may be parties in cases before the Court.
2. The Court subject to and in conformity with its Rules, may request of public international organizations information relevant to cases before it, and shall receive such information presented by such organization on their own initiative.
3. Whenever the construction of the constituent instrument of a public international organisation or of an international convention adopted thereunder is in question in a case before the Court, the registrar shall so notify the public international organization concerned and shall communicate to it copies of all the written proceedings.

Article 35

1. The Court shall be open to the states parties to the present Statute.
2. The conditions under which the Court shall be open to other states shall, subject to the special provisions contained in treaties in force, be laid down by the Security Council, but in no case shall such conditions place the parties in a position of inequality before the Court.
3. When a state which is not a Member of the United Nations is a party to a case, the Court shall fix the amount which that party is to contribute towards the expenses of the Court. This provision shall not apply if such state is bearing a share of the expenses of the Court.

Article 36

1. The jurisdiction of the Court comprises all cases which the parties refer to it and it matters specially provided for in the Charter of the United Nations or in treaties and convention in force.
2. The states parties to the present Statute may at any time declare that they recognize as compulsory *ipso facto* and without special agreement, in relation to any other state accepting the same obligation, the jurisdiction of the Court in all legal disputes concerning:

(a) the interpretation of a treaty;

(b) any question of international law;

(c) the existence of any fact which, if established, would constitute a breach of an international obligation;

(d) the nature or extent of the reparation to be made for the breach of an international obligation.

3. The declarations referred to above may be made unconditionally or on condition of reciprocity on the part of several or certain states, or for a certain time.

4. Such declarations shall be deposited with the Secretary- General of the United Nations, who shall transmit copies thereof to the parties to the Statute and to the Registrar of the Court.

5. Declarations made under Article 36 of the Permanent Court of International Justice and which are still in force shall be deemed, as between the parties to the present Statute, to be acceptances of the compulsory jurisdiction of the International Court of Justice for the period which they still have to run and in accordance with their terms.

6. In the event of a dispute as to whether the Court has jurisdiction, the matter shall be settled by the decision of the Court.

Article 37

Whenever a treaty or convention in force provides for reference of a matter to a tribunal to have been instituted by the League of Nations, or to the Permanent Court of International Justice, the matter shall, as between the parties to the present Statute, be referred to the International Court of Justice.

Article 38

1. The Court, whose function is to decide in accordance with International Law such disputes as are submitted to it, shall apply :

(a) international conventions, whether general or particular, established rules expressly recognized by the contesting states;

(b) international custom, as evidence of a general practice accepted as law;

(c) the general principles of law recognized by civilized nations;

(d) subject to the provisions of Article 59, judicial decisions and the teachings of the most highly qualified publicists of the various nations, as subsidiary means for the determination of rules of law.

2. This provision shall not prejudice the power of the Court to decide a case *ex acquo et bono*, if the parties agree thereto.

CHAPTER III
PROCEDURE

Article 39

1. The official languages of the Court shall be French and English. If the parties agree that the case shall be conducted in French, the judgment shall be delivered in French. If the parties agree that the case shall be conducted in English, the judgment shall be delivered in English.

2. In the absence of an agreement as to which language shall be employed, each party may, in the pleadings, use the language which it prefers; the decision of the Court shall be given in French and English. In this case the Court shall at the same time determine which of the two texts shall be considered as authoritative.

3. The Court shall, at the request of any party, authorize a language other than French or English to be used by that party.

Article 40

1. Cases are brought before the Court, as the case may be, either by the notification of the special agreement or by a written application addressed to the Registrar. In either case the subject of the dispute and the parties shall be indicated.

2. The Registrar shall forthwith communicate the application to all concerned.

3. He shall also notify the Members of the Untied Nations through the Secretary-General, and also any other States entitled to appear before the Court.

Article 41

1. The Court shall have the power to indicate, if it considers that circu stances so require, any provisional measures which ought to be taken to preserve the respective rights of either party.

2. Pending the final decision, notice of the measures suggested shall forthwith be given to the parties and to the Security Council.

Article 42

1. The parties shall be representated by agents.
2. They may have the assistance of counsel or advocates before the Court.
3. The agents, counsel, and advocates of parties before the Court shall enjoy the privileges and immunities necessary to the independent exercise of their duties.

Article 43

1. The procedure shall consist of two parts: written and oral.
2. The written proceedings shall consists of the communication to the Court and to the parties of memorials, counter-memorials and, if necessary, replies; also all papers and documents in support.
3. These communications shall be made through the Registrar, in the order and within the time fixed by the Court.
4. A certified copy of every document produced by one party shall be communicate to the other party.
5. The oral proceedings shall consists of the hearing by the Court of witnesses, experts, agents, counsel, and advocates.

Article 44

1. For the service of all notices upon persons other than the agents, counsel, and advocates, the Court shall apply direct to the Government of the state upon whose territory the notice has to be served.
2. The same provision shall apply whenever steps are to be taken to procure evidence on the spot.

Article 45

The hearing shall be under the control of the President or, if he is unable to preside, of the Vice-President; if neither is able to preside, the senior judge present shall preside.

Article 46

The hearing in Court shall be public, unless the Court shall decide otherwise, or unless the parties demand that the public be not admitted.

Article 47

1. Minutes shall be made at each hearing and signed by the Registrar and the President.
2. These minutes alone shall be authentic.

Article 48

The Court shall make orders for the conduct of the case, shall decide the form and time in which each party must conclude its arguments, and make all arrangements connected with the taking of evidence.

Article 49

The Court may, even before the hearing begins, call upon the agents to produce any document or to supply any explanation. Formal note shall be taken of any refusal.

Article 50

The Court may, at any time, entrust any individual, body, bureau, commission, or other organization that it may select, with the task of carrying out an enquiry or giving an expert opinion.

Article 51

During the hearing any relevant questions are to be put to the witnesses and experts under the conditions laid down by the Court in the rules of procedure referred to in Article 30.

Article 52

After the Court has received the proofs and evidence within the time specified for the purposes, it may refuse to accept any further oral or written evidence that one party may desire to present unless the other side consents.

Article 53

1. Whenever one of the parties does not appear before the Court, or fails to defend its case, the other party may call upon the Court to decide in favour of its claim.

2. The Court must, before doing so, satisfy itself, not only that it has jurisdiction in accordance with Articles 36 and 37, but also that the claim is well founded in fact and law.

Article 54

1. When, subject to the control of the Court, the agents, counsel, and advocates have completed their presentation of the case, the President shall declare the hearing closed.

2. The Court shall withdraw to consider the judgment.

3. The deliberations of the Court shall take place in private and remain secret.

Article 55

1. All questions shall be decided by a majority of the judges present.

2. In the event of an equality of votes, the President or the judge who acts in his place shall have a casting vote.

Article 56

1. The judgment shall state the reasons on which it is based.

2. It shall contain the names of the judges who have taken part in the decision.

Article 57

If the judgment does not represent in whole or in part the unanimous opinion of the judges, any judge shall be entitled to deliver a separate opinion.

Article 58

The judgment shall be signed by the President and by the Registrar. It shall be read in open Court, due notice having been given to the agents.

Article 59

The decision of the Court has no binding force except between the parties and in respect of that particular case.

Article 60

The judgment is final and without appeal. In the event of dispute as to the meaning or scope of the judgment, the Court shall construe it upon the request of any party.

Article 61

1. An application for revision of a judgment may be made only when it is based upon the discovery of some fact of such a nature as to be a decisive factor, which fact was, when the judgment was given, unknown to the Court and also to the party claiming revision, always provided that such ignorance was not due to negligence.

2. The proceedings for revision shall be opened by a judgment of the Court expressly recording the existence of the new fact, recognizing that it has such a character as to lay the case open to revision, and declaring the application admissible on this ground.

3. The Court may require previous compliance with the terms of the judgment before it admits proceedings in revision.

4. The application for revision must be made at least within six months of the discovery of the new fact.

5. No application for revision may be made after the lapse of ten years from the date of the judgment.

Article 62

1. Should a state consider that it has an interest of a legal nature which may be affected by the decision in the case, it may submit a request to the Court to be permitted to intervene.

2. It shall be for the Court to decide upon this request.

Article 63

1. Whenever the construction of a convention to which states other than those concerned in the case are parties is in question, the Registrar shall notify all such states forthwith.

2. Every state so notified has the right to intervene in the proceedings; but if it uses this right, the construction given by the judgment will be equally binding upon it.

Article 64

Unless otherwise decided by the Court, each party shall bear its own costs.

CHAPTER IV
ADVISORY OPINIONS

Article 65

1. The Court may give an advisory opinion on any legal question at the request of whatever body may be authorized by or in accordance with the Charter of the United Nations to make such a request.

2. Questions upon which the advisory opinion of the Court is asked shall be laid before the Court by means of a written request containing an exact statement of the question upon which an opinion is required, and accompanied by all documents likely to throw light upon the question.

Article 66

1. The Registrar shall forthwith give notice of the request for an advisory opinion to all states entitled to appear before the Court.

2. The Registrar shall also, by means of a special and direct communication, notify any state entitled to appear before the Court or international organization considered by the Court, or, should it not be sitting, by the President, as likely to be able to furnish information on the question, that the Court will be prepared to receive, within a time limit to be fixed by the President, written statements, or to hear, at a public sitting to be held for the purpose, oral statements relating to the question.

3. Should any such state entitled to appear before the Court have failed to receive the special communication referred to in paragraph 2 of this Article, such state may express a desire to submit a written statement or to be heard; and the Court will decide.

4. States and organizations having presented written or oral statements or both shall be permitted to comment on the statements made by other states or organizations in the form, to the extent, and within the time limits which the Court, or, should it not be sitting, the President, shall decide in each particular case. Accordingly, the Registrar shall in due time communicate any such written statements to states and organizations having submitted to similar statements.

Article 67

The Court shall deliver its advisory opinions in open court, notice having been given to the Secretary-General and to the representatives of Members of the United Nations, of other states and of international organizations immediately concerned.

Article 68

In the exercise of its advisory functions the Court shall further be guided by the provisions of the present Statute which apply in contentious cases to the extent to which it recognizes them to be applicable.

CHAPTER V
AMENDMENT

Article 69

Amendments to the present Statute shall be effected by the same procedure as is provided by the Charter of the United Nations for amendments to that Charter, subject however to any provisions which the General Assembly upon recommendation of the Security Council may adopt concerning the participation of states which are parties to the present Statute but are not Members of the United Nations.

Article 70

The Court shall have power to propose such amendments to the present Statute as it may deem necessary, through written communications to the Secretary-General, for consideration in conformity with the provisions of Article 69.

INDEX

Standard Text Books on Law (Subject-wise)

❖ **Administrative Law**	
U. P. D. Kesari	**Administrative Law**
K. C. Joshi	**Administrative Law**
❖ **Arbitration & Conciliation**	
S. C. Tripathi	**Arbitration & Conciliation**
Anupam Kurlwal	**An Introduction to Alternate Dispute Resolution System**
S. C. Tripathi	**Alternate Dispute Resolution System (ADR)**
❖ **Banking Law**	
Anjani Kant	**Lectures on Banking Law**
R. N. Chaudhary	**Banking Law**
❖ **Business Law**	
R.N. Chaudhary	**Business Laws**
❖ **Company Law**	
S. C. Tripathi	**New Company Law**
V.L. Mony	**Hand Book on Company Law**
Deepankar Sharma	**Law of Corporate Governance**
❖ **Competition Law**	
S. C. Tripathi	**Competition Law**
❖ **Civil Procedure Code**	
Avtar Singh	**Civil Procedure Code**
D. N. Mathur	**Civil Procedure Code**
❖ **Constitutional Law**	
Avtar Singh	**The Constitutional Law of India**
Kailash Rai	**Constitutional Law of India**
K. C. Joshi	**Constitutional Law of India**
G. P. Tripathi	**Constitutional Law-New Challenges**
Jai S. Singh	**Constitutional Law of India (Cases and Materials)**
Shatakshi Johri	**Lectures on Constitutional Law (with Power Point Presentation)**
June L. D'Souza	**World Constitutions**
Ullas Kumar Saha	**Constitutional Law I**
Ullas Kumar Saha	**Constitutional Law II**
Kush Kalra	**Leading Judgments on Constitutional Law**

❖ **Consumer Protection Act**	
S. C. Tripathi	**Consumer Protection Act**
❖ **Law of Contract**	
S. S. Srivastava	**Law of Contract — I & II with Specific Relief Act, Sale of Goods Act, Partnership Act & Negotiable Instruments Act**
Kailash Rai	**Contract-I & Specific Relief Act**
Prabhat K. Gupta	**Contract-I with Specific Relief**
K. Swamyraj	**Lectures on Law of Contract**
❖ **Copyright Law**	
Ishita Chatterjee	**Copyright Law**
❖ **Criminal Procedure Code**	
S. N. Misra	**The Code of Criminal Procedure**
Caesar Roy	**The Probation of Offenders Act, 1958**
❖ **Criminology & Penology**	
N. V. Paranjape	**Criminology & Penology with Victimology**
K.D.Gaur	**Criminal Law, Criminology and Administration of Criminal Justice**
❖ **Cyber Law**	
J. P. Mishra	**An Introduction to Cyber Law**
B.A. Deshpande	**Text Book on Cyber Law**
❖ **Easement Act**	
H. P. Gupta	**Indian Easement Act**
❖ **Law for Engineers**	
Vibha & Kunwar Arora	**Law for Engineers**
❖ **Environmental Law**	
S. C. Tripathi	**Environmental Law**
Sukanta K. Nanda	**Environmental Law**
Sanjeev K. Chadha	**Lectures on Environmental Law**
❖ **Equity & Trust**	
S. C. Tripathi	**Equity & Trust**
❖ **Evidence**	
Avtar Singh	**Principles of The Law of Evidence**

❖ **Forensic Science**	
Ishita Chatterjee	**Law of Forensic Science**
❖ **Family Law**	
Shivani Gosawami	**Family Law - I**
❖ **Hindu Law**	
U. P. D. Kesari	**Modern Hindu Law**
Basant K. Sharma	**Hindu Law**
❖ **Human Rights**	
H. O. Agarwal	**Human Rights**
Bhagyashree A. Deshpande	**Human Rights : Law & Practice**
Barun Kumar Das	**Human Rights Law and Domestic Violence**
❖ **Health Law**	
Nandita Adhikari	**Law & Medicine**
Ishita Chatterjee	**Health Law**
❖ **Indian Penal Code**	
K.D. Gaur	**Commentary on India Penal Code**
K.D. Gaur	**Commentary on the Indian Penal Code (Abridged Edition)**
S. N. Misra	**Indian Penal Code**
R. N. Saxena	**Indian Penal Code**
N.V. Paranjape	**Indian Penal Code**
Kumar Askand Padey	**Principal of Criminal Law in India : Cases and Materials**
K.D. Gaur	**Leading Cases on Criminal Law**
Ishita Chatterjee	**White Collar Crimes**
❖ **Information Technology**	
Ishita Chaterjee	**Law on Information Technology**
❖ **International Law & Human Rights**	
H. O. Agarwal	**International Organisation**
H. O. Agarwal	**International Law & Human Rights**
H. O. Agarwal	**A Concise Book on International Law & Human Rights (Nut shell)**
❖ **Private International Law**	
V.L. Mony	**Private International Law**
Sai Ramani Garimella	**Private International Law (Conflict of laws)**

❖ **International Trade Law**	
Ishita Chatterjee	**International Trade Law**
❖ **Intellectual Property Rights**	
J. P. Misra	An Introduction to **Intellectual Property Rights**
M. K. Bhandari	An Introduction to **Intellectual Property Rights**
Kush Kalra	**Landmark Judgments on Intellectual Property Rights**
❖ **Law of Insurance**	
Naresh Mahipal	**An Introduction to Insurance Laws**
R. N. Chaudhary	**General Principles of Insurance Law**
❖ **Interpretation of Statutes**	
R.D. Srivastava	**Text Book of Interpretation of Statutes & Legislation**
D. N. Mathur	**Interpretation of Statutes**
❖ **Judicial Process**	
G. P. Tripathi	**Judicial Process**
❖ **Jurisprudence**	
Nomita Agarwal	**Jurisprudence & Legal Theory**
S. P. Dwivedi	**Jurisprudence & Legal Theory**
M. K. Das	**An Introduction to Jurisprudence (Legal Theory)**
❖ **Labour Laws**	
S. N. Misra	**Labour & Industrial Laws**
Sunil Yadav	**Labour Laws**
Ullas Kumar Saha	**Hand Book on Labour Laws**
❖ **Land Law**	
R. R. Maurya	**U. P. Land Laws**
R. R. Maurya	**Land Revenue Code, 2006**
D. N. Mathur	**Maharashtra Land Laws**
Harshali Chowdhary	**Punjab & Haryana Land Laws**
❖ **Legal Dictionary**	
Arora	**Supreme Law Dictionary** (English – Hindi)
❖ **Legal Ethics**	
Kailash Rai	**Legal Ethics, Accountability for Lawyers & Bench-Bar Relations**
D.N. Mathur	**Professional Ethics, Accountability for Lawyers & Bench-Bar Relations**

❖ **Legal GK**	
Sushil Kumar Garg	**Legal General Knowledge**
S. C. Tripathi	**Legal Essays & Short Paragraphs**
Kush Kalra	**Legal Essays (For Competitive Examinations)**
❖ **Legal Method**	
G. P. Tripathi	**Legal Method**
❖ **Legal Language**	
S. C. Tripathi	**Legal Language, Legal Writing & General English**
Anirudh Prasad	**Outlines of Legal Language in India**
❖ **Legal & Constitutional History**	
S. C. Tripathi	**Indian Legal & Constitutional History**
G. P. Tripathi	**History of Courts & Legislation**
❖ **Indian Limitation Act**	
H. P. Gupta	**Limitation Act**
❖ **Law & Social Transformation**	
G. P. Tripathi	**Law & Social Transformation**
Bhagyashree A. Deshpande	**Law & Social Transformation in India**
❖ **Media Law**	
Sukanta K. Nanda	**Media Law**
❖ **Muslim Law**	
M. A. Qureshi	**Muslim Law**
Mohd. Nazmi	**Mohammadan Law**
❖ **Moot Court**	
Kailash Rai	**Moot Court (Pre-Trial Preparation and Participation in Trial Proceedings)**
Satyendra Mani Tripathi	**ARGUENDO : A Moot Court Handbook**
❖ **Practical Training**	
D. N. Mathur	**All India Bar Examination Guide**
D. N. Mathur	**Hand Book on Court Visits (An Essential Readings for Law Students & Budding Lawyers)**
J. K. Upadhyay	**UGC-Net (JRF) Examination Guide on Law**
Amlanika Bora	**UGC-Net/JRF (Law) Examination Solved Papers**
Sharma, Diwakar &	**CLP's Ultimate Success CLAT & LLB Entrance**

Saraf	**Examination**
Kunwar Arora	**Solved Papers for LL.M. Enterance Exam.**
Gurjit Singh	**The Art of Cross Examination**
❖ Partnership Act	
H. P. Gupta	**Indian Partnership Act**
S.C. Tripathi	**Indian Partnership Act**
❖ Pleadings, Drafting & Conveyancing	
R. N. Chaturvedi	**Pleadings, Drafting & Conveyancing**
❖ Psychology and Law	
Nagma Javed	**Psychology and Law**
❖ Public Interest Litigation	
Ajay Gulati	**Public Interest Lawyering, Legal Aid & Para Legal Services**
Kailash Rai	**Public Interest Lawyering, Legal Aid & Para Legal Services**
❖ Research Methodology (Legal)	
Mona Purohit	**Legal Education & Research Methodology**
G.P. Tripathi	**Legal Research & Research Methodology**
G.P. Tripathi	**Legal Education in India**
❖ Right to Information Act	
A. S. Yadav	**Right to Information Act, 2005 : An Analysis**
❖ Sale of Goods Act	
S. C. Tripathi	**Sale of Goods Act**
❖ Socio Economic Offences	
Nuzhat Parveen Khan	**Law Relating to Socio-Economic Offences**
❖ Taxation Laws	
Atal Kumar	**Taxation Laws**
Ullash Kumar Saha	**Principles of Taxation Laws with GST**
❖ Transfer of Property Act	
G. P. Tripathi	**Transfer of Property Act**
Ashok Kumar Srivastava	**The Transfer of Property Act with Easement Act**
Rajani Malhotra Dhingra	**Transfer of Property Act and Indian Easement Act**

❖ **Law of Torts**	
J. N. Pandey	**Law of Torts**
Siddharth Dubey	**Lectures on Law of Torts and Consumer Protection**
K. Swamyraj	**Lectures on Law of Torts**
❖ **Women & Children**	
Anjani Kant	**Law Relating to Women & Children**
S. C. Tripathi	**Law Relating to Women & Children**
S. K. Chatterjee	**Offences against Children & Juvenile Offence**
S.S. Singh	**Offences against Children & Juvenile Offence**
Ishita Chaterjee	**Gender Justice and Feminist Jurisprudence**
Samiya Tabassum	**Women and Law**
❖ **Women & Criminal Law**	
S. C. Tripathi	**Women & Criminal Law**
❖ **Political Science for Pre-Law Students**	
Preetam V. Jain	**Political Science I (Political Theory)**
Alok K. Gupta	**Political Science II (Political Obligation)**
Neelam Kant	**An Introduction to Political Science**
❖ **Economics**	
Ratna Chatterjee	**An Introduction to Economics**
Surbhi Arora	**Economics for Law Student**
❖ **Sociology**	
Navendu Thakur	**An Introduction to Sociology**
❖ **General English for Law Students**	
S.C. Tripathi	**General English for Law Students**
Shweta Gupta	**General English and Legal Language**
❖ **Logic**	
R. Kale	**Logic - I**
R. Kale	**Logic - II**
❖ **History**	
Farhat Khan	**Indin History (For Law Students)**
❖ **Reference Books**	
Dr. Amita Verma	**Cyber Crimes in India**
Dr. A. Verma	**Cyber Crimes & Law**
Dr. S. Kaur	**Female Foeticide—A Frightful Reality**

Dr. Kavita Singh	**Human Rights and Anti-Terrorism Law's in India**
Dr. Bandopadhyay & Dubey	**An Introduction to Environmental Rights**
Dr. Sharma, Jaswal & Singh	**Protection & Promotion of Human Rights in India**
G. S. Randhawa	**Victimology & Compensatory Jurisprudence**
Dr. H.O. Agarwal	**Kashmir Problems – Its Legal Aspects**
Ishita Chatterjee	**Techno Legal Aspects of Scientific Evidence**
Dr. Anshuman Mishra	**Election Laws With Special Reference to Corrupt Practices**
Devinder Singh	**Child Labour & Right to Education**
Dr. Sharma & Jaswal	**Law as a Facilitator of Socio-Economic Reforms**
Dr. Chintamani Rout	**Personal Liberty and Human Rights**
Dr. Ajay Pratap Singh	**The Arms Act in India : A Study in Criminological Perspective**
Kush Kalra	**Matrimonial Disputes**
Kush Kalra	**Freedom of Speech and Expression**
June L. DSouza	**International Law of Billergency & Occupation : A Pedagogic Introduction**
Usha Tandon & Sidharth Luthra	**Human Right : Trafficking of Women and Children Legal and Policy Framework**
Dr. Sanjeev K. Chadha	**Environmental Jurisprudence**
Dr. Kamaljeet Kaur	**Narco Terrorism**
Virendra M. Pandit	**Private Investigation**
Dr. Harpreet Kaur	**Elder Abuse**
Indira Srivastava	**Medical & Environmental Sociology**
Dr. Inderpreet Kaur	**The Emerging Trends of Compensatory Jurisdiction in India**
V.M. Pandit	**Intelligence and Investigation in Security Management**

Dear Reader,

- **Thanks for choosing this book published by our publication house.**
- **Register yourself and your colleagues on our website www.clplawbooks.com at student/teacher corner and get promotional offers and free legal updates.**
- **Connect with us by giving feedback/ mistakes/critical evaluation and suggestions for our books.**

Thanks

CLP Editorial Team

Central Law Publications

107 Darbhanga Castle, Allahabad-211 002 (India)
Tel.: [0532] 2461178, 2461123.
Mobile : 9415340927

E-mail: clp.editorial@gmail.com
Website: www.clplawbooks.com
Follow us on Facebook: www.facebook.com/clplawbooks